080539

P9-ARV-593

A DA CAPO PRESS REPRINT SERIES

The Lyric Stage

GENERAL EDITOR: DALE HARRIS
SARAH LAWRENCE COLLEGE

Serge Diaghilev

HIS LIFE, HIS WORK, HIS LEGEND

An Intimate Biography

by

SERGE LIFAR

DA CAPO PRESS . NEW YORK . 1976

Library of Congress Cataloging in Publication Data

Lifar, Serge, 1905-
    Serge Diaghilev, his life, his work, his legend.

    Translation of Diagilev is Dîàgilevym.
    Reprint of the ed. published by Putnam, New York.
    1. Dîàgilev, Sergeĭ Pavlovich, 1872-1929.
2. Ballet. I. Title.
GV1785.D5L48 1976   792.8'092'4 [B]   76-25041
ISBN 0-306-70839-6

This Da Capo Press edition of *Serge Diaghilev* is an unabridged republication
of the first edition published in New York in 1940.

Published by Da Capo Press, Inc.
A Subsidiary of Plenum Publishing Corporation
227 West 17th Street, New York, N. Y. 10011

SERGE DIAGHILEV

SERGE PAVLOVITCH DIAGHILEV, 1872-1929

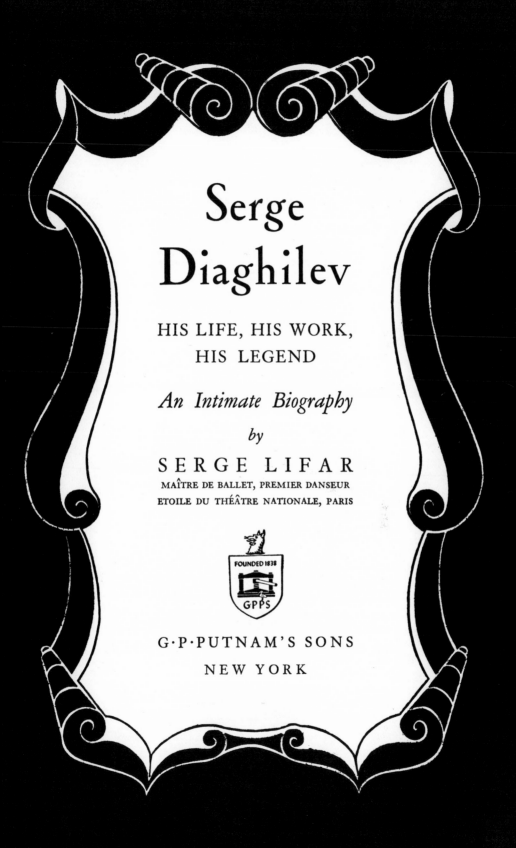

Serge Diaghilev

HIS LIFE, HIS WORK, HIS LEGEND

An Intimate Biography

by

SERGE LIFAR

MAÎTRE DE BALLET, PREMIER DANSEUR
ETOILE DU THÉÂTRE NATIONALE, PARIS

FOUNDED 1838

GPPS

G·P·PUTNAM'S SONS

NEW YORK

PREFACE

NOW THAT this book is about to be delivered to the public, I must confess myself moved and somewhat apprehensive, so intimately is it bound up with my life, and so many years has it taken to write. I began to work on it, very soon after Diaghilev's death, and while still profoundly affected by that event. Aware how swiftly the memory of even the greatest among us fades, and cannot be resuscitated, if there be none to record it, I resolved to set down everything I myself remembered of Diaghilev, from the first days to the last. Then, lest I should omit any of those vivid fleeting details which seem meaningless alone, but in the absence of which I could not hope to evoke him, and again, because they might seem out of place in a formal biography, I decided it preferable to relate—not Diaghilev's life—but my own, in so far as it linked with his in the years 1923-29. The task then flowed easily, and my *Memoirs* wrote themselves, so to speak, one reminiscence spontaneously evoking another. Besides, it was all so recent, so undimmed, and there were my diaries, Serge Pavlovitch's letters to myself, his personal papers, to help my memory and prevent possible lapses.

However, even from the very beginning of my task, certain difficulties made themselves felt, since much of the material involved others, and I had resolved neither to weaken the truth, nor even to amend it. Thus, the obstacles seemed insuperable, and for a time I relinquished the idea. But then, a possible solution presented itself: that of continuing the work, but postponing publication for half a century. This left me free to set down the *truth*, exactly as it had presented itself to me, sparing neither myself nor others, for where individuals are historically important, it is my firm conviction that nothing should either be modified or concealed.

I therefore continued with my task, and by 1933 had completed it according to my original conception. Then it was put under seals, and set aside for posthumous publication.

Nevertheless, although the picture of Diaghilev which this version presented is both vivid and true, it now seems too personal to me, too intensely concentrated on Serge Pavlovitch the individual, rather than on his career in the service of the arts, as champion of a new artistic culture and aesthetic, founder of *The World of Art,* and creator of the Russian Ballet.

And here it is of interest to recall that, when others pried curiously into his life, Diaghilev would always reply:

"I, personally, can be of no interest to anyone: it is not my life that is interesting, but my work."

Thus, the *Memoirs* to which I refer contained much that dealt with Diaghilev personally, but little that dealt with his work; the reason being that it had not occurred to me then—so soon after his death—to attempt to gauge, or survey, the importance of this lifework. Besides, I was well aware how inadequate were my powers to do it justice, and how greatly lacking in me was the necessary erudition.

I therefore waited for such a work to appear from some other hand: one which would reconstruct his career, reveal the ideals behind the work, and do full justice to perhaps its most remarkable feature, the Russian Ballet, though at the same time allowing full significance to all his strenuous efforts in the dissemination of Russian art—painting, music, dancing —and his revolutionary influence upon the whole of scenic art.

Time passed, but no such work appeared. Finally, in 1934, inadequate though I felt myself to be, I decided to attempt that task myself,[1] hoping to make publication coincide with the Diaghilev exhibition I was arranging for 1939, in commemoration of the tenth anniversary of his death. This exhibition was to be held at the Louvre, and though it was to devote itself exclusively to one side only of Serge Pavlovitch's many activities, the Russian Ballet, I hoped that my monograph would be valuable in collecting and supplementing the scattered material already published, embracing as it did the whole of the man's lifework. Dry though it might seem as a compilation of fact, I hoped it would remain as a permanent memorial and tribute. Unfortunately, this somewhat barren relation of dry fact was unavoidable, seeing how much had necessarily to be compressed into it. Indeed, so manifold, so varied, were Diaghilev's activities, that to describe them in detail would have needed, not one, but several volumes.

It is not for me to say how far I have succeeded in adequately appraising what I feel to be most characteristic and distinctive in the man: that vision which enabled him to detect artistic genius, to foster and fan it to flame; that ability to bring artists together and unite them—often to their surprise—in a common achievement, in which he himself played the most prominent part. The proof lies in that "Diaghilev imprimatur" borne by every venture with which he was connected, and if I can bring this home to my reader, I shall consider my task well achieved.

When this study of Diaghilev was finished, I recognized that it could not stand alone. Diaghilev, the inspiration behind so many artistic developments, the creator of a new artistic culture, obscures the image of Diaghilev, the man. Thus, I had of necessity to revert again to my first conception—the *Memoirs,* and to compose another book which should be personal and intimate in character. There would be two works: one called *Diaghilev;* the other *With Diaghilev.* It was impossible to think of

---

[1] In the course of my work on this book, various reminiscences dealing with Diaghilev saw the light. I have at times made use of some of this material, but do not mention it here, since, wherever quoted, I give the reference in the text.

fusing the two works, for the divergent approach—the first a scientific monograph, the second a personal account—naturally precluded such a treatment. Eventually, however, the problem was solved by juxtaposing both within the same volume. But even this task involved a vast amount of modification, not so much in eliminating matter which might be considered unsuitable by the censor, but in so arranging the contents as to make it possible to delete whatever did not directly bear on Diaghilev, or bore too directly on third parties. After which it became essential to reduce the bulk of the volumes, so that both might be enclosed in the same pair of covers. I still hope to publish these *Memoirs in toto,* at some date in the future, but that time is not yet.

Certain extensive deletions have been necessary for a special reason. I refer to Diaghilev's perpetual quarrels and estrangements. He was a man of many, very many, friends, and a man of unique, irresistible charm. Nevertheless, a surprising number of these friends became his enemies with time, not because of any disappointment in his capacities, but because something had happened to instill profound feelings of injury and bitterness.

Diaghilev loved friends and mankind, and was faithful to that love; but individuals were purely *episodes* in his creative activity, *necessary* at one moment, but *nuisances* when new horizons, incomprehensible or unacceptable to these friends, opened before him. From that moment, they ceased to exist for him, and though he in no wise denied his ancient friendships or repudiated them, they simply dropped from his mind. It was this attitude of his, painful indeed to those who found themselves mere *episodes* in his life's work, which was found so hard to forgive, and which motivated the relentless bitterness of so many of the accounts which take him for their subject. Again, others in their jealous rage have never forgiven Diaghilev because he always led, but was never led by, them. . . .

This attitude to others as *episodes* in his life, must be recognized and accepted: but individuals, and whole periods of his life and creative activity, stand outside this category—his stepmother, for instance, Mme. H. V. Panaev-Diaghilev in youth, and Mme. Sert in later life. *Non-episodic,* too, was his creative will! For though its varied manifestations may appear episodic, the passionate flame at the core of his unrelenting urge to reveal to the world a new creative beauty was not episodic, but the innermost heart of the man.

SERGE LIFAR

ACKNOWLEDGMENTS

The Author wishes to make grateful acknowledgment for invaluable information and extracts which he has drawn and quoted from many sources. He is specially indebted to the following: M. Leon Bailby, M. Alexandre Benois, M. Robert Brussel in *Revue Musicale* and *Figaro,* M. G. Calmette in *Figaro,* Madame Karsavina, M. Pierre Lalo, Madame Nijinsky, M. Marcel Prevost, M. Stravinsky and M. J. L. Vaudroyer. All those who are interested in Diaghilev and his period are advised to acquaint themselves with the writings of these eminent authorities in the original.

The Author also wishes to thank E. P. Dutton & Company, Inc., for permission to use material from Madame Karsavina's *Theatre Street;* Greenberg Publisher, Inc., for permission to use material from W. A. Propert's *The Russian Ballet;* and Simon and Schuster, Inc., for permission to use material from Madame Nijinsky's *Nijinsky.*

CONTENTS

ILLUSTRATIONS

BOOK I: DIAGHILEV

PART ONE: THE YOUNG DIAGHILEV

TO THE
GLORIOUS MEMORY
OF
DIAGHILEV

CHAPTER I

ANCESTRY

The Mask and the Face

TO THE observer, what was most striking in the mask of Serge Pavlovitch Diaghilev, was no doubt its strangeness and mobility, for every feature seemed to be endowed with its own vitality, and to speak a separate language. And yet that face impressed one as curiously monumental, and even indestructible, so much health and power did it radiate. It reminded one of Peter the Great. Even from a distance there was something in the curve of the lips that instantly provoked the same comparison. And indeed, Diaghilev himself was proud of this resemblance, accentuated by his clipped mustache, and would boast at times that the great Peter's blood flowed in his veins.[1]

But what seemed to emphasize this monumental impression still more, was the extraordinary size of his head, which no ready-made hat would fit, and which somehow seemed out of proportion to his body.

If one refers to his photographs, an odd feeling begins to take possession of one, a feeling that the man's face and mask have merged. The first impression is of the all-but-immobile mask, but little by little the real face begins to show through.

That mask was exceedingly expressive, so expressive that there were times when it actually seemed Diaghilev's real face and indeed he himself often gave the impression of having made the same error.

It was the mask of a Russian aristocrat. There was lethargy, hauteur, contempt in it; some snobbishness, a certain degree of squeamish antipathy to life and its more seamy sides, a gourmet's studied interest in food and wine, the tepid interest of the art patron, who, now and then, "manages to find time" to indulge in "artistic" emotion, while prizing elegance more than real depth. But even the mask of the patron may occasionally split into laughter, and that so infectiously, that it reveals how much sound healthy vitality the snob-mask manages to hide.

But that is not all, for this kind of decadent snob likes an occasional bit of clean honest fun, such as smashing glasses at rowdy parties; and an occasional rage when the chairs and tables fly through the air, for none may thwart his domineering, autocratic almightiness, which admits no higher authority than itself. Nor is he averse to some small philoso-

---

[1] His grandmother, Khitrovo, belonged to the famous family of the Rumianzovs. The family tradition had it that one of Rumianzov's sons, he being then one of Peter the Great's orderlies, bore a striking resemblance to the Tsar. Diaghilev's mother was a Yevreinov. (Ed.)

phizings at times, on elevated subjects, since he rather admires intellectuality, provided no one takes it too seriously. So fearing to live, he lives in shackles.

Yet the longer one looks, the clearer his real face shines through.

First, with a smile, or rather a quivering of the muscles round the harsh lips, so reminiscent of Peter the Great, and in that smile are kindness, softness, unbelievable warmth. This ghost of a smile, Diaghilev's "charm," is what one sees first, interpreting it as kindness to others. It seems to be saying how helpless its owner must be in practical matters, how utterly defenseless a man must be to smile in a fashion so charmingly childish, so virginally tender; and it is just that smile which charms and conquers and draws your eyes to his face, so that you *see* it at last.

Thereupon, one becomes conscious of Diaghilev's eyes, their sacred melancholy, their sacred torment, their Quest for the Holy City, their memory of a distant heaven, and their search for a new.

All these things were to be discovered in Diaghilev's eyes: tenderness, kindness and, least expected of all, sentimentalism.

Through the mask and the face, the true image of Diaghilev appeared.

The Diaghilev Heritage

In the mask and face of Serge Pavlovitch Diaghilev, that first and last of his line, a shoot which gave no scion, we find many of the qualities which I shall call "diaghilevism." To us Diaghilev, diaghilevism, stand for one man and one man only, Serge Pavlovitch, one of those men by whose efforts "was put in motion our land." Russian history needs no other Diaghilev, save only his aunt, Anna Pavlovna,[2] perhaps the most prominent social worker of the nineteenth century.

But to supply an answer to S. I. Mamontov, when, meeting Seriozha[3] Diaghilev in 1896, he asked: "From what soil has this mushroom sprung?" we must refer, not to Diaghilev, but to the Diaghilevs, whose family chronicler[4] soon makes clear that S. P. Diaghilev inherited his full share of the Diaghilev patrimony.

"They," she says, "men, women and children, handsome or plain, all manifestly belong to the same strain, all have the same distinguishing traits.

"First and foremost of these is the mouth. However charming, however ugly, it is always a variant of one basic conformation: the lower lip is always plump and sensuous.

"Next the hair and the way it springs from the scalp. Always thick and lustrous, though ranging from palest gold to raven black through

[2] Married Filosofov. (Ed.)
[3] Diminutive of Serge. (Ed.)
[4] Mme. Panaev-Diaghilev, S. P. Diaghilev's foster-mother. (Ed.)

every intermediary shade, always it frames the forehead in the same way.

"Then, despite an inherent cheerfulness, the family eye is characteristic, for whether blue, hazel, black, green, and whatever the shape may be, the same sad expression is characteristic of them all.

"An inclination to *embonpoint* in middle life—an *embonpoint* distinctly Russian, though in varying degrees—is also one of the family characteristics.

"All these factors, and a host of other barely noticeable traits, give them an *air de famille,* which makes them recognizable, wherever they may be. It is not of the kind which makes one brother the double of the other—they were never mistaken for each other—but frequently, in some drawing room, or railway carriage, no matter where, a friend or acquaintance of one member of the family would approach another whom he had never seen in his life, with the words: 'A Diaghilev, I presume?'

"Another characteristic, no less striking, was a certain natural gaiety which made them seem at home wherever they might be. To which must be added a certain oddity of speech, often found in members of large families, who invent a private language of their own, and thus form a sort of secret society."

In addition to these family traits common to all the Diaghilevs, Serge Pavlovitch had much that seemed directly inherited from his father and grandfather. And, just as his real face would materialize from the mask, so through the father, and *behind* the father—who had much in common with his brilliant son—it was possible to feel and visualize Serge Pavlovitch's grandfather, Pavel Dmitrievitch Diaghilev.

His father we know of as one of the adornments of the Imperial Household Guards, handsome, witty, easy-going, cheerful; of average learning and intellect, a good friend, a man of the world, active and interested in many things, with a gentleman's psychology which made him impatient of "cursed problems" or "life's mysteries," a man essentially forthright in all his responses.

Gifted with an excellent tenor voice, he was also an accomplished musician, and had, as a young officer, studied under the famous Czech Rotkovsky. Drawing-room ballads, gypsy songs, serious music, all came alike to him, and helped him to become a fashionable heartbreaker. Wherever he went, he was always welcome. At balls and restaurants, in the drawing room or at home, his gaiety and good spirits were proverbial.

Many of these traits were inherited by his son, Diaghilev—his mask-face, in addition to other qualities which this easygoing cheerful Guardee owed to his own father, a man of highly complex, interesting and original personality. Passionate, impetuous, with no bounds to his enthusiasms, before the moral crisis which overtook him in 1855, at forty-seven, Diaghilev's grandfather combined in himself an intense emotivity and passionate adoration of life, with an ascetic's yearnings, and was at one and the same time, part sybarite and epicure, part monk and scatter-brain. For so, his chief at the Treasury, Count Kiselev, once called him, on account of his refractory, unsettled temperament.

Pavel Dmitrievitch, his grandson P. G. Koribut-Kubitovitch tells us, "was an unusual man." Descended from an old family of Moscow gentry, he passed into the army by way of the St. Petersburg School of Military Engineering, but resigned his commission after a short period of service, to take up a position in the Ministry of State Domains under the famous Count Kiselev, only, however, to abandon it shortly owing to a trivial difference of opinion. Like his grandson, he found discipline intolerable.

At that period, he was exceedingly high-spirited, a first-rate executant on the piano, and proud of having studied under the then famous Field. He was also married, on excellent terms with his wife, and the father of eight children.

In 1850, however, he moved from the city, to settle in the province of Perm, where his father had left him an important estate.

This estate, "Bikbarda" of about 15,000 *desyatin* (some 40,000 acres), was situated partly in the Osinsk district of Perm province, and partly in the neighboring Birsk district of the province of Ufa, a large house being attached to each property, while in addition each part of the estate boasted a distillery.

Another item in his inheritance was a mansion of some thirty rooms, complete with lodge, garden, stables, ice-cellars, etc., in the main thoroughfare of Perm, capital of the province. But though he made his estate his home for six months of the year, the family remained in St. Petersburg for the education of the children, living in a large house on Furstadskaya Street, only the first two floors of which it occupied.

That he was broad-minded and of liberal views is proved by the fact that, disliking the idea of possessing serfs, he took care only to employ hired labor in his town house. It appears too that in his treatment of his peasant serfs he was always a kind and humane master.

It was natural, therefore, that with the reforms introduced by Alexander II, Pavel Dmitrievitch should be elected by the landowners of Perm province, to represent them on the famous committee for the liberation of the serfs, which was then sitting in St. Petersburg. Meanwhile, having an excellent head for business, his affairs and distilleries prospered, so that soon, from enjoying a modest competence, he became exceedingly wealthy.

Nevertheless, the richer Pavel Dmitrievitch became, the less store did he seem to set by his wealth and worldly possessions. And now he began to frequent the monks, those monks whom his wife accused of being responsible for the change which began to take place in him.

"It was they," she said, "who put into his head the idea of renouncing all his earthly possessions. He, poor man, cannot reconcile himself to it at all, you can see that by the way he's struggling with himself, for say

Grandfather of Diaghilev

what you will, he has a kind and loving heart." However, a different and far more convincing explanation of the change that was taking place in him, is provided by the reminiscences of H. V. Panaev-Diaghilev, when she writes:

"Anna Ivanovna, Pavel Dmitrievitch's wife, considered that the following incident which occurred, as she puts it herself, 'in the year Nonochka was married' (Nonochka being their eldest daughter Anna, who in 1855 married Vladimir Dmitrievitch Filosofov, one of the best men alive), was what inaugurated the family drama.

"It all happened in Peterhof. They had just rented a splendid big villa which formerly belonged to Rubinstein, and which still exists. There, the whole family migrated for the summer, including the young Filosofov couple, and their new-born baby Julinka. In addition to the nine Diaghilev children, there were also five Buickov children (the orphans of an elder sister of Anna Ivanovna's, adopted by Pavel Dmitrievitch) and the two half-grown sons of Count Fedor Petrovitch Litke, first cousins to Anna Ivanovna.

"Tutors, governesses and nurses added to the tale of the great gathering, and made innumerable mouths to feed, a fact on which Anna Ivanovna strongly insisted in telling the story, to give some idea of the difficult position in which she found herself, when Pavel Dmitrievitch, having gone to the Treasury for money one fine morning, failed to return, either that day, or the next three. Knowing that he had meant to collect a rather large sum, she began to fear he had been robbed or even murdered.

"She waited a bit longer, and then, as he still did not put in an appearance and there was no news of him, decided the matter needed looking into, and went off to St. Petersburg, no mean expedition in those days. There, the *dvornik*[5] of her town house informed her that the master had indeed been home, but that after a visit from a lame, redheaded monk, both had set off for an unknown destination.

"Not for a fortnight did Pavel Dmitrievitch return to Peterhof, and then he arrived pale, gloomy, obviously thinner, and without a penny piece in his pockets. Nor was it possible to make him disclose where he had been.

"We may assume that this episode indicated a crisis in Pavel Dmitrievitch's relations with his family, but that it should have initiated the ensuing drama seems to me exceedingly dubious. On the contrary, I should say that it marked the conclusion of, and resolved, an earlier hidden period of great stress and torment. It seems difficult to believe that this escapade could have been the result of a premeditated impulse.

"Some time later he fell ill, and began to behave in a way that was very abnormal. One symptom was his refusal to see anybody, even his chil-

[5] Yard porter. (Ed.)

dren, the one exception being his wife. Anna Ivanovna told me
that this was a terrible time, for whole days would be spent wandering
through the streets of St. Petersburg, and the nights in endless pacings
about the bedroom, to the interminable strains of the mechanical organ,
which we all knew so well from the ballroom at Bikbarda. At times,
these paroxysms brought him very near to frenzy. At other times, she
would find him oblivious, stretched out before the holy icons, like one
crucified. Again, there were times when he would attempt to swallow
mother-of-pearl Jerusalem crosses, broken up small, which she only just
managed to pull out of his mouth.

"This very bad period did not last long, but it left indelible traces.
The ancient, portly Pavel Dmitrievitch, sybaritic, gay and devoted to
music, receptions, the theater and masked balls, had vanished as completely as though he had never existed. In his place a new man appeared
—the ascetic: and to this ascetic, Anna Ivanovna was unable to reconcile
herself, even to the end of his days. With the vehemence and pride
which distinguished everything she did, she now began to oppose, and
passionately resist, his new way of life. Nevertheless, his own determination was as passionate and stubborn, with the result that neither would
make the least concession.

"As if to make things worse, money problems, as often happens,
began to crop up. As I see it, the steadily increasing family income helped
to provide ever-new reasons for discord, for as a result, Pavel Dmitrievitch
was enabled to donate enormous sums to the monasteries (I believe there
was hardly one which was not so favored), for the building of churches
and the endowment of religious hostelries: and in short, to hand out
money, right and left.

"All this made Mama furiously angry. One could not have called her
mean. True, she was economical where small things were concerned,
but that to my mind is often the sign of a liberal disposition, and this
she certainly had in larger matters, however much she might have been
astonished had anyone dared to tell her so. What made her so furious
was not the amounts that were lavished—she herself spent huge sums
freely—but the causes on which they were spent. The result was that
the clergy became an absolute nightmare to her, the object of a raging
hatred, because certain of its members were not above turning Pavel
Dmitrievitch's religious exaltation to their own advantage.

"The following story well illustrates how intense was her feeling on
this subject. It was their custom to attend divine service together, accompanied by the rest of their family, in the Cathedral of St. Sergius on
the Liteinaya. One Sunday, as they were standing side by side and the
offertory was made, Pavel Dmitrievitch put a bank note for a thousand
rubles into the plate. Whereupon, without a moment's hesitation, Anna
Ivanovna removed the note from the plate and placed it in her pocket,

leaving one ruble in its stead,[6] declaring meanwhile to her husband that she would go to the Metropolitan, tell him the whole story, and ask whether it was right for a God-fearing man so to despoil his own children."

When his grandfather died in 1883, Serge Pavlovitch was eleven, and vividly recollected his grandmother, Anna Ivanovna. How odd it is to recognize, in these portraits drawn by H. V. Panaev-Diaghilev, which cover the early part of Pavel Pavlovitch's life, the numerous traits that bring Diaghilev himself to one's mind.

This, therefore, was the Diaghilev soil from which that mushroom, Serge Pavlovitch Diaghilev sprang. Though of the same genus, he was wholly distinct, with traits we find in no other Diaghilev.

---

[6] P. G. Koribut-Kubitovitch told me it was not a "thousand-ruble note" (they did not exist then), but a large wad of one hundred ruble notes to the value of 5,000 rubles.

CHAPTER II

CHILDHOOD AND ADOLESCENCE

The Birth of S. P. Diaghilev

DIAGHILEV WAS born in the Selistchev barracks (province of Novgorod) on March 19th, 1872.

These barracks were situated on Count Arakchyev's historically famous estate, "Grusino," on the banks of the river Volkhov, and it was there that Diaghilev's father had been posted by his regiment for a year, and had taken his young wife. As the confinement drew near, they were joined by his favorite sister, Maria Pavlovna Koribut-Kubitovitch, some seven years his senior, widowed but two months before, and left with three children. Thanks to the regimental doctor, and Maria Pavlovna's assistance, the baby was safely delivered, in spite of an excessively difficult labor, due to the unusual size of the baby's head; but a few days later Mme. Diaghilev died in the arms of her sister-in-law.

"I remember," so writes Diaghilev's youngest aunt, J. P. Parensov, "how, when I had just left the Institute,[1] a great sorrow suddenly overwhelmed us; for we heard that Jenia had died in childbed. I remember how impressed I was by Mama's grief, the fuss and worry about getting mourning, our hurried departure for the Selistchev barracks. When we arrived, there was Jenia on the table, little Seriozha in an adjoining room crying, and Polushka completely overwhelmed by his grief (he was twenty-five at the time). I remember how sympathetic all the young people in the barracks were, how we all, and a great number of officers, followed the coffin down to the River Volkhov, to put her on a steamer for Kuzmino, where the funeral was to take place. All the time, little Seriozha was unconcernedly asleep in his nurse Dunia's arms, with young, handsome Alexandra Maximovna, Jenia's maid, standing by in case of need. We all became very fond of Seriozha and treated him with the utmost kindness.

"Then we held a family council, at which it was decided that the two orphaned families should be united, and soon after, Pavel Pavlovitch was gazetted Squadron Commander in the Chevaliers-Gardes, with handsome quarters in St. Petersburg, at the barracks in Shpalernaya Street.

---

[1] A high school for the daughters of noblemen modeled on the French convent school. (Ed.)

The Nanny Dunia

"I remember," says P. G. Koribut-Kubitovitch, sixty-six years later (he was six years and six months older than Serge Pavlovitch), "how, sometime in spring, they brought us the fair-haired, dark-eyed Seriozha; and how I began to look him over as he lay in the arms of his magnificent, red-haired wet nurse, while nanny Dunia, in the typical white-pleated cap worn by all nurses of good families in those days, stood beside. Then our nanny, Avdotia Adrianovna, wearing a similar cap, began lovingly to fondle the newcomer, an orphan from the very first days of his life."

Born a domestic serf into the Yevreinov family, nanny Dunia had brought up Seriozha's mother, and when she married, accompanied her, so to speak, as part of her mistress's dowry. Faithful, loving and beloved, she spent the whole of her long life, which reached into extreme old age, with only two families, the Yevreinovs and Diaghilevs. In addition she looked after Serge's two half-brothers, Valentine and Yuri, his father's sons by his stepmother Elena Valerianova Diaghilev. (Serge Pavlovitch had a great fondness for his half-brothers, and in particular Yuri.) Dunia represented a type of nurse which has now vanished entirely—a type we find exemplified in Pushkin's Arina Rodionovna—and Serge's whole life, down to 1912, was closely linked with hers.

When, as an undergraduate, Diaghilev moved from the Filosofovs' apartment to his own flat in Galernaya Street, it was nanny Dunia who came from Perm to look after him. When, founding *The World of Art,* Diaghilev took a large apartment at 45 Liteiny Prospect, two of the rooms of which were reserved as editorial offices, nanny Dunia followed him there. All Seriozha's friends and collaborators knew her well. In his well-known portrait by Bakst, she is there to be seen in the background: and, at the gatherings of the editorial staff, and the famous *World of Art* Mondays that were held during the winter, nanny Dunia, wearing a black lace cap, would preside over the samovar in the big dining room; no light task, when thirty to forty guests were assembled for tea.

P. P. Diaghilev's Second Marriage and Life in St. Petersburg

Seriozha did not long remain with the Koribut-Kubitovitchs, for his father, having lived down his despair, in 1874, two years after his wife's death, married Helena Panaev. Though the Diaghilev family had adored Seriozha's mother, and grieved sincerely at her death, a time came when they grew even fonder of the stepmother, a woman admirably suited to the Diaghilev family, who, attaching herself to them all, with the whole warmth of a generous heart, soon merged her interests completely in theirs. Clever, generous and warm-hearted, it was not long before all the Diaghilevs were at her feet. According to Serge Pavlovitch, there was no better woman in the world.

There is little need to enlarge on her feelings towards her new family; indeed, nothing could be added to the testimony she herself provides in her memoirs, extracts from which we have already quoted, and from which we now quote again, providing as they do, sure and reliable, vivid and interesting testimony to the conditions surrounding the life of the young Diaghilev.

Comfortable and easy with others, they were comfortable and easy with her, for she seemed to possess in the highest degree the art of creating a comfortable, homelike interior. So Serge Pavlovitch found it, whether in St. Petersburg, or Bikbarda, where his childhood and adolescence were spent.

We can reconstruct Diaghilev's life in St. Petersburg from what has been told us by D. V. Filosofov.

"Helena Valerianovna never had, and never could have had what is called a *salon mondain,* with all the conventionalities one is accustomed to attach to that sort of function. But not because she was unsociable. On the contrary, the door of her house always stood wide open to guests. But she made her acquaintances in an entirely different, 'non-*salon,*' spirit. She never tried to sort out people according to their usefulness, or reputation; she never ran after people, and as a result, everybody who came to the house became an intimate. Her husband's regiment, the Diaghilev and Panaev families, provided the extensive circle from which her many and various intimate friends were drawn. And it all happened quite naturally, as if by itself. To society folk—in the narrow sense of the word—to the special St. Petersburg type of them, in a word to all those who used their social connections for advancement in their careers, or for making useful friends, Helena Valerianovna's house was no good at all, and even a place that was rather boring. Nor did the hosts themselves do anything to attract this alien, unsuitable element, for they had no time for tiresome guests or guests who needed entertaining. But those who felt at home in the Diaghilev house, soon became constant visitors.

Music in Diaghilev's Life

"Sometimes, at her Thursdays, whole operas would be performed in amateur fashion. Much later, when those 'lovely days of Aranjuez' were over, I myself, late in the '90's, would sometimes hear a quartet from *Rigoletto* or *A Life for the Tsar,* executed by family forces. All the Diaghilevs were musical, but their interest was dilettante in comparison with the natural musical talent presented by the Panaevs. A good deal of information, from many sources, is available about the musical interests of the Diaghilevs. We learn, for instance, that 'Polushka,' Diaghilev's father, knew the whole of Glinka's opera, *Russlan and Ludmila,* by heart, besides others. . . . In her own recollections, Diaghilev's stepmother lays emphasis on their unusual enthusiasm and talent for music, and the way in which all the Diaghilevs seemed to breathe music like the very air. In her descriptions of Bikbarda, she writes . . . 'The sound of a piano rings out from the ballroom. All talk, shouting, laughter, movement dies away . . . everyone hurries to a seat; even the children arrive on tiptoe and sit quietly, and a silence reigns which seemed inconceivable even a moment before. Everyone has become all ears. . . . This family of musicians, in which even the smallest boys whistle a Schumann quintet or Beethoven symphony as they stroll about, is starting its ritual . . .'

"Among these boys, Seriozha's passion for music was especially marked. Greedily he absorbed everything that he heard, and was deeply affected by it. He had a really enthusiastic cult for Tchaikovsky, many of whose songs had long been familiar to him through hearing them sung by his stepaunt, A. V. Panaev-Kartsov. She sang Tchaikovsky's songs with great skill and understanding. Tchaikovsky himself highly esteemed the manner in which she rendered his songs. Strange as it seems now, in the latter part of the '80's, Tchaikovsky was far from enjoying any real popularity, and Mme. Panaev-Kartsov's efforts contributed greatly to his future success. I believe that the famous song *Den li Tsarit* was written especially for her. All his life, Diaghilev remembered how, as a child, he had visited 'Uncle Petia' in Klin, and it was always a pleasure to him to recall his connection with Tchaikovsky, and speak of him as 'Uncle Petia.' This, too, may have encouraged his cult for the composer, but the main reason for his infatuation, his quite extraordinary infatuation for Tchaikovsky, lay no doubt in the deeply absorbing and emotional qualities of the master's music. Diaghilev also met Mussorgsky in childhood. That composer, barely known at the time, played his aunt's accompaniments at the piano.

"Seriozha, like all the Diaghilevs, and this ingenuousness was perhaps the most striking and significant feature of their natures, never pondered whether the music was good music or bad music, never asked himself was he to like or dislike it, and for this or that reason, or whether a particular enthusiasm were praiseworthy or not. Diaghilev, like all the Diaghilevs, reacted to music, to all art in fact, with his *entrails,* emotionally, even sentimentally. In later life, he was often to become the prey of a conflict between his intellectual concept of what a work of art should be, and what he *felt* it should be. But at other times this inner self would lead him infallibly along the path of true art, and that, even intellectually."

Indeed, it would seem that so profound was the effect which Tchaikovsky's music had had on his soul, so deeply rooted in him was this first musical love and the emotional concepts with which it was linked, that, strive as he might in subsequent years to sever his allegiance, the effort was always foredoomed to failure.

Later, and even in the last London article, dated 1929, Diaghilev was to take up the cudgels "against the cult of Gounod, Tchaikovsky and Donizetti," who "inflicted both melody and simplicity upon us," and made "poor music seem merely banal." Yet, less than three weeks before his death, he was listening to Tchaikovsky's *Sixth Symphony,* and at the end, when all false and transitory things had fallen away, and all that was real and true in him rose up again with renewed power, in those last days, on the brink of eternity, he was recalling Tchaikovsky's melodies, those slow and long-drawn Russian melodies, with tears; and, overcome with emotion, would hum the *Symphonie Pathétique* to himself, and then say that in all music nothing could vie with the *Sixth Symphony, The Meistersingers,* and *Tristan.* And this though Diaghilev, in the years of apostolic servitude to new and modern forms, had come to consider that second god of his, the god he had learned to love so passionately in adolescence, to be the evil genius of the music of the nineteenth century.

I have lingered so long on Diaghilev's emotional responses to music through the *entrails,* because so much in him was linked with it. The same might be said of his responses to literature and painting. His environment during childhood was an environment where painting and literature, loved and cherished, made part of the family background. "The words of Turgeniev, Tolstoy, and Gogol in particular, hovered about us like old beloved friends." Though the family approach was to some extent dilettante, nevertheless it was understanding, and this, combined with an unusually powerful innate artistic sense, provided the boy with a compendious cultural and artistic baggage. There were no professional artists or workers in the arts to be found among the Diaghilevs, and yet this culture was in no wise abstract, mental or "intellectual." The Diaghilevs (and Diaghilev) loved the arts, and busied themselves with the arts, not with the routine connected with the arts.

It was this sort of enlightened dilettantism, which so much influenced Diaghilev, if not the Diaghilev of the Russian ballet, certainly that of *The World of Art,* in which, in 1900, he wrote:

"I hardly think many people would be found nowadays prepared to discuss the superiority of classical forms of art over the naturalistic, or vice versa. Modern workers in the art do not dazzle themselves with the task of propagating *coûte que coûte* the 'one true' vision, as it was seen twenty to twenty-five years ago. All trends have the same right to exist, for the value of a work of art does not in the least depend on its trend. Because a Rembrandt is fine, that does not mean that a Fra Angelico becomes any better or worse."

Life in Perm and Bikbarda

In 1882, when Serge Pavlovitch was ten, the Diaghilevs removed their household to Perm, and P. G. Koribut-Kubitovitch has kindly provided me with the details.

Pavel Pavlovitch Diaghilev
Father of Diaghilev

Jenia Yevreinov-Diaghilev
Mother of Diaghilev

Helena Valerianovna Panaev-
Diaghilev
Stepmother of Diaghilev

Diaghilev as a Baby
with His Father

"Pavel Pavlovitch Diaghilev remained in his regiment until he was gazetted Colonel, and would probably soon have taken command of a cavalry regiment, but just at this time, his creditors began to press him seriously, his debts having by now amounted to a sum considered particularly large in those days (some 200,000 rubles). This sum was chiefly owed to the moneylenders, who exacted extortionate interest, and when bills fell due for renewal, would almost double the original amount. When the news was broken to his father, Pavel Dmitrievitch agreed to clear his son's debts, but only on condition that he resigned from the brilliant Chevaliers-Gardes and moved to Perm, where he and his family could live comfortably and cheaply in a large, well-run house. In this house the grandfather now lived alone, save for a bachelor son. The daughters had all married, and were now established in St. Petersburg—as was their mother, to be near them. The eldest son lived at Bikbarda, where he was a justice of the peace, and his two sons attended the local high school. In the summer, however, all the members of the family would gather in Bikbarda, together with offspring, governesses and nurses; and then, in the autumn, the whole family would disperse, and the grandfather would be left alone in his great stone house. Thus, the arrival of his son, with a wife whom Pavel Dmitrievitch respected highly, and their three sons, Serge, Valentine and Yuri greatly altered his life and introduced a certain excitement.

"Fortunately for Diaghilev's father, the commanding officer of the Reserve Infantry Battalion stationed in Perm happened to be removed elsewhere, and by dint of using his connections, he managed to get himself gazetted to the vacant position. This was a great stroke of luck, even though it meant something of a descent, for with no knowledge of agriculture, or any interest in it, he would otherwise have been doomed to complete inactivity.

"The Diaghilevs therefore started on their long journey from St. Petersburg. In those days neither Perm nor Kazan were on the railway line, and it was necessary to alight at Nijni-Novgorod, then travel down the Volga on a Lubimov steamer for four days, and at Kazan branch off into the Kama River. To the children, the whole journey was a delightful, exciting adventure. All his life Diaghilev remembered the lovely banks of these rivers, their hills, their forests, their vast plains and pastures, the old villages, the small provincial towns, and the ancient Nijni-Novgorod and Kazan.

"To the grandfather, it was a great delight to see the huge house fill and become alive, and no longer feel overawed by the immense dining room capable of seating some sixty people. A new life began for him, cheerful and gay; with plenty of music, books and conversation. Cards were never seen in the Diaghilev house, no one ever played whist or preference, but art and literature were always welcome. Barely a year was out before the house had become the center of the town's artistic activities. To be admitted to the house was considered an honor to which all the neighbors aspired. Little by little a musical circle was formed, its nucleus being Seriozha's father and stepmother, who both sang beautifully, and Uncle Vanya, who, from childhood, had studied under the best St. Petersburg teachers, and was an excellent executant on both the piano and 'cello. Two or three times a year a charity concert would be given by this circle in the Assembly Rooms of the Nobility. Soon, a small amateur orchestra organized itself, again conducted by Uncle Vanya, and during rehearsals in the big drawing room, Seriozha would be permitted to sit up till ten. He was also allowed to sit up when Uncle Vanya and Danemark played pieces for four hands from Mozart, Beethoven, Haydn, etc., on a splendid Bechstein. This Danemark taught German in the Perm classical high school, but was also a distinguished musician, who was soon teaching Seriozha music. A strict and exacting teacher, he supervised all Diaghilev's music until he left school. Aunt Helena, Serge's stepmother, read aloud beautifully, and once or twice a week there would be a literary evening.

"On the dining-room walls, and in grandfather's huge study, hung large old prints of works by Rembrandt, Raphael, etc., and the bookcase contained magnificent illustrated works devoted to famous collections and the museums of Munich, Florence, Paris and other great cities. These Serge was allowed to handle in his grandfather's presence; and thus, at an early age, was already familiar with the names and works of many great artists.

"At this time, too, he was kept very busy with his lessons in music, French and German, though to the latter he proved particularly recalcitrant."

For this period of his life we must once again turn to the memoirs of H. V. Panaev-Diaghilev, and her description of the family life and countryside of Bikbarda. It is difficult to say what influence most profoundly affected the growing Diaghilev, but one thing may be asserted with confidence, namely, that if Diaghilev, thanks to an essentially direct and candid nature, was but little inclined towards childish musings and philosophizings, there was nothing in the way life was lived at Bikbarda, to encourage any such tendency.

"Never and nowhere, except in imagination," she writes, "did I ever see a veranda like ours at Bikbarda. Real terraces of earth and stone, flower beds and spurting fountains, may of course have been bigger, wider, and perhaps finer.... But ours was just a plain Russian wooden veranda, with pillars and a roof, that stretched along the whole southern wing of the one-storied timber house, and even beyond, seeing that it ended in a big loggia, which projected past the corner of the house and ran out over the garden gate, and alongside the road bordering a ravine. Beyond this hollow were the distillery, the village and a forest that seemed to stretch illimitable as the sea. Here on this loggia, we would generally sit to take tea, as we watched the sun slowly setting.... In summer, part of the loggia would be used for meals, and could easily accommodate some fifty people. On the balcony itself, near the loggia, numbers of sofas and old shiny chintz-covered stools were arranged, while the wall at the back was almost completely obliterated by a living screen of plants and creepers. Along the balustrade, and between the pillars, stretched rows of variegated summer flowers in boxes, and the big garden trees and their foliage made a kind of bower of the place.

"The descendants of the owners of Bikbarda consisted of four sons and four daughters; and these, with their wives, husbands and children, altogether totaled some fifty souls. Let us picture an occasion when, as frequently happened, all, or nearly all, were present. The characters are the Diaghilevs, and some total·stranger, just arrived, for the first time, let us say, on business. He is asked to stay...he agrees...and the party moves off to our dear Bikbarda veranda. As they proceed, there comes a drone of voices and peals of merry laughter, which goes on 'increasing until the bewildered guest suddenly finds himself in the midst of a noisy, irrepressibly gay crowd. Fashionably dressed women, children, officers, students, schoolboys, hurry to and fro, or bustle hither and thither, to the sound of loud kisses on every side.

"Astonished, he attempts to discover the source of such merriment. Is it a wedding, an anniversary, a baptism, someone's return from a distant journey, or some other occasion for rejoicing, of which he knows nothing? Meanwhile, he confounds himself in apologies for his unsuitable clothes, or explains he had not expected to interrupt some family celebration,· or break in on the assembled guests.

"Laughingly, they explain that nothing unusual is on foot, that it is just an ordinary day, that he is the only guest, and that all are members of the family.

"Perplexed, he draws apart to be out of the way of some young officer galloping astride a chair, or a tall man in mufti, frantically conducting an imaginary orchestra, miming every instrument to perfection, and singing the overture with faultless accuracy. Next, the stranger finds himself darting aside, for a covey of children dashes past like an avalanche from the mountains, and makes for the garden, where it disperses in all directions to play at expresses, or rushing troikas as the drivers shout in Tartar fashion—*Aititama-a!*

"Abashed, the guest begins to throw anxious glances round him, and strives to catch what people are saying, though not one word does he understand, even though they seem to be talking Russian. His head seems almost bursting with the effort, as watching his hosts, he mutters to himself, 'Madness, nonsense, sheer insanity.'

"Almost everyone who later became the friend, or as often happened, the enthusiastic admirer of the family, went through some such similar phase at their first meeting with the Diaghilev family *en masse.*"

Diaghilev's Love of Scenery

Immensely significant for his latter life, was to be the fact that Diaghilev had been reared, not in St. Petersburg or Moscow, but in Bikbarda; indeed, all his approaches and reactions to art were profoundly conditioned by this fact. There he lived surrounded by all that was Russia, there he learned to love the simple Russian landscape, and the banks of the Kama and Volga, for the memory of his trip down the Volga to the Caucasus, was to remain all through his life an abiding memory. There, too, he learned to love everything Russian, and it was that immense, whole-hearted, anxious love, which in a great measure determined not only the artistic bias, but the artistic predilections of the later Diaghilev, founder and editor of *The World of Art*.

Diaghilev was considered, and still is considered, a snob and cosmopolitan aesthete. And it is true that he was indeed both these things, while being receptive to all forms of art, and able to accord them all his admiration and enthusiasm. But the foundation of his *love* for art, was his love of Russian scenery, whereas any tendency towards a national or nationalistic Russian art, left him indifferent or hostile, as did everything that was narrow and artificial. This can be seen in the way he took up arms against "pseudo-Berendeis" [2] and "Stenka Razins" and in his claim that nothing could prove more harmful to an artist's integrity than a nationalist bias. Nevertheless, he was capable of writing, "The only admissible nationalism is the unconscious nationalism of the blood. This is a rare and valuable treasure. But it must be one's very nature that is nationalist, which—even, it may sometimes be, against one's will [as actually happened in Diaghilev's case]—automatically and eternally reflects the fires of a fundamental nationalism. Nationalism can only be an integral part of oneself; one must be, as it were, a noble scion in whom the pure blood of one's nation still flows. Then its value is real, incalculable, I may say."

Diaghilev the aesthete, could admire Aubrey Beardsley, but his true love was reserved for Levitan, Maliutin, and Mashenka Yakunchikova. As soon as he speaks of his favorite artists, how different are the words that spring to his lips! Lyrical, colloquial, plain matter-of-fact words which clearly reveal that Diaghilev, fundamentally, could have been no "aesthete." How beautifully he writes of Levitan, "who succeeded in making us realize that we had lost the art of appreciating and seeing Russian scenery with Russian eyes; making us realize that he alone of Russian painters was able to depict the infinite charm of all those emotions which, in morning coolness, or twilight's languorous warmth, in some remote north Russian village, each of us so blissfully feels. How much true understanding of Russian nature, worthy of Pushkin himself,

---

[2] Berendei: A mythological figure representing "the good old times of yore," somewhat similar to Old King Cole. (Ed.)

we find in all his work; in his blue moonlit nights, his avenues of sleeping, century-old birches, which slowly lead one to that old house in the country, which all of us know so well, where Tatyana waits and dreams....

"There was nothing sensational about his work: the bits of scenery he painted seem to have flashed past, and been forgotten, as though they themselves had fused with Nature. But one fact remains indubitable, and will never be forgotten. That very moment we leave the stifling atmosphere of the town for Nature, we recall with gratitude the great lessons of this painter of the Russian soil. Whether it be some village belfry, some tattered hedge or bluish lake, in all his work we see Nature *through* him, *by means of* him, as he himself saw it and revealed it to others."

With the same love Diaghilev writes of the work of Maliutin, in connection with the building of a tower at Talashkino, "that proper Russian countryseat" owned by Princess Tenishev. "What a delightful and artistic impression, all these elaborate, yet simple towers, make on the beholder! It is impossible to say where the charm of Maliutin's artistic imagination begins, or where the charm of the Russian landscape ends. Ornamented with fantastic birds, gates lead into the forest, and their ramifications mingle with the pine tree branches against a haze of deep dazzling snow."

And then the lyrical obituary Diaghilev wrote for Mashenka Yakunchikova, that real lament for a sister-artist. "Yakunchikova's time was all too short for all the things she might have done. But in all that she had time to do, harassed by baby-napkins and the bustle of Paris, she revealed the depths of a lovely talent, a profound feeling and affection for our Russian forests, oh, so remote, 'those little pines and firs' which for her were instinct with religious feeling, and which she longed for all her life. Her whole existence was a drama.... She could not cope with it all, she, the dear poet of Russian forests, pastures, village churchyards with their lopsided crosses, convent gates, and village porches. How could she, she so gentle and frail, find it in her to struggle with life?"

With what emotion must Diaghilev have looked at the portrait of Yakunchikova, depicting an immense open lawn facing the pillared terrace of Vedenskoye, so touchingly reminiscent of the Bikbarda veranda described by his stepmother. Childish memories persisted in Diaghilev all through his life and in Benois' décor for the *Götterdämmerung* it is as though some tiny corner of Perm province haunts him still.

Diaghilev attributed so great an importance to the Russian landscape in its influence on Russian painting, that, writing of the Moscow Exhibition of "The 36" painters, he says: "The Moscow public, from the very opening, greeted this venture by 'The 36' with unanimous approval. And it was right that they should do so, for one cannot but approve of these pleasing and modest canvases by our truly Russian landscape painters, revealing as they do how closely and perseveringly these painters have studied the beauties of our Russian springs, the poetry of thawing snow, and every fascinating shade of golden autumn."

Here it is necessary to qualify, somewhat, what has been said about *his kind* of love for the familiar Russian landscape, and *his kind* of approach to Russian painting. In art, Diaghilev searched for, and valued, familiar emotions dear to him, though he was far from being indifferent to what the picture represented. But this value acquired importance and interest for him, only when the picture had its own artistic value, independent of any "anecdotal" quality. The theme, the "what" of painting, not only did not exist for him, he felt it alien to him. He was as actively hostile to it, as he was deeply sympathetic to the whole of the "Independent" movement which was then beginning to arise.

The second qualification relates to the depicting of Russian nature. What Diaghilev loved most was not the heroic or fantastic, but the elegiac, lyrical, tender. For that reason Bilibin, both Vasnetzovs, and even Helena Polenova, one of the goddesses of *The World of Art,* left him comparatively cold, whereas the profoundly lyrical Levitan and Yakunchikova moved him deeply. In the same way, Tchaikovsky's elegiac tenderness made Diaghilev, about the same time, say of him, "that dear and near poet, that dearest of all Russian musicians."

I have dealt in some detail with the problem of Diaghilev's conception of art, because the origins of that attitude were rooted in childhood and adolescence, when as a small, healthy and turbulent boy, he roamed the woods and fields of Bikbarda. In that normal and healthy environment, there was but little likelihood that he would indulge in abstract analytical processes, in place of a direct assimilation of nature. No, Diaghilev was never a *Wunderkind!* He was a country-bred boy, surrounded by others, nurtured on Nature and Nature alone, very different from that other, Nikolenka, in Tolstoy's *Childhood and Adolescence,* "whose spiritual sustenance was abstract discussion and deadly introspection." Leaving the question of Diaghilev's later development to a future chapter, all I would say here is that, as time went on, he more and more inclined to the "Left" where art was concerned, only however to return, before his death, to what was traditional and *real,* for that was the very basis of his being.

Diaghilev's childhood must have been very happy. I do not get this impression of his happiness, and the joyous fullness of his life at this time, from books or memoirs—for who can pierce the candid, mute soul of a child?—but from things recalled by Serge Pavlovitch towards the end of his life: memories of youth, remembered with joyful tears, and assurances that only then had he been truly happy.

The Gymnasium [3]

In the early years of the '80's, though the exact year is not known, but probably in his first year at Perm, i.e., 1882, Diaghilev entered the Perm gymnasium. Though we know little of these years, we should know less but for the recollections, published by a schoolmate, O. Vassiliev, whose friendship with Diaghilev began in 1886.

"Our gymnasium in those days," he writes, "was an old-fashioned, provincial institution, with somewhat patriarchial customs and observances. From time immemorial the headmaster had been old Gracinsky, who was already past eighty when I first went to the school. He was a venerable old man, with snow-white hair, who, puffing and blowing, would roam about the corridors in a nightgown and dressing gown. This nightgown was very symbolic of the way things went on at our gymnasium, for the whole place was run in the most homely manner. Classes often began late, the teachers would at times arrive not too sober or with obvious hang-overs, having done themselves well the night before, and order and cleanliness, in the austere and somber old building, were mainly conspicuous by their absence.

"Nevertheless our 'Granddad' as we used to call him, was the very soul of kindness and decency.

"True, he looked stern, would frown, and take one to task rather severely, even pull one's hair a little, but that was only to hide his fundamental kindness and good nature. The smallest boy in the lowest form would have no fear of him.

"Soon after I began going to the school, 'Granddad' retired to make way for a young, energetic head of the 'climber' type, who immediately started 'smartening' the school up, with the result that very soon feathers were flying in all directions.

"The new head went to the other extreme. Alfionov by name, he was by way of being a public figure, and had achieved some notoriety, on account of a public pronouncement concerning the 'Sons of Cooks.' [4] One frequently saw his name in the newspapers and reviews, and the expression he invented became a byword.

"In those days, Seriozha Diaghilev, the son of very wealthy and important people in our town, attended our school. His father, a colonel, owned a large distillery.

"He was a tall, bulky boy for his age, with an unusually big head and expressive face. His education and development were well beyond average, and far in advance of his class. He knew things of which we, his schoolmates, had no notion, such as Russian and foreign literature, the theater and music. French and German he also spoke fluently, and

[3] Secondary school, equivalent to a grammer school. (Ed.)
[4] The Minister of Education had issued regulations which tended to restrict the rights of children of domestics to attend high school. (Ed.)

could play the piano. Externally, too, he was very different. There was an elegance, a refinement, even a stateliness in his carriage. He was a perfect 'little gentleman' in comparison with us.

"Seriozha Diaghilev had a funny attractive manner, which seemed to go with him, and to be part and parcel of that elegance of his. In talking, he would frequently give an abrupt shake to his hand, and end with a snap of the fingers. It was a purely imitative gesture adopted by one in search of a pose and picturesque mannerism, but already it corresponded to something in the boy's nature.

"There is no need to insist how exceptional he appeared in our eyes, the eyes of his classmates and contemporaries, mostly modest, unnoticeable and even drab and colorless provincial schoolboys, or on the impression which he created on us. The teaching staff, too, considered him exceptional.

"His scholastic progress, however, was less remarkable. Not because he lacked the capacity for academic distinction: everything, on the contrary, testified to his outstanding gifts: but because all our school-world, with its dreary learning, its gray teachers and classmates, was too remote from his nature. He lived in a different world, more beautiful, more refined, and altogether richer in content.

"The Diaghilev home was one of the most brilliant and intellectual in Perm. Indeed, it was Perm's 'Athens.' There, artists, musicians, and the most cultured progressive inhabitants of the town congregated for private theatricals, balls, concerts or recitals of chamber music. Diaghilev's father was very hospitable, a perfect host, and his mother (his stepmother, rather) was a woman of great culture, a musician and singer, who often performed at charity concerts.

"Seriozha Diaghilev moved among the *élite,* and so was in no way interested in a dismal, gray, provincial school and what it could teach him. The Diaghilev house was a large, magnificent mansion at the end of the main street—Great Siberian Street—near the park. Indeed, it was like the palace of some feudal prince. Inside, too, all was luxury and wealth.

"Living in such a palace, and accustomed to such an *élite,* Diaghilev no doubt only remembered school and all connected with it, when the moment came to pick up his satchel and go off to his lessons. Probably it was the dreariest moment of his day at that time.

"He would arrive in class totally unprepared, and immediately set to work to mug up his lesson, with the help of the best pupils. No one ever refused to help him, and when his turn came to be 'called,' there would always be lots of zealous prompting, while during written lessons numbers of helpful notes would be passed to him. Owing to this help and his own dexterity, plus a natural resourcefulness, he generally emerged from critical situations completely victorious. One must add that the teachers assisted him in every possible way. Most of them frequented the Diaghilev house, and enjoyed the attentions and hospitality of its amiable and enlightened hosts.

"Often on coming to school, Seriozha would say: 'I 'll be called at one of the Greek lessons today.'

" 'Why do you think so?' we would ask.

" 'Our teacher in Greek was visiting us last night, and told me.'

"And he actually would be called at the Greek lesson that day, and perfectly prepared, receive full marks. Needless to say, I confess we were all rather envious of him on such days, for we were questioned unawares, and the teachers did not visit our parents' houses.

"I reached the fifth form with Seriozha Diaghilev, after which, my parents moving to a different town, I began to go to another school."

These memoirs provide a veracious, living picture of the spoiled, happy-go-lucky Seriozha. One's only regret is that his classmate says nothing of his hot-tempered, dictatorial and arbitrary nature, nor of his pranks and fights at school, for we know that Diaghilev, the youth, often ended his discussions with blows.

In spite of the many true and vivid traits described by O. Vassiliev, the memoirs sound somewhat sanctimonious, and to be written from a viewpoint that seems to reveal an eye to his future greatness and fame.

Legends about Diaghilev

In 1890, at eighteen, Diaghilev completed his studies at the Perm gymnasium. But actually his childhood and adolescence had come to an end the year before, when he "fell"; when for the *first* and *last* time in his life he had intercourse with a woman. This episode played so enormous a part throughout the remainder of his most unusual, though fundamentally normal, man's life, that it is necessary to inquire more closely into the actual circumstances, in order to seek a clue to Diaghilev's difficulties.

Should we, can we, investigate a matter so delicate?

These two questions demand separate answers. To my mind, it is a matter that needs discussing, and to which an answer should be found. Diaghilev was of such importance, indeed so historically important, that whatever we can learn of his life must be valuable to us. In my opinion, no truth about Diaghilev can detract in the least from his greatness. Be that as it may, however, so much gossip and rumor has been spread about in connection with Diaghilev's "abnormalities," that they are now, and have been for years, public property.

Thus, it is altogether too late to attempt to suppress these rumors, and further silence would only result in establishing them more strongly, though they in fact distort and defile Diaghilev's character. Not silence, but truth must be the weapon to battle against all these travesties.

To the second question, can we investigate this matter, the reply must unfortunately be in the negative. For the answer to the riddle involves people now living, though of no importance historically, save for the legendary Nijinsky, whose relation to Diaghilev has been written about elsewhere.

But to return to the "episode." As Serge Pavlovitch told it me, it appears he was then seventeen, and the girl, young, charming, and a cousin of sorts.... Then suddenly to his horror and astonishment, he found himself infected. This occurrence made a dreadful impression on Diaghilev, and eternally inspired him with a sort of aversion to women. Eternally! We know from life and literature (I am thinking of Tolstoy, but especially of Andreyev, whose *The Abyss* had such amazing success in the early years of the twentieth century, because of its profound psychological truth), that the first youthful "falls," absurd and aimless though they may be, are practically always disillusioning, and inspire an *eternal* disgust. But this *eternity* is hardly protracted, for a time comes when the blood once more stirs, and overcomes the disgust. Then, given a true relation, disgust vanishes, and makes way for love. This is normal, and is what should have happened in Diaghilev's case, since he was normal himself. And so it would have done ... according to certain information which has come to me, but which unfortunately I have been unable to verify. For Diaghilev did meet a woman whom he learned to love and desire, but a woman who rejected his suit. It was with bitterness, therefore, that Diaghilev recalled his rejected love, remarking that, but for this rebuff, he would never have glanced at another person....

We do not know whether there was actually such a woman in his life, but, be that as it may, even when Diaghilev's intimate life had already taken another direction, there were times when love and desire for woman would awake in him, though fated never to find expression or fulfillment.

Highly sexed, with strong erotic instincts, Diaghilev's creative erotic energies were directed into "abnormal" channels, not so much because of his repulsion towards women, but because he happened to frequent a certain fashionable *milieu,* and because of a friendship with a young handsome writer....

At that time—the '90's—both he and Diaghilev attacked "abnormal love" with such heat, that even their friends did not suspect the existence of any such intimacy between them.

According to Diaghilev, had he been able to marry the woman he loved, no one else would ever have mattered to him, and he would have remained faithful to his *one woman.* Since fate, however, willed otherwise, his life became a quest for the *one beloved.* Unless this is understood, it is impossible to understand Diaghilev and his eroticism, or its importance in his devotion to the arts.

Above all, Diaghilev was *constant.* Though he loved many, it was not because, his whim satisfied, he passed easily from love to love; but because *they* abandoned him, *they* betrayed him, and left him to his agony, and the shattered fragments of his dream of *one beloved*. Diaghilev had no use for "lovely boys"—more, he was always drawn to normal people— and nothing can be more erroneous than such a view of him.

The truth was very different. What attracted him in people was their talent, or some exceptional gift adumbrating genius, a genius pure and simple, for everything in Diaghilev humbled itself before the supremacy of art. Love, Eros, was not only linked to, and bound up with art for him, but came to him through art.

First he would be struck and enthralled by some discovered "genius," then he would wish to bring that genius to life and reveal it to the world, and only then would he begin to love the possessor of that genius, tenderly, timorously, self-sacrificingly; begin to love and desire and long for the chosen one to be his, all his.

True to the family type, for all the Diaghilevs had numbers of children and saw themselves as so many *paterfamilias,* Diaghilev all his life dreamed of a family and strove to build one up with the help of his *one beloved,* though that *one beloved,* time after time, abandoned him for some woman, to create a family with that woman. Then once more Diaghilev would be left alone in his fearful abandonment, to a world made desert.

This was Diaghilev's tragedy, repeated over and over. First that brutal shock when Romola robbed him, fate's spoiled child, of *his* Nijinsky. Then, as successive favorites, one after the other, abandoned him for women, he came to realize by degrees how inevitable that betrayal must be. And so Diaghilev became jealous of women, where his beloved were concerned, and feared the eventual rupture, knowing how inevitable it must be. He knew too how stimulating his own intimacy was, and that the more he hedged his "elected" round, the more alluring and desirable women found them. Thus, in a very self-protection, he would seek to arouse a disgust in them for the female form, by demonstrating its lack of ideal beauty. Again, knowing that what was most terrible, most dangerous in women was not their bodies, which were rarely beautiful, but their romantic halo, their femininity and charm, he would seek to protect himself by encouraging the physical intimacy of his "elected" with women, so long as that intimacy remained on a physical plane, for then no opportunity would exist for the dream to crystallize, that being what he most feared.... Nevertheless, all this conflict moved and excited him strangely.

More and more, with time, was Eros killed in him, and ever more clearly appeared the futility of his dream of establishing a family about him. An abiding sadness took possession of his soul. This longing for a family, given his paternal nature, was intensely deep-rooted. Towards the end he began to think of another family, not this time his own, but one very near to him. I remember how, in 1928, the year before his death, he said to me, with a sad affectionate smile, "Seriozha, marry, please marry!

I'll stand godfather to your son. He'll call me Granddad and love me. When I'm old, he'll be such a joy to me, perhaps my only joy...."

All this has taken me a long way from Diaghilev's childhood, but how disentangle youth from maturity and their endless repercussions? And is it not in youth that we find the spring which feeds maturity, and more or less determines the whole of a man's future development?

CHAPTER III

PRELUDES TO "THE WORLD OF ART"

Diaghilev's arrival in St. Petersburg and his meeting with
A. N. Benois

SOMEONE LEAPS through the window of the Ratkov-Rozhnov's villa near St. Petersburg, and a gay, clear, baritone voice cries out, "I'm Seriozha!"

It was 1890, and Diaghilev had but lately arrived from Perm.

The story is now taken up by his friend at that time, A. N. Benois.

"I first met Diaghilev," he says, "in the summer of 1890. That year, I remained in town, and D. Filosofov, who had gone off to his estate, Bogdanovskoye, entrusted me and our common friend V. F. Nouvel, with the task of seeing that his cousin, Seriozha Diaghilev, who had just matriculated in Perm, and was about to enter the university, 'was made comfortable.' One fine morning, therefore, I was informed that Seriozha had arrived, and the very same day was able to take a look at Dima's cousin, in Valetchka's apartment. What struck us all was his look of abounding health. He had full rosy cheeks, vermilion lips and perfect white teeth, revealed whenever he smiled. It was seldom that this smile did not turn into an infectious, though quite childish laugh. On the whole, he seemed 'a nice chap' to us, 'a boisterously healthy country lad,' and if we then and there decided to allow him to join 'our band,' it was only because he was a relative of one of us, Dima. He was the same age as Filosofov, two years younger than I, and one year younger than Valetchka.

"The memory of this meeting recalls something that happened either in the same, or the following year, at a time when I knew Serge very much better, but when many things in him still had a way of unexpectedly revealing themselves. Seriozha had just come back from the country, and wanted me to go with him visiting Valetchka, then staying in a villa at Pargolovo. As it happened, Valetchka was out, and we went looking for him, but as I wanted to revisit certain places remembered from childhood, we went towards the Viukhi Hills, which bound Pargolovo to the north. It was very hot, and we were forced to cross some rough, boggy ground. After a bit, tired out, we decided to rest in a field, and then, having discovered a dry spot, stretched out on the grass. As we lay there looking up at the sky, I began to put him through a sort of cross-questioning. This kind of friendly inquisition was pretty usual among us at the time. It was a way of finding out how 'suitable' the other fellow was, a way of assuring ourselves his views did not diverge too hopelessly from our own. Even at our first meeting it had transpired that, though Seriozha was musical, and even a 'composer,' and intended, in addition to his studies, to take courses in voice-training and musical composition, his musical tastes did not quite correspond wth ours. Even then, he ranked Glinka above all other composers (his father Pavel Pavlovitch knew the whole of *Russlan* by heart), but though he appreciated Borodin, at the same time, too, he enjoyed all sorts of 'Italian stuff,' while being somewhat indifferent to our idol Tchaikovsky, and even Wagner.

"This 'serious' conversation was suddenly interrupted most unexpectedly, in the worst schoolboy manner. Lying on my back, I could not see what Seriozha was doing, and so was completely taken aback when I suddenly found him astride of me, belaboring me with his fists, and at the same time roaring with laughter. Naturally, a fight started. But still, nothing of this kind was ever allowed in our group. We were all 'well brought up, mothers' little boys,' and according to the then prevailing custom, were rather averse to any kind of 'physical exercise.' What was more, I soon discovered that I should not be able to deal with such a strong, heavy chap as Seriozha then was, and that, in fact, the 'senior' had got into a very unprofitable and even humiliating situation. A ruse seemed the only way out, and I uttered a loud cry, and said that my hand was injured. Nevertheless, he did not immediately stop, and his eyes, only a few inches from my own, went on gleaming in triumph and the desire to get the better of me. At last, meeting with no further resistance, and yielding to my prayers, he stopped the silly game, jumped to his feet, and even helped me get up. To make him believe I was hurt, I went on nursing my hand for some little time, though in fact it did not pain me at all.

"I have remembered this episode all my life, and in my subsequent relations with him, I often recalled it whenever he 'got me under' (though in a figurative sense), or when I had somehow got my own back and was 'victorious.' In any case, our relations throughout the succeeding years continued in terms of competition and struggle, and as I see it, this gave an added vitality and strenuousness to our friendship and collaboration....

"...For years I had been one of Seriozha's chief 'pedagogues,' one of his 'intellectual guardians.' But all through those years, Seriozha, while 'wringing out' of me (and everyone else) whatever we could be made to yield, would at the same time, with a strange facility, pass from peace to strife, would 'throw' his man, or again, for no apparent reason, take a hiding, though now he employed 'persuasive' means of a moral, or business order, instead of having recourse to brute force."

Friendship with D. V. Filosofov and first journey abroad

The incident referred to above must have taken place in 1891, for Diaghilev only spent a few days in St. Petersburg during the summer of 1890, after which he left for Bogdanovskoye, the Filosofov estate in Pskov province, preparatory to starting out with his cousin on their "European tour."

This journey abroad marks the beginning of that deep friendship which united the two men for the next fifteen years. Abroad, people would often turn round to stare or gaze after them with open admiration, so gentlemanly did Diaghilev appear, so aristocratic Filosofov. Benois tells how Filosofov with his great influence over Diaghilev introduced him to art. The extent of Filosofov's influence over Diaghilev cannot be denied, not only in the early '90's, but during *The World of Art* period. Nevertheless, it must remain an open question, whether this influence was either positive or of great significance. I shall, however, treat this matter in greater detail when discussing the editorial staff of *The World of Art*.

Among those surrounding Benois, Dima Filosofov undoubtedly knew most about art, though least sensitive to it. This organic alienness, never suspected by the "Pickwickians," will be comprehended only by artists. Dima was useful in helping to propound the problems of art to Diaghilev —at that epoch abstract considerations meant little to him—but as to conveying any understanding of art, or helping him to assimilate it, that he could not do. Indeed, endowed as he was by nature with artistic perceptions and a sensitivity given to but very few of the disciples of Apollo, this was perhaps what he least stood in need of. Let us be grateful, therefore, to Filosofov for guiding Diaghilev in the direction of the arts.

This first journey abroad was but short, for both had to be back in time for the new term. Nevertheless, they had managed to visit Berlin, Paris, Venice, Rome, Florence and Vienna. What made the deepest impression on Diaghilev were Venice, Florence and Vienna. Here it was he heard his first performance of *Lohengrin*. It swept him out of himself, and from that moment he began to rave about Wagner. From *Lohengrin* and *Tannhäuser* he progressed to *The Nibelungs* and *Parsifal,* and from *Parsifal* and *The Ring* to *Tristan and Isolde* and the *Meistersinger,* the two latter works remaining his most beloved operas to the end of his days.

In 1900, in *The World of Art,* we find the following words from his pen: "The most important musical event of the season was that which passed least noticed. We refer to the production, on the Russian stage, of Wagner's opera *Tristan and Isolde.* Generally speaking, it is always works of genius which least appeal to audiences. This axiom, though far from new, always excites an involuntary protest. *Tristan* was composed some forty years ago, and consequently sufficient time should have elapsed for our audiences to have accustomed themselves to it; nevertheless, to date, we fear the courage has been lacking. Not that we disapprove, since the longer a work of genius remains hidden from the enthusiasms of the multitude, the completer and more intact will it remain for the lovers of true art."

About Venice, which later became for Diaghilev the most beloved place on earth—a Diaghilev place—I shall have to tell again and again. His delight in it was endless, he was always talking of it, and after his first return he would, to all and sundry, proudly display a large photograph depicting himself and Filosofov reclining in a gondola.

Revelation, however, came in Florence, and with it a standard to appraise all art. Significantly, *The World of Art* for 1899 contains the following words under his name: "There is no objective norm for the evaluation of a work of art. But in every, or almost every, work of art there is a moment of maximum creative genius, and that and that only must be our scale. Only that is worth while and exciting. One must climb the pinnacles of Florentine art to pass judgment on contemporary art."

This belief in Florence as earth's most priceless treasure house of art was reaffirmed in him with every subsequent visit.

The "Neva Pickwickians" and the influence of A. N. Benois

Back in St. Petersburg, Diaghilev lived for a time with his aunt, A. P. Filosofov—Dima's mother—well known for her pioneer work in connection with women's rights, and their freedom to enter the universities. Here he took his degree in law, as did his new friends, D. V. Filosofov, A. N. Benois and V. F. Nouvel. Not that the university played any important part in his life, for neither the life nor the work interested him. His whole outlook differed fundamentally from that of the average undergraduate—the herd instinct frightened him—and politics, whether of the Right or Left, left him indifferent. Nor did the subject he had chosen much attract him, for he seldom attended lectures, and time and again absented himself from examinations, with the result that he was soon outstripped by his fellows (as was, owing to illness, Dima Filosofov). It was only the necessity of completing the course, and taking a degree, in those days considered essential to a career, which made him finally pass the required examination. It was now 1896, and Diaghilev had spent six years at the university instead of the customary four.

What interested him much more deeply was a group formed in 1890, the year in which he reached St. Petersburg. The story of the group, or "society," which came to play such an important part in Russian art life, is told in detail by its chief inspirer, A. N. Benois.

"The active members of the 'society,'" he says, "the real cradle of *The World of Art,* were myself, its elected president, V. F. Nouvel, D. V. Filosofov, L. S. Rosenberg, who in the following year adopted the name of his grandfather, Bakst, G. F. Kalin and N. V. Skalon. All these were foundation members, and as such enjoyed certain honorary privileges. Bakst held the office of speaker (and maintained order by means of a brass bell only too frequently employed), and Grisha Kalin was the secretary.

"As associate members, though not very regular in their attendances, we had C. A. Somov, my childhood friend V. A. Brun de St. Hippolyte, who later vanished completely from our world, J. N. Fenoult, J. A. Mamontov, N. P. Cheremisinov, D. H. Pypin and S. P. Diaghilev... Diaghilev himself never lectured, and disliked attending our 'real' lectures, but on less formal evenings he, together with 'Valetchka' Nouvel, would treat us to pieces for four hands, or would sing in his fine powerful baritone....

"The subject of some of our lectures were: 'Some characteristics of the great masters of painting,' delivered by myself and in which I managed to deal with the lives of Dürer, Holbein and Cranach; 'French Painting of the XIXth Century,' also by myself, but this time, I believe, I got no further than Girodet and Gérard; 'The Belief in a Future Life among Various Peoples,' read by Skalon, who alone among us was distinguished by a materialist conception of the universe; 'Turgenev and his Time,' by Kalin, a very lively and witty lecturer; 'Russian Painting,' by Levushka Bakst, who had only time to acquaint us with the work of G. Semiradsky and J. Klever, sundry landscape painters and C. Makovsky, for which we twitted him unmercifully; 'The History of Opera,' by V. Nouvel, who accompanied his lecture with some interesting musical illustrations; 'Alexander I,' by our youngest member, D. Filosofov, though, as I remember, he barely got further than 1806. But there is no need to give these lectures in further detail, for the themes treated at our gatherings provide a sufficient proof of the part they played in originating the future *The World of Art.*

"By the middle of the first winter, however, the 'Neva Pickwickians' began to reveal a certain impatience towards the society and its statutes. Associate members grew irregular in their attendances, lecturers tried to shirk lecturing and the unbridled spirit of youthful exuberance tore wildly about, and strove to destroy the existing order. As for the Speaker's bell, it was rarely silent.

"In the autumn of 1891, the society's meetings were resumed, only to be discontinued almost immediately, and were never held in that form again. But the thing had been done. We realized we represented a definite kernel, or, as we liked to call ourselves, remembering Balzac, *'un cenacle,'* composed of personalities 'out-of-the-ordinary,' that being one of our jocular [1] ways of describing ourselves, and one which continued perma-

---

[1] A. N. Benois says that the term "personalities out-of-the-ordinary" was used jocularly by the members, but this must be an error, for all the members at that epoch were seriously interested and attracted by Nietzsche and Nietzscheanism—with its consequent influence on *The World of Art.* Though they may not all have been positive of becoming "Napoleons" they most certainly believed themselves to be "Supermen."

nently in use. In time, however, the membership of the group changed. The pillars, Valetchka, Levushka, Dima and I, remained through all the metamorphoses of *The World of Art,* but by degrees Skalon, Kalin and many associate members left. In their place some who had remained at a distance, such as Diaghilev, Somov, and—no longer a boy—my nephew Lanceret, now attached themselves the more closely. In the course of 1892 and part of 1893, my friend Charles Birlé, an official at the Consulate in St. Petersburg, and later French Consul in Moscow, became a regular attendant. To him we owe the change in our attitude towards contemporary art. He was also responsible for bringing A. P. Nourok into our group, a man several years our senior but with a soul considerably younger.

"At this time our society was contemplating the publication of its own journal, and had even taken some preliminary steps, but of course nothing came of it. I say of course because Diaghilev had nothing to do with the matter, for during the first five years of the '90's Seriozha Diaghilev was somewhat aloof from the other members."

Benois seems to complain that Diaghilev was seldom present at the society's meetings, and that some time had to elapse before his friends, engrossed in art and its attendant problems, were able to consider him "one of them." Nevertheless, Diaghilev was profoundly interested in art, though much less in its problems. But the society's members (A. N. Benois in particular) were irritated with Diaghilev and his "provincial lack of culture, his indifference to aesthetic and philosophical argumentation," and even more by what Benois calls his foppishness. "There were times," says Benois, "when Seriozha's behavior was really offensive. In the theater, for instance, he would behave in a quite peculiar and most objectionable manner, stalking about with his nose in the air, barely deigning to acknowledge his friends yet—what was worse—all nods and smiles to socially important acquaintances."

This "vainglorious snobbishness," it may be said in passing, accompanied Diaghilev through life. Only towards the very end did I observe any change, when reality—dearly paid for—had taught him wisdom in this respect.

Benois notes, too, that "in the first years after his arrival from Perm, Diaghilev on the whole rather ignored art. He was interested in the theater, busy establishing social connections, occupied with his music, and —infinitely less!—with his university studies. He avoided exhibitions, did not visit the museums, and only very spasmodically attended the meetings of our group, which at that time was deeply interested in painting and the plastic arts."

We may note, in passing, Benois' somewhat obvious slip, for clearly it is painting he means when he writes: "Diaghilev on the whole rather ignored art." This is proved by the next sentence where he says he was interested in the theater and music. It should be emphasized, however,

Diaghilev at the Lycée
"Seriozha"

Dmitri Vladimirovitch Filosofov
"Dima"

Alexandre N. Benois
"Shura"

V. F. Nouvel
"Valetchka"

that Diaghilev's indifference to painting attaches only to his very first years in St. Petersburg, and that even so "indifference" is altogether too strong a word. Diaghilev *was* interested in painting, but music predominated over all else.

This interest in painting was developed and stimulated chiefly, though not entirely, by Benois himself, and that he learned much from his teacher, Diaghilev himself does not deny, for in reviewing Benois' *History of Russian Painting* he wrote: "Benois' influence on contemporary Russian art is incomparably greater than appears at first glance. If, prejudice aside, it seems to us that the whole future of Russian art now resides in the exhibitions organized under the aegis of the so-called *The World of Art* group, and that their banner stands for a noteworthy and coherent grouping, then it must be admitted that Benois played an all-important part in inspiring that unity and its steadfast convictions.

"I must confess candidly that though in fact I was the organizer of these exhibitions, but for Benois' influence, that art group which gave us Somov, Lanceret, Bakst, Braz, Maliavin and even Serov, could never have been rallied to one purpose, for each would have gone his own way.

"Of wide culture and profoundly responsive, Benois' tendency to involve himself in pedagogic activities was always remarkable. Even as a young man he was always, automatically as it were, inculcating a real love of art in his friends, a love he has never deserted to this day. We are all eternally in his debt for our knowledge, relative though that may be, and for our absolute faith in our mission."

We need feel no astonishment at the fact that the cultured Benois, a denizen of the capital, descended from a family of *professional* artists, should have proved so excellent a teacher for the young provincial from Perm, whose family were only cultured dilettantes, and who, though remarkably gifted by nature, was certainly not plagued by any of the problems of art, nor, generally speaking, prone to philosophizing; whereas Benois and his friends, particularly Nouvel, might even then, in the '90's, have been considered *blasé*. What is astonishing is that the healthy, rosy-cheeked, and apparently unthinking provincial—the youngest of them all —should have been able to "throw his men" so soon, and become not only their leader but that of *all artistic Russia*.

Friendship with V. F. Nouvel and interest in Music

In the sphere of music, however, Diaghilev was infinitely more independent. At the time of his arrival in St. Petersburg, he was not only an accomplished singer, and excellent performer on the piano, but had the right to consider himself a serious musician and composer, with several works to his credit. Thanks to a common enthusiasm for music, V. F. Nouvel, one of the members of the "Neva Pickwickians," soon became his closest friend. This was "Valetchka," as he was known to the other

members, in the editorial offices of *The World of Art,* and eventually in
Diaghilev's Russian Ballet.

Valetchka Nouvel, known to everyone who had anything to do with
art, was on intimate terms with every outstanding personality in that
world, though most perhaps with Diaghilev, Somov, Kuzmin, Sudeikine
and Stravinsky.

His whole life was spent among art and artists, yet he himself was
neither artist nor patron, but only an extremely enlightened and devoted
dilettante. Nevertheless, the opinions and judgments of this dilettante bore
great weight, especially in the period of *The World of Art.*

An exceedingly vivid picture of the Nouvel of those days is to be found
in Mme. Ostroumova-Lebedeva's *Autobiographical Notes.*

"A young, uncommonly active, cheerful man. Terribly restless. He
makes one think of champagne, when it sparkles and fizzes. The moment
he entered a room, everyone became cheerful. He was very clever, really
clever. He would laugh at, mock and tease everyone, but his particular
victim was always Nourok,[2] whom he buzzed round like a horse-fly,
planting sting after sting. At first Nourok would begin by retaliating,
parrying the taunts with often rather venomous shafts, but Nouvel was
indefatigable. So mercilessly indeed did he pester Nourok, that the latter
would begin to howl with anguish. Nevertheless, they never quarreled,
for when he had reduced Nourok to the very depths of despair, he would
burst out laughing, and they would become friends again. They were
really great friends. Nouvel was an excellent musician. Later, they both
founded the Contemporary Music Society. Both were remarkable for their
passion for freedom, and a complete absence of all ambition."

This absence of ambition, of initiative in any large sense, somewhat
obscured Nouvel in the eyes of the public, so that it is not generally
realized how important a part he played on *The World of Art,* or what
his connection was with the Contemporary Music Society. Nevertheless,
this undogmatic, skeptical aesthete, whose sense of beauty was infinitely
more developed than that of Filosofov, just as he was infinitely lighter
than Dima, was content to continue in his part as Attaché Extraordinary
to art, as, in life, he never aspired to be more than Attaché Extraordinary
at the Ministry of the Imperial Court, where all his official life was spent.[3]

Fate played queer pranks with these two friends of Diaghilev's, for
Filosofov, a born functionary, turned author and became a man of no
profession, whereas lazy, casual Nouvel became a servant of the public.

I have dwelt in some detail, though hardly sufficiently perhaps, but I
shall have to return to him frequently, with Valetchka Nouvel, for not
only was he Diaghilev's friend but, what is more, he was the confidant
to whom Serge Pavlovitch opened his soul and confessed his sins, and

[2] I shall have more to say about Nourok, one of the most active workers on *The World
of Art.*

[3] Attaché Extraordinary was often used in Russia in a slightly derisive, or as here,
deprecatory sense, implying very light duties, if any. (Ed.)

in whom he found an antidote to the narrow dogmatism of Dima Filosofov.

A mutual passion for music had led to their intimacy. Together they played piano duets, went to concerts, solemnly discussed music and their common idol, Tchaikovsky. When in 1893, Tchaikovsky was dying, Nouvel tells us that Diaghilev, who lived fairly near "Uncle Petra," would call several times a day to inquire, and would then pass on the news at once to Nouvel. Diaghilev was the first to arrive at Tchaikovsky's deathbed, bearing a wreath.

An incident with N. A. Rimsky-Korsakov

Throughout these years, in fact, until 1895, it was music and musical activities which dominated everything in Diaghilev's life. With regard to his singing lessons it seems to be generally agreed that Cottogni was his master. But where theory was concerned, the witnesses differ. Benois says: "As regards the theory of music he had the advantage of studying under Rimsky-Korsakov," and this information is confirmed by Igor Grabar.

Diaghilev himself told me he had studied composition under that composer.

However that may be, certain of Diaghilev's friends, Koribut-Kubitovitch, Nouvel, and others, claim to remember an episode which could only have been told them by Diaghilev himself, and which, from internal evidence, would seem to make it impossible for the latter ever to have been the pupil of Rimsky-Korsakov. In Koribut-Kubitovitch's memoirs we find: "So far as I remember, Seriozha studied theory and composition, not with Rimsky-Korsakov, but with Sokolov, a professor at the Conservatoire. Serge, however, having a high opinion of his own musical talent, wished to obtain the former's opinion on his work, and to that end paid him a visit, expecting to be met with praise and encouragement; only, however, to be forced to listen to some by-no-means flattering criticism, and a warning that he still had very much to learn. Angry and hurt, he left the composer, saying, 'Take it from me, you'll hear very different opinions when I'm famous,' as he slammed the door." Nouvel's version however is even brusquer (though equally improbable). "Time will show which of us history considers the greater."

What did happen, and when, between the two men, it is impossible to say in the absence of actual eye-witnesses, but what seems certain is that Rimsky-Korsakov's chill reception considerably damped Diaghilev's ardor for music. The only way of reconciling the conflicting accounts would appear to be by assuming that this episode occurred, not at their first meeting, but some time after Diaghilev had begun to study under the famous musician, and that it was this episode itself which caused him to transfer his allegiance to Sokolov.

An even chillier reception, however, awaited him in 1894, this time from his friends. Diaghilev had invited numerous guests to a party, at which the fountain scene from *Boris Godunov* was to be played, for which he himself had written the music, and which, though obviously deriving from Mussorgsky, contained no small infusion of broad melody. In addition, he himself was singing in the role of Dmitri, the Imposter, while his aunt, A. V. Panaev-Karstov was filling the role of Marina. But the whole scene turned out an utter and awful fiasco, after which Diaghilev renounced composition forever.

Thus, to all intents and purposes, his musical apprenticeship was over. Nevertheless, his love for music continued, and he went on assiduously attending concerts. At that epoch his god was Wagner. In the same year he became a subscribing member of the Imperial Musical Society, and made great efforts to infuse new life and blood into it ... but with little success.

Disappointed with his lack of success in the domain of music, Diaghilev more and more began to turn to painting. ...

Diaghilev at Bogdanovskoye

From 1890 to 1895, Diaghilev spent every summer with Dima Filosofov, either at his Bogdanovskoye estate, near Pskov, or abroad. This estate was in the heart of the Pushkin country, and only a few miles from Mikhaelovskoye, Trigorskoye, Vrev, and Sviati Gori. With its "Turgeniev" ponds, its lovely old parks and gardens, its broad avenues of trees and winding footpaths, its century-old limes and hills and strip-fields, it seemed the very heart of Russia, picturesque and colorful in a way not often met with in the North.

Everything at Bogdanovskoye reminded one of Pushkin, while at Trigorskoye there still lived that Maria Ivanovna Osipova who had actually known the great poet, and his "Zizi's" daughter, Baroness S. B. Vrevskaya. In these surroundings, "where two years flashed by in hermit solitude," where so many of Pushkin's masterpieces were written, one enters more deeply into the great poet's works. Diaghilev had always loved Pushkin, but after these visits to Bogdanovskoye, that love became a veritable cult.

However, even here in the country village, the conflict of two ideologies made itself felt, the clash of two generations. Not that it involved Pushkin in any way, though each side interpreted him differently, but one side, that of the " '60's," with its doctrine of social service, demanded that art should be useful and propagandist, and thus opposed any aesthetic approach, whereas that of the " '90's" laid its emphasis on individuality in art, and art as its own justification. Tchernichevsky [4] was emblazoned

[4] The leading spirit and writer of the "Back to the People" revolutionary movement of the Russian intelligentsia in the '60's and '70's. (Ed.)

on the banner of the former group, which Anna Pavlovna Filosofov had borne aloft all her life, while Nietzsche was the rallying cry of the son and favorite nephew.

One may well imagine Mme. Filosofov's feelings, bound up as were her ideas with Tchernichevsky's concepts of an "art for the people," on hearing, and then, in cold print seeing her idol described as "that unhealthy influence which still persisted" while "those who judge our art, still sometimes sigh after that barbaric image which strove to murder art, or at least befoul it with its unclean fingers."

Upon which, entering the fray, Mme. Filosofov herself wrote: "My children are wonderful and I love them dearly, but I can't help feeling like a hen who has hatched out ducklings. They're ducklings, not chickens. Possibly they are better than myself, nevertheless they are assuredly not myself. Sometimes it makes me miserable, so different are our views.

"To begin with their disputes and arguments. When our young people (not mine alone) meet, and I listen to their discussions and wrangles, there are times when I really feel sick. Always the same small talk that you get in drawing rooms; music, painting, poetry the whole time.... And when I remember how passionately we used to argue about how we could best serve the people! Where is that feeling now, and that activity, that yearning to help the weak, etc.? Why, one's head used to swim sometimes with it all, everyone was so alive, so eager.... But the young men of today are prematurely aged. Who knows, perhaps they are right, but what use is that to me?"

"Who knows, perhaps they are right," Anna Pavlovna exclaims, though she could not resist challenging them, or defending her own point of view. But when it came to arguing, they always got the better of her, so soundly had they established their attitude to art. Mme. Filosofov held solid unflinching views on social service, but her aesthetics was less convincing, for she herself was a Diaghilev and as such endowed with a strong artistic instinct, which try as she would, she could not suppress in favor of what she considered "more important." But it was only in words they got the better, she still remained unconvinced.

Nevertheless, so persuasive was Seriozha that at length she was forced to surrender to these new spiritual forces and accept them.

"The Russian decadent movement," she wrote, "was born here, in our Bogdanovskoye, because the pioneers were my son Dmitri Vladimirovitch, and my nephew S. P. Diaghilev. Here it was that *The World of Art* was conceived. To me, a woman of the '60's, the whole thing seemed so mad, that it was all I could do to restrain my indignation. They merely laughed at me. Imagine my wretchedness at seeing the birth pangs of the decadent movement actually occurring in my house. Like all new movements it was extravagant in the extreme. Nevertheless, when the edge had worn off my initial antagonism, I began to take a certain interest in their ideas, and frankly, to sympathize with much in them. The tense, false atmosphere began to clear, a number of things were bundled away, till at last one great idea remained outstanding, namely, the seeking and creation of Beauty. Even if Serge had not founded *The World of Art,* this would have been a sufficient claim to fame."

If only this truly clever and sensitive woman could have suspected that though "beaten" she, too, was partly in the right, and that her son, as time would show, was no real duckling!

A second journey abroad

Towards the close of 1893, Diaghilev and D. Filosofov made a second journey abroad. Some interesting details of the trip are provided by P. G. Koribut-Kubitovitch.[5] "It was February, 1894, when I met Seriozha and Dima in Nice. The latter had been seriously ill, and the doctor had ordered him off to the South of France. I found him convalescing at the famous villa, Château Valrose, which at that time belonged to P. von Dervis, a friend of Dima's brother, and his fellow-student at the Cadet College and Cavalry School. Before reaching Nice, Serge had spent some time in Berlin, and there had visited the famous portrait painter Lenbach, from whom he had bought a study for the well-known portrait of Bismarck in the uniform of the Cuirassiers. Afterwards, in Munich, he had bought a painting by Liebermann. He was very proud of these purchases. I believe that this was the beginning of his hobby of collecting pictures, and his dream of founding a museum. Then, towards the end of March, Serge and I went to Italy and visited a number of towns, including Genoa, Milan, Venice, Bologna, and Florence. In Venice and Florence, Serge began buying fifteenth- and sixteenth-century furniture. We went the rounds of the antique dealers and found some wonderful things. Astonishingly good were a leather armchair and some low Savonarola stools, a magnificent long table and several chairs, and in Naples and Rome, a number of marvelous bronze vases and statuettes.

"I had been collecting antiques ever since my student days, and so could give Diaghilev the benefit of my experience. When all our purchases eventually arrived in St. Petersburg, and were installed in Diaghilev's new flat at Zamiatin Pereulok, all Serge's friends, including Benois, were loud in admiration, and Diaghilev himself was very proud of them. If I am not mistaken, these objects which were so precious to Serge were not destroyed in the Revolution, for it appears that Benois saw and recognized them in a depôt for confiscated antique furniture, and managed to get them moved and deposited in the Hermitage Museum."

[5] P. G. Koribut-Kubitovitch reached Nice in carnival time. Suddenly, among the merry crowd, he found himself being attacked and hustled. Imagine his astonishment when his assaulters took off their masks...and disclosed S. P. Diaghilev and D. V. Filosofov.

Apostle of the Arts

The year 1895 was a fateful one for Diaghilev, for it marked the break-away from his youth, and the beginning of his future activity as Apostle of the Arts. In that year he began to try out his wings, immature though they were, but even these first attempts presage the soaring heights to which he was finally to attain.

That summer he once more went abroad, but now without his former companion Filosofov. On June 15th he was in Antwerp, from which he wrote as follows to M. and Mme. Benois:

"Dear Anna Karlovna and friend Shura! For a long time now I've been wanting to drop you a line to remind you of my existence, but could not manage to write anything worth sending, because there simply hasn't been time to extract the quintessence of all I've seen and felt, what with visiting four and twenty museums and calling on fourteen painters in their studios. For that reason, too, I must put off, till we meet, any real discussion of certain artistic problems, of the greatest interest, which have cropped up in the last month.

"But here and now I swear that next winter, I shall put myself in Shura's hands, and solemnly declare him curator of the Diaghilev museum. I mean this seriously: who knows, a few years hence we may really have something worth while. But whatever happens, the foundations will have been well and truly laid; however ... silence! I refuse to reveal all the acquaintances I have recently made, lest I should spoil the effect. ... I hope Shura will hearken to my call, and agree to become curator of the museum, for it now seems clear to me that so long as one does not attempt anything too ambitious, it would be possible to create something quite decent with three or four thousand rubles a year. There you have the practical side of my trip. Forgive this disjointed letter.

"Your friend, Seriozha Diaghilev."

On this journey he bought paintings by Bartels, Dagnan-Bouveret, Israels, Liebermann, Menzel and, idol of the artists associated with *The World of Art,* a Puvis de Chavannes. These he brought back to Russia. But also, he brought back his project for founding a museum, a tremendous enthusiasm, and an unbelievable energy dedicated to the cause of achieving something great in art. This enthusiasm and energy were never to abandon him. On the contrary, they were to augment year by year, and with every fresh obstacle to the unconquerable creative energy of his will.

The scheme for founding a museum died stillborn, "But," says A. N. Benois, "from that moment Seriozha was on an equal footing with us all, and his receptions, in a certain degree, began to rival my own."

This phrase, however, needs elaboration, for year by year, Diaghilev, though not an artist, began to outstrip his painting friends, and make them more and more believe in him. One of the first to be convinced of Diaghilev's genius was V. A. Serov, undisputed leader of the new school of Russian painters, who then placed his talent at the service of Diaghilev's cause.

Yet others doubted, in spite of the convincing, the surprising testimony of Diaghilev's profound knowledge and intense sensibility in matters of art: an understanding so deep that, years later, it was to take Igor Grabar "completely aback."

True, this instance is posterior to the period of which I am writing, yet none the less is it typical of the man who "at first glance" could pierce to the inner significance of any work of art.

"Diaghilev," he wrote, "was extraordinarily well informed where painting was concerned, very much better indeed than many painters. His visual memory was remarkable, and his flair for finding attributions quite astonishing. I remember an incident which particularly amazed us, when we were hanging the pictures for an exhibition of historical paintings in the Tauride Palace, which he himself had planned and organized. Now and again we would find ourselves completely at a loss to attribute either a sitter's, or artist's name to some portrait sent from the country. Whereupon Diaghilev would be sent for, and looking in for half an hour, having torn himself away from other interests, with a mere glance, a pitying smile would say: 'Why come, that's surely a Luders, and that must be Prince Alexander Mikhailovitch as a boy.'

"In the features of a boy, painted under the Empress Anne, this man could discern the future senator as he would be painted under Paul I, or vice versa, attribute to some admiral who had fought at Sebastopol, the name of a man known only by his portraits as a child, painted in the time of Catherine the Great. His judgments were quick and peremptory, and of course he occasionally blundered: but never so grossly or frequently as others."

In that year, too, 1895, Diaghilev published two articles in *The News,* with the sole object, as he put it, "of somewhat opening our public's eyes ... and those of our painters."

During the constant expansion of Diaghilev's social and artistic activities, the two chief pillars of the *cenacle,* Benois and Somov, had established themselves in Paris. Thus, all the credit for conceiving and carrying out his ideas for inculcating a new approach to art must be attributed simply and solely to Diaghilev.

His first highly successful "manifestation" was the 1897 exhibition of English and German water-colorists, about which, in 1924, Benois wrote:

"It may seem strange for Diaghilev to have started off now with the English, Germans and Scandinavians, and to have attached such importance to painters in water color, i.e., second-raters and their affectations. But that may be explained in many ways, and chiefly perhaps, by our own immaturity. There was an instinctive urge in us to escape from the backwardness of our Russian artistic concepts, to rid ourselves of our provincialism, and establish contact with Western culture and its untiring experimentation in the arts. We wanted to get away from the literary approach, the tendentiousness of our 'independent,' the hopeless dilettantism of our pseudo-innovators, and our expiring academism. But we still lacked a background that would enable us to discern what was most precious outside our borders, and to concentrate all our faculties on that alone."

Dreams of a Museum and Review

Having revealed to the Russian public one aspect of artistic achievement in the West by means of this small though impressive "manifestation," Diaghilev began to dream of new and more grandiose schemes, schemes which he alone could execute.

"I want," he said, "to peel Russian art of its trimmings, give it a thorough clean-up, and serve it up to the West in all its glory. If the time is not yet ripe, however, then hail to Krylov's 'Swan, pike, and crayfish.'"

Now Diaghilev's mind begins seething with plans, each more grandiose than the last. He dreams of arranging an "exhibition of Finnish and Russian painters, of organizing a group of people with advanced ideas, of founding his own review." And also it seems to him "that the opportune moment has come to rally together into a group, able to take its place in European Art." Thus he writes to his friend Benois, and adds: "...I'm trying to organize a new group of people with advanced ideas. In the opinion of certain young painters who recently met at my house, we ought to arrange a show some time within the year, for which I shall be *solely responsible,* that is, not only for all the arrangements, but even to the *very pictures* we select. This exhibition is scheduled to take place from Jan. 15th to Feb. 15th, 1898, at the Stieglitz gallery. You can imagine the sort of people who're joining us: young St. Petersburgites, immensely enthusiastic Muscovites, Finns (aren't they Russian, too?), as well as a few Russians established abroad: Alexandre Benois, Yukunchikova, Fedor Botkin."

On October 8th, 1897, he again wrote to Benois in connection with his art journal. "I'm frightfully busy, and really haven't time to reply to your dear letter. You've already heard through Kostia [Somov] that I'm completely immersed in my schemes, each more grandiose than the last. At present I'm thinking of starting a periodical which will focus all our artistic activities, and in which I can give reproductions of real paintings and frankly speak my mind. When that's settled, I hope to organize a number of shows of contemporary work, under the auspices of our journal, and also to include the most recent developments in applied art from Moscow and Finland. You'll guess, therefore, that I'm seeing the future through a magnifying glass. But for that I've need of help, and who should I turn to but you? Anyway, I count on you, as I would on myself, and with reason, eh? The least I shall expect from you is five articles a year, but what about hardly matters so long as they're good and interesting! Kostia has already offered his help, and promises a cover design, and a poster. How talented he is, by the way, and how he delights and interests me. He swears that all my enthusiasm is hot air. Well, why not, dear friends, when it's so pleasant to be carried away? You wouldn't believe the progress he's made; the things he's done this summer are simply magnificent. I expect no less from you. The Finns are remarkable, and two or three youngsters have an extraordinary delicacy and color-sense. They're serious competitors, watch out or they'll beat you. I'm all impatience to see what you're sending me. The Princess [Princess M. Tenishev—*The World of Art's* first patron] is in St. Petersburg, and we're the *greatest friends*. She's cramful of energy, and money, too, I believe. She intends to buy some pictures at the Scandinavian exhibition, and asks me to advise her. I certainly won't encourage her to buy duds. In the near future I'm expecting Zorn, Thaulow and Edelfeld. Just imagine, the two former are going to stay with me. The Princess has commissioned Zorn to paint her portrait. When I was in Finland, I spent all my time cracking up Kostia. Very soon I mean to show her all he's done; and trust me, I'll see she buys some of his things.

"What do you think of Vrubel? Anyhow, write to me soon how all this strikes you. I haven't yet decided what the review is to be called. What about Ober? Couldn't we get him to exhibit (ordinary size canvases)?"

Diaghilev's grandiose schemes eventually came to fruition, but at the cost of how much effort and disillusion! His dream, however, of "founding an advanced group" went unrealized, and it was his very "friends" who were responsible.

"When I stated, two years ago," he wrote to Benois, "that I would have nothing to do with Russian painters, beyond making them pay for their outrageous caddishness, I was absolutely right. In all my dealings with French, German, English, Dutch, Scottish and Scandinavian painters, I have never encountered anything like the difficulties I found in dealing with the home product. And now even you and Bakst have to put your spoke in, and add to them. Bakst, with that mercenary spirit so typical of him, demands I do nothing the first year about forming the 'group,' and yet wants me, at my own cost, and with my own efforts, to organize an exhibition of young Russian painters. Serov took up the same stand, but for different reasons. He's sick of bureaucracy, and loathes 'groups.' I must say that Bakst is at the back of it all. I know it's all Greek to you, but honestly, up to the neck in mud as I am, I don't feel the heart to talk about it. Anyway, I'm sick of everyone and everything. There hasn't been a decent, disinterested person among them. They can't separate their pockets from their artistic principles. A worthless, cowardly lot, that's what they are."

Still more disillusioning, however, was to prove the foundation of the journal.

In January, 1898, a second exhibition of Finnish and Russian painters, organized by Diaghilev, was opened at the Stieglitz Museum in St. Petersburg. It was a brilliant, magnificent success, but how much effort, negotiation, argument, and reconciliation it had demanded of its organizer! This exhibition proved an event of great importance to Russian art, and paved the way for numerous developments.

The public reacted in diverse ways, but always passionately whether for or against it. A. P. Ostroumova-Lebedeva, whom no one could suspect of being personally favorable to Diaghilev, notes in her memoirs:

"The exhibition of Finnish painters, which also included a number of Russians, impressed me as being exceedingly alive and stimulating. Serov is wonderful. His portrait of the Grand Duke on a black horse is a real masterpiece. Then Purvit, Korovin, A. Vasnetzov and Levitan! What names and what paintings! How it uplifts one to look at them! Then there is the famous trio, Alexandre Benois, Bakst and Somov. Répin's opinion on the latter was, 'It's stupid, it's done for effect.' "

A great many other visitors went away enthusiastic, but one also heard others repeating Répin's words—"it's stupid, it's done for effect," as well as another word, which they applied to anything new, living, that fell outside their accepted, really moribund, academic standards...the word "decadent."

Now, with this exhibition, began the onslaught on *The World of Art* and heaven alone knows how much mud and opprobrium was slung at Diaghilev and his friends. Suddenly the swamp had come alive, and in all directions terrified frogs could be heard croaking disapprovingly at those who had actually dared to be...talented, new, and themselves. And it was this onslaught, or rather this mean-spirited baiting, which really occasioned the bellicose tone of the review.

In founding *The World of Art* Diaghilev's idea had been to start a simple artistic review. But being attacked, he had, in spite of himself, to turn it into a weapon for both attack and defense.

This exhibition had many consequences, one in particular being the large amount of space devoted to Finnish artists in *The World of Art*. It was no accident that the very first issues contained reproductions from paintings by Edelfeld, Blomsted, Gallen, Ernefeldt, Enkel and Galonen, or that Diaghilev wrote of them: "In spite of the marked divergences observable among these painters, in spite of the opposition of the two trends which split them into painters with a nationalistic outlook and those who follow the aristocrats of the West, they still manifest a common viewpoint, fully conscious of its collective strength. And this strength their art reflects. One feels it in their innate love of the stern national type, in their touching affection for their arid landscapes, and in their enthusiasm for their old legends. It is just these nationalistic elements in their painting, which, though they have so long held up the development of our own painting, have enabled them to gather their forces so that now they can stand erect. And that because they have been able to enter deeply into the soul of their people, instead of photographically reproducing their less attractive aspects.

"Edelfeld's illustrations (and they can be nationalist enough), Gallen's stage settings, Galonen's interiors, all reveal how profoundly these artists have penetrated into and expressed the spirit of their people. But what captivates one especially in their works is their mastery of their art, their original technique which need fear no comparison with that of the West. All served their apprenticeship in Paris, and there is not one for whom drawing is that rock on which so many good painters have come to grief."

Even more clearly did Diaghilev express himself in an article published in 1903, again in *The World of Art*. It is a particularly interesting article, because it adumbrates an attitude which only found complete expression when the Russian Ballet was in full swing...the idea of "the future."

"Here is a country which has no artistic past, no kind of art history at all: everything it has is in the present, or rather in the future, a near future rich with promise.... This little Finnish exhibition is made vivid by the strivings of an unfolding, youthful freshness....In spite of their environment, these painters live a life that can be led only by races in whom immense reserves of artistic energy still remain unexpended.

"That charm does not reside in any single work by one of them, Zimberg, Rissanen, Enkel, Engberg or Ernefeldt, but in their common genius, and in the unique impulse of their youthful art.

"But though a great love of their country, and its people, shines in their works, it is something totally different from the German's adoration of his 'Fatherland' or the Frenchman's devotion to his 'co-citizens.' What the Finnish painters have discovered and learned to love in their country, is its beauty as seen through the astonishing charm of each individual artistic temperament...that is where their chief merit lies.

"Every one of their exhibitions is an enchantment, whereas we, giants in comparison with that small northern land inhabited by such near neighbors, can feel only shame for our lethargy and the poverty of our artistic life."

This exhibition, too, had other consequences worthy of mention. It gathered together into a compact group the young school of Russian painters and made them conscious of their significance and power, while on the other hand it provided striking proof of Diaghilev's organizing abilities to his Maecenases, Princess Tenishev and Sava Mamontov, and proved his capacity to undertake the editing of an important periodical devoted to the arts. It, in fact, decided the fate of *The World of Art*. Princess Tenishev became responsible for publishing the review, which

Diaghilev was to edit, and Mamontov provided the financial backing, the agreement being signed on March 18th, 1898.

Diaghilev's friends welcomed the new magazine warmly, Alexandre Benois writing: "I sincerely hope, that one way or another, we can manage by our common efforts to knock a little sound sense into the public's head. We must be positive and courageous, but only after carefully thinking things out; our outlook must be broad but uncompromising. There must be no despising of the past, even that which is near to us, but we must be pitiless to all its debris, however fashionable, admired, or likely to procure us a facile or resounding success. In connection with the applied arts, we must avoid everything artificial, baroque, hybrid and pretentious, but do our best to propagate, like Morris, principles based on sound reason, or put otherwise, real beauty. Why not call the magazine *The Renaissance,* and as its program, declare merciless war on everything 'decadent'? True, here in Russia, we call decadent everything that is really fine, but of course it's not that naïve ignorance I'm thinking of, but true decadence, which menaces all beauty with destruction. My whole being revolts against all that is fashionable, against fashion itself. Our mission, it seems to me, is to devote ourselves to something greater, more important, and in all justice I must admit that Seriozha with his exhibition has struck just the right note. We must not yield an inch, but neither must we ever rush headlong forward. But above all, I hope to God, he can stand up to Mamontov, who, important and respected though he may be, is all the more dangerous in that he lacks the least vestige of taste. Yes, Seriozhinka will have his work cut out! But tell him I'm with him heart and soul, and that more than anything else, I wish him *strength."*

This letter is significant, for it expresses the views, unrevolutionary though they be, of one of the most "radical" collaborators of *The World of Art.*

On the other hand, V. Nouvel wrote as follows:

"I am now spending all my evenings with Seriozha. We are all keyed up and excited about his magazine, and working at fever heat. Meanwhile we spend all our time passionately arguing. It absorbs me completely. Perhaps it's all mean and petty (!) but there it is, and I won't, I can't, violate my nature. I shall only move on to better things, when I feel a natural irresistible need to do so."

Yes, Benois was right in saying, "Seriozhinka will have his work cut out." Soon enough it was obvious that the only person he could count on was Dima Filosofov, for Shura Benois, who had welcomed the magazine with such warmth, cooled off quickly, and on July 5th, we find him writing:

"Three years ago all I dreamed of was starting a magazine, and I used to subscribe to quantities of them. But since, I've realized I dislike all the existing ones, and again, that the thought of helping to start a new one leaves me cold. There is something about a magazine that inevitably reduces everything to a common denominator. We mustn't forget, however, that there are lots of young artists (and old ones, too) to whom it may be of the greatest service. That's why, in principle, I'm in favor. But from that to warmly supporting it, there's a long distance between. If I were in St. Petersburg, I don't doubt that by force of argument, the ice round me would somehow have been melted (fine metaphor!), but here, far from you all, it only hardens and gets thicker."

Even "champagne" Valetchka had lost much of his enthusiasm, and on July 1st was writing to Benois: "Dima and Seriozha have gone into the country until Aug. 1st, and as a result all the excitement round the magazine has died down for a time. I understand only too well your lack of enthusiasm about our review. I should feel the same way myself, no doubt, if I had some other interest, but I haven't (I've given up music, and it seems to me I've done right). The magazine provided an excuse for long abstract discussions, which I enjoy, but as we've stopped having them now, I cling to the idea. When it comes to practical details, however, I get bored and begin yawning. It seems I'm fated to think and argue about things no one wants and no one has any need of. I assure you I'd much rather be doing that than all we're doing at present. This business of trying to raise the general public to one's own level, comes to exactly the same thing as lowering oneself to theirs. But anyway, what do I care about the general public? If I do take part in all this activity, it's only to help those round me, and make my own life more endurable."

What Diaghilev's own state of mind was like, abandoned by all his "friends," at the most critical moment of his career, we know him from a letter addressed to Benois and dated June 2nd, 1898: "When you're building a house, Heaven alone knows how much fuss and worry you're laying up for yourself. Now it's beams, now bricks, now wallpaper, and an infinity of trifles. All you know is you'll have a fine housefront because you've trust in your architect's talent, and his friendship. But then, exactly the opposite happens, for when, covered with dirt and sweat, you creep out of the scaffolding and timbers, your architect turns up and reports he's incompetent to build a whole house, and anyway is there any point in going on with the thing, and so on, and so forth? Then and then only, do you really realize how filthy the bricks are, how the glue stinks, how stupid the workmen are.... And that, roughly, was the effect your letter had on me. If even Valetchka started to do something about it, it was because he realized all it stood for, all that had to be done. But you, you begin by discussing whether it's necessary, whether it would be right to offer a welcoming hand to the old lot or Vasnetzov....

"In exactly the same way that I can't demand that my parents shall love me, so I haven't the right to demand that you support me morally and physically, by contributing your blessing and the fruits of your labors. Put shortly, I can't beg you, or prove my case to you, and as God is my witness, there isn't time to give you a good shaking—a moment's carelessness and the whole thing will fall about my ears! That's all. I hope these amiable scoldings will have their effect, that you'll stop behaving like a total stranger, and that you'll slip on an overall and come and help us stir the quicklime."

Nothing happened, however. Diaghilev and Filosofov had to stir the quicklime alone. Nevertheless, in spite of everything and everyone, the first number of *The World of Art* appeared on November 10th, 1898.

PART TWO: "THE WORLD OF ART" EPOCH

CHAPTER IV

"THE WORLD OF ART" EPOCH

Russian Art and Culture before The World of Art

I HAVE called this part of my book *The World of Art* epoch, because it represents a definite phase in Diaghilev's life. Nevertheless, the title can be read in a wider sense, given the fact that *The World of Art* marked an epoch, and a great epoch, both in regard to Russian art and Russian culture.

It is impossible to overestimate the significance of this magazine of the arts; indeed, such was its importance that words alone cannot do it justice.

Today, it is almost impossible to cast the mind back to a period as remote as were the '90's of the last century, particularly in Russia; an epoch in which that country, for the first time in its history, had a review devoted to the arts in the fullest, most generous interpretation of that word.

That springtide burgeoning of Russian art and culture, of a high artistic level, which marked the early years of the nineteenth century was followed by a period of decadence, more and more accentuated with the years—a decadence visible even towards the end of Pushkin's life, and which caused him to write, "the new generation cannot find time even to talk of poetry": and that "the merchants, to whom 'an earthen pot' is dearer than a 'marble God,' for whom art exists but for purely utilitarian ends, must be driven from the temple."

And indeed, an "iron age," was beginning, an age which boldly proclaimed that "boots are more than Shakespeare." Had Russia, in Pushkin's time, attained to such a perfection of culture, as witness its masterpieces and even its smallest trifles, only to fall so low? Was it fair that two decades of light and culture should have to be paid for at the cost of nearly half a century of decadence, and that not the so-called "decadence" pilloried by the enemies of progress, but an almost final impoverishment of art.

Round the '40's a gleam still reaches us, the afterglow of the blazing sun of Pushkin's time; but from the '50's on, the shadows gradually encroach until the whole of Russia's *artistic* culture is finally extinguished. If I emphasize so much the word artistic, it is because in the '60's, the '70's and '80's, great poets and painters (and genuises, too) alike appear, but they were always alone and isolated, and their light did little to pierce the mortal surrounding gloom. Culture had ceased to exist, as we knew it in Pushkin's time, with music perhaps the sole exception.

Two trends clearly predominate in the latter part of the nineteenth century: on the one hand that of an old-fashioned classicism deriving from Pushkin, and on the other the crassest utilitarianism. True, there seems at times a sort of moral beauty in the vital necessity of the second, essentially anti-aesthetic though it was. But the first fades completely away, a pale reflection of the culture of Pushkin's era, whose true light, extinguished, leaves a sapless, traditional imitation, a formal bureaucratic art, lacking all beauty and vitality.

But now a new school sprang into being, "Vagrants" they called themselves, after those traveling exhibitions which in the past had reflected similar tendencies, with purely philanthropic, utilitarian aims, calculated to promote "good feeling" and help the people, that luckless people deprived of liberty and the right to think for themselves. A school which even dared to say to the poet:

> "You can refrain from being a poet,
> But citizen you must be!"

Art in those days meant fulfilling noble, and in its way, fine and heroic deeds of civic duty, but how dismal and drab were those heroics, and how depressing it is to turn the pages of the fat reviews of the time, printed in hideous type on cheap paper! How depressing to read their sapless, lame verses, and gaze at endless reproductions, wretched falsifications of mean lives, each more drab and well-meaning than the last. We might say, paraphrasing Oscar Wilde, that art had ceased caring about the *how* and only bothered about the *what*. Put differently, all that seemed to matter was the subject, not the treatment. Thus beauty disappeared from life and art—killed by propaganda.

But, as I say, happy exceptions did exist, a few lone figures dared brave the current, though often only to go under.... The whole feeling of the time was opposed to art.

Nevertheless, a longing for art, beauty, and "the feast of life" though timid at first, waxed bolder with the '80's. By the '90's, that longing could be stifled no longer. New painters, new poets, came into being, with totally different orientations.

The World of Art *as a significant factor*

When Diaghilev, at eighteen, first settled in St. Petersburg, the ground for *The World of Art* had already been cleared and a new and nearing epoch was giving form and content to a fresh orientation which was rapidly growing sentient. Soon everything was to be swept before it. Russia was already prepared for its artistic renaissance.

Diaghilev's great merit lies not in having opened up new paths by means of his magazine *The World of Art* and his exhibitions of painting, but in grouping together the new school of painters, and in enabling them in some degree, to embody and formulate their ideas. All in all, he made it possible to continue these new paths, though he did not carve them out. But, first and foremost, *The World of Art* was a prime necessity to painters, musicians and even writers, and as such, its importance can hardly be exaggerated.

To *The World of Art* must be attributed the whole of the cultural renaissance which occurred in Russia at the beginning of this century, one of its main contributions being the manner in which it raised the whole standard of publishing. Never before had really fine editions existed in Russia, editions that were helped immensely by succeeding developments in the graphic arts, and the increasing technical perfection of color printing.

This group, organized by Diaghilev, stimulated the birth of other groupings. A. P. Nourok and V. F. Nouvel, both collaborators, founded the Contemporary Music Society, and V. V. Rosanov, O. S. Merejkovsky, N. M. Minsky, Mme. Zinaide Hippius, and D. V. Filosofov, all contributors to *The World of Art,* founded a religious and philosophical group with its own journal, entitled *The New Way.* Meanwhile, with *The World of Art* for inspiration, new interest began to be focused on the treasures of old Russia, and a veritable cult developed for the masterpieces of architecture and sculpture which adorn the two capitals, St. Petersburg and Moscow. As a result *The Artistic Treasures of Russia* was born, which laid particular emphasis on the past, and devoted much of its interest to the applied arts of the period. Its first editor was A. N. Benois, and it was succeeded by *The Forgotten Years,* and finally by *Apollo,* the spiritual successor to *The World of Art.*

It is impossible to search out all the proliferations of *The World of Art,* for its tentacles went on penetrating ever more deeply into Russian life, creating a new society, a new culture, a new outlook on art, and even on the universe....

Yet, while grouping together artists and those active in the arts, and while providing them with an opportunity for embodying their dreams and tracing new paths, *The World of Art* was creating an atmosphere, an environment, particularly encouraging to the arts. Never before had Russia had so large an élite of intellectuals, of people knowledgeable and interested in the arts.

Another great merit of the new review was the manner in which it organized immense exhibitions, on which Diaghilev himself could draw for material. And whereas an exhibition shown in Moscow, St. Petersburg, Helsingfors, Paris or Berlin, could only be accessible to the inhabitants of those capitals, *The World of Art,* containing numerous excellent reproductions, drawn from these very exhibitions, could circulate all through Russia, and that with greater success, seeing its cheapness, since a yearly subscription of ten rubles entitled subscribers to twenty-four issues.

Aims and main trends of The World of Art

What exactly were the aims of *The World of Art?* One would be hard put to it to find an answer which should clearly define the position it adopted. In our opinion it seems more satisfactory to talk of the *content,* and leave the theoretical discussion until later.

The general orientation of *The World of Art* was passionately discussed during its existence, and perhaps even more once it had ceased publication.

This is what Igor Grabar, one of the contributors, wrote on the matter: "Above all, it would be profoundly wrong to consider *The World of Art,* though an error frequently made, as a sort of ideological and aesthetic front, composed of artists of the advanced groups, who, with a symbolism borrowed from the West, opposed our native rationalism.

"There never was, either in its dawn or evening twilight, a moment when *The World of Art* presented a common united front, whether political, social or even purely artistic. Nor, in any exhibition arranged by Diaghilev, even before his review was started, would one find a single painting that could be deemed incomprehensible, or provide an excuse, whether for the public or critics, to cry 'decadence,' or even 'symbolism.' However, seeing that these exhibitions were a hundred times finer than anything shown at Mussard's Mondays or The Society of St. Petersburg Painters or The Water-Color Society, these groups and their adherents began to attack him, and that was why he was assailed by almost universal opprobrium.

"The names of the European painters who exhibited at these shows is sufficient to prove the absence of any particular orientation. There was not one Symbolist among the Russian painters exhibiting, just as there was no symbolism among the first contributors to *The World of Art.*

"According to a different viewpoint, as utterly false as the first, the contributors to *The World of Art* appear to have been suffering from an acute attack of 'historicity' and 'retrospectivist' poisoning, and to have lost themselves amid the graphic arts. But if this poison had been as deadly as was claimed, surely there would have been no room for the most original of the new French painters in our review? And anyway, where is the 'historicity' of Vrubel or Serov? As to its devotion to the graphic arts, thanks to which they were to attain a rare perfection in Russia, that was but one form—admittedly prominent—of the multiple activities of our review, and the many artists gathered about it. . . ."

When *Apollo* succeeded *The World of Art* the greatest importance was attached by it to the part played by the first of our Russian art journals. Referring to the absence of a single viewpoint, or rather to *The World of Art's* various eclecticisms, by which it managed to "reconcile irreconcilables," the editor, Vsevolod Dmitriev, naïvely and unreasonably considers these inconsistencies the prime cause of its premature decease.

"A mere ten years ago *The World of Art* seemed to stretch out to the very horizon, and to be dowered with everlasting, illimitable, creative capacities of renewal.... There, at its exhibitions, Dobuzhinsky's exquisite accuracy and detachment hung side by side with Maliavin's unassuageable passion. The cerebral Somov with his hard, cold, acid line, found himself perfectly complemented by Serov's picturesque broad simplicity. But if they complemented each other, that proves a sort of underlying unity? No, for that same *The World of Art* made us participate in things which seemed almost done for a wager, such as trying to link Bakst and Surikov together; Borovikosky and Cézanne.... All these efforts," in V. Dmitriev's words, with their mutual contradictions, "led *The World of Art* into a blind alley, to which, in any case, its retrospective bias was surely guiding it."

While V. Dmitriev sees the Achilles' heel of the review in its ideology and eclecticism, N. E. Radlov, in the same number of *Apollo* thinks, and probably with more reason, that the strength of Diaghilev's review lay in its tendency to draw upon a multiplicity of ideologies and trends. Worth quoting here is the beginning of an article, devoted to one of Diaghilev's collaborators, E. E. Lanceret. "Whatever the judgment of posterity may be concerning the painters connected with *The World of Art,* their function as an educative influence will be rated infinitely higher than their practical achievement as artists.

"As masters they have done infinitely more than as painters. Their opposition to the 'sermon' in paint expresses itself in 'sermons' so eloquent and fine, that all their practice, valuable though it is, seems only the illustration and application of a number of 'examples.'

"We must always bear in mind the many new worlds which have had to be rediscovered by art, and those which have had to be thrown open to the public.... The theater, book-making, art criticism, the modern art of the West, the inexhaustible reservoir of the applied arts, Russian architecture, and especially that of 'Old St. Petersburg.'

"What was effected in these respects by the group of painters associated with *The World of Art* is no doubt very unequal both in quantity and quality, yet none the less history will praise it for having revealed these new worlds! Whenever the slightest progress was made, which brought the public nearer to a real understanding of modern art, of our inheritance from the past, *The World of Art* was primarily responsible for it....

"This cultural art, which would have been a surprising phenomenon in the Russia of the second half of the nineteenth century, coincides with the apparition of numerous problems in aesthetics, new themes, new forms of expression so far undreamed, and stylizations of many a kind. But what helped especially, it must be admitted, was the complete absence of any kind of specialization, in many cases deriving from inadequate technique. These art pioneers transmitted their discoveries to a generation whose artistic culture was no longer so many-sided, but among whom were to be found a number of specialists who only needed to begin to dig, in order to unearth the artistic treasures which their predecessors had discovered.

Finally, to quote from another issue of *Apollo* of the same year, I find certain lines I myself could have wished to have written: "We got more and more to love *The World of Art*, because a unifying thread ran through all its exhibitions, and because of the artistic novelty of everything it showed.

"From the time of the 'Vagrants,' with their clean-cut, definite program, no one, until Diaghilev appeared, had managed to organize the painters in so homogeneous and convincing a group. That whole was essentially a work of art, for though individual contributions, it is true, were at times unequal in value, the whole could lay claim to artistic unity. Their experiments, often daring, but always deeply interesting, were informed by a single spirit in pursuit of a common purpose."

But if *The World of Art* group manifested a single spirit and common purpose, revealing a clear-cut trend—for one there was, in spite of all that was said to the contrary—it was entirely indebted for it to the complex, though homogeneous personality of its main organizer and founder, Serge Diaghilev.

And though he had never in his life painted a picture, nevertheless that "whole" of which *Apollo* speaks "as an artistic unity," must be considered Diaghilev's great contribution to the arts.

The cult of Personality

What was unique in *The World of Art*, and what gave it direction, was its search for new paths, new formulas in the arts. But even more praiseworthy perhaps, though less obvious or capable of definition (whence perhaps its real importance), was its awareness, the originality of its aesthetic standards where both life and art were concerned, its search for beauty, beauty unalloyed, in its own right, freed from all questions of utility. Literary and historical as the aesthetic standards of *The World of Art* may have been, they made an impact, and propagated the new doctrine of aesthetics.

That this tendency to approach art through the history of culture, was very marked at the time, in Diaghilev and his collaborators, many articles in the review clearly reveal. But even in this approach, as in the attitude of the group to the art of the past, it was possible to gauge a new viewpoint, which demanded of every work that it be valued or revalued in relation to contemporary needs. What was new in it was its negation of traditional standards and accepted canons. This attitude is clearly expressed in Diaghilev's first editorial, introducing the review.

Referring to his own generation's passion for "modernity," for seeing present and past, with the same eyes, Diaghilev writes: "Those who accuse us of blindly loving whatever is modern, and of despising the past, have not the slightest conception of our real point of view. I say and repeat, that our first masters and our Olympian gods were Giotto, Shakespeare and Bach, yet true it is that we have dared place Puvis de Chavannes, Dostoevsky and Wagner at their sides. Nevertheless, this is a perfectly logical development of our fundamental position. Having rejected every accepted standard, each and every one of these artists has been weighed up strictly in accordance with what we, personally, demand. We have gazed at the past through a modern prism, and have worshiped only what we, personally, found worthy of adoration. We have submerged ourselves in the past, and have sought to evaluate Shakespeare according to our personal development and understanding, exactly as we have done with Wagner and Böcklin. What we demand, first and foremost, is independence and freedom, and though we reserve for ourselves the right to judge, we do not in any way seek to modify the artist's standards."

And again: "...Could we make our *credo* the faith of our fathers and ancestors, we, in our search for individuality, we who have faith in nothing but what we personally believe? This is what marks us out from all others, for whoever desires to come closer to us must first relinquish the thought that, like Narcissus, we love none but ourselves. Our standards are wider, more comprehensive, than those of the past; nevertheless, they can only be applied through us and our own personalities, and to that extent, therefore, our self-love may be said to exist. Yet, if, incautiously, one of us may some day have said that we love ourselves as we love the Deity, we must interpret it as meaning that all things must be contemplated through our own prism, and that only within ourselves can be found the divine authority which will help us to resolve our most terrifying enigmas."

In this attitude to art, which manifests an individualism so deep-rooted that it verges on the extremest subjectivism, we find the Alpha and Omega of the inspiration guiding *The World of Art*. It is the cult of personality, rooted in a fundamental viewpoint that art must express an artist's individuality. It was a view shared by the majority of *The World of Art's* collaborators, a view unremittingly proclaimed by them, particularly in the first years. Diaghilev, still in the same article, refers to it as follows:

"...At the root of the whole world of creative activity, as its primary cause, sole link in all its divergences, is the King omnipotent, the one creative force, the human *personality,* the single star that lights our darkness, and silences the warring schools of those who fabricate new art religions."

And again: *"Beauty in art is feeling, told in images.* It matters to us but little what those images are, for the importance of a work lies not in itself [1] but in its revelation of a creative personality. The history of art

---

[1] What a risky, heretical thing to say.

is not a list of masterpieces, but a series of records consecrated to the expression of human genius as seen through works of art ... *the importance and significance of a work of art lies in how clearly and sharply it defines the personality of its creator, and the degree to which it establishes contact with the personality of the beholder."*

Today the part played by the creative personality, in the creation of works of art, is generally admitted, though all are agreed it is not the only factor. But under the influence of his friend, D. Filosofov, himself influenced by the couple, Merejkovsky and Mme. Zinaide Hippius, (the facts themselves are easily proved), Diaghilev was considerably overstating his case, possibly because his predecessors had gone too far in the opposite direction.

This concept of Diaghilev's relating to the importance of personality in art was taken up and carried further by a number of his collaborators, and to such a degree, in fact, that at times it fringes on the absurd. Thus V. Brussov, in an otherwise excellent article "Unnecessary Truth," published in 1902 in *The World of Art,* very convincingly takes up the defense of theatrical conventions, against the ultra-realistic trends of the Moscow Art Theater. The article is excellent, as I have said, but how confused and strangely it begins!

"Art is born in the very moment an artist seeks to make manifest his innermost sensations. Where no such effort takes place, there is no creation; while, by revealing his innermost sensations, a man ceases to be an artist. The artist, in creating, transfigures his very soul, and in this transmutation lies all his artistic aesthetic delight. A work of art is the artist's spirit, his soul, his feelings and sensations. The soul is the content of a work of art but its legend, its concept are its *form.* Its images, sounds and colors are the *substance* it employs. What is the content of Goethe's *Faust?* And what is the legend Goethe uses, and the philosophic, moral concepts that round the play out? They are its form. Faust, Mephistopheles, Gretchen and other figures focus the lines. They are the substance Goethe employs. So, too, a piece of sculpture represents the very soul of the sculptor at the moment it is conceived: its subject is its form; the marble, bronze or wax its substance."

To discover "aesthetic delight" in the revelation of innermost depths, and to see art as the "making manifest" of an artist's innermost sensations, I must confess, seems to me somewhat excessive. But yet, all that he says about the "soul" does not necessarily relate to art; and again, can one possibly agree to limit art, creation, and aesthetic delight in this manner? ... Admitting that "personality" plays an important part in the creation of a work of art, and that it is *necessarily* reflected in the product, are we justified in claiming that personality exists nowhere but in the product, and that it alone characterizes art, and gives aesthetic feeling its value? If indeed this could be claimed, then many things would be art which are totally unrelated to it, since personality reveals itself in all things made by man and not alone in the arts. Besides, given such a standard, much that we think beautiful and eternal would need to be excluded. But again, where in all these lucubrations on personality in art do we find even a hint that creation is always revelation, a startling upsurge, always *bigger* than the artist's personality, always a sort of miraculous *plus,* and to such an extent that there are times when one is tempted to define the act of creation of a work of art, not as an achievement *by,* but *through* the artist, by a force *loftier* than himself, which guides his chisel, pen or brush?

Yet what is even more inexplicable and strange is that such a point of view should be defended, not by Filosofov or Diaghilev, but by Brussov, a poet and one of the pillars of our new-born Symbolist Russian poetry. Indeed, so powerful was the cult of "personality" at the beginning of the twentieth century, that it might well have seemed that everything was to be sacrificed to it.

The Program of The World of Art

With its Nietzschean cult of the "individual" (we must remember the discussions at Bogdanovskoye), *The World of Art* was addressing its public in a language with which that public was still unacquainted. And indeed there was much that needed saying in the six years of its existence, though what it said was often contradictory. But that was natural enough, given the fact that the review was a living organism, and as such continually changing and growing. Added to which was the fact that no ideological bias united the staff at the editor's council table, and that every contributor was at liberty to say what he thought. Indeed, *The World of Art* was averse to any kind of sectarianism, its chief object being, not to encourage one or other sectarian viewpoint, but to educate the artistic sense of the Russian public. It was the world of art which Diaghilev hoped to reveal to it, a pure, self-centered art, in all its forms and through all its ramifications.

These aims were proclaimed in the "Program" which was attached to every subscription slip inserted in the first issue.

"The review will comprise three sections: I. The Arts; II, Applied Arts; III, Art Chronicle.

"Part I will be devoted to Russian and foreign masters of all periods, in so far as their works relate to, and throw light on, the contemporary spirit in art.

"Part II will particularly devote itself to the work of individual craftsmen, with special reference to outstanding examples of ancient Russian art. With the object of improving the standard of our native industrial art, all Russian artists will be asked to link themselves in this common task.

"The literary contributions to both sections will be mainly of a critical nature, covering every art manifestation of interest, whether at home or in the West. Exhibitions will be analyzed, music chronicled, the latest art journals reviewed, etc. The brothers Vasnetzov, V. Polenov, H. Polenova, P. Sokolov, V. Serov, M. Nesterov, I. Levitan, I. Ostroumov, C. Korovin, S. Korovin, M. Yakunchikova, Alexander Benois, S. Maliutin, Ober, L. Bakst, M. Vrubel, C. Somov, A. Golovin, Prince Trubetzkoy, I. Davidova and others will be among the review's collaborators. We are assured also of the co-operation of the Finnish artists Edelfeld, Ernefeldt, Gallen, Blomsted, etc.

"The first issues will contain articles by P. D. Boborikin, Prof. A. Prakhov, Prince S. Volkonsky, D. Merejkovsky, V. S. Solovyev, C. Balmont, Mme. Zinaide Hippius, N. Minsky, I. Yassinsky, V. Rosanov and others.

"Published by Princess Tenishev and S. Mamontov.

"Editor: S. Diaghilev."

Later in the year a further statement was published to the effect that, beginning with the new century, a further section would be devoted to literature and literary criticism.

Neither this prospectus nor Diaghilev's main editorial articles can be considered in any way bellicose, nevertheless, they soon aroused fierce opposition. Today it is difficult to imagine the fierce abuse flung at *The World of Art,* or the filth hurled by respectable "fat reviews" and the Press.

It was a challenge impossible to ignore, and one which compelled *The World of Art* to define its position. Two hostile camps sprang up, those for the new journal and those against. And what especially exacerbated the division was the Répin incident.

The Répin incident

Ilya Répin, that talented and most important figure among the "Vagrants," a leading influence in the Academy of Arts, and altogether of wider tolerance than his comrades, in his fear of being called "backward" or branded conservative, warmly defended the new movement, so contemptuously called "decadent." In *The World of Art,* for instance, we see him testifying to the following effect: "All who now feel fear for the future of art will assuredly one day be saying: 'Yes, it is a legitimate factor, it cannot be gainsaid.' Then this strange movement will be seen as the revelation of a new creative impulse, and will be accorded full citizen rights. Yes, my friends, all this struggle is futile. Your Chinese principles will get you nowhere."

Diaghilev, to whom talent, real talent, was of more value and greater importance than any "movement," considered Répin to be one of Russia's greatest painters, and begged him to collaborate on *The World of Art,* a request which was warmly accepted. Thus, the very first issues contained a number of colored reproductions of Répin's paintings, while the tenth issue was devoted entirely to Répin's work. But now events began to force Répin into a completely opposite position. For, on the one hand, *The World of Art* inspired such unanimous and almost indecent opposition, that Répin began to feel somewhat frightened, and to doubt whether a few new friends were worth the loss of so many. Again, it was impossible for him to remain indifferent to *The World of Art's* merciless attacks on the Academy and "Vagrants," attacks which made his position very difficult with his academical colleagues. What brought the issue to a head was a note, evidently by A. Nourok, as follows: "Whenever a new museum is opened, it is of course impossible to guarantee that nothing mediocre shall be included; nevertheless, precautions should be taken to omit works beneath contempt, or those which compromise the creative impulse of our nation. Works of this kind, totally devoid of even historic importance, should be removed both energetically and swiftly. We therefore recommend that the following paintings shall forthwith be removed from our National Museum"—after which followed a long list, proscribing works by Aivazovsky, C. Makovski, Moller, Flavitzky, Kotarbinsky, Jacoby, Sedov, etc.

Thereupon, Répin broke with *The World of Art* publicly, in a letter published in *The Niva.*[2] In this letter, Répin deplored its "dilettantism" and "decadence," and retaliated by attacking both the works it reproduced and the exhibitions arranged by it. One of the choicest extracts refers to the Belgian painter, Léon-Fréderic, "whose dead, bloated children look as though they had been preserved in spirit, and whose utter ignorance of his art positively makes one sick." Of another painter, Gallen, Répin wrote: "He is the image of the artist gone wild. It is the delirium of a madman, akin to the scrawlings of a savage." Again: "Rodin's sculpture bears a close relationship to the stone women found on Scythian tombs in South Russia, while the young Finns, and our own C. Somov, A. Benois, Maliutin, and other half-educated painters, with pious fervor, imitate the mannerisms of those who seek to make ignorance prevail, such as Monet, Rosier, Anctan, Conder, and other contemporary painters."

C. Somov was especially singled out for attack. He is a "poor crippled monster," cries Répin, and goes on: "I know this talented youth, and cannot understand his hypocrisy in using such childishly foolish color, as for instance the green of his grass, or the idiocy of certain of his compositions, full of misshapen dwarf monsters." Alone of all Diaghilev's collaborators, Serov, the academician, Riabushkin, Edelfeld, Golovin, Davidov and Polenov were spared.

Surprisingly enough, Répin ends his attack... "with my compliments

2 *The Field: A Weekly Review.* (Ed.)

to Diaghilev," but whether this was because he feared making a dangerous foe, or because Diaghilev seemed to him more conservative than
the others, or because he, Diaghilev, highly appreciated Répin's talent,
we have no means of knowing. However, we have his testimony to the
following effect: "In *The World of Art* what I particularly esteem in
M. Diaghilev is his energy, his ability to get things done, search out
exhibits, and enlist the sympathies of connoisseurs and owners of famous
art works. These are rare gifts, and one cannot but value highly the efforts
of this cultured young man in fostering so great a love for the arts. Yet,
it is difficult to believe that so socially polished an individual, and one
with such comprehensive tastes in every branch of the arts, including
singing and music; that so distinguished an aristocrat, can tolerate such
horrors in painting as the works of Léon-Fréderic, Gallen, or that of
such pitiable monsters as C. Somov, Anctan, Conder, etc., though one
cannot deny them a certain superficial interest."

In spite of this letter Diaghilev refused to be drawn, and produced
his tenth issue, containing numerous reproductions of paintings by Répin,
for the which the latter had earlier given his permission. The first pages
contained Répin's letter to *The Niva* and were immediately followed
by Diaghilev's crushing reply. This "Letter to Répin" is one of the finest
examples of Diaghilev's literary method. The form used was an astute
one, that of refuting Répin sentence by sentence. Where Répin attacks
The World of Art's tendency to destroy everything academic, Diaghilev,
on the opposite page, quotes his article "The Pupils' Exhibition," in which
he himself states that "it is as obsolete and unreasonable to attack the
Academy as it is to attack any school." In another place he quotes an
article by Répin, dated 1897 (eighteen months earlier), in which the latter
attacks the academies, and states that they "atrophy free creativity and
its forward impulse." Later again, Diaghilev quotes Répin's crushing remarks on the "decadence" of *The World of Art,* while opposing them
with Répin's own refutal of the same charge which was quoted earlier.
In subsequent issues, *The World of Art* often returned to the attack,
but we must say in justice that, although attacking Répin the critic,
Diaghilev continued to write of the painter with great respect, and in full
recognition of his importance and talent.

After this incident the review became still more belligerent. But this
was due to no wish of Diaghilev's, whose artistic eclecticism made him
naturally tolerant, and whose views, in any case, at that epoch, were
neither particularly radical nor Left.

Foreign contributors to The World of Art

To return to *The World of Art's* program, and the degree to which
it was achieved.

That program, which was published in 1899, named a lengthy, though not too exact, list of collaborators, including some who were thrown overboard with the first issues, such as P. D. Boborikin, Prof. A. Prakhov, Prince S. Volkonsky, V. Solovyev, and I. Yassinsky. Again, the names of certain important contributors are found to be absent, such as Igor Grabar (who went on writing the art criticisms until 1902, after which he collaborated as illustrator) or Maliavin, to give but two, and no mention at all is made of the foreign contributors. Though Diaghilev did his best to attract foreign contributions, they played no great part in his review, and eventually almost ceased to appear. On the other hand, many reproductions were published of works by foreign artists. Between 1899 and 1900, however, the review published quite a number of articles by foreign writers and painters. It is enough to quote Maeterlinck on "Everyday Tragedy and Contemporary Drama," E. Grieg on "Mozart and Ourselves," H. Lichtenberger on "Wagner and his Attitude to Art," F. Nietzsche on "Wagner in Bayreuth," H. Bahr on "Artists and Critics," Huysmans on "Whistler," Liebermann on "Degas," Lenbach on "Academies and Technique," Madsen on "Eric Verenskjold," R. Muther on "Gustave Moreau," MacColl on "Aubrey Beardsley," Sizeran on "The Prisons of Art," Nicholson on "Williams," and John Ruskin on "Pre-Raphaelitism." It is worth noting, too, that Diaghilev did not seek out "celebrities" to adorn the pages of *The World of Art,* but men whose outlook and interests were in harmony with the review. For instance, MacColl's article on Beardsley, whose drawings, greatly admired at the time, were already well known to the group which later constituted *The World of Art,* and much influenced Russian painters, begins as follows: "The editor of *The World of Art* has asked me to contribute an article which, being complementary to the photographs of Beardsley's drawings, will help to make Russian readers better acquainted with the work of this artist, explain the spirit behind his work, and deal with the peculiarities of his personality. The editor has asked me to do this, because of my personal acquaintance with this remarkable youth, whose short career, which began so suddenly and ended so abruptly, I watched with the greatest interest both as friend and critic."

The appearance of O. Solovyeva's translation of Ruskin's article was somewhat unexpected, since Diaghilev had always, from his first leading article, disputed the views held by Ruskin on art; nevertheless its appearance is explained in this characteristic note by the editor: "Although disagreeing with certain of the principles expounded in this article, the Editor has decided to publish it, in order that his readers may acquaint themselves with the attitude to art expressed by the famous English writer, John Ruskin, whose death so recently occurred."

These "guest-painters," however, played but a very small part in the life of *The World of Art.* It was the permanent contributors who were infinitely more important. Though some died, others appeared to take their places. It is hardly necessary to take note of all these changes, but some of the contributors are worth putting on record.

Helena Polenova died in 1898, I. Levitan in 1899, M. Yakunchikova in 1902, all three being a great loss to Russian art, *The World of Art,* and Diaghilev personally. In 1899 A. Ostroumova joined the paper, and M. Dobuzhinsky; Valerii Brussov and Andrei Biely joined it in 1902, while V. Borissov, Mussatov, and the architect Fomin joined it the following year.

A. Nourok's part in the Review

In the last line of the prospectus quoted earlier we find the words: "Editor: S. Diaghilev." As we shall see, Diaghilev was not only the titular, but actual editor, a task he prosecuted so actively, particularly in the first two years, that he must be considered the true soul and creator of *The World of Art,* its cause the Diaghilev cause, and the review Diaghilev's review. Neverthless, he had zealous assistants and advisers— for he loved surrounding himself with others, though frequently going contrary to their judgment—in addition to his editorial board, consisting principally of D. Filosofov, who took up an extreme Right position on matters of art, V. Serov, L. Bakst, A. Benois, who represented the Center, and V. Nouvel and A. Nourok, the extreme Left. We are already acquainted with the other members, but a few words remain to be said in connection with A. Nourok.

Though one does not usually find a man's contemporaries in common agreement upon his character, such testimony as we have relating to Nourok is surprisingly unanimous. To all he was a man of transparent, pure soul, who sought to appear both dissolute and a cynic. "Space does not permit me to linger," writes A. Benois, "on the description of this great crank—and thus I am ready to describe my dead friend in all sincerity, just as I would my god Hoffmann—I will merely record that it was Nourok who, among us, filled, as it were, the role of the positivist-materialist Skalon, much to the irritation of the fierce 'mystics,' which we then were. To us he stood for everything that was ultra-critical, iconoclastic, overcynical and affectedly lewd. Huysman's *A Rebours,* banned by the censor, Baudelaire's *Les Fleurs du Mal,* Ver-laine's erotic poems, the novels of Laclos, Louis de Coudray and the Marquis de Sade were his favorite literature, and some such book always peeped out of his pocket. Absurdly, naïvely, he would strive to mystify us, and feign fearful dissipations, while living a peaceful, respectable and thoroughly bourgeois kind of life. Nourok would have liked it thought he smoked opium, inhaled ether, or brutalized women: his whole behavior affected mystery and had that odd bias to which we, for no particular reason, attached the 'Hoffmannish' word: *Skurrilität.* He was the first to acquaint us with Beardsley's drawings, and to make propa-

Diaghilev, by Serov

Diaghilev, by Bakst

ganda in favor of Fidus, Steinlen and Heine, all of whom strongly influenced our outlook on art."

A. Ostroumova-Lebedeva and Igor Grabar testify much to the same effect. To the general public, however, as also to readers of *The World of Art*, his name meant nothing, for he never signed his articles except by initials, or with the pseudonym Silenus. He and V. Nouvel were in charge of the journal's music section, but he also contributed to other sections, and notably that of painting. Here his wit, his sarcasm, his merciless onslaughts on ignorance and second-ratism, however popular it might be, soon made him prominent, and incurred much enmity for the review. "The dispassionate Filosofov," says Grabar, "would reject Nourok's shafts when they were too bitter, considering they overstepped the bounds of permissible malice; yet even that which was printed sufficed to instil its poison month by month into the frozen blood stream of our art pundits."

Nourok was also active in collecting numerous notes for the *Artistic Chronicles*. Since the majority were unsigned it was as impossible then, thirty-five years ago, as it is now, to guess at their authorship, these chronicles being a collective effort to which Diaghilev, Filosofov, Nourok, Nouvel, Serov, Benois and Bakst all contributed.

The influence on Diaghilev of D. Filosofov and A. Benois

During the early years, and especially while A. Benois was living abroad, D. Filosofov, Diaghilev's bosom friend and right-hand man, exerted considerable influence. Placed in charge of the literary section, he was inclined to consider himself, if not the editor, as certainly the co-editor of the review. Indeed, so excessive seemed his pretensions that A. Benois wished completely to abandon his connection with the review. "Seriozha's dictatorial manner," he wrote to Bakst, "hardly helped to attentuate the unpleasant impression caused by Dima's patronizing ways, which he vainly sought to mask under a mass of paradoxes and sophistries." This same Benois, who seems to have been as closely in touch with Filosofov as anybody, admits, however, that throughout the "whole existence of *The World of Art* Filosofov was a true helmsman, who, in addition, was forced to bear the burden of much of the purely technical work of the review. With true self-sacrifice he never sought to avoid any of the paltry details connected with all great undertakings, and would meticulously supervise printing, block-making, etc. He it was who whipped up our flagging energies, saw we had drawings on hand, strove to ensure punctuality (though, alas, generally without success!) and in every way spared no effort to reconcile adversaries, and pour balm on wounds caused by Diaghilev's sharp temper."

This function, it may be said in passing, formed no small part of Filosofov's activities, for though Diaghilev the charmer, when he wished and took the trouble, could with the greatest ease charm others, in which case he would win yet another devoted slave yet he could as easily wound them deeply, though not from any particular desire, for that was foreign to his nature, but because he was thoughtless and but rarely thought of others.

One example of this ministering to the wounds caused by Diaghilev is provided in the account given by that talented Russian etcher A. Ostroumova-Lebedeva who, in 1897, was asked to contribute to *The World of Art*. "I did not like Diaghilev," she writes, "though he has an intelligent face and one full of character. Yet his whole person breathes such self-satisfaction, such limitless assurance. As soon as we met he began to talk of my etchings, and his wish for me to work on *The World of Art*. But he did it in such a way, and in such accents, that I was instantly driven into opposition. I answered shortly and we parted. Benois and Filosofov did their best to reconcile our mutual antagonism, and frequently, in later days, would take a good deal of trouble to smooth out the differences which were always arising between us."

There can be no doubt that D. Filosofov exerted considerable influence on Diaghilev in the early years of the review, and thus to some extent on its whole trend. The signs are visible in the search for individuality, for subjective standards, in the literary and symbolic approach to painting, and in the nationalism, to which, under Filosofov's influence, Diaghilev was prepared to sacrifice his wide cosmopolitanism, as is shown by the prospectus and the review's enthusiasm for the work of Vasnetzov. 1899 was a significant year for Diaghilev, for in it he, with Filosofov, visited Kiev and the Vladimir cathedral, which Vasnetzov had decorated (together with M. Nesterov and M. Vrubel). So deeply impressed were they that Diaghilev, spurred on by Filosofov, began not only to rave of Vasnetzov as the greatest of living Russian painters, but was almost prepared to enlist under Vasnetzov's banner, however foreign it might be to his nature, with its rallying-cry, "Deny the West and Western art for the sake of our national Russian culture." Diaghilev's article, "On Vasnetzov's Exhibition," begins with a statement which Benois found it impossible, for a long time, to forgive, as he could never forgive *The World of Art* for including reproductions of Vasnetzov's icons and paintings in its first issue: "Just as, in time to come, the important names of our epoch, such as Levitan, Nesterov and Serov will be held up and burned at the stake, so today the great names of Surikov, Répin and Vasnetzov are linked in our imaginations. This is the group which determines the direction of contemporary Russian painting." Later, again, Diaghilev says that the chief merit of Surikov, Répin and particularly Vasnetzov lies in the fact that they are not "afraid of being themselves," and that never before has Russian art revealed a national consciousness as powerfully as it does in the works of these masters.

In these first years Diaghilev was always singing Vasnetzov's praises, but as Filosofov's influence began to abate and that of Benois to grow stronger, his attitude changed. By 1904 his tone in regard to his one-time demigod is totally different, and not only does he not spare the latter in his decline, but he is also far more cautious in his appraisal of works which once had his whole-hearted enthusiasm.

"The Vasnetzov of Kiev Cathedral is in the direct tradition of his own 'stone age.' Here we see him at his most characteristic; here, whether for good or ill [he had written very differently once], he is himself, and with extraordinary power expresses his own cherished images. But a time came when the intensity of that creative vision waned, till at last we come to the tragedy we now witness at his exhibition. Heavens above! how changed from his former state! Well was it that the catalogue stated we were to see 'Professor' Vasnetzov's paintings! Yet, it should have said, too, 'Member of the St. Petersburg Academy,' 'the modern icon-painter,' 'renowned painter of Madonnas,' and every doubt of the fearful collapse of this artist would finally have vanished. I have respected Vasnetzov in the past, and value his importance to Russian painting too greatly to wish to recall these mediocre religious compositions which his fatigued imagination has wrought for the new churches at Darmstadt and St. Petersburg. This last exhibition, I repeat, is a tragedy...."

In this new period Filosofov's influence declined, while that of Benois grew stronger, until we find the latter Diaghilev's co-editor. Greatly influenced by Benois, Diaghilev's views underwent considerable modification. The literary attitude was abandoned in favor of pure painting, and an interest developed in the artistic treasures of his own country, its architectural riches, and all its ancient arts and culture, as exemplified in even the simplest domestic utensils. Meanwhile, both Benois and Grabar were devoting themselves to converting both their readers and editor to the art of their contemporaries with special reference to the French Impressionists. At the outset Diaghilev was hostile to Impressionism, and in his first article, dated 1898, wrote as follows: "I must say that the technique illustrated by Ruskin is just as incomprehensible to me as that of the Impressionists. I cannot bear all this elaboration in the design which reveals nothing but effort and meticulousness, just as wild and chaotic painting reveals only chicanery and insufficient thought. Of the first, their merit, it seems, lies in the fact that a magnifying glass is needed to examine them, while the second, it appears, are meritorious because what look like daubs are, by some trick, transformed into objects at a distance. But what we demand of technique, first and foremost, is that it shall remain in the background, as though it did not exist. One of the charms of listening to a pianist is that no one needs to know what difficulties have been overcome. And one of the aims of art should be to subordinate technique to aesthetic aspects."

"What I most dislike is reckless daubing," wrote Diaghilev, and yet, not very long after, we find that more and more space in the review is being allotted to critical articles upon such reckless daubs and reproductions of them. Impressionism had become as much a keynote of *The World of Art* as was its infatuation with Symbolism: two trends which pointed clearly enough to Benois.

Dispute between Filosofov and Benois

In 1901 a series of polemical discussions between Filosofov and Benois began to appear in the review, in which may be read the struggle for control of the policy of the review, and incidentally of Diaghilev. What evidently provoked it was Benois' *History of Russian Painting in the XIXth Century,* a work of which Diaghilev could not but wholeheartedly approve, while deploring its, to him, incorrect historical perspective and ideological dogma. Benois' opinion that no one but Venetzianov, Ivanov and Fedotov mattered as painters in the early days of our century, and that a liberated art only began with Serov, Levitan and Korovin, seemed to Diaghilev quite unacceptable.

"Everyone who has even once looked into *The World of Art,*" wrote Diaghilev, "must know how much I love and respect Serov, Korovin and Levitan, but to state that by the end of the '80's, every technical discovery had been made, both in regard to color, drawing and chiaroscuro, or that nothing new remained to be discovered, one would need to be a very Stassov, with all that painter's self-assurance. Stassov maintains that Russian painting began with Verestchagin, Kramskoy, Shishkin, and the 'Vagrants,' while for Benois it begins with Serov, Korovin, Levitan, and the birth of *The World of Art.*

Not, however, that there was very much in these disputations, for their sole effect was to weld the two men ever closer.

More serious was the dispute between Filosofov and Benois, the point at issue being Benois' disrespect for Vasnetzov, that demigod, who to him seemed both transmitter and apostle of a religion pecularly Russian; that Vasnetzov, by whose instrumentality Diaghilev had founded *The World of Art,* and whose work and ideas he had always sought to further. Whereupon, Filosofov decided to teach Benois the painter a lesson, for daring to ponder high matters considered by Filosofov solely his own and Merejkovsky's preserve. The immediate result was that a long article entitled "Ivanov and Vasnetzov as seen by Benois" appeared in the review, its main theme being that Ivanov, admired as he was by Benois, was nevertheless a Catholic and follower of Strauss, whereas Vasnetzov represented the true mirror of the soul of Russia. It ended: "It is a pity that M. Benois approaches the high mystery of our national culture in a spirit of such levity. I repeat that he should never have departed from a purely aesthetic point of view. The roots of our national spirit and religion are sufficiently complex, and cannot with impunity be approached in a spirit of levity."

These preliminary skirmishes, however, did not end their rivalry. The following year, 1902, Filosofov encroached on a domain *naturally* foreign to him, art, and in the literary section, for which he was solely responsible, published an article entitled, "Contemporary Art and the Tower of San Marco." To this Alexandre Benois replied with an article entitled "Ancient and Contemporary Art." In this article Benois administers the *coup-de-grâce* to the point of view adopted by his fellow workers in art. It was a new and much more rigorous attitude than that which had led him to accept Diaghilev into his circle, merely because he was "Dima's cousin."

"It is unusual for me to find something that could wound me more than Filosofov's article on the Tower of San Marco. Really, it makes one feel one would like to stop writing, fighting for art, sharing one's enthusiasms with one's friends, when one realizes the abyss that divides even the closest friends, when one realizes the atmosphere of total indifference in which one works and lives. In spite of all Filosofov says in favor of modern art, progress, life, through it all I detect his basic indifference to art, to beauty. Though he attaches due importance to hygiene, our changed conditions, the progress of culture, and a virile attitude, he has nevertheless omitted from his calculations beauty, the eternal origins of art, eternal, not only in the sense of becoming, but in its past and present. Filosofov seems intent on rushing forward, without one backward glance; to him all is in the future and nothing in the past, and such a creed is like having no creed at all."

No doubt the victory remained with Benois, for in 1904 we find him, in word and deed, Diaghilev's co-editor. In that year, too, we find Filosofov writing: "I had the great honor of being one of the founders of *The World of Art*. For six years I have been responsible for the literary section of the Review, and its 'Chronicles,'" Now, however, the literary section was beginning to recede into the background, while Filosofov's own contributions become progressively rarer. It must finally have begun to dawn on Diaghilev that his "bosom friend," to whom French draftsmen represented "brothel art," was a long way from any real understanding of art, and that the latter's connoisseurship ended with Puvis de Chavannes and Vasnetzov. (Aubrey Beardsley seemed "equivocal" to him, and the paintings of Maurice Denis merely "naïve.") What must perhaps have shocked Diaghilev most, was Filosofov's reactions to the work of Levitan and Somov, the two painters Diaghilev most admired. We have a letter from Nouvel to Benois, saying: "Dima went on obstinately asserting that the one great figure in Russian painting was Vasnetzov, while Levitan was merely 'mediocrity' in comparison." No doubt the final straw for Diaghilev was Filosofov's contemptuous criticism of Somov's painting as "conventional, somewhat sugary sentimentalism," whereas he himself appreciated that artist's work very highly.

Diaghilev as Editor

Important as was the work done by Filosofov and Benois in editing *The World of Art,* and great as was their influence upon Diaghilev, none the less did he remain its acting editor; the dictator of its artistic policy. He it was, who invited this or that artistic contribution: he who chose the larger part of the illustrations (I say "larger part," for to a certain degree they were determined by the articles themselves and Benois' "letters"); he, who regularly provided many of the bi-monthly notes; and he, again, who was responsible for the journal's main articles, articles which expounded his own outlook, whether or no it pleased his collaborators. Very frequently, his opinions would be at odds with those of his friends, especially Filosofov and Benois; but in return it must be said that Diaghilev never put any obstacle in the way of their freely expressing their thoughts, however little he personally might agree with them.

Diaghilev's personal enthusiasms at this period undoubtedly find their completest expression in the issues of 1898, 1899, and 1900. The first issue as I have said, a double number, contained reproductions of works by Vasnetzov (at that time Diaghilev's god), Korovin, Levitan, Helena Polenova and Maliutin (several by the two latter), and the Scandinavian Eric Verenskjold; but succeeding issues reflected Diaghilev's tastes with equal eloquence, as we see from the reproductions of works by Levitzsky, Prince Trubetzkoy, Puvis de Chavannes, Somov, Beardsley, Vrubel and P. Sokolov, those of some of the Finnish painters he most admired, and others by Brullow and Borovikovsky. "Brullow means much to me," Diaghilev was never tired of repeating, and even from the very first issues spared no effort to popularize the work of this artist. Thus we may see how clearly, how single-mindedly Diaghilev pursued his dictatorial path, and at what point he and his "master" Alexandre Benois parted company, for to the latter Brullow meant little. Indeed, in this very same journal, Benois was subsequently to write: "Brullow is a vulgarian, and if no one has polished him off as he deserves, it is because society, and even our painters, lack any real and true feeling for art."

"Decadence" in fact and theory

If we take a rough cross-section of Diaghilev's contributions, we find he was seeking to expound certain ideas near and dear to him, in connection with the intrinsic values of works of art, irrespective of schools. Remarkably unprejudiced and independent in his judgments, even his eclecticism was notable for its catholicity. The origins of this outlook are revealed in the very first article contributed to *The World of Art.*

"Classicism," says Diaghilev, "the romantic school and the strident realism which derives from both, these everchanging shapes of the past hundred years, seem to demand, that we too, shall adopt preconceived forms and labels. We, however, refuse to soil ourselves, by contact with such works as have been specially devised and painted for us, or even to be tempted by them: a phenomenon so astonishing that many have interpreted it as a symptom of our decadence. But we continue to preserve our skepticism, and accept, or deny, in equal degree, all that has gone before."

For the heading of this first leader of his in *The World of Art* Diaghilev borrowed a quotation from Michelangelo: "He who follows will never lead." All his innovating activity may be summed up in this phrase. Diaghilev instinctively hated everything that was derivative, imitative, *réchauffée* or static, for this was what real "decadence" represented to him. And this attitude was to be perpetually reiterated, from that first article entitled "Our Pseudo-Decadence," to the last.

Thus, when modern art was accused of "decadence," Diaghilev wrote: "Whether something is decadent or not has nothing to do with whether Répin is better than Brullow (highly problematic though that may be). Each in his way, represents the culminating point of a period of artistic tension, summits painfully conquered, though disastrous, for each and all of their imitators. (That is when the real decadence begins!) The Mollers, Flavitzkys, Semiradskys, represent the 'decadence' of Brullow; the Savitskys, Pimonenkos, Kasatkins, on the other hand, the 'decadence' of Répin. But that, too, is precisely why modern art is not 'decadent,' for it neither imitates, nor is better nor worse. All it seeks is to express itself at its most characteristic, whether in the work of one man or many.

"It is very possible that, where ultimate values are concerned, our epoch may well prove inferior to that of 'classical art,' or that of 'realistic,' and may be unable to claim any such important figure as Répin or Brullow. If that be so, its rôle in the history of culture will be but a minor one, though none the less, armed with its own justification. Nevertheless, our epoch, where painting is concerned, can never be considered a "decadent' one, an age which accepts ready-made ideas, or one that is always mouthing established truths; on the contrary, we shall be credited with what we deserve, because we have so unflinchingly pursued new paths."

It is clear, however, that Diaghilev was no servile worshiper of modernism. Real decadence he attacked, as he attacked "flashy modernism," and was later to attack painters he had crowned with bays in the columns of *The World of Art*. One instance is that article entitled "Omnipotent Munich." "Thirty years ago, the schools of Düsseldorf, at that time the world's artistic center, played no small part in destroying much promising talent, for with their academism, they froze it stiff. Now again, Munich, which leads the van of Western art, is proving responsible for the destruction of a number of remarkably gifted individuals. Secessionist art is now the most hideous routine procedure, and has provided a formula

for the fabrication of thousands of paintings. Obvious effects, mass production, decadence, these are the evils it is necessary to combat."

Hatred of derivative, repetitive and static art

It was this attitude towards decadence and formulas, which provoked
such hatred in Diaghilev for whatever smacked of repetitiveness, imitation, or static art. We know how greatly he admired Zorn, Carrière and
Dagnan-Bouveret. But that does not prevent his writing in 1901: "You
see a magnificent portrait, the latest, by that spoiled baby of Paris, Zorn.
When two years ago his sky-blue 'American woman' was exhibited, its
main feature being a huge dog, the whole town rushed to see it, spoke of
nothing but Zorn, his energy, vitality, spontaneity, and general devil-may-
care-ness. All that is still there: a white silk frock, fascinatingly painted
by a master's hand, a red sofa, an *art nouveau* background, and Japanese
dwarf trees. The woman herself is beautifully placed on the canvas, the
tones, the composition are exquisite, and yet, in spite of all this perfection,
one feels, though why I know not, a small chill breath which seems to
say there is nothing one cannot acquire by practice—not only design and
anatomy, but even passion, even the ingenuousness of adolescence: in a
word, all those condiments more precious than diamonds to the painter.

"Zorn's dramatic effects, his excess of feeling shock us at times: but
now they have become merely a formula, imitative, superficial, however
skillful it may be, and like, for example, the last 'fogs' by Carrière.
Carrière is a divine poet, the Rodin of painting. How often have we not
shuddered with a sacred shudder, before his sublime portraits of mothers
and children? But why is it always the very same thing, except that only
the inspiration is lacking, an inspiration which has always stood him in
such good stead? It is obvious that every one of us has some quality
specifically his own. That was why Rembrandt remained always himself,
and never became a Leonardo. This was the vast asset of all the great
masters. Whatever they did, they were always true to themselves: they
were never imitative. But nowadays things have changed. Rafaelli, Carrière
emerge out of the blue; they 'discover themselves,' and then begin feeding
on themselves and their 'discovery,' after which one of two things happens: either they get lost in the mazes of their own mannerisms like
Dagnan-Bouveret, Lenbach, Zwill, Meunier, Friant; or else they begin
imitating themselves, so that it is no longer a Carrière we are looking at,
but a pseudo-Carrière, a pseudo-Ménard, and so on. Having by chance,
made a fortunate discovery, nothing will ever drag them off it again. And
by careful study of each of their mannerisms, they finally create a veritable factory, and succeed in turning out some excellent specimens. But ...

"We could say as much on the subject of Aman-Jean. His famous portrait of Suzanne Poucet has appeared in innumerable books and reproductions; there is real inspiration in it, it is a veritable Aman-Jean,

feminine, pensive, tender. But why ruin one's own reputation by exhibiting, on the last wall of the show, and surrounded by pastels, a series of self-imitations, of mass-produced females swathed in filmy gauzes against motley backgrounds, that might be bits of wallpaper bought at Liberty's?"

This holy hatred of Diaghilev's for repetitiveness, a hatred which endured all through his life, might lead one to think that alone the present and future mattered to him, but never the past. That, however, was not the case. Enlightened as he was in matters of art, past cultures and what they have passed on to us could not be indifferent to him. What he hated was not, properly speaking, "the past," but the past when it laid claim to govern the present. The past, as such, provided he could subscribe to its art, possessed in his eyes, an eternal value. It would be an understatement to say that Diaghilev loved the art of the past, for he adored it, devoted himself to it (hence his eclecticism) and was constantly reiterating that every artist, no matter who, if he deserved the name, must have studied, and drawn his inspiration, from the teachings of past cultures, built up through the ages. Throughout the whole of his life, in the period of *The World of Art,* as also in that of the Russian Ballet, *Diaghilev delved in the past, and piously guarded what he found in it: that past determined his present, and through the present, his strivings towards the future.*

The Applied Arts

The applied arts, both Russian and foreign, occupied much space in *The World of Art* as indeed had been announced by the prospectus. "Part II will devote itself particularly to the work of individual craftsmen, with special reference to outstanding examples of ancient Russian art."

Actually, much more space was finally allotted to the home product, from ancient tapestries, needlework and domestic utensils to modern furniture designed by Benois, Bakst, Maliutin, Yakunchikova, Ober, etc., than to the products of the West. But, although Diaghilev much admired certain foreigners, such as Olbrich, he did not care for the *art nouveau* which was swamping the European market, and much preferred what was being created in Russia. Thus, we find him writing: "The applied arts in the West have succeeded in making considerable progress, much to the despair of no small number of tourists who, in their search for novelty, have found the productions of Darmstadt, Turin, Vienna and many another 'sacred wood' crowded out by the innumerable imitators of Olbrich, Baur-de-Velde, Eckmann, etc., crammed down their throats.

"*Le style nouveau,* having utterly swamped Europe, is now as cosmopolitan as one of those Continental expresses which speeds through Germany, Belgium, France in one day. I do not know whether the difference in track gauge, or a certain sluggishness about our goods trains, is responsible for the fact that this, by now, universal convention, has failed to catch on here. Actually, such efforts as Russia has made to develop the applied arts have so far produced results diametrically opposed to what we find in the West. Instead of finding oneself up against a mass movement, as it is over there, here we find only individual efforts, isolating and charming though they be, such as those of Vasnetzov, Vrubel, Polenova and Maliutin."

Owing to the extraordinary variety of the "Art Notes," Russian readers were enabled to follow every contemporary artistic development, whether at home or abroad, the section devoted to "Notes and Queries" being exceptionally interesting. Indeed, this section was admirably adapted to fulfill the mission which *The World of Art* had set itself, namely that of completing the artistic education of Russia. The material covers an extraordinary range, dealing in turn with D. Levitzky (to whom Diaghilev dedicated the only book he ever wrote), the sculptor Prince P. Trubetzkoy, P. P. Sokolov the painter, I. Davidova, the Porcelain Factory, Churches and Chapels of the seventeenth century, Ancient Sculpture, the Sculptor Seidl, the Korovins, Ober, Maliutin, etc. . . . but it is impossible to go through the whole list.

Music

The section devoted to music in *The World of Art* was very adequate, being serious, comprehensive and sound rather than brilliant. Neither the editor, nor staff, however, were responsible for this, and every possible effort was made to improve the standard. The general arrangement of the section was very similar to that devoted to painting: it was intended to educate the reader and acquaint him with the best work of the past, as well as with contemporary activities, both at home and abroad.

This section was in charge of A. Nourok, a man of wide culture and with a keen sense of music. Outside contributions were invited and thus, in the first two years, we find articles such as those by Laroche entitled "A Certain Performance," or "Pseudo-Conquests by Russian Music Abroad," "A Few Words anent the Programs of the Russian Music Society's recitals," "Program Music"; or those by A. Koptaiev on "Latest events in Musical Literature," "Portraits of Musicians," "Scriabin and the Moscow Opera Season." Nourok did his best to enhance the quality and interest of the few pages *The World of Art* was willing to devote to this subject, but he himself had little talent as a critic. Indeed, at that time, no outstanding Russian critic of music existed—a fact as true of today.

Nevertheless, Nourok and V. F. Nouvel certainly contributed largely, both in *The World of Art* and "The Contemporary Music Society," to the development of public taste, and to familiarizing the general public with the work of rising Russian composers (one of Nourok's special enthusiasms being Rachmaninov). We owe it to them, too, that the names of César Franck, Debussy, Ravel, Vincent d'Indy, Richard Strauss and Max Reger, became familiar to the Russian public.

Literature

This section, edited by D. Filosofov, differed so greatly from the main portion of the review devoted to visual art, that it might almost have seemed a totally independent effort. That difference was already indicated in the advance prospectus, where it was stated that the literary section would solely devote itself to "literary and aesthetic criticism."

As with painting, Russian poetry at that time was largely experimental. Thus, the first step to be taken was that of classifying our St. Petersburg poets by schools. One group consisted of the more timid experimentalists, who might more or less be classified as followers of Nadsen, such as Minsky and Merejkovsky, and who, by some strange misunderstanding at the beginning of their careers, considered themselves to be poets. The other group comprised some powerfully individual and truly original poets, such as Sologub and Mme. Zinaide Hippius, the Muscovite, C. Balmont, "poet by the grace of God," and the Moscow Symbolists, at their head being V. Brussov, Koniavsky, the young Andrei Biely, and the "Genevan," V. Ivanov, in addition to the St. Petersburger, Alexandre Blok, then almost at his zenith.

Russian poetry, therefore, needed a *World of Art* of its own, in every way comparable with that of painting, a lack which Diaghilev's review was only too ready to supply, and could and should have done. Actually, however, it failed to do so, not because D. Filosofov lacked the necessary organizing ability, but because, absorbed in other ideas, he failed to perceive the new poetic movement. Suffice it to say that throughout the whole of 1899 and 1900, not a single poem, not one major literary work appeared in the review, nor a single story, even though, at the time, Remisov, Biely and Sologub were charging Russian literature with new vitality. In 1901, however, appeared the first swallow, and poems by Balmont, Mme. Hippius, Sologub and Minsky and Merejkovsky were published. But no spring followed. It was the first herald—and the last. One cannot therefore help wondering, whether it was not merely because they served as themes for illustrations by Benois, Bakst and Lanceret that they were ever published at all. Even when, later, as a result of Diaghilev's reiterated demands, and that of some of his collaborators more responsive to modern poetry, the work of Brussov and Biely was admitted to the review, it was their theories, uninteresting though these were, which were printed, and not their poems.

The World of Art, instead of giving due publicity to the rising school of Russian writers, as it did to the painters, was content to restrict itself to bare criticism, and criticism, I repeat, which, owing to Filosofov, remained untouched by the new trends.

Why was this? Are we to assume a dearth of talented writers? Yet it is enough to recall the list of original contributors (a list which was to grow with time) and which included such names as Balmont, Mme. Hippius, Merejkovsky, Rosanov, V. Solovyev and F. Sologub, to realize what brilliant talents were already connected with the review. But—save for one issue, dated 1901, in which certain of his poems were printed— all that Balmont ever contributed to the review was two articles, one on Goya ("The Poetry of Horror") the other on Calderon's tragedy "The Adoration of the Cross." Sologub, again, contributed but one article in the whole period of the review's existence, an essay on Pushkin, "On the Pushkin Celebrations," while Solovyev abandoned the journal indignantly the moment its special Pushkin number appeared.

That issue was intended to coincide with the Pushkin centenary cele- brations of May 26th, 1899. Judging by the degree to which Diaghilev adored the great poet, and the fervor with which Filosofov described Pushkin's own visits to Bogdanovskoye in the days of his father, who, as a child had actually seen him, a particularly brilliant issue might have been expected. Diaghilev indeed had done all he could to ensure its success, and had filled the review with numbers of reproductions of works by contemporary painters, such as Th. Tolstoy, Kiprensky, Venetzianov, Aleyev, Legachev, Terebenev, Chernetzov, Nottbek, Tropinin, Reutern, Brullow, Selentzov and Orlovsky and by publishing an article of the greatest interest in the "Art Notes" entitled "Pushkin Illustrations." [3] However, the issue from a literary standpoint proved a total failure, for Filosofov had seen fit to insert articles by Rosanov, "A Note on Pushkin," Merejkovsky, "The Pushkin Celebrations," Minsky, "Pushkin's Teach- ing" (perhaps the best of them) and F. Sologub, "A Pan-Russian Ritual," all of which, in one way or another, jeered at the official celebrations and their bureaucratic organization, though none had any positive or alter- native suggestion to make. This article by Rosanov, which was to shock Solovyev and countless others so profoundly, took for its main theme the immense difference which its author saw between the lives of Gogol, Lermontov and Dostoevsky, who spent their nights writing, and that of Pushkin, who "gambled his nights away." In Rosanov's words: "Push- kin's soul did not compel him, on lovely, starry nights, or perfect days, to seat himself in front of a sheet of paper; whereas the first three were

---

[3] In this article Diaghilev, among other things, pleaded that illustration should remain subjective. "If we," he said, "demand that an illustrator's art be mainly descriptive, we limit his scope, and set insuperable difficulties in his path. It is sheer madness to demand of illustration that it render the soul of the poet or his most secret thoughts: for what it amounts to is asking that the painter shall become a poet, also, which is neither possible nor helpful. The whole significance of the illustrator's art lies in its utter subjectivity; all that we ask of him is his own interpretation of a poem, story, novel. An illustration should never be expected to complement some piece of writing, nor merge into it; far otherwise. It should light up the creation of the poet with the strictly personal illumination that emanates from the painter. The more startling that vision is, the more completely it expresses the personality of the painter, the greater will be its importance. In a word, it is a matter of complete indifference that the poet shall be able to say, 'Yes, that indeed is how I see it.' What really matters is his saying, 'Ah! so that's how *you* see it.' "

unable to help themselves. Their search for an absolute freedom, whether in Rome or 'the wide world,' where none would come to invite them, and none should be their guest," was the prime condition of their existence.

Another curious feature greatly distinguished the literary section from the rest of the review. That was its almost total neglect of foreign literature, all its interests being concentrated, very unfairly at times, on the home product. At the most, towards the end of its career, a number of articles and notes dealing with Polish literature by Peremilovsky were published. This, with practically no exception, was all the interest Filosofov manifested in literature abroad.

As for *belles lettres,* practically no space at all was allotted to it. Short stories and poems were completely missing, and the literary criticism was characterized both by its poverty and paucity. We must ask ourselves, therefore, how the literary section came to take up so much of the review —a fact which elicited heated protests from the painters.

The truth was that Filosofov, in his unbounded enthusiasm for the ideas of Merejkovsky and Mme. Hippius, his intimate friends, and in pursuit of his own ideals, wished to convert *The World of Art* into a philosophic and religious review, and the immense amount of this material which therefore found its way into the pages, pushed literature well into the background. For these ideas he was prepared to sacrifice all that *The World of Art* stood for. This explains why Merejkovsky's book *Leo Tolstoy and Dostoevsky* ran as a serial during the years 1900, when possibly just for Merejkovsky's benefit, the literary section was started, and 1901. True, the work was exceedingly talented, and made some stir on its appearance, but does that justify its occupying the whole of the space allotted to literary matters, when the only result could be to enfeeble and impoverish the review? Finally, in 1902, "An Epilogue" to this work was printed, after which the name of Merejkovsky disappears from the review, except for a short article "Giants and Pygmies," published in 1903.

It must be said, however, that 1902 marked the appearance of a review entitled *The New Path,* its tendency being much more sympathetic to both Merejkovsky and Filosofov than Diaghilev's review. Thus the former no longer needed *The World of Art,* and the latter, though himself beginning to cool off, at the same time found it necessary to invite new contributions, with the result that work by Brussov and Andrei Biely begins to appear in the same year.

One of the most talented contributors to the review at this time was the V. V. Rosanov already mentioned. As a result of his intimacy with the editorial staff, he well appreciated the nature of the review, and for that reason refrained from contributing lengthy articles which could only be published in installments, while doing his best to lend variety to his contributions. Thus, we find him writing "A Note on Pushkin," "Beauty in Ancient Egypt," "Diana—Aphrodite," "Further Considerations relating to Pushkin's Death," "Notes on a Lecture by V. Solovyev," "An Entertaining Evening," "Development of Russian Sculpture," "Some Interesting Ideas by Slabichevsky," "Paestum and Pompeii," etc. Of some importance, too, were P. Pertzov's regular contributions to the literary section.[4]

Drama and the Theater

On the other hand, *The World of Art* proved a faithful mirror for achievements in the theater, both in regard to opera and the drama, though rather less, strange though it seems, to the ballet. Not that there was much scope for critical writing in connection with the Imperial Theaters, bound as they were by tradition, and making only the rarest concessions to modernity. Nevertheless, we find articles by Mme. Hippius on A. Tolstoy's *Tsar Boris* staged at the Théâtre Alexandre, and by Diaghilev, Filosofov, Rosanov, Benois and Mirovitch dealing with productions in the Imperial Theaters. *The World of Art* also showed a lively interest in the production of works by Sophocles and Euripides, given at the Théâtre Alexandre; perhaps to some extent because they had been translated by Merejkovsky.

Such rare concessions as the stage made to modernism and decadence, or to a production that occasionally "came off" left Diaghilev unenthusiastic, for as he wrote: "These are but tepid and unconvincing efforts at modernity which make no effort to understand either its true nature or its needs. It is easy enough to pose at being modern, but an altogether different matter to satisfy the deep needs of contemporary culture. That is why our theatrical pundits have thrown up the sponge, preferring to furbish themselves with modern trappings, rather than bother with what lies beneath, for they consider that such glory as they have earned thanks to 'their decadent bric-a-brac' is amply sufficient and indicative."

The publication of *The World of Art* coincided with the appearance of another individual venture, namely the Moscow Art Theater, which revolutionized our theatrical art, and may be considered one of the greatest events in the history of Russian culture.

It was an event, the importance of which was immediately realized by *The World of Art,* for during the whole six years of its existence, it always manifested the liveliest interest and concern in the vicissitudes and development of this group. Although it allowed its contributors the fullest liberty to say what they thought—I say it in all seriousness—and though at times they would draw attention to the real dangers inherent in Tchekhov's repertoire, the editorial staff of *The World of Art* was none the less convinced that the establishment of the Moscow Art Theater was an event of the greatest importance, and one which might exert a very real influence on the whole development of art.

---

[4] His *Literary Reminiscences* were published in Soviet Russia during 1933. The eighth chapter is of great interest, for it is entirely devoted to *The World of Art*.

The first article to deal with this new theatrical group appeared in 1900. It was contributed by P. Gneditch, and was entitled "The Theater of the Future." Attacking the established theater, it waxed highly enthusiastic over the new venture, and went on to say "Every company that strikes out a new path has first to solve three problems: (1) how to repudiate once and for all traditional convention, (2) how to substitute for it the reality of everyday existence as conceived and envisaged by the author, (3) how to learn to choose from this realistic art, works of the greatest integrity, vitality and interest, i.e., the most successful artistically." Later, he adds that these three problems have all been successfully solved by the Moscow Art Theater (absolutely, for modern plays; less so, for costume or historical plays) and boldly asserts [it is 1900 remember!] that "the production of *Uncle Vanya* and *The Sea Gull* marks an epoch in the art of the stage."

By 1902, we find a more critical attitude towards the viewpoint and trends of the Moscow Art Theater, both from Filosofov and Brussov; the latter, in a brilliant article entitled "Useless Truth," expressing alarm at what were considered Stanislavsky's excesses and their probable effect on the conventions of the stage, which seemed to them both quite indispensable to any future developments in that art.

Diaghilev, too, contributed a number of articles (two particularly outstanding) on the same group. All his life, he had manifested a lively interest in the theater, and this was to become still greater when, in 1899-1900, he was appointed assistant to the Director of the Imperial Theaters.

Thus, any opinion expressed by the future founder and director of the Russian Ballet must be precious to us, and particularly, because many of the tendencies in the Moscow Art Theater were later reflected in the ballet. We will pause awhile therefore, to consider Diaghilev's pronouncements and begin with an extract from an article entitled "The Originality of the Moscow Art Theater." "The chief prerogative of this group," he says, "lies in the fact that it can allow itself to take risks which any other daring innovator, enjoying less popularity, less authority, would dearly pay for. Here you have a group to whom everything will be forgiven: more, every effort will be made to give credence to its sincerity and the seriousness of its aims, however outrageous they may seem." [5]

Among these daring experiments must be numbered the production of Maeterlinck's three plays.

All these plays proved to be failures, both in the eyes of the partisans of the Symbolist school, to whom a new approach seemed needed, totally foreign to the realism of the Art Theater, and those of Stanislavsky's customary admirers, who saw Maeterlinck's Symbolism as mere affectation. Further on, in the same article, Diaghilev takes up the defense, and asserts that "the production of *The Blind* was a clever and subtle solution

[5] Might not the very same words have been said fifteen to twenty years later apropos Diaghilev's Russian Ballet?

of a problem which seemed beyond the powers of a theater whose roots penetrated so deeply into existence. And yet that burst of music, so suddenly interrupted, which introduces the performance and closes it, seems still to continue all the time one is watching this profoundly moving and mysterious tragedy."

The second Diaghilev article, "More about *Julius Caesar*" was evoked by V. Mirovitch's article "First Night at *Julius Caesar*, by the Art Theater," a writer also responsible for two other articles: "The First Performance of Gorky's *Lower Depths*" and *"The Pillars of Society* at the Art Theater." Diaghilev, however, disagreed with Mirovitch's contention that "the center of gravity in the theater has been transferred from the domain of the actor and the artist's individual inspiration, to that of the mechanics of their art," or that, "lacking, as it did, tragic actors, the Art Theater should never have embarked on producing Shakespeare."

So aggressive and eloquent was Diaghilev's refutation of this statement that I think it essential to reproduce it here in detail:

"This is a reproach to which every new development in art has had to submit, identical with that twenty-year cry that Rimsky-Korsakov's and Glazunov's music was nothing but musical theorems solved by musically minded mathematicians. Are not reproaches still being hurled at Sarah, that divine genius, for the super-perfection of her technique, as prejudicing acting 'from the heart,' *à la Duse?* Think of the sarcasms heaped on the Meiningen players when they appeared in countries educated in the tradition of psychopathic enthusiasm for all sorts of art tricks from Tamberlic's *contre ut dièze* [6] to Komisarjevska's sour tears! All this 'straight from the heart' business, these 'moments of inspiration,' this bestial pursuit of 'the soul' which seem impossible to throw off, have greatly harmed our art.

"Just as a portrait is no good unless it 'comes out of its frame,' so we refuse to accept our classical theater unless it contains at least one 'great tragic actor.' Any flabby seventy-year-old Othello—say, Salvini—will make all the Yuri Beliaevs lie flat on their backs: that is the charming custom we have inherited from the rabid admirers of the great Karatigins, Samoilovs and other Rubinis."

Remarks such as these from Diaghilev are infinitely more precious and interesting to us than whether Vishnevsky was suitable in the part of Antony. Contrary to the general opinion, and that of Mirovitch, Diaghilev claimed that there was no real "soul" in Vishnevsky's conception of the part, and that it bordered perilously upon Tamberlic's holy *ut dièze.*

---

[6] Tamberlic. Italian tenor of immense international fame: at the height of his powers, 1850-60. In common with all the great singers of his time and school, he attached, as did his public, an exaggerated importance to the highest note of his register, C, C-sharp (*ut dièze*), and sometimes even D. When one of these was due in the part, everyone on both sides of the footlights stopped, and prepared to listen to the marvelous sound produced by the singer, with extreme deliberation and absolute contempt of the dramatic situation and even of the musical sense of the moment. The post-Wagner style condemned this practice as inartistic and senseless; the ordinary listener still raves about it. (Ed.)

This same article ends on an exceedingly interesting note: "I should find it difficult to say whether the Art Theater was justified in putting on *Julius Caesar,* but one thing is certain, and that is that it is a perfectly legitimate and natural thing to want to build up a classical repertory. We were delighted to observe that the Moscow actors were able to put on a classic, and produce it in a most finished manner such as befits a modern, a most modern spectator.

"There is a great tendency in our Alexandriinsky Theater to create 'types,' according to the 'artistic temperaments' of every actor on its roster, as a result of which, where the classics are concerned, however 'great' an actor may be, he must perforce relearn everything from A to Z, and most important, forget his 'greatness.'

"The Moscow actors, however, know what discipline is, and that, more important than temperament or 'the sacred fire,' is what combines all colors into one single picture. Their great merit lies precisely in what they have been reproached with, namely, 'transferring the center of gravity in the theater from the domain of the actor, and the artist's individual inspiration to that of the mechanics of their art.' Bondage to inspiration is what enslaves our theater."

The Opera

The article "More about *Julius Caesar"* is dated 1903, that on "News of the Moscow Art Theater," 1904. The latter is certainly the best article contributed by Diaghilev to *The World of Art,* and coincides with a period when he was already losing interest in the review, and perhaps already contemplating devoting his energies to some new activity. Meanwhile, where opera was concerned, Diaghilev manifested an interest and enthusiasm which far outshone that of any of the other contributors to *The World of Art.* Apart from two notes by A. Nourok, dealing with Delibes' *Lakmé* and Rimsky-Korsakov's *Le Coq d'Or* and two others by A. Benois, one dealing with a new production of *Russlan and Ludmila,* the other with *The Valkyries* (the latter of the greatest interest in that it reveals how similar were Benois' and Diaghilev's views where productions of Wagner were concerned), every other article was written by Diaghilev. Not that these were very numerous or varied, since, for the most part, they deal exclusively with Wagner's operas. Such enthusiastic Wagnerism in the pages of *The World of Art* finds its explanation, not only in the adoration felt by both Diaghilev and Benois at about this time for the genius of Bayreuth, nor in the fact that the Mariinsky Theater, though lacking all modern apparatus, nevertheless, managed to stage his operas, but in their anxiety to convey to the management of the Imperial Theaters how the works of this composer should be staged. That was the real, the underlying, motive for Benois' article on *The Valkyries.* While admitting that these productions were far superior to those of Paris, and needed to fear no comparison with those of Bayreuth, Vienna or Dresden, he never-theless claimed that an immense amount still remained to be done, and stated that in his opinion "steps should be taken to exorcise the weird fate of Wagner's operas," for, as to the visual side of his works, the composer had been only too easily contented, approving whatever the stock scene-painters had turned out.

Diaghilev, for his part, demanded that the sets, the acting, and even the vocal renderings be re-interpreted. According to him the operas needed to be produced in a totally different fashion "from that demanded by Cosima, who has reached a stage where she is confusing her own whimsies with the wishes of her genius-husband. The *Nibelungs* must be produced without the assistance of the German 'Wagner-experts'—a task which would prove both important and impressive."

In the end *The World of Art* proved triumphant, for in 1903 Benois and Korovin were commissioned to design the sets for a new production of *Götterdämmerung* (the former preparing the designs, the latter being entrusted with the scenery). Diaghilev applauded the innovation, and claimed that the opera had now been produced in a manner far su-perior to that of its own country. Nevertheless, he was not entirely satisfied, declaring that he had expected more from Benois, and that he particularly disliked its realism. But as ever, Diaghilev was too exacting.

"In so far as he is a fine painter," he wrote, "Benois has produced some delightful water colors, which would adorn any exhibition. But one ques-tion remains to be asked. What has Wagner to do with all this, and what has become of the twilight of the gods? Stated otherwise, what connection is there between these landscapes, veritable works of art though they be, and Wotan, Brünnhilde, Valhalla, the Rhine Maidens, and the whole phantasmagoria which is the very essence of Wagner's creation? We are shown a fine northern landscape, with pines and some large stones left lying about, the kind of stage stone no one believes in, though why they are there, heaven alone knows! And this charming spot in the province of Perm is meant to stand for that rock, pregnant with terror, on which Wotan lulls his winged daughter to sleep. This is the heroic scene, that is to be peopled by gods and heroes."

However, Diaghilev did not only concern himself with certain pro-ductions, for "the reform of the opera" was also a matter of keen in-terest to him. Among other schemes, he worked on an idea that had long been cherished by Prince S. Volkonsky, director,[7] for a short time, of the Imperial Theaters: namely, that of establishing a second opera company, in addition to that attached to the Mariinsky Theater.

---

[7] In 1902, when Diaghilev wrote his articles on the necessity for such a reform, Prince Volkonsky was no longer in office.

The Ballet

Between 1899-1901 Diaghilev, as I have said, was associated with the management of the Imperial Theaters, where, as he wrote and said later, he hoped to be able to introduce certain innovations, which were eventually to find their application in the Russian Ballet. A number of facts appear to bear out this statement, and principally that of his resignation after the Sylvia episode, the costumes and décor for which he had wished to entrust to certain young painters, worthy of the name, instead of applying to the professionals. It will be necessary to revert yet again to the important part played by painting in the Russian Ballet, and more generally the "ballet-scena." In this respect, Diaghilev's attitude in 1909-1910 was exactly what we find it in 1899-1900. Meanwhile, we find his closest collaborator, that right hand of his, both on *The World of Art* and the Russian Ballet, Alexandre Benois, writing in the review that "the co-operation of artists like Golovin and Korovin is a first step towards raising the ballet to its level in the days of Fanny Elssler and Taglioni."

"Even if it is possible to claim," wrote Benois, "that their first attempt has not proved wholly successful, nevertheless one cannot deny the glowing spark of life which must eventually flare into an immense beacon. Now at last we can see real painting in the theater, instead of the backgrounds of the professional scene-painter. It is an event of the greatest importance, for it foretells a total rebirth of the art of the stage in this country."

A. Benois proved to be an excellent prophet, and "the glowing spark of art and life" did, indeed, with time, flare up into an immense beacon.

If, however, we assume that Diaghilev, from the very beginning of his connection with the Imperial Theaters, had a clear-cut program and definite ideas about the ballet, as he himself was to state in later years, how surprising does it seem that no parallel effort was made to propagate these ideas through the medium of the review? Actually, it is not until 1902 that we find the first mention of the ballet in its pages, a period when both Benois and Diaghilev were beginning to develop an interest in this art. One explanation may be that, being attached to the Imperial Theaters, and thus exclusively occupied with practical matters, he was willing to leave its theoretical aspects in abeyance until such time as, free to follow his own devices, he might hope, in writing, to influence the future development of the ballet. Nevertheless, even between the years 1902-1904, we find no mention of any project for reforming the ballet, while such notes and articles as do exist prove excessively meager. One thing alone seemed clear to Diaghilev and Benois, namely, the need for employing real painters to provide finer, more evocative settings for the ballet. Benois, too, though well aware of the bonds which linked ballet and painting, found much difficulty in providing any definition of these bonds. This, however, was much the case with all the contributors to the review. Each felt vaguely that change and reform were needed, but no one could say precisely in what way. Indeed, all that Benois can find to say is, "our ballet, the most famous in Europe, where ballet is either dead or has long since become something unsavory, this ballet of ours, of which we have every reason to be proud, is, we must confess, on the decline. It is on the decline, in spite of Vsevolojsky's [8] charming productions, in spite of Tchaikovsky's inspired music, or the lovely music Glazunov provides...and in spite of its dancers, among whom the most worthy of mention are MM. Legat, Gerdt, Lukyanov, and Mlles. Preobrazhenskaya, Kshesinskaya, Pavlova II, Sedova—though there are many others.

"Yet the fault does not lie in the interpreters, but in the tottering system, and such absurd, idiotic productions as that of *Raymonda,* in which it is physically impossible for a dancer to create a part for himself, or elfin ballets in which there is practically no dancing, or utterly nonsensical ballets stuffed with 'character' parts. When it comes to real pearls like *Giselle, La Fille Mal Gardée, Coppélia, Sylvia,* the whole production is dictated by outworn traditions, that is, of course, when they are not cast cynically aside like a bundle of old rags. As for creating new ballets, the question simply does not arise. The dances themselves eternally repeat the old patterns—and though we do not deny M. Petipa's talent, for, indeed, many of his groupings and folk dances are effective and charmingly designed, yet from that to real creation is a very long step. Little compositions are what they are, admirably executed, but altogether lacking in soul or meaning."

Benois treated the ballet with the utmost seriousness; to him it was one of the great arts, and thus we find him writing the following memorable words: "The Ballet is a universe in itself, which no one has yet exploited, or even understood what mighty reserves of expression, harmony, beauty, *meaning* it may conceal, even in comparison with tragedy."

No doubt Benois was setting his standards high, as may be seen from the manner in which he criticized *Don Quixote,* the first production to be put on by Gorsky, that young and talented ballet master of the Moscow ballet, at the Mariinsky Theater. Yet, though Benois applauded the reforms introduced by Gorsky, they did not entirely satisfy him. However, from his article, one would be hard put to it to say what these reforms were and why they needed to be applauded. "Clearly the ballet master has ignored the legend, the 'atmosphere,' in composing his ballet. What he has sought instead is to charm the public by a sort of firework display of the costumes, a mad whirling of masses, of individual items introduced at just the propitious moment; not for a moment has he bothered about the beauty of the sets, dramatic contrasts, rhythm, or plastic

[8] Read Vsevolojsky's *Costumes.*

effects. It would really be most regrettable if M. Gorsky were to continue in this easy, though somewhat unworthy, path. Another step, and
we shall be finding ourselves in the very midst of those famous Viennese
ballets, full of women whirling coquettishly to the sounds of an interminable waltz. Why, then, should we pay honor and glory to Gorsky
if, seriously speaking, nothing has been gained by changing M. Petipa
for a new 'decadent' routine of which we are tiring already?"

Another thing, too, astonishes us. If Benois attaches such significance
to rhythm and plastic art, why does he say that "the co-operation of
artists like Golovin and Korovin is a first step towards raising the ballet
to its level in the days of Fanny Elssler and Taglioni"?

But whereas Benois saw a spark of art in the new ballets, Diaghilev,
in an article on the "Ballets of Delibes" fiercely criticizes the theatrical
management for the manner in which it produces its ballets, and notably
those by Delibes, *Coppélia, Sylvia,* and *La Source. "Coppélia,"* he wrote,
"is the most adorable ballet in the world, a unique pearl in the history of
dancing. But heavens! how much effort it must have cost to tarnish and
denature it to the extent this wretched evening has revealed....As for
the second ballet, *Sylvia,* the entire management of the Imperial Theaters
half killed itself trying to turn it into a complete failure last year....
But I shall not waste time describing what *Sylvia* is, for anyone who
knows Delibes must know the position he occupies in music, choreography and the plastic arts. There is only one thing that surprises me:
how is it that in the entire directorate of the Imperial Theaters, there does
not happen to be one man who realizes that if one loves choreography,
classicism, and plastic art, it is impossible to love rubbish, or utterly pointless transformation scenes like that in Minkus' *Don Quixote,* or Pugni's
far-too-celebrated *Koniok Gorbunok,*[9] which one can see at any fair;
and first and foremost that the sets must not be entrusted to Korovin and
Golovin? What an idea, to waste the time and strength of such talented
painters in burdening them with so elementary a task!"

Eventually, on December 8th, 1902, the Mariinsky Theater put on *La
Source,* the third of Delibes's ballets, whereupon *The World of Art*
reported: "There is not much to be said about the production of this
ballet, for the sets and décor were uglier and more intolerable than those
made ten years ago. One novelty there was, however, for the dances are
no longer produced in Petipa's old manner, but as they are on the boards
at the Zoo-Theater. Throughout the whole performance, the *corps de
ballet* marched from one end of the stage to the other in perfect align-
ment, performing every kind of gymnastics, while the ballerina danced
up by the footlights. The management can now plead with perfect justice:
'a few more productions of this kind, and we shall have finished with
every artistic tradition of the ballet.'"

It would be futile to seek, in Diaghilev's articles, for the reforms that

[9] The hump-backed pony of the fairy tales. (Ed.)

that ballet really required. All he does is sharply to attack the complete absence of any artistic feeling in the official productions—nothing more. A far better idea of his opinions can be gained from the articles he contributed on the theater, than from the few lines inspired in him by the ballet.

I have lingered too long perhaps on the art of the stage as reflected in *The World of Art,* and yet I consider it justified, for so little was said about the theater by the founder of the Russian Ballet, during his twenty years of devotion to it, that we must catch at every allusion made by him, or his closest collaborators. In this respect our most prolific source is *The World of Art.* From it we may learn Diaghilev's point of departure, and his guiding ideas in the task he was soon to assume.

CHAPTER V

EXHIBITIONS OF "THE WORLD OF ART"

Exhibitions at the Stieglitz Gallery

THE EXHIBITIONS organized by *The World of Art* exercised a great influence on the review, for they greatly helped it to recruit both contributors and material for reproduction in its pages. Indeed, the material brought in in this way was far richer than that supplied by the usual contributors, or by the notices on Western art, or by the articles devoted to individual artists as selected by Diaghilev.

The two first exhibitions of this kind, which took place in 1899 and 1900, unlike those which followed, were exclusively expressions of Diaghilev's taste. The first, which opened on January 18th, 1899, and was held in the rooms of the Stieglitz Museum, was an international exhibition in the fullest meaning of the word. Round a nucleus of Russian artists such as Bakst, Benois, Golovin, Botkin, Vasnetzov, Vrubel, Lanceret, Levitan, Miliavin, Maliutin, Nesterov, Purvit, Polenova, Polenov, Perepletchikov, Répin, Svetoslavsky, Somov, Serov, Yakunchikova, were gathered works by foreign painters such as the Finns, Blomsted, Gallen, Ernefeldt and Enkel; the Frenchmen, Aman-Jean, Besnard, Blanche, Dagnan-Bouveret, Degas, Carrière, Latouche, Lhermitte, Ménard, Puvis de Chavannes, Rafaelli, and Simon; the Germans, Bartels, Dill, Liebl, and Liebermann; the Englishman, Brangwyn; the Belgians, Bergren and Léon-Frédéric; the Americans, Alexander, Tiffany, and Whistler; the Swiss, Böcklin; the Italian, Boldini; the Scotchmen, Patterson and Thomas; the Norwegian, Thaulow, and the Swede, Zorn.

It is impossible to conceive what efforts it cost Diaghilev to organize this exhibition, which, in spite of proving a huge success in the eyes of the rising painters, the public, and society, was, with its organizer, bitterly criticized by the Press.

The second exhibition organized by *The World of Art,* i.e., Diaghilev, was opened on January 28th, 1900, and was again held at the same gallery. It too proved very successful. On this occasion only the works of Russian artists were shown, among whom Serov, Levitan, Nesterov, Benois, Yakunchikova, Vrubel, Golovin, Maliutin, Somov, Lanceret, Bakst, Dossiekin, and a number of paintings of the eighteenth and early nineteenth century, composed of works by Levitzky, Borovikovsky, Brullow, Kiprensky, etc.

The third of these exhibitions was opened on January 5th, 1901, but since Baron Stieglitz had ceased to rent his gallery, it was held in "enemy country," i.e., at the Academy of Arts. Officially at least, Diaghilev was no longer assuming complete control, but actually it was hardly possible to withstand his dictatorial will, for well he knew both how to command and persuade.

Difficulties of Organization

Soon after the opening of the 1900 exhibition, on February 26th, a council meeting was called by *The World of Art* for the purpose of establishing a set of regulations under which subsequent exhibitions should be held. A central committee was also formed, consisting of two members—subject to annual election—in addition to the editor of *The World of Art*. As a result, the third exhibition was in fact organized by Diaghilev, A. Benois and V. Serov. As for the exhibitors, these were divided into three categories: "permanent" members, with the right to decide what paintings they would send, "guest" painters, specially invited, one at least of whose paintings must be selected by the organizers, and finally, painters who might occasionally be invited to exhibit if approved by seven permanent members.

Many difficulties attended the organization of the 1901 exhibition, and much negotiating, both oral and written, before the Academy of Arts was prepared to lend its galleries. In Diaghilev's words, "they were loaded with insults, and beset with cunning intrigues, official protests and hosts of petty annoyances."

"What were we met with," he wrote, "in response to our perfectly legitimate wish to organize our exhibition as tastefully and comfortably as we could? First, innumerable protests. When we substituted for the easels, wooden screens covered with canvas, we were told they were dangerous and highly inflammable, and as a result found ourselves involved in endless correspondence, committee meetings, negotiations. Our honorable professors and academicians actually tried to strike terror into the hearts of the public through interviews 'that just happened to get' reported in the newspapers. Others, and some of the most 'venerable' at that, went so far as to state that our adversaries would not even hesitate to set fire to our show, so much did they hate us. In fact, now or never was the moment to hum that air from the *Huguenots,* 'Charles has Enemies.' When, in spite of all these miserable protests, the exhibition was finally opened, all our art critics found nothing better to do than mock at our 'decadent' venture, and declare that, 'in boosting Zionglinsky, we were forgetting Titian.'"

Finally, as we have said, the exhibition was opened, the outstanding works being those by A. Benois (one, "The Pond in front of the Grand Palace," was bought by the Emperor, who himself visited the show on February 3rd), I. Bilibin, I. Braz, A. Golovin, Korovin, Lanceret, Nesterov, Ostroumova-Lebedeva, Perepletchikov, Purvit, Rushitz, Somov, Serov, Prince Trubetskoy, and Zionglinsky; sculpture by Golubkina and objects by Yakunchikova. In addition there were on show works by Bakst, Baksheyev, Vasnetzov, Vinogradov, Vrubel, Dossiekin, Maliutin, Maliavin, Mamontov, Ober, Okolovitch, Pasternak, Rylov, Riabushkin and Svetoslavsky. Comparing this exhibition with those of 1899 and 1900, some new names are to be found: S. Vinogradov, who exhibited three pictures, Okolovitch (a pastel), Pasternak, Rylov and Riabushkin. The contagion of "decadence" seemed to be spreading.

The 1902 exhibition opened on March 9th in the "Arcade" galleries. Though also organized by *The World of Art*, it enjoyed the collaboration of "The 36," a group of Moscow painters, and proved brilliantly success- ful. But in 1903 a scission took place and "The 36" held their own exhibition. Diaghilev's criticism of the separatists was a typical one, revealing yet again how completely objective he was in matters of art, an objectivity that was most clearly defined in his attitude to Répin: "I do not know," he wrote, "which of the two aforementioned exhibitions suf- fered most from the parting. All I can say is, that those who control the fates of 'The 36' have too much taste to admit anything coarse or in- artistic, and thus their exhibition, as was to be expected, looked fresh and made a good impression."

Death Warrant of The World of Art

In 1903, yet another exhibition was organized by *The World of Art* and on February 15th a meeting was held by the various exhibitors about which we find A. Benois speaking somewhat reticently: "Our ex- hibitions, under the banner of *The World of Art*, came to an end a full year before the review. What was responsible for this catastrophe were the complications arising from the connection of our own exhibition with that, somewhat similar in character and composition, held in Moscow by 'The 36.' This, however, was merely the excuse, for underneath lay an awareness that it was 'time to stop.' In passing, however, it may be added that our own exhibition, held in the rooms of the 'Society for the Protection of Art,' proved unsatisfactory, both as to the pictures exhibited and the general effect."

More summary was the résumé provided by *The World of Art*: "This spring, *The World of Art* review will not hold its usual exhibition. The new 'Society of Artists,' comprising participators in the exhibition held by 'The 36' in Moscow, and the majority of the fellow workers on *The World of Art* will, however, hold an exhibition in Moscow towards the end of December at the Stroganov school. The same exhibition will be shown in St. Petersburg during Lent. The absence of a constitution, and a severely critical selection committee—such was the foundation on

which *The World of Art* exhibitions were organized. A strict constitution, and no selection committee is the basis of the 'New Society.'"

On the other hand, Igor Grabar provides us with rather fuller details
in regard to the historic meeting of February 15th. "At the outset of
1903, we having opened our exhibition in St. Petersburg, all the members of *The World of Art* group suddenly appeared in St. Petersburg.
Never before had such a concourse of artists gathered together, for all
the Moscow painters seemed to have made a special point of appearing.
Diaghilev opened the meeting, which was held in the editor's office, and
made a speech in which he said that, according to the information he
had received, certain exhibitors felt they had grievances against the selection committee, and that thus it was his duty to ask whether the moment
had not come to plan their exhibitions on a new basis. He also alluded to
certain of the Moscow painters who had openly expressed their dissatisfaction with the dictatorial powers arrogated by Diaghilev.

"At first reluctantly, then more boldly, people began speaking. Eventually, it was agreed that what would be preferable would be a larger
selection committee, one with less power, and also less subject to 'dictatorial outbreaks.'

"I remained silent, for I saw that the Muscovites had mustered in such
force to render a good account of themselves in the struggle against the
St. Petersburgites. But what surprised me was to find that some of our
painters, like Bilibin, Braz, etc., were suffering from a sense of injury,
and fully agreed with the Muscovites.

"The real thunderbolt, however, was Benois' declaration, that he too
was in favor of a new society. At this Diaghilev and Filosofov looked at
one another. The former seemed very disturbed, the latter remained
calm, though a sarcastic smile hovered on his lips. Eventually, the Muscovite demands won the day. Everyone got up, and Filosofov, in a voice
audible to everyone, said: 'Thank God! this is the end.'

"The meeting broke up. A few of us remained. We were silent. What
was there to say? We all knew that *The World of Art* had come to an
end. It was a painful, anguished moment.

"On February 15th, the death warrant of our exhibitions was signed,
and with it, therefore, that of *The World of Art*."

CHAPTER VI

THE IMPERIAL THEATERS

Diaghilev's connection with the Imperial Theaters

IN JULY, 1899, Prince S. M. Volkonsky had been nominated director of the Imperial Theaters, and on September 10th of the same year, Serge Diaghilev was appointed his special assistant. The two men had long known each other, for Prince Volkonsky had published (his only contribution, it is true) an article, entitled "Art," in issues 3 and 4 of *The World of Art,* for the year 1899.

Diaghilev, then aged twenty-seven, was both handsome and seductive. The white lock in the dark hair had won for him the sobriquet of "Chinchilla," and his appearance on the managerial staff of the Imperial Theaters made a great impression on a number of artists, in particular, on the greatest and most influential of the stars of the Mariinsky Theater!

> "I've just discovered
> Chinchilla in his box:
> And I'm horribly afraid
> I may make a misstep in my dancing."

So sang Mlle. Mathilde Kshesinskaya, as she danced her variation in *Esmeralda.* Her liking for Diaghilev was exceedingly obvious, and astonished no one. Indeed, the other ballerinas would join in, too:

> "And I'm horribly afraid
> I may make a misstep in my dancing."

After her dance, Kshesinskaya would come up to the footlights and bow to the Chinchilla, whereupon Diaghilev would loudly applaud. They were very great friends. It flattered Diaghilev that the prima ballerina paid so much attention to him, when she herself was such a favorite with the Emperor and Grand Dukes, and so justly celebrated for her dancing throughout Russia. And Kshesinskaya herself was proud of the approbation of the young balletomane, whose artistic taste and connoisseurship were so universally admitted, who edited *The World of Art,* and whose exhibitions had earned for him the praise of even their Imperial Majesties.

Altogether, several special assistants were attached to the management of the Imperial Theaters (for instance, in 1889 there were seven) though their duties were of the lightest. Nevertheless, Prince Volkonsky decided

to make use of Diaghilev's determination, energy and sure taste, by
employing him on several "missions." The editor of *The World of Art*
could not be expected merely to adorn the directors' box, with a monocle
screwed into his eye.

The Imperial Theaters' Annual

The first of these special missions, therefore, was that of editing the
Annual of the Imperial Theaters. Heretofore, this task had been entrusted to Moltchanov, the famous Savina's husband, who had performed his task in the most thoroughly bureaucratic manner. "But the
moment Diaghilev was attached to the directorate of the Imperial
Theaters," wrote Prince Volkonsky, "Moltchanov himself had the bright
idea of resigning his position as editor of the *Annual,* for he had guessed
that the task would be entrusted to Diaghilev, and no doubt secretly
hoped that 'the decadent' would destroy himself in the process. Thus,
we all awaited the first issue with the greatest impatience. Most of our
functionaries connected with the arts, as well as the academically minded,
were already highly incensed with *The World of Art.* Its youth and
freshness seemed pure insolence to them, while the painters who had
grouped themselves under its banner and who were later to be world-
famous, such as Benois, Somov, Bakst, Maliutin, Serov, Maliavin, Roehrich, etc., were ridiculed by the whole Press, and *The New Age* in
particular.[1] Diaghilev felt he was being treated as a sort of ragamuffin;
an ignorant helot in the arts. And the whole attitude of the Press, in
announcing the approaching publication of the first issue of the *Annual*
under a new editor, was both malevolent and mocking.

"Nevertheless, when it finally appeared, it exceeded the most optimistic expectations, and sowed terror and dismay among those who had
expected failure.

"This first issue of Diaghilev's *Annual* was to mark an era in the
history of Russian bookmaking, an epoch notable for the production of
such periodicals as *Apollo, Bygone Years, The New Art,* and examples
of bookmaking such as those by Lukomsky, Benois' monographs, and the
'Sirius' editions; in fact, a mass of material impossible to enumerate."

That Prince Volkonsky to some extent exaggerates the importance of
Diaghilev's *Annual* may be admitted. It was a judgment which would

---

[1] It must be admitted that Diaghilev, too, hardly bothered to consider *The New Age's*
feelings, as we see by this telegram published by Filosofov in *The World of Art* signed
Bejanitzky, one of Diaghilev's favorite pseudonyms.

"In thanking you for your invitation to participate at the ceremony in honor of A. S.
Souvorin, I send my cordial congratulations to *The New Age.* With all my heart, I
hope that this periodical, one of the most important published in Russia, will venture
a backward glance and admit that, during the whole twenty-five years of its activity,
the evolution of Russian art has taken place irrespective of, and in opposition to, every
idea ever expressed by *The New Age.*

"The Editor: *The World of Art,*
"BEJANITZKY."

have been perfectly justified, had the *Annual* for 1899-1900 (including a supplement dealing with 1898-1899) appeared not towards the end of 1900, but early in 1898, for instance, before *The World of Art* yet existed. If Diaghilev did indeed inaugurate a new epoch in the history of Russian bookmaking, it was his review which was responsible, and not the *Annual*, epoch-making though that may have been in comparison with previous *Annuals*. Certainly, it was impossible ever again to issue it as in Moltchanov's days, and Baron Driesen, who succeeded Diaghilev, did his best to maintain it at the same level.

This *Annual*, indeed, proved a most notable *édition de luxe* (though it practically "did for" the Office, since it cost twice as much as any previous number to produce), one that was outstanding from every point of view, as much for the variety and abundance of the contents, as for the quality of the reproductions and the technical perfection of the printing.

In addition to the material dealing with the activities of the Imperial Theaters, which had, perforce, to be included—covering productions, anniversaries, obituary notices, and itemized lists, such as plays, actors, staff, etc.—the *Annual* contained a number of articles of the greatest interest, such as V. Svetlov's ninety-one pages dealing with "Choreography in Classical Times," and a somewhat shorter article by Alexandre Benois on the "Alexandriinsky Theater." More, I myself consider its itemized list of "Ballets performed at the Imperial Theaters in St. Petersburg from the year 1828," to be of the greatest value: indeed, on several occasions, I found it exceedingly useful when writing my *Ballet Traditional to Modern*.

But the real worth of this *Annual* lay in the artistry of its typography, for the volume abounded in vignettes, head and tail pieces, facsimile reproductions of eighteenth-century playbills and programs, and numerous insets. Of the latter, the most noteworthy were a portrait of the Empress Elizabeth Petrovna dressed for a masked ball, by G. H. Grott, two portraits of F. Volkov and A. P. Sumarokov by Losenko (engraved by Walker), a portrait of I. Vsevolojsky by Serov, another of Moltchanov by Bakst, two portraits of César Cui and Gay by Répin, another of Wagner by Lenbach, still another of M. Savina by Braz, three programs designed for the Hermitage Theater by Bakst and Somov, and many other items.

In addition, many reproductions illustrated the various plays, operas and ballets staged by the Imperial Theaters, such as *Othello, Oedipus Rex*, Boborikin's *The Crime*, Rostand's *Cyrano de Bergerac*, Lopukhin's *From the Moon to Japan*, Glazunov's *The Ordeal of Damis* and *The Seasons*, Drigo's *Harlequinade*, Petipa's *Dupré's Pupils*, Pugni's *Esmeralda*, César Cui's *The Saracen*, Puccini's *La Bohème*, Wagner's *Tristan and Isolde* and *Tannhäuser*, Berlioz's *The Trojans at Carthage*, Serov's *Judith*, Goethe's *Egmont*, etc., etc. The illustrations for a new comedy by Borisov, *Biron*, are particularly interesting. (Baron Driesen erroneously ascribes it to A. V. Polovtzov, and places the action in the reign of the Empress Elizabeth instead of that of the Empress Anne.) Each portrait of the main characters in the play, such as Biron, Prince Cherkasky, Tretiakovsky, Count Minich, Count Bestuzhev-Riumin, was accompanied by contemporary photographs of the actors in the costumes they wore for their impersonations (a procedure employed, though to a lesser extent, in illustrating other plays).

Curious, too, were the reproductions of designs for ballets made by I. A. Vsevolojsky, Prince Volkonsky's predecessor. And again, thanks to the co-operation of the painters associated with *The World of Art*, the photographs of actors and dancers were transformed into little masterpieces by being touched up with the addition of appropriate backgrounds. It was clear, therefore that Prince Volkonsky had acquired a very unusual collaborator. As he himself wrote:

"Through Diaghilev I was able to avail myself of the co-operation of a number of painters. Apollinaire Vasnetzov, for instance, designed the sets and costumes of *Sadko* for me, and made of it something original and beautiful. In his posthumous *Musical Chronicles,* Rimsky-Korsakov speaks very favorably of this production, which means something in a book all bristling with prickles. I also made the acquaintance of other painters round Diaghilev. Everything seemed to be moving actively forward—as actively, that is, as was possible on dangerous ground, and managing the Imperial Theaters was certainly that—when suddenly, the incident happened."

But here, one is tempted to insert: "when suddenly Prince Volkonsky proved weak and vacillating and incapable of protecting Diaghilev."

Prince Volkonsky and the "Diaghilev Incident"

Prince Volkonsky must have known perfectly well that, by appointing Diaghilev to edit the *Annual,* he would be bound seriously to annoy the permanent functionaries who managed the Theaters. Nevertheless, in spite of numerous protests, he adhered to his decision, with the result that Diaghilev was able to complete his task. Unfortunately, Prince Volkonsky's courage soon failed him, with the result that an incident occurred in connection with Diaghilev's succeeding "mission." Here is the Prince's version:

"Diaghilev," he writes in his memoirs, "possessed in the highest degree the quality of making himself disliked wherever he went. An underground revolt began to spread against him, in the office, in the wings, in the sewing-rooms. I paid no attention, in the hope that the artistic results of his activity would make people overlook what they thought his arrogance and tactlessness.

"Then one day, I handed the head clerk a written order stating that Diaghilev had been entrusted with the production of Delibes's ballet *Sylvia.* This notice was to appear next day in the official order paper.

Two Studies of Diaghilev

That evening, two of my colleagues in the Office arrived, and warned me that my decision threatened to provoke so much discontent among the staff that they very much doubted whether any such order would be executed. I yielded...the order was not printed, and I had to tell Diaghilev that I was withdrawing my promise."

Two observations seem necessary here. In the first place, anyone familiar with Russian bureaucratic institutions, especially those under the Ministry of the Imperial Court, must know that, though an "underground revolt" may be within the bounds of probability, it might easily have been dealt with, and was in no wise likely to affect the successful prosecution of a scheme envisaged by the director, whatever his "two colleagues" might have said. But the term is ill-chosen, for as director of the Imperial Theaters, Prince Volkonsky could only have underlings in his employ, and certainly not collaborators. In the second place, Prince Volkonsky's account seeks to convey that having entrusted Diaghilev with the production of *Sylvia*, that very same night, in deference to the plea of his two collaborators, he reconsidered his decision. Actually, something quite different had happened, for Prince Volkonsky changed his mind only when considerable progress had already been made with the designs for the new ballet. This fact is corroborated by a remark on *Russlan and Ludmila* made by A. Benois, which appeared in 1904 in *The World of Art*. Referring to the reforms which Prince Volkonsky proposed introducing, Benois remarks that "his stay at the head of the Imperial Theaters has been all too short to permit him to carry out the many reforms in his mind. To give some idea of them, we may mention the new sets for *Eugen Onegin,* and the production of *Sadko* from designs by Vasnetzov, the very first attempts to co-operate with *real* painters and not professional scene-painters. These plans should have reached fruition with Delibes's *Sylvia,* and a certain number of painters had been called in to work out a setting, even to the minutest details, of this most admirable ballet. But the cowardice and indolence of the management have put a sudden end to these plans, and the building, with only its foundations laid, is left unfinished."

But to continue with Prince Volkonsky's account: "Next morning, I received a written statement from Diaghilev in which he resigned the editorship of the *Annual*. This was followed by a whole bundle of letters from the painters, commissioned to redesign the ballet, declaring that they refused to work for me any longer. Whether I was right or wrong in breaking my promise is not the question. But I could certainly not tolerate such opposition on the part of an employee under my orders. I therefore demanded his resignation. He refused. I then submitted a demand for his dismissal: and at this point began all the pother."

Here again, we must complain not so much of the inaccuracies, as of the way things are glossed over. In the first place, was it a crime for Diaghilev to resign from his position as editor of the *Annual:* Moltchanov had done as much, and Prince Volkonsky, pleased at his departure, had made no objection to his resignation. On the other hand, could Diaghilev, in so far as he was a public servant, be held responsible for the fact that a number of "free," independent painters had sent in a "whole bundle" of letters refusing to work any longer for the management? But also, two infinitely more important facts are glossed over: (1) that it was he himself who called on Diaghilev, *at his own home,* instead of sending for him, and formally demanded his resignation, a fact which greatly influenced the future course of events; (2) while telling us he submitted a demand for Diaghilev's dismissal, he slurs over the full significance of such a "dismissal without petition," for in those days such a dismissal carried a much dreaded stigma. Indeed, any official dismissed under "Article 3" was deprived forever of the right to enter the Government service, and a "wolf's passport" became his lot through life.[2]

And it was this, this "wolf's passport," which Prince Volkonsky was intending to fasten on a man whose "artistic taste and connoisseurship were so universally admitted" and whom he himself admired for these very reasons.

But to return to Prince Volkonsky: "Diaghilev's will was like iron; nothing in the world could have stood in his way. Everything was set into motion: Kshesinskaya, the Grand Duke Serge Mikhailovitch, even the Emperor, heard of it. And what was strangest of all, was that the very people who had opposed me when I took up Diaghilev, now turned against me and defended him. Oh, human inconstancy! It was war to the knife. General Rydzevsky, acting for the Minister of the Imperial Court, Baron Frederichs, who was then ill, called on me bearing a letter from the Tsar, in which His Majesty demanded that no steps be taken to dismiss Diaghilev before he himself had discussed the matter."

This "war to the knife" might easily have been avoided, for all Diaghilev's old enemies, having got their way, were now on his side, and the Tsar himself had asked for delay.... But at this point Prince Volkonsky reveals that though he might lack energy, one thing he did not lack—obstinacy. Whatever the cost, he was determined to win. And so he did...and by very odd means.

Let us continue with his account of General Rydzevsky's second visit.

"I have just been talking to the Emperor, and have succeeded in getting his consent to the dismissal. It was lucky that you gave me the copies of your correspondence with Diaghilev: I showed them to the Emperor, and he said:

"'If that's the way things are, let the order be published.'

"'So it's all finished and done with?' I said.

---

[2] Used here metaphorically: literally "wolf's passport" was a term applied to a document given to undesirable tramps to prevent them remaining in the same locality. This procedure had been obsolete for some considerable time. (Ed.)

" 'Who knows?' answered the General. 'The notice cannot be published till the day after tomorrow. But tomorrow the Grand Duke Serge Mikhailovitch might easily go and see the Tsar and get the whole thing changed. Anyway, I've made up my mind that if anyone telephones when I'm at home, they're to say I've gone out and don't know where I'm to be found.'

"The next day I was rung up several times and asked whether General Rydzevsky was not at my house. And the following day the order notifying Diaghilev's dismissal appeared. Thenceforth Diaghilev and I always cut each other."

Here Prince Volkonsky over-simplifies the negotiations which took place in connection with Diaghilev's dismissal. It was not once, but several times, that the Grand Duke Serge Mikhailovitch and General Rydzevsky sought out the Emperor at Tsarskoye Selo, and strove to make him reach a decision. "Pardon," "dismiss," "pardon," "dismiss," "pardon," "dismiss," so it went on. Even on the Grand Duke's first outlining of the matter, hearing that Prince Volkonsky had called on Diaghilev at his home, the Emperor at once sided with Diaghilev, and said:

"If I were Diaghilev, I should not have resigned."

The final decision of the Lord of all the Russias was also in Diaghilev's favor. But we know how shady was the trick by which General Rydzevsky got the order dismissing Diaghilev published "pursuant to article 3."

Feeling somewhat conscience-stricken—for had he not agreed "he would not have resigned"? (though Diaghilev, uncompromising if ever a man was, needed no such justification)—the Emperor, anxious to compensate him in some way, requested the Secretary of State, A. S. Taneyev, to provide Diaghilev with an appointment. But the Minister himself, Baron Frederichs, now back from his "cure," pointed out that such a thing was quite impossible, in view of the "wolf's passport." Whereupon His Majesty exclaimed: "What a stupid law!" and forthwith ordained that a post be found for Diaghilev.

In his book entitled *The Russian Ballet, 1921-1929,* W. A. Propert reproduces a most interesting letter from Diaghilev, dated February 17th, 1926, answering two questions set him by the author: the first, what was his opinion of Isadora Duncan; the second, asking details about his connection with the Imperial Theaters. To this last Diaghilev answered as follows:

"From 1899 to 1901, I was attached for special duties to the director of the Imperial Theaters. I was young and full of ideas. For a year I edited the Imperial Theaters' *Annual;* that went very well. I wanted to turn the theater into the path I have gone on following to this day. It did not succeed! A terrific scandal took place, in which Grand Dukes, Princes, Delilahs and aged Ministers all took a hand—in a word, *fourteen reports were sent in to H.M. the Emperor to get me cleared out.* For two months St. Petersburg could talk of nothing else. Thanks to it, the director of the Imperial Theaters was thrown out, too, immediately afterwards. To the amazement of the whole bureaucracy, one week after my downfall, the Emperor had me appointed to his Personal Chancery. Soon after, I left Russia. The Emperor did not like me. He thought I was a 'wily' one, and once told my cousin, the Minister of Commerce, that he was afraid one day or other I might play him some scurvy trick. Poor Emperor, how ill-placed were his fears! How much better for him would it have been could he have summed up correctly those who did eventually play the fatal trick." [3]

Not for long, then, did Prince Volkonsky keep his post, for, some weeks after, an incident which brought him into conflict with Kshesinskaya and the Grand Duke Serge Mikhailovitch, forced him to resign. Mlle. Kshesinskaya had been fined for some breach of the rules, and the Grand Duke sought to have the order rescinded, whereupon Prince Volkonsky, opposing it strongly, was eventually forced to hand in his resignation. This happened in July, 1901.

We may now turn back to the end of Prince Volkonsky's story.

". . . Thenceforth, Diaghilev and I always cut each other. Nevertheless, I rejoiced at each of his successes, not only from the point of view of art, but also because they silenced his detractors.

"Ten years after those wonderful exhibitions I saw him in Rome, at the restaurant Umberto, dining with many of the people with whom he was then working. I went up to him, and said:

"'Serge Pavlovitch, I have always been a fervent admirer of all you're doing, and I feel I owe it to myself to tell you so personally.'

"'It's a long time since we met,' he replied, 'it makes me happy to be able to shake you by the hand again.'"

"Thus ended the Diaghilev incident."

Anyone aware of Diaghilev's uncompromising nature at moments may feel some astonishment that he manifested so little resentment. It may be explained, however, by the fact that his moods fluctuated greatly, and also by the fact that he had no great liking for his position with the Imperial Theaters, much preferring a career as a "gentleman free lance." Thus the dismissal itself was in no way a blow to him. Nevertheless, his contact with the Imperial Theaters, to some extent, affected all his later activity, for it introduced him to a number of dancers, among others Fokine, who greatly aided him in the practical realization of the reforms he wished to introduce into the art of the stage, and so helped him to penetrate to the very core of the life of the theater.

[3] The continuation of the letter in answer to the first of Propert's questions throws much light on the origin of the Russian Ballet and its founder's ideas. "I knew Isadora well in St. Petersburg, and with Fokine I was present at her first appearance. Fokine raved about her, and Duncan's influence on him was the very foundation of all his creative activity. I've known Isadora all her life, as well in Venice where she wanted to marry Nijinsky, as in Monte Carlo, where she danced the tango with Massine, explaining meanwhile that in all dancing only one thing mattered—'the basic movements.' Classical ballet in Imperial Russia never recovered from the impact of Isadora's dancing."

CHAPTER VII

THE LAST YEARS OF "THE WORLD OF ART"

Diaghilev's departure for abroad: he criticizes "modernism"

FOR EIGHTEEN months after his dismissal, Diaghilev was never seen at the theater. True, very soon after the "incident," in the late spring of 1901, he went abroad, and there he stayed till practically the end of 1902, except for very short visits to Russia. But although he continued to edit *The World of Art,* maintained connection with the office, and sent it material from time to time, to all intents and purposes he had delegated the work to Benois and Filosofov, and his interest in the review was obviously declining.

For the first six months of 1901 we find but one article contributed by Diaghilev, and that deals with art exhibitions. Therein he contended, *inter alia,* that Répin was fundamentally much closer to his "enemies" of *The World of Art* than to his friends—the "Vagrants."

While abroad two articles were all that was received from Diaghilev's pen: "The Paris Exhibitions" and "Painting Exhibitions in Germany." Though somewhat heavy in their treatment, these articles, both for size and content, were worth many shorter ones. A number of reproductions of paintings by Aman-Jean, A. Besnard, Anglade, Ch. Cotta, A. Dauchet, M. Denis, Simon, Zorn, Edelfeldt, Zuloaga, Carrière, La Gondara, Leibl, Leistikov, Olbrich, etc. etc., illustrated them.

The Paris exhibitions, both that of the "Salon des Champs Elysées" and that of the "Champ de Mars," seem, on the whole, to have proved disappointing. He was also somewhat dissatisfied with the modern school, which seemed to have "aged and gone gray," a dissatisfaction which was to make him swing over to the "old masters." "The main defect of all contemporary, so-called semi-advanced modernistic exhibitions," he wrote, "is the abundance of advanced paintings on show. It is as though a remarkable discovery had been made—a formula for 'modernism.' Of late years, and especially since the World Exhibition, this formula has been more and more frequently employed. Even the very young seem to be marking time, have become well behaved, moderate, and fearful of advancing too far, though careful of lagging behind. Not enough mistakes are being made; one feels that the Claudes in the Louvre are no longer possible now, and that Corot, Monet and Besnard have done enough fighting to have the right to a little rest.

"Meanwhile, the innumerable paintings at the 'Champ de Mars' trail in an endless stream across the rooms: really one might cut them up by the yard. All one sees are little Whistlers, Cazins or Simons; gray, 'soulful' landscapes, endless portraits, 'symphonies in gray and green,' and rugged Bretons either fishing or eating fish.

"Happening to talk about the Salon to some French painters in somewhat critical terms, they seemed astonished: 'Is it really so bad? Isn't it much as usual?' *'As usual,'* that is the enemy!"

Zuloaga, de La Gondara, Maurice Denis and Anglade greatly delighted him. In Zuloaga Diaghilev at once saw "a painter of great importance, powerful to a degree to which we have long grown unaccustomed."

There is, however, no indication of a diminished interest in modern art in the conclusion of this article, for it ends on a personal note, in which the author seeks to transmit his own feeling about art to his readers, a feeling that objectivity can only be realized through the medium of the subjective.

"Admittedly Besnard, Zuloaga and Gondara are excellent. That indeed, even on a world-wide scale, should be enough for a year: one can't expect a genius to be born every minute! If it were only that! Unfortunately, the real trouble, the depressing side of it all, is the complete absence of any vital enthusiasm, the fact that the fires are burning low, have indeed gone completely out on numbers of altars which now stand cold, magnificent, unchangeable and useless."

Exhibitions of Painting in Germany

Now let us take a rapid glance at the very long letter devoted to "Painting Exhibitions in Germany" and sub-divided into three sections, "Darmstadt," "Dresden" and the "Berlin Secessionists." It is a polemical letter directed against Richard Muther, one of the ablest critics of the history of art, and in it Diaghilev ardently supported the Darmstadt venture, which bore the resounding title "A Document of German Art," and its efforts to create an artistic colony by way of protest against the "infinite hideousness in which the greater part of contemporary society exists without even being aware of the fact."

This "Dresden letter" is a sort of dithyramb in honor of the exhibition held in that city. There is no need to linger in detail on its enthusiasms, for the only painters mentioned are those we know already from *The World of Art.*

We shall note only one new feature in this exhibition, for it corresponded with much in Diaghilev's thought and trends at the time, and thus enabled him to express, in high relief, such ideas as were most dear to him, and were indeed the prime source of all his eclecticism: "Last spring, at a meeting of those exhibiting at *The World of Art* exhibition, a proposal was made which provoked some very lively argument. It was suggested that, for the future, contemporary paintings should be hung side by side with the paintings of the past, and not in a separate room as heretofore. Thus a Serov would be succeeded by a Levitzky, a Boucher by a Somov, and so on. The idea seemed deserving of serious consideration, for after all, we spend a good deal of time nowadays talking about freedom in the arts, its infinite variety, while on the other hand deploring its decadence. If then, indeed, contemporary art is as decadent as some would have it, it will be bound to collapse under such a test: but if, again, as we venture to think, it has sufficient vitality and freshness of its own, then it has nothing to fear in comparison with its illustrious predecessors. The suggestion therefore was accepted, and this comparative exhibition was to have been held. No idea, however, it appears, can claim originality, for to my surprise I found our plan had already been carried out in Dresden. And I must admit that the effect was most impressive. Though the productions of contemporary art preponderated, they seemed both enriched and sanctioned by the contiguity of the great classical painters of the past. There was a quite unusual feeling of opulence and completion about that line of pictures in which Besnard alternated with Van Dyck, Zuloaga with Leibl, Velasquez with Watts, and so on. Not one of these contrasts proved in any way startling; on the contrary, the various masters complemented each other perfectly and provided triumphant proof that real works of art *are created irrespective of formula or epoch."*

In this letter Diaghilev says but little about individual artists. One exception, however, is made in regard to the French sculpture, Carriés, then recently deceased, an exhibition of whose work held in 1895 had already greatly impressed him.

Since the "Berlin Secessionists" were of "very minor importance," there was obviously but little need to write much about them. Nevertheless, Diaghilev goes at some length into the then vexed question of "secession," for in his eyes, small exhibitions, held all over the place, were pure waste of time, and held no promise for the future. Their one justification might be their purely local effect (like that of a provincial newspaper), but that justification no longer existed, since a certain number of painters, always the same, had made a habit of seceding, transferring themselves to one group after another, in the attempt to get themselves shown as frequently as possible.

Diaghilev's plans for a Russian National Gallery

Diaghilev returned from abroad a greatly changed man. The wild enthusiasms were now tempered, his conversation was more restrained, and he was altogether less boisterous and optimistic. Most striking of all, his interest in contemporary art had practically vanished. As for *The World of Art,* it interested him little.

Nevertheless, *The World of Art* rested on so sound a basis, and those guiding its fortunes had acquired so much experience, that it continued to appear as before, and even to grow, thanks to a number of new contributors. Meanwhile, its orientation was, little by little, changing.

It would hardly be true to say that Diaghilev had totally abandoned *The World of Art,* for he still took an interest in it, but to a far less degree, and with altogether less enthusiasm and energy than he had manifested in the years 1899 and 1900. For the moment he was completely engrossed in other and more grandiose plans. But such indeed was his nature, since he was constitutionally unable to remain satisfied with one thing, and one thing only, for any length of time. It was impossible for him to stabilize himself, or to find peace in something already achieved. He said little, however, about his new plans, having by now grown altogether less expansive. Nevertheless, they were not difficult to guess. His principal scheme, or dream, if you will, was the creation of a National Gallery of Russian Art, on a scale more vast than anything that existed in Europe, to embrace the whole history of Russian painting. Another dream was that of writing a full and *documented* account of the history of Russian painting beginning with the eighteenth century.

These plans were no castles in Spain, for Diaghilev immediately set to work to bring about their realization with all the energy and enthusiasm of which he was capable. When it was essential to shut himself up for days in his study, or bury himself amid dusty archives, Diaghilev, to whom such work was abhorrent, let nothing deter him. When it was necessary, for the same purpose, to drive over miles and miles of our abominable roads, unendurable as that must have been to one so accustomed to the comfortable railways of Europe, none the less he would set out.

A glimpse of these schemes is provided by a long article "On Russian Museums" and a short notice, both of which appeared in *The World of Art* for the year 1901.

What strikes one immediately about the lengthy article "On Russian Museums" is the style, by no means journalistic, and the documentation, which reveals how much preliminary research had already gone to the project. In it a number of the most important galleries are dealt with, such as the Tretiakov Gallery and the Alexander III and Rumianzev Museums; but through it all his dream is constantly appearing—that of creating a unique National Gallery. After a brief animadversion on the Tretiakov Gallery, which he sees as a collection illustrating but a single page of Russian painting (almost wholly devoted to the years 1860-1890), he goes on to discuss the Alexander III Museum, which provides "a unique opportunity for gathering together representative works of the whole of Russian art (both painting and sculpture) from its origins, i.e., the time of Peter the Great, to our own day."

After discussing the manner in which this museum was founded, he goes on to deal with its disparate elements, drawn from various sources:

the Russian room in the Hermitage, the museum in the Academy of Arts, the collection in the Palace of Tsarkoye Selo, the collection of Prince Lobanov-Rostovsky, and that of Princess Tenishev, and their lack of any real unity. At the time this article was written the museum had been in existence for five years, but nevertheless nothing had been done to arrange the items, the curators themselves had but the vaguest notion of the contents, and in spite of numerous acquisitions, not one single outstanding painting had been acquired. As for more recent acquisitions, all Diaghilev could say of them was: *"Invariably the worst pictures at any show are always bought by this museum."* After which, he went on to say that to his mind the museum had far more important problems to solve, the chief of which was to gather together the Russian paintings still to be found scattered about the Imperial Palaces, "whose wealth of art treasures is beyond imagination." Whereupon there follows a detailed list, derived from his visits to the archives, of all the objects which might enrich the National Museum. "The Alexander III Museum might at this moment, were the Government willing to co-operate, possess, *without making a single purchase from any individual,* thirty-nine of the best works of Levitzky, and, as a cursory glance at the Palace inventories shows, at least forty-eight paintings by Borovikovsky, of which three-quarters are absolutely first-class...." Diaghilev further suggests that all old masters be collected from the Chinese Gallery in the Gatchina Palace, the Treasury of the Ministry of the Imperial Court, the Moscow Armory, the Academy of Sciences, the Academy of Arts, the Holy Synod, the Alexander-Nevsky Monastery, the Rumianzev Museum, etc. A number of serious reforms are also suggested by him, "...the actual structure must be radically altered. Paintings having absolutely nothing in common, belonging to different schools and with no common link, are hung together, thus robbing them of all beauty and individuality, and making them clash with each other. As for the catalogue, the information it provides is a model of inexactitude [and here Diaghilev gives some illuminating examples].

"This museum should be representative of our history as revealed in painting," he continues. "Our great men have been painted by our most famous masters, and our sovereigns have time and again commissioned notable masters to come from abroad and paint their portraits. These painters often established themselves in Russia for years. It is of the utmost importance that all this should be gathered together into one unique whole. Would not that be an impressive undertaking?"

Diaghilev also demanded the introduction of reforms in the manner in which the gallery was administered, and in the preservation and restoration of the paintings.

All in all, this article must be considered as a report, admirably presented, by a lover of the arts; one who had studied his subject profoundly, was perfectly at home in it, and was prepared, with all the energy at his disposal, to take a hand in carrying it out. It would therefore only have been logical, and may we not assume that, secretly perhaps, Diaghilev was hoping something of the kind, for him to have been entrusted with the task of reorganization? But, alas, nothing happened, for the "powers" turned a deaf ear. Fortunately, however, the material collected by Diaghilev proved far from useless. Indeed, it contributed largely towards the realization of another project which followed as a natural consequence of the first: namely, the organization of an Exhibition of Russian Portraits, chosen in regard to their artistic and historical importance.

Diaghilev as historian of Russian painting: his book on Levitzky

In an earlier passage I referred to a note published in *The World of Art* towards the end of 1901. It is so short that I quote it fully:

"We have pleasure in announcing the appearance next January (1902) of the first volume of an illustrated work to be published by *The World of Art*, entitled *Russian Painting of the Eighteenth Century*. The complete work will comprise three volumes, the first of which will be devoted to D. G. Levitzky, the second to the following painters of the second half of the eighteenth century, Rokotov, Anthropov, Drozgin, Shibanov, Argunov, Shchukin, Shchedrin, etc., and the third to V. L. Borovikovsky.

"Given the fact that the majority of the works painted by the above-mentioned artists are only to be found in private collections, the editors appeal to all who may possess examples to communicate with them, at Fontanka 11, St. Petersburg. In regard to the critical material and text, this will be contributed by V. P. Gorlenko and A. N. Benois. The work is intended to assemble a mass of dispersed and largely ignored material, illustrating the lives and work of some of our most remarkable painters and will be accompanied by the best reproductions available."

Nevertheless, the work was not completed by January, 1902, nor even by February, 1902 (as a fresh announcement in *The World of Art* promised). But, in the course of 1902, there appeared an important monograph by S. P. Diaghilev entitled: *Russian Painting of the Eighteenth Century,* Vol. I, D. G. Levitzky, 1735-1832, which, in 1904, was to receive the highest award of the Imperial Academy of Sciences, the Prix Uvarov.

This volume proved to be a most magnificent specimen of the printer's art, the whole production being a very model of good taste, for the paper was excellent, the typography perfect, and the title-pages had been designed by Lanceret and Somov. In addition, the pages were enriched with remarkable collotype reproductions of contemporary documents, besides containing numerous vignettes, head and tail pieces, and reproductions of 121 portraits painted by Levitzky, of which 63 were insets, the rest being grouped together in the appendix.

The text also revealed itself as a document of the utmost importance for the history of Russian art, in every way deserving of the award made by the Academy of Sciences. But what most clearly revealed the vast stores of knowledge, the devoted effort which had gone into the work, was the convincing manner in which Diaghilev had identified a number of works by the painter. Here at last was permanent proof of the profundity of Diaghilev's intuition, a quality indispensable to the expert, and of his analytical, synthesizing, intellect. This work reveals Diaghilev at his best. And yet it illustrates his great weakness. For though brimming over with original, creative ideas, he had the utmost difficulty in expressing them in an illuminating and inspiring manner. And that was doubtless why, giant though he was in matters of art, he has left us so little of *his own*.

In this work Diaghilev has set himself a double task: that of tracing a number of portraits no longer in the possession of their original owners, and that of "tracing works of which no mention is made in contemporary documents." "This latter task," he continues, "seems to me far more important and exciting. To that end I have approached numbers of people whom I had reason to think owned works by Levitzky (thirty-six replies). I also made use of the Press, at first in the form of an announcement in the Art Notes (one reply), and then in the shape of a letter to the editor (twenty replies). Finally, towards the end of 1901, I sent a circular letter to all the governors of provinces, and district marshals of nobility, about 600 in all (28 replies)."

The activity manifested by Diaghilev was fully rewarded, and he was soon in a position to publish a list of works, which, for completeness, far exceeded anything so far compiled on the history of Russian painting. It was a list which classified the works of Levitzky in two categories: "(1) those undeniably his, or obviously attributable to him; (2) such portraits as were known to exist, but were no longer discoverable." Here, in masterly fashion, Diaghilev dealt analytically with ninety-two existing works, two other works known to have been copied by the painter, and fifteen portraits impossible to trace.

Another feature of the work was a "chronological list of portraits painted by D. G. Levitzky between 1769 and 1818," the critical notes to each work being accompanied by additional material relating to the painter and sitter. "This list also contains," he says, "much biographical detail relating to the personages painted by Levitzky. A certain amount has been borrowed from the works of Rovinsky and Petrov, but the rest is so far unpublished, having been culled from documents, memoirs and works personally discovered in the Department of Archives. Generally speaking, I have confined myself to externals in the lives of the sitters, since it is their vital activities which, more than anything, throw light on the manners and customs of the epoch." In fact, the "list" proves to be a *catalogue raisonné* which occupies sixty of the seventy-four pages which make up the whole book. Preceding it, we find a preface, and the following statement by Diaghilev: "The object aimed at in this work is not that of resurrecting an episode in Russian art, but of reconstructing, as fully as possible, its most brilliant epoch; an epoch rich in talented artists, which came to a sudden flowering after the timid, apprentice-efforts of the period of Peter the Great, but which as suddenly faded away in the stentorian neo-classicism of the early nineteenth century.

"In a word, in so far as it is concerned with the nineteenth century, this work gathers together all those elements which prepared the way for Kiprensky and Venetzianov, while omitting whatever might bear on Lossenko and his school, those dead and affected precursors of Brullow's triumphs."

What an admirable and tempting task! For Diaghilev, with his profound knowledge of the whole range of eighteenth-century Russian painting, his profound understanding of Levitzky, might well have succeeded in realizing his program...had he only possessed the slightest talent as an author, the slightest gift for creative expression. Unfortunately, Diaghilev had no notion of, no liking for, writing: and that is why his book does infinitely less than justice to either his learning, or flair. It is obvious that, in order to arrive at his conclusion and successfully accomplish his task, much research had been necessary and from numerous angles—though most important of all was the emotional response. Unfortunately, he was utterly incapable of expressing anything of all this, and his monograph, therefore, remains a *compilation* admirably documented. Much as we might expect a vital, inspiring approach, we do not find it...and though it was there, deep inside, as part and parcel of his very being, the means to express it were utterly lacking. The very "conclusion," is a confession of the tragic impotence of its author. "With all my heart, I hope that this list of Levitzky's works will be enriched by the discovery of other products of his *fragrant talent.* Should I have gone astray in thus surveying the works of *the beloved master,* I shall be grateful for any information which may put me right."

This conclusion is followed by some twenty pages devoted to the painter's life. It is not, however, by Diaghilev, excellently well-informed though he was, but by Gorlenko. The tragedy of this great man was, that profoundly sensitive though he was in matters of art, in spite of his undoubted originality and arresting conversation (though only in private), in spite of his inspiration and enthusiasm, he was unable to communicate anything of it at all in writing....

Monograph on the portrait painter Shibanov

Meanwhile, Diaghilev continued to study eighteenth-century Russian painting, and in 1904 published an admirable article dealing with Shibanov, the portrait painter. His researches in connection with Shibanov had led him to an important discovery, namely, that there had in fact been two painters of that name, one Alexis, the only example of whose work was a copy after Guercino, a "St. Matthew," preserved in the Academy of Fine Arts; the other, Michael, Potemkin's serf, painter of the famous Kiev portrait of Catherine II wearing a fur hat, of that of Mamonov, her squire, and of the two portraits of the Spiridovs. Having proved that neither of these latter portraits could justly be attributed to Alexis Shibanov, the subject of his article, Diaghilev turns to Michael:

"It is at this point," he says, "that this article on Shibanov's 'famous portraits,' should really begin. Unhappily, we know nothing about that painter's life, and only some lucky chance may eventually enable us to pierce the mystery which enshrouds the existence of this great Russian painter, and the conditions in which it was possible for his talent to ripen."

This, and the preceding work, mark the emergence of Diaghilev as a serious and competent critic of eighteenth-century Russian painting, a connoisseur in fact. In 1902, for instance, it is Diaghilev as expert, who in *The World of Art* criticizes both the "Exhibition of Russian Historical Portraits," and its *"Catalogue Raisonné* of 150 Years of Painting," edited by Baron N. Wrangel with A. N. Benois' close collaboration. In a masterly and authoritative manner, he corrects a number of errors in both, such as the statement that Lossenko was a pupil of Jacob Argunov, when in fact he had studied under Jean of that name; and the classification of a work as by Borovikovsky when it was merely a poor copy, and vice versa.

In 1901, A. Benois was appointed editor of a periodical entitled *Artistic Treasures of Old Russia,* and since Diaghilev's interest in old Russian masters had, if anything, deepened, the two men found themselves more closely linked than ever by this interest. It was an interest which could not fail to affect *The World of Art.* Thus in 1902 we find it devoting considerably more space than before to "Russia's Artistic Treasures." As a result its pages began to teem with reproductions of works by Borovikovsky, Venetzianov, Voile, Grott, Daw, Kiprensky, Levitzky, Rokotov, Count Rotari, Torelli, Count Raslin, the architect Voronikhin, Prince Gagarin, Zakharov, B. Rastrelli (Smolny Monastery), Rossi, and many photographs of monuments in St. Petersburg, etc.

The end of The World of Art

It was not difficult to foresee that 1904 was destined to mark the final disappearance of *The World of Art.* Only the first issue bore the imprint of the dictator, "Editor-Publisher, S. de Diaghilev." All in all, this first issue was an exceptionally well-balanced one, containing as it did, thirty-three illustrations by A. N. Benois to Pushkin's "Bronze Horseman," twenty-eight reproductions from works shown at the exhibition

of Finnish painting by Vickstroem, Vlassov, Hallem, Hallonen, Daniel-
sen, Ernefeld, Zimberg, Thomé, Edelfeldt, Enberg and Enkel, as well as
a number of engravings by Ostroumova-Lebedeva of a project for a
monument to Peter the Great. The next issue, however, was to contain
the additional words "Editor, A. N. Benois."

Diaghilev, engrossed in organizing his "Art and Historic Exhibition
of Russian Portraits," and by the incessant journeys it necessitated, now
lacked time for *The World of Art*. In addition, he felt that some public
and striking gesture should be made on behalf of Benois, who, in 1903,
had been forced to resign from the editorship of *The Artistic Treasures
of Old Russia*. This he accomplished by relinquishing *The World of Art*
into his hands.

The World of Art, however, continued in its old path, though with a
more marked bent towards archaeology, and greater efforts to familiarize
its readers with the "art treasures" of the past, tendencies obviously determined by the new editor. By degrees, too, the latter was successful in
diminishing the number of pages allowed to Filosofov, as may be seen
from the contents list of the 12th and last issue. It is as follows:

A. Benois: Exhibition of Historic Works of Art. St. Petersburg, 1904.
I. Bilibin: Popular Art in Northern Russia.
V. S. Veniaminov: Archangelskoye.
A. Ivanov: Loge Siegfried.
P. Nicolaev: The Poetry of the Middle Ages, depicted in miniatures
(with a headpiece by Lanceret, and other decorations from German
works of the fifteenth century).
A. Uspensky: The Patriarchal Vestry in Moscow.
I. Fomin: Moscow Classicism.

It is worthy of note that every illustration in this issue refers to one
or other of these articles.

During the second half of 1904, there was included a new section
devoted to "Art History," the preliminary announcement for which appeared in the following terms:

"For some time past, *The World of Art* has felt the need for a section
which would correspond to the 'Notes,' etc., found in foreign periodicals.
We propose, therefore, to include in such a section, whatever may be
considered outstanding in the way of Russian or foreign art material
which would otherwise find no place under any of the headings to which
we devote the major portion of each issue. An enormous amount of the
most interesting material is thrust aside, and so remains unknown, simply
because our editors fear to mention it, not knowing under what head,
what label, what system, to classify it.

"In the past, something of what we have in mind formed part of the
first issues of *The Artistic Treasures of Old Russia*. And something of

the sort, we may add, was attempted in *The World of Art,* under the heading 'Information,' during the first years of its existence."

In this, the last year of *The World of Art's* existence, all we can find are two articles contributed by Diaghilev, one devoted to the "Exhibition of the Union of Russian Painters," the other to "News from the Moscow Art Theater."

After which, *The World of Art* came to an end, as is generally supposed, on account of financial difficulties.

Causes of the discontinuance of The World of Art

Financial difficulties had arisen at the end of the very first year of the review's existence, and may be attributed largely to the resignation from the editorial board of Princess M. K. Tenishev and Sava Mamontov, and their refusal to contribute further financial assistance. A. N. Benois tells the story as follows:

"S. Mamontov was the first to withdraw his subsidy, his affairs having taken a turn for the worse and now being in a somewhat shaky condition, to be followed soon by Princess Tenishev. My own relations with the latter and E. C. Chetvertinskaya had changed considerably, too, and really for a very trivial reason (the truth probably being that both ladies had had enough of being dictated to by someone they considered a mere 'schoolboy,' given the fact they had known me as a lad). Thus, there was a complete break in our relations. On the other hand, our Maecenas, then recently returned from abroad, had fallen under the influence of Adrian Prakhov, who was in every way opposed to us. But, whatever the reason, her attitude towards 'her spiritual godchild' suddenly changed, and actually, shortly before, she had presented her Russian collection to the Alexander III Museum, and was no longer interested in Western art. Anyway, she sent for Diaghilev and Filosofov, and informed them they could no longer count on her financial support. This, for them, meant a considerable loss, since the review was so luxuriously printed that mere subscriptions could not hope to cover the cost. To some extent, she could hardly help behaving as she did, considering the way in which the newspapers had begun to attack her, often very humorously; though in the most tactless and scandalous manner. For instance, the *Bouffon* published some caricatures in which 'Old Judge' (Shcherbov) made a point of ridiculing not only the Princess's generosity, but also Diaghilev's wholly disinterested devotion to the arts.

"The ragtag and bobtail of the art world, too, was highly incensed with the Princess for purchasing a decorative panel painted by Vrubel, who, if I remember rightly, had only just appeared in St. Petersburg. In the caricature mentioned above, the Princess Tenishev was depicted as an ugly common woman of the people, bargaining with Diaghilev, as a second-hand furniture dealer, for a sort of greenish counterpane, bearing a vague resemblance to a panel, which she was attempting to purchase for one ruble (a very poor pun on Vrubel). In another caricature, she was depicted as a cow being milked by Diaghilev."

Diaghilev's exhibitions enjoyed the high favor of the Tsar, who visited them all, and on each occasion had long talks with the organizer. About this time, too, Serov was painting the Tsar's portrait, and was able without much difficulty to persuade his royal sitter to accord *The World of Art* a yearly subsidy of 30,000 rubles. Later, when Nicholas II lost interest in Diaghilev and Serov, this subsidy was withdrawn, and the founder of *The World of Art* was forced to rely on his friends, and his own far-from-bulging pockets.

A. Benois also recounts the financial difficulties which arose in 1904, but his very words reveal that these were rather the pretext than the cause. "The paper had to come to an end, for we already knew...that the year 1904 was bound to be its last. True, just as it was on the point of expiring, we all felt exceedingly regretful, and Diaghilev, who had had his official subsidy withdrawn, by now being very anathema to the court, once more decided to approach our first Maecenas, the Princess Tenishev, whereupon the latter, who no longer bore us any ill will for the trivial incidents which had driven us apart, immediately responded to his appeal. Nevertheless...'it had to come to an end.' We were all obsessed by the thought, one proof being the unbelievably (for him) dilatory way in which Diaghilev conducted his negotiations with the Princess. Just when it all seemed arranged, the whole thing came to an absolute full stop, the pretext being a wholly insignificant point which the Princess wished inserted in the agreement. The Princess, influenced by Prakhov and Roehrich, still hoped to foster a renaissance of our National art. But, in spite of that hope, the review failed to appear the following year."

This tale of A. Benois' is so inaccurate that it calls for substantial correction. To begin with, the negotiations were not interrupted in the middle, but were brought to a successful conclusion. Furthermore, it was not "us," i.e., Diaghilev and friends, who "broke them off," but Princess Tenishev, who made it known, through the Press, that she was no longer inclined to participate in its publication. Lastly, it was again not "we" who had taken exception to an "insignificant point," but the Princess; that "minor point" being of a nature hardly to be forgotten by A. Benois.

This is what really happened. Princess Tenishev was insisting that one of the conditions for her participation in the publication of *The World of Art* must be A. Benois' retirement from the editorial board. This condition was accepted by Diaghilev during the negotiations, but in the end he was unable to bring himself to betray his friend and co-editor. "Soon," so the Princess relates, "the papers announced that subscriptions to the review were now being taken, and mentioned my participation in it as co-editor. In the list of collaborators I saw the name of A. Benois. Diaghilev therefore had again gone contrary to his promise, and, as before, regardless of my feelings. I immediately made it known, through the medium of the same papers, that I had nothing to do with the review, or any intention of collaborating with it in the future. And that was the end of *The World of Art*.

This refusal, however, only proved fatal to *The World of Art* because many other causes were working in the same direction—to cite only one, the meeting held on February 15th, 1903, which pronounced the death sentence of those exhibitions which had been so intimately part of *The World of Art*.

What was decisive for the fate of *The World of Art* was the fact that it was *no longer* needed by Diaghilev. A dreadful *memento mori* had struck his ears, the oracle to which he had alluded in his article devoted to the Moscow Exhibition of the Union of Russian Painters. I quote the end, it is very revealing.

"It is terrible to think of the future of the 'Vagrants' now that the 'Union' has lured away their last remaining forces. Indeed, it is a most instructive example, one that might serve as a dreadful *memento mori* for the 'Union' itself. The birth throes of a new 'cause' are always painful, though profoundly interesting, and possessed of 'all the intoxication of Spring.' But a moment comes when the first autumnal leaves begin falling, and then, beware! It is all too easy to turn into toothless old 'vagrants,' to that well-known refrain from *The Queen of Spades*, 'yesteryear's days and poets.'

"But though it be an historic, ineluctable law, must the end mean always decay, and can one not be 'borne living into the heavens'? Surely it is infinitely more possible in art, than in any other province."

Diaghilev believed that his mission on *The World of Art* was ended. He *was utterly unable* to continue with it, or, marking time, to drag it after him. Thus, refusing to accept decay, he was, with *The World of Art* "borne living into the heavens."

So ends the first period of Diaghilev's apostolic service to art.

"The Art and Historic Exhibition of Russian Portraits"

In a note written in 1900, relating to the portraits painted by the great Russian Masters of the eighteenth century, at that time scattered about the country, we find V. Veniaminov, in the "Chronicles" of *The World of Art* writing as follows:

"Anyone who organized a general exhibition devoted to Russian painting of the eighteenth century would be rendering a priceless service to the historiography of our art. Such an exhibition would help us to resolve many problems and perplexities."

Was Venianimov here expressing one of Diaghilev's ideas, or something he was thinking himself? In any case, this was the moment chosen by the founder of *The World of Art* to begin organizing an exhibition devoted to Russian painting of the eighteenth century.

By 1902, the whole plan has been outlined and begins to take precedence over all else in Diaghilev's mind. His plan for reorganizing the Alexander III Museum, or rather his plan for founding a National Museum, having failed, Diaghilev set to work to realize a new dream, and began to manifest much resentment at such opposition as he met. This resentment was clearly expressed in an article devoted to the "Art and Historic Exhibition of Russian Portraits" which appeared in 1902. "It was with the keenest interest that we visited the Academy of Sciences, but it was with a feeling of profound disappointment that we left the rooms in *which a noble, a splendid idea has been so pitilessly travestied*. That idea was the gathering together in one place, for the second time in thirty years,[1] of the works of our illustrious dead painters, whose finest paintings are now scattered throughout the land, in many cases in the possession of those who do not even suspect their value.... This last exhibition, organized in aid of charity, is a clumsy ultra-dilettante undertaking. Haste appears to have been its watchword, for there is absolutely no plan. The lack of space has limited it still further, and as a result the exhibition is meager, one-sided, and, worst of all ... aimless. Which is not to say that it does not contain worth-while paintings. Indeed the case is far otherwise, for of the 260 wretched canvases crowded together there, a good half must be considered of exceptional merit! But what does it prove? That a dozen people happened to collect all the paintings in their possession, and named the result an exhibition. Yet, is that the way so tremendous an undertaking as an exhibition of Russian portrait painting should be organized? No doubt, it will be said that the organizers never claimed to have anything so grandiose in view. Agreed, but do not let us forget that by their *wretched attempt* they have prevented such serious institutions as the Historic Society, the Russian Museum, and others from carrying out the idea borrowed by the present organizers, for the simple reason that neither the Palaces, nor the private or public collections, are able to lend their pictures every year. *From that angle, the Exhibition of Historical Paintings has done infinite harm.*"

Nevertheless, such exasperation as Diaghilev may have felt, in no wise changed his plans. With tenfold energy and all the unswerving stubbornness so characteristic of the man, he continued the relentless pursuit of that second dream, that second miracle of his. Thus, in the fifth issue of *The World of Art* dated 1904, among the "Chronicles," we find the following note:

"Under the exalted patronage of His Majesty the Emperor, during

---

[1] An exhibition of historic paintings had been organized in 1870 by A. A. Vassiltchikov, Prince A. B. Lobanov-Rostovsky, Count S. G. Stroganov, D. V. Grigorovitch and P. N. Petrov.

February, 1905, an exhibition of historic Russian portraits, from 1705 to 1905, will be held, in aid of the widows and orphans of those fallen in battle.

"This exhibition will be held in the halls of the Tauride Palace, and will comprise portraits by Russian Masters, as well as those of Russian notables by foreign painters.

"The President of the Organizing Committee will be H.I.H. the Grand Duke Nikolai Mikhailovitch, the members being I. A. Vsevolojsky, Count I. I. Tolstoy, Count A. A. Bobrinsky, P. N. Dashkov, S. A. Panchulidze, S. P. Diaghilev, A. N. Benois and S. P. Franck. The general organizer appointed by the Organizing Committee will be S. P. Diaghilev. The exhibition offices are to be found in the palace of the Grand Duke Nikolai Mikhailovitch (Millionmaya 19). The purpose of this exhibition is to gather under one roof, Russian portraits at present widely distributed in the Imperial Palaces, in private collections, and especially in individual possession, whether in the two capitals, provincial towns or country seats.

"It is earnestly to be hoped that those who have such portraits in their possession will notify the organizers, and so contribute to both the historic and the cultural value of this great undertaking."

Officially, Diaghilev was satisfied to remain the "general organizer" and so-called "appointee" of the Organizing Committee. Actually, no other organizer existed. The "exalted patronage," the presence of a grand duke at the head of a committee which numbered so many influential persons, were but so many pretexts to make possible the loan of the halls of the Tauride Palace, at one time the residence of Prince Potemkin. In addition, these names would greatly help him to obtain the loan of the paintings he might need.

It is worth noting that this announcement stresses the "cultural and historic value," though not the artistic worth of this gigantic undertaking; Diaghilev was far too modest in terming it merely "great."

Diaghilev's activity, and the energy expended by him in connection with this exhibition, were almost inconceivable. Nothing affrighted him—neither the distances, nor the discomfort of the journeys it necessitated at times; neither the bumpy roads nor the peasants' carts, which bruised both back and sides, while he went in search of provincial governors, or rural landowners lost in the vast expanse of forests and steppes. Then, that caressing baritone, that delightful smile, those sad eyes, would be brought into play, and the victim would finally succumb. Who could resist that especial charm, whose value he himself was now beginning to realize so well? Besides, the times themselves were propitious: sporadic unrest seemed to foreshadow the flames that in the following year would cast their scarlet glow over Russia, a year in which many masterpieces were to perish, including a number of the portraits Diaghilev had promised to "safeguard" in the event of disturbances.

Between journeys, Diaghilev would haunt the Public Record Office, the libraries, or bury himself in ancient books and periodicals, searching for traces of suitable material. Or again, he would send out circulars, or pester the mighty, and, in fact, take an infinity of trouble. Finally, the canvases began to pour in, first in hundreds, then in thousands. Whereupon other problems arose, such as attributing dates, signatures, the names of sitters, etc. And again, every work needed to be classified, and the whole given an artistic unity, after which each item needed arranging in such a manner as to illustrate the whole range of Russian life, art and culture, in the two hundred years from 1705 to 1905. Not for an instant, however, did Diaghilev's creative energy, his determination to succeed, falter. Finally, the exhibition was opened with all due ceremony. But now the question must be asked: "Had it been worth the fearful effort expended?" No two opinions are possible, for even had Diaghilev been forced to expend fifty, one hundred times, the effort, had he collapsed with sheer exhaustion the day after, there would have been nothing for him to regret, and he would still have "been borne living into the heavens." That one miracle of the exhibition held in the Tauride Palace would have sufficed to render his name forever illustrious in the annals of Russian culture, for *it was a great miracle which Diaghilev, the magician, had performed.*

The official opening took place in February, 1905, during a period of intense social disturbance, when political events alone might have been thought to absorb the interest of the public. In the preceding days Diaghilev was depressed and uneasy, and A. P. Filosofov was able to write: "The boys look very down in the mouth, Seriozha is almost unrecognizable."

Nevertheless Diaghilev's miracle could not be thrust aside by hurrying events, and day after day enthusiastic crowds thronged through the halls of the Tauride Palace. Very significant in this connection is Mme. Filosofov's letter to Diaghilev's stepmother.

"Dear Laelia,

"You, no doubt, too, must be feeling the same terrible anxiety and depression we all feel here.... It is difficult to write in times of such great distress, and that is why you have not heard from me lately. But my thoughts are often with you, and I write now, because I have just undergone a complete spiritual metamorphosis—alas, temporary, no doubt —which has raised me to the skies. I have been to the exhibition in the Tauride Palace, and you cannot imagine—not the liveliest imagination could picture it—the superhuman grandeur of what I saw. I was transported into a world that seems infinitely nearer than our own."

A month later she is writing again: "I keep going to Seriozha's exhibition: it brings balm to my soul. It's something amazing!"

And so indeed, must the majority of visitors have felt, since many of them returned *day after day* for a month, two months even, such was their anxiety to see and absorb all that was shown: a fact only too comprehensible, given the immense variety and richness of the works presented. Diaghilev, in his announcement, had emphasized the cultural and historical aspects as most likely to interest the general public, and no doubt this largely explains the intense popular interest, but since many of the works were veritable masterpieces, the effect was, willy-nilly, to indoctrinate the beholders with the rudiments of aesthetics. At sundry times, I have happened to meet some of the habitual visitors to this exhibition, and invariably they have told me that certain halls, such as that devoted to the time of Catherine the Great or Paul I (and especially the latter, no doubt because of the strange mad look of his face), so tangibly, so convincingly revived their epochs, that a sort of hallucination was experienced, which seemed to transport the beholder out of his own time into the past. After a few hours spent in either of these halls, people would go home promising themselves never to return, in order to do justice to the rest of the exhibition. Yet, next day, as though drawn by a magnet, they would return, unable to tear themselves from the portraits which had moved them so deeply on the preceding day. So rich, so varied was the exhibition—for it included about 3,000 portraits—that many months would have been necessary to make oneself *fully acquainted* with everything it contained.

This exhibition of historic portraits was important, too, in another way which Igor Grabar thus defines: "The services rendered by Diaghilev in the domain of the history of Russian art are of the utmost importance. His exhibition of portraits was an event of world-wide significance, for it brought to light a host of Russian and non-Russian painters and sculptors, ignored till then, among whom were dozens of really first-class artists. This exhibition, initiated by Diaghilev, inaugurated a new era in the study of Russian and European art of the eighteenth and first half of the nineteenth century. In place of conflicting data and vague facts, it became possible, for the first time, using the gigantic quantities of material gathered from all over Russia, to establish fresh data, and throw new light on interlocking sources, relations and influences, unsuspected before. One result, was a whole series of drastic, and at times unexpected, revaluations of the work of many artists; much that was obscure before now became plainer, and new and tempting vistas for deeper investigation were thrown open."

But now arose the problem of how to hold together what Diaghilev had managed to create with such effort!

Whereupon Diaghilev began to busy himself with efforts to get the Tauride Palace handed over to a special commission, charged with the duty of regularly organizing similar exhibitions. In addition, he was anxious to arrange for the permanent installation in the same building of the portraits discovered by him in the depths of the country—subject, of course, to their owners' consent. Many, if not the great majority, would certainly have agreed, following on the events of 1905. Unfortunately, all these efforts were doomed to failure, and it was necessary, therefore, to return the paintings, with the result that the greater proportion perished in the "illuminations" of 1905. When, as occasionally happened, some were spared, they suffered a similar fate in 1917, with scarcely a single exception. For that reason this exhibition of Diaghilev's, his miracle, can never be resuscitated. Our elders saw it, and that memory they still preserve; but my own generation (I was born soon after it opened) can only envy them, and note the immense significance of the event, from its catalogues and contemporary accounts.

The young Diaghilev, in the years 1890-1895, took little, if any, interest in politics, and might have been called a skeptical conservative. But the destruction of so many of the treasures he held dear was bound to make him still more antagonistic to revolution. Thus, it is all the more strange to observe him, to some extent, affected by the wave of liberalism which, in 1905, swept over the country, understandable though it may be in view of the shifting, unsettled state of public opinion. In congratulating her daughter on the manifesto of October the 17th of that year, Mme. Filosofov writes: "We are rejoicing. Yesterday, even, we had champagne. You would never guess who brought the manifesto...Seriozha, of all people. Wonderful!" The dots before "Seriozha," and the concluding "Wonderful!" need no comment.

Diaghilev's personal disappointments

On his appointment as special assistant to the Director of the Imperial Theaters, Diaghilev had begun to dream of regenerating opera and ballet in Russia. Now, however, these dreams were to be doomed to frustration.

His plans for founding a vast national museum had come to nothing, and *The World of Art* had ceased to exist. His plan for reserving the Tauride Palace as a permanent center for successive exhibitions, and to house the portraits he himself had collected, had also proved fruitless, and the portraits themselves were being destroyed, as it were, in front of his eyes...Diaghilev began to feel cramped in Russia...new lands, new worlds, were calling to be conquered.

Departure for abroad

In the spring of 1906 Diaghilev, accompanied by his secretary, Mavrin, left for a lengthy tour, visiting in turn Greece, Italy, France and Germany. But first he decided to organize, in his own old dictatorial manner, just one more of *The World of Art* exhibitions as a last farewell to the St. Petersburg public. If we are to believe Benois, who assuredly cannot be accused of exaggerating Diaghilev's merits, the exhibition proved a triumphant success. In Benois' words: "It was held during that difficult winter of 1906, when even the energies of those managing the 'Union' had flagged. The demoralization of our successors [2] inspired Diaghilev for the last time to demonstrate all the virtue which lay in dictatorship, and to prove that, where he was concerned, the wish was father to the deed."

Immediately the exhibition ended, Diaghilev left for abroad and the conquest of Europe.

Serge Pavlovitch loved repeating that the blood of Peter the Great flowed in his veins, and that he modeled himself upon that illustrious Tsar, whose indomitable passion for work he sought to emulate. It pleased him greatly to be told he even appeared to resemble him physically. And, indeed, they well resembled each other in thir profound and all-embracing love for Russia. But whereas Peter the Great, in order to bring about his reforms, had found it necessary to transplant the culture of Western Europe to our soil, Diaghilev sought to transform the art of the world by familiarizing Europe with Russian art.

Here we begin an entirely new chapter in Diaghilev's life and work; at first as the apostle of Russian art in Europe, and then as revolutionizer of that universal art form, the ballet.

[2] The Exhibitions Committee of *The World of Art*.

PART THREE: THE RUSSIAN BALLET

CHAPTER VIII

FROM "THE WORLD OF ART" TO THE RUSSIAN BALLET

The Paris Exhibition of 1906

AND NOW Diaghilev made his bow to Western Europe with a first "Russian Season," represented by his exhibition of Russian art, held in the Paris Salon d'Automne. He had set to work the moment he reached that city.

This exhibition was intended to provide a comprehensive survey of two centuries of Russian painting and sculpture, and in addition Diaghilev meant to exhibit the N. P. Lukachev collection of ancient icons. The whole exhibition, therefore, would provide a conspectus of Russian representational art throughout its existence. Yet, ambitious as the plan was, it was the Russian painters associated with *The World of Art* whose works preponderated. Among them may be mentioned Anisfeld, Leon Bakst, A. N. Benois, Borissov-Moussatov, Dobuzhinsky, Igor Grabar, Korovin, Kusnetzov, Larionov, Maliavin, Millioti, Roehrich, Somov, Serov, Sudbinin, Sudeikine, Steletzky, Tarkhov, Prince Trubetzkoy, Vrubel and Yakunchikova, while their predecessors were represented principally by Borovikovsky, Brullow, Chubin, Kiprensky, Levitzky and Venetzianov.

Presiding over the organizing committee, and patron of the exhibition, was the Grand Duke Vladimir Alexandrovitch; but in addition three honorary presidents were appointed, namely, the Russian Ambassador, M. Nelidov, the Comtesse de Greffulhe, and M. Dujardin-Beaumetz. The name of the general organizer, S. de Diaghilev, only occurs at the foot of the long list of members of the committee, headed by Count I. Tolstoy.

As ever, Diaghilev spared no pains to make his exhibition comprehensible to the general public, and to that end issued an elaborate catalogue, copiously illustrated, which included an introductory article by A. Benois on Russian art, and a short foreword by himself, in which it was stated that:

"The aim of this exhibition is not the provision of a complete and scrupulously methodical conspectus of Russian art through all the stages of its evolution. Adequately to accomplish such a task would offer insuperable difficulties, and be of questionable value. Many names, once famous, are today shorn of their glory; some for the moment, but others

for ever. Many an artist, to whom their contemporaries once attached
an exaggerated importance, nowadays seem wholly without value, their
influence on modern painting having been nil. That is why the work of
certain painters has been deliberately omitted; painters who, in the West,
have too long been considered solely representative of artistic Russia,
who too long have offered only a distorted vision of the true nature and
real importance of Russian national art to the eyes of Europe. This
present exhibition is a glimpse of the development of our art as seen
through modern eyes. Every aspect which has exerted a first-hand influence on the contemporary spirit of our country, will be found represented. It is a faithful image of artistic Russia today, in its strenuous
seeking, its respectful admiration for the past, and its ardent faith in
the future."

So remarkably successful did this exhibition prove that Diaghilev immediately began to think of arranging further exhibitions to familiarize
the Paris public with yet other aspects of Russian art.

Russian painting had proved eminently successful. The exhibitors were
delighted. Their work had been understood and highly appreciated, and
as a result many were invited to send to the Salon d'Automne. Diaghilev
himself had been offered the *Légion d'Honneur,* which he refused in
favor of Bakst. Thus, all things seemed to indicate that another branch
of Russian art, so far unknown to Paris, namely music, might enjoy an
equal success. Whereupon, Diaghilev organized a "trial" concert, held in
the Palais des Champs Elysées. Many musicians and artists were invited,
and its enthusiastic reception paved the way for the season of 1907.

Acquaintance with the Comtesse de Greffulhe

Meanwhile Diaghilev had made many valuable connections, and acquired numerous influential friends in French society. He had also managed to secure the patronage of the Comtesse de Greffulhe for all his
future seasons, support which was to prove of inestimable value. Mme.
Guy de Pourtalès was responsible for this introduction, on which occasion Diaghilev immediately asked whether he might not call in connection with a certain "scheme."

Only recently the Comtesse de Greffulhe gave me some interesting
details of this visit, as, sitting in her immense drawing room, surrounded
by many masterpieces of painting and sculpture, she talked of Serge
Pavlovitch with an all but devotional reverence....

"Yes, it was there in that armchair that he sat....This is a statue he
often admired....There is the piano on which he played...."

I asked the Countess what impression Diaghilev had made on her,
and whether, indeed, he was as handsome as was said. Her only reply,
however, was that Diaghilev had made practically no impression on her

at all, and that at first she had taken him to be a sort of young snob or shady adventurer, with a remarkable conversational gift.

"At first I kept on wondering what on earth he wanted? There he sat, staring at that statue. Then suddenly he got up, and began looking at my pictures, and, I must say, some of the things he said were extraordinarily interesting. I soon realized that he was remarkably well informed, and that I was dealing with a man of very great culture...that made me begin to like him. But when he went to the piano, and began playing things by Russian composers whom I had never even heard of, I began to understand him, and why he had come. His playing was excellent, and the music was so fresh, so altogether wonderful and lovely, that when he explained he intended organizing a festival of Russian music in the coming year I immediately, without the slightest doubts or misgivings, promised to do everything in my power to help make it successful."

Following this visit, therefore, Diaghilev might rest assured that his 1907 season would take place. Thereafter, until the outbreak of the Great War, year after year, Paris had its Russian, its Diaghilev, season.

In all justice, it must be said that Diaghilev had perfectly chosen the place and moment. Paris, at that time, was indisputably the world's spiritual capital, and the tardy springtide of the Franco-Russian *entente* was inspiring the intensest interest and enthusiasm for everything connected with our country. In addition, both Governments spared no effort to foster a closer relationship between the two States, and what language is more communicable, more comprehensible, than that of the arts?

Thus, Diaghilev's efforts admirably suited the plans of the Imperial Government, which explains the lavish subsidies granted by the Court, the support of the Russian Embassy, and his ability to borrow the best artists, no matter whom, even when he himself had quarreled with the Court, and had dispensed with His Imperial Majesty's exalted patronage....Had Diaghilev not fulfilled this mission it is exceedingly possible that it would have been delegated to another: but what a stroke of luck for Russian art that it was he, and not some artist-bureaucrat who would have striven to thrust pseudo-nationalistic "Berendeis and Stenka Razins" on Paris!

Exhibitions in Berlin and Venice

It must not be assumed, however, that because Diaghilev had made Paris his center, he was content to confine his activities to that city alone, or even to France, for already he was dreaming of world-wide conquests. That same year the whole Salon d'Automne exhibition was transported to Berlin, and the following year, though reduced in compass, to Venice.

The Berlin exhibition was held at the Salon Schulte, where it proved very successful, though far less so than in Paris. Igor Grabar tells us: "The Kaiser expressed a wish to visit the exhibition with his family, the day before the opening ceremony, and it was mainly myself who, because of my good German, was entrusted with the task of taking him round. Diaghilev's knowledge of the language was poor, and he therefore conversed in French with the Kaiser. As for the latter, his behavior was both objectionable and stupid, for he struck one attitude after another, and the platitudes he uttered were in the worst possible taste. Stopping in front of a portrait by Levitzky, he said:

" 'What nobility in the pose and gesture.'

" 'But men then were noble, Your Majesty,' ventured Diaghilev.

" 'And some still are,' the Kaiser interjected, obviously displeased, and no doubt referring to himself.

"This brush did not, however, affect his friendliness towards Diaghilev, editor of that *The World of Art* in which, as Prince he had at times been so cruelly treated. He even stopped for a considerable space in front of Bakst's portrait of Diaghilev, and questioned him at length about his old nurse Dunia...."

Success of Russian Music in Paris

Triumphantly returning to St. Petersburg, Diaghilev set about preparing for his second season in Paris, the famous concerts of "Russian Music Through the Ages." A committee was formed, presided over by A. S. Taneyev, Chamberlain to the Imperial Court and himself a distinguished composer, consisting of Diaghilev, A. Khitrov, de Reinecke, A. von Gilse von der Pals, R. Gailhard, Messager, Broussan, Chevillard, A. Nikisch, F. Blumenfeldt, N. A. Rimsky-Korsakov, A. Glazunov, and S. V. Rachmaninov. As honorary presidents there were elected the Russian Ambassador in Paris, M. Nelidov, his by then devoted patron the Comtesse de Greffulhe, and Aristide Briand, at that time French Minister of Education and Fine Arts. Exactly as before, on the occasion of the Portrait Exhibition in the Tauride Palace, Diaghilev's name was dissimulated among those of the numerous members of the committee, for what mattered to him was not the advertisement, but the achievement. In the same way the posters for the ballet season of 1909 announced, *"Saison Russe avec le concours des artistes, l'orchestre et les choeurs des Théâtres de Saint-Petersbourg et Moscou,"* without so much as even mentioning Diaghilev's name.

For these concerts the most celebrated figures in music were enlisted, the conductors being Arthur Nikisch, with his unique understanding of Tchaikovsky's music, Rimsky-Korsakov, Felix Blumenfeldt, Rachmaninov, C. Chevillard and Glazunov. The solo pianist was Josef Hofmann and the singers numbered among them the Felia Litvin, Feodor

Feodor Chaliapin in *Boris Godunov,* 1908

Chaliapin (his reputation dates from this epoch), Cherkasskaya, Zbrueva, Petrenko, Smirnov, Kastorsky, Matveyev, Filipov, etc. The programs were carefully chosen and included many of the masterpieces of Russian music, such as Glinka's overture to, and first act of, *Russlan and Ludmila,* and his *Kamarinskaya;* Rimsky-Korsakov's symphonic poem *Christmas Eve,* the introduction to the first act and Liel's two songs from *Snegourochka,* the third scene from the opera-ballet *Mlada, The Night on Triglav Mountain,* the symphonic suite from *Tsar Saltan* and the sub-marine-kingdom scene from *Sadko;* Tchaikovsky's second and fourth symphonies, as also the arioso from *The Witch* (Charodeika); many excerpts from Borodin's *Prince Igor;* Mussorgsky's *Trepak, Song of the Flea* and the second act of *Boris Godunov,* together with other excerpts from the same opera and *Khovantchina;* Taneyev's *Second Symphony;* Liadov's *Eight Folk Songs,* and *Baba Yaga;* Scriabin's *Piano Concerto* and *Second Symphony;* Rachmaninov's *Second Piano Concerto* and the Cantata *Spring;* Balakirev's *Thamar;* Glazunov's *Second Symphony,* and a small "Symphonic Impression"; Liapunov's *Concerto for Piano and Orchestra,* and César Cui's "Romantic Piece" from the opera *William Ratcliff.*

Obviously, it was hardly possible to present the whole of Russian music from the end of the eighteenth century to the beginning of the twentieth century in five concerts, nevertheless such works as were performed proved a veritable and far-reaching revelation to the Parisian public.

In this case, too, the printed program provided an elaborate text designed to familiarize the listener with the main outlines of Russian music. Biographical and analytical notes dealt with Glinka, the father of Russian music, Borodin, Cui, Balakirev, Mussorgsky, Tchaikovsky, Rimsky-Korsakov, A. E. Taneyev (though his nephew, undeniably more gifted, was not included), Liadov, Liapunov, Glazunov, Scriabin and Rachmaninov. It also included reproductions of portraits of these musicians as painted by Répin, Bakst, Kusnetzov, Serov and Zak, analytical notes on the various items, illustrations of the singers in their costume-parts (in particular many of Chaliapin), and reproductions illustrating a number of sets from Russian operas, etc., etc.

Now, thirty years after, when hardly a concert takes place at which one or other of these items is not presented, it is difficult to imagine the tremendous impression they then created. If they interest us now, however, that interest is largely a historical one, which revolves round the particular items chosen and their interpreters, such as Nikisch, Hofmann, Chaliapin, Litvin, Zbrueva, and Cherkasskaya. And yet, it is just this fact which makes Diaghilev so important, for what today seems so ordinary and accepted was a new world when first revealed to Europe.

Of all these composers it was Rimsky-Korsakov, Borodin, and Mussorgsky who made the deepest impression on the Parisian public, little attention being paid to the work of either Tchaikovsky or Rachmaninov, although the latter was already beginning to find enthusiasts in Russia.

"Boris Godunov" with Chaliapin

The most powerful influence was that excited by Mussorgsky, for it profoundly modified the life and soul of all modern French music. Not only did it influence so pronouncedly individual a composer as Ravel, but even so mature and original a master of his art as Debussy was to be immensely indebted to him. True, the younger generation of French composers learned many a valuable lesson from Rimsky-Korsakov's miracles of orchestration, but their real god was Mussorgsky. Even now, thirty years later, that influence still persists. Wagner alone is his compeer, though it is difficult to say which proved the greater creative influence.

In any case, the greatest successes were those borne off by Mussorgsky and Chaliapin, and we may assume, therefore, that this was what determined Diaghilev to produce *Boris Godunov* in Paris the following year. The preparatory work proved long and arduous, for Diaghilev was determined to stage a veritable reconstitution of late sixteenth-century Russia, and to that end ransacked the length and breadth of peasant Russia in search of ancient costumes, genuine old sarafans and seed-pearl embroideries, all of which, including the sets, were afterwards presented to the Opéra National.

Serge Pavlovitch often talked to me about this first opera season of his in 1908. The dress rehearsal, it seemed, went off brilliantly, the first performance was to take place next day, and Diaghilev was at peace, sure of success. But that very evening, Chaliapin, huge, enormous, and laboring under some deep emotion, came seeking him at his hotel.

"I shan't be able to sing tomorrow...I'm in a funk...I'm terrified... it doesn't sound...."

And in fact the clipped phrases (for he often spoke in this way) were hardly audible. Utterly helpless, he sank into a chair, shaking with fever, the fever of the creator awaiting the inspired moment, which he senses will *descend on him next day.*

Diaghilev did all in his power to reassure, to calm, to distract and drive away his fears, but in vain. In body and soul, in every fiber, Chaliapin had collapsed. They spent the whole evening together, till finally Chaliapin began to feel somewhat more sure of himself. But, as they were parting, his fears overwhelmed him again; he was terrified of being alone, and felt he could not possibly manage without Diaghilev to sustain him.

"I'll stay with you, Serge; I'll sleep no matter where, on one of the chairs," he said, and so spent a very uncomfortable and feverish night on a sofa half his size, in the drawing room of Diaghilev's suite.

The next night, the miracle of *Boris Godunov* was revealed to Paris, and through Paris, to the whole world. Before, the work had only been known in Russia, but not even Russia had ever heard or seen a Boris, as Chaliapin sang and acted the part that night.

The effect it produced on Paris was indescribable. The usual cold and fashionable audience of the Opéra was utterly transformed. People stood on their seats, yelled as if possessed, waved handkerchiefs, and wept in an unrestrained and Asiatic manner very different from European tears. Europe had taken Mussorgsky and his *Boris Godunov* to its heart. From that moment it was to become part of every operatic repertoire in America and Europe.

Chaliapin's personal success too was tremendous. As a result, singers all over the world, whether opera singers or not, whether in *Boris Godunov* or some other opera, began to copy his every mannerism, to apply every lesson he had taught. After that memorable night, singing and acting became something *altogether different* from what they had been. The sets, designed by Golovin and Juon were also immensely appreciated, and particularly that for the fourth scene designed by Alexandre Benois.

Friendship with Madame Sert

Another memorable event, indeed one of the most important in his life, was associated with this production in Paris, for through it he made the acquaintance of Mme. Misia Sert (Mme. Edwards, as she was then) of whom he said, shortly before his death, that she was his greatest, his best friend. That friendship, which weathered twenty stormy years, arose out of this very production, when Misia, in her enthusiasm, would book a whole tier of boxes, and never miss a single performance.

Mme. Sert and the Princess de Polignac, whom he met at the same time, may be said, to some extent, to have been Diaghilev's muses: for, during the whole period of the Russian Ballet, they were the inspiration of practically all his creative activity. Most of the ballets were, in fact, dedicated to the Princess, and the preliminary rehearsals generally took place at her house: but ideas for new ballets were first discussed, and then decided on in concert with Misia Sert. Diaghilev knew he could always count on the latter for material and moral support, for she was genuinely devoted to him. And it was this devotion, thanks to her position in Parisian society, which was so instrumental in assuring Diaghilev's success.[1]

The Princess de Polignac greatly admired Diaghilev's artistic achievement. Mme. Sert, too, admired the Russian Ballet, but she also admired Serge Pavlovitch, and to such an extent, that it was a standing joke in

[1] She had been associated with music and musicians all her life. As a child she had known Liszt. At this period she was the wife of the editor of *Le Matin*. Her second husband was the Spanish painter Sert.

the ballet that some day our "woman-hater" would end by marrying her.

Whenever Diaghilev arrived in Paris, almost the first thing he did would be to telephone Mme. Sert, then settle down for a long comfortable chat, and afterwards go off to visit her at her house. True, their conversations often ended in mutual recriminations and quarrels. She would accuse him of turning to her only when in trouble, of neglecting her the rest of the time; and he, suspicious, doubting, and jealously possessive in a way that refused to brook what he imagined even the slightest infidelity, even in thought, would resent what he considered her indifference to both his work and himself. Thus, these two strong natures seemed in permanent conflict, each imagining the other indifferent or lackadaisical; and yet, strange though it seems, Diaghilev almost always would prove the weaker, for though more jealous, he was also both more conciliatory and more passive. On one occasion, deeply offended because Diaghilev had asked her help on a matter of passports, Mme. Sert wrote that it was not him she loved, but his work; whereupon, in a letter dated January 1st, 1919, he replied:

"You say it isn't me that you love, but my work. Well, I can say the opposite to that, that I *love* you with all your faults, and the feelings I should have had for my sister, if I had ever had one. Unfortunately, I never had, so all these feelings crystallize round you. Please remember that not so very long ago *we* came to the conclusion, in all seriousness, that you were the one *woman* on earth that we loved. That is why it is so unworthy of a *sister* to make such a to-do about not having had any letters for some time. When I write—and you know how seldom that is —it is when I *have something* to say: not of my London 'successes,' which you no doubt have heard of already, but of my hopes, schemes and projects...."

Whenever Mme. Sert missed a show or supper party at which she was expected, pleading sudden business, Diaghilev would experience these jealous furies. As he saw it, it was but an excuse masking a total indifference to him and his work.

"Nothing could be more absurd," he writes to her on April 23rd, 1917, "but fate, it seems, wills it that you should turn up always and everywhere, just as I am on the point of departing; or that you should be 'called away' the very moment I arrive, or when I specially want to stay for *a few hours.* I say *want,* but perhaps it would be better to say *wanted,* because, honestly, these last weeks you've shown yourself so cold and indifferent to all that matters to me, all that lies near my heart, that it's better to be quite frank about it. I know very well that friendships don't last for centuries, but one thing I do beg of you, and that is never to tell me again that you've been 'urgently called away,' because *I know it already.* I can predict these urgent 'calls' with the utmost certainty, though I only consider them 'calls' in the sense that they 'call' for the laughter of my friends to whom I prophesy them beforehand. I quite understand that José [2] may be called away on business, but that you, you, should treat me thus, seems both unkind and unmerited. Yes, the truth at times seems to me best."

Diaghilev often left Paris at enmity with Mme. Sert, but on his return, he would immediately telephone, start chatting, then go to her house, and the old dispute would not even be mentioned....

Preparations for the Paris season of 1909

Immediately on returning to St. Petersburg, Diaghilev threw himself into preparing for the forthcoming season in Paris. A great deal was at stake, for Diaghilev was not only exporting the Russian Opera, but for the very first time, the Russian Ballet.

How did the Ballet come to be included? Let us give the answer in his own words, from a letter written in 1928.

"From opera to ballet is but a step. At that time there were more than 400 ballet dancers on the roster of the Imperial Theaters. They had all had a remarkably good training, and they danced the traditional classical ballets....All these ballets I was very familiar with, having been attached to the Director of the Imperial Theaters for two years or so.

"I could not help observing, however, that among the younger members of the St. Petersburg ballet, a sort of reaction to the classical tradition, which Petipa so jealously preserved, was beginning to make itself felt.

"From that moment, I began wondering whether it would not be possible to create a number of short new ballets, which besides being of artistic value would link the three main factors, music, decorative design, and choreography far more closely than ever before.

"The more I thought about it, the clearer it seemed that a real ballet could only be created by the perfect combination of all these factors.

"That is why when I am producing a ballet, I never for a moment lose sight of one of these factors." [3]

These words, to which not nearly enough attention has been paid, go a long way towards explaining why Diaghilev devoted practically all the remainder of his life to the Ballet. To him, it was the perfect synthesis of decorative design and painting, music, and the dance.

But to return to St. Petersburg, where Diaghilev was already hard at work on his season for 1909!

Nothing could have seemed more promising. The Imperial Court had taken him under its exalted wing, a heavy subsidy had been granted, and

---

[2] Mme. Sert's husband. (Ed.)

[3] The rest of the letter is worthy of quotation for the light it throws on Diaghilev as a director. "Thus, I often visit the scene-painting studios, the sewing-room, attend orchestral rehearsals, and every day visit the production studio to watch my artists at work, from the stars to the boys in the *corps de ballet,* completing their training."

last but not least, the Hermitage Theater had been lent for rehearsals. Meanwhile, an unofficial committee, a sort of artistic nucleus, met daily at Diaghilev's house. In addition to Alexandre Benois, the artistic manager in Paris during the 1908 season, it consisted of Leon Bakst, Prince V. N. Argutinsky-Dolgoruky,[4] N. N. Tcherepnine, composer of the *Pavillon d'Armide* and ballet conductor to the Mariinsky Theater, the ballet critic, V. Svetlov, who had become an enthusiastic admirer of Diaghilev and his achievements, and finally, the well-known balletomane, General Bezobrazov. At these meetings the program for the following season would be worked out, the lists of dancers to be engaged in St. Petersburg or Moscow be gone through, and an active correspondence maintained with Paris. An interesting account of the unofficial committee is fortunately provided by V. Svetlov.

After exposing the old ballet *Vampuka*[5] to the most devastating criticism, on account of the complete absence of any co-ordination between the efforts of musician, designer, costumier, librettist and choreauthor (i.e., choreographer), Svetlov continues:

"How different things are in the new Diaghilev ballets. Composers, painters, ballet masters, authors and those interested in the arts come together and plan the work to be done. Subjects are proposed, discussed, and then worked out in detail. Each makes his suggestions, which are accepted or rejected by a general consensus of opinion, and thus in the end it is difficult to say which individual was responsible for the libretto, and what was due to the common effort. The real author was, of course, he who first proposed the idea, but the amendments, the working-out, the details, made it the work of all. So too with the music, the dances; all is the result of this collective effort. A painter, too, who feels a particular subject congenial, will be entrusted with all the artistic details. Not only will he be made responsible for providing the designs for both sets and costumes, he will also be expected to design all the properties and other accessories: in a word, to be responsible for the whole scenic presentation of the new ballet down to its smallest details.

"Thus, both artistic unity of design and execution are achieved. Artists, who all their lives deal with epochs, styles, plastic forms, color and line, i.e., elements with which no ballet master can hope to be equally familiar, must in the very nature of things, be their closest and co-equal collaborators in the process of creating a ballet. Then, in full awareness of

[4] Prince V. N. Argutinsky-Dolgoruky, Secretary to the Russian Embassy in Paris, and Diaghilev's friend. In 1909 he more than once helped him out of financial difficulties. In particular, when Diaghilev had lost his subsidy, it was the Prince who guaranteed his bank account for a considerable sum, and thus made it possible for him to leave for abroad. (Ed.)

[5] The title of an extremely successful satirical *pastiche* on Italian opera, produced shortly before by a troupe of St. Petersburg actors calling themselves "The Crooked Mirror." This company was the precursor and parent of Balaieff's *Chauves-Souris*. The tunes and text were on everyone's lips, and the word is still used to denote a ridiculous operatic production. (Ed.)

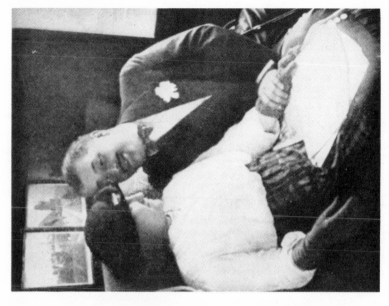

Diaghilev and Misia Sert

Stravinsky, Diaghilev, Bakst, and a Relative of
Diaghilev—Princess X

the scenic effect of décor and groupings, the ballet master works out his choreography accordingly...."

Diaghilev himself undertook the task of inviting such dancers as he wished to collaborate with him. Everywhere he met with delighted acceptances: not a single person refused. Of those in St. Petersburg, he enlisted first and foremost the dancers forming the "young revolutionary group," kneaded together by M. M. Fokine, himself a splendid dancer, and just beginning his ballet master's career, Anna Pavlova, Tamara Karsavina, the brilliant Kshesinskaya, Bolm, Monakhov, and a certain young dancer who but the previous year was still completing his studies in the school of the Imperial Theaters, though now hailed as the world's eighth wonder, that genius of dancing, Nijinsky. Among the artists engaged in Moscow may be cited, in addition to Chaliapin, the prima ballerina of the Bolshoi Theater, Coralli, and the dancer Mordkin.

Such distinguished ballerinas and dancers as Baldina, A. and V. Feodorov, Smirnova, Dobroliubiva, Kozlov, Bulgakov, and Petrov were also included, as were also the best dancers in the *corps de ballet*.

In addition, Diaghilev was able to secure the services of some of the best-known singers, and with Chaliapin there went to Paris Lipkovska, Petrenko, Smirnov, Kastorsky, Sharonov, Zaporozhetz, Damaev and Davidov.

Tamara Karsavina, the most faithful of the great dancers who worked with Diaghilev, gives us a description of his first visit to her.

"Little did I think what changes it would bring into my life when, one afternoon I sat waiting for Diaghilev in my small sitting room. I was married by now, and had my own home. 'The red plush of that suite—like a provincial hotel,' I thought, looking at my furniture. A piece of Dresden china, my first acquisition in the bibelot line, seemed alone capable of bearing witness to my taste. I moved it from the *étagère* to the piano; it looked better where it was before, though not so conspicuous. I moved it back again. Six o'clock; he should have come at five. My agitation grew. It was not on account of an offer to be discussed; there was an emotion of a different kind making me conscious of the red plush, and apprehensive of what Diaghilev, the aesthetic, might think of me.... He was now coming to seal his offer by a ceremonial visit. I was not then aware of his unpunctuality, amazing even from a Russian point of view. I had almost given him up, when I saw his coupé stop at my door. Diaghilev never would drive in an open cab for fear of being infected with glanders.... From the windows I could see the river Jdanovka and the always empty Petrovsky Park, a bit of sylvan scenery in town. Duniasha made me blush by her grotesque mispronunciation of my visitor's name when showing him in. 'A meeting for discussing various artistic questions had kept him so late,' Diaghilev explained. I had a first glimpse of the feverish activities that he had called to life. Maquettes for scenery and costumes were painted, productions elaborated by conclaves of artists and musicians. Diaghilev himself was then just back from Moscow, where he had engaged all the best and prettiest dancers as well as Chaliapin himself.... 'The high patronage of the Grand Duke Vladimir, and a subsidy is given to us,' he told me with satisfaction. 'By the way, I will send you your contract signed tonight; or is it Monday today—unlucky day, I will do it tomorrow,' he said at parting.

"The setting sun had in places illuminated the red plush to the brightness of pomegranate. I wore a copy of a Paris model. My talk had been easy, *mondaine* I thought it. My real nervousness in the presence of a personality that fascinated and intimidated me did not show.

"Diaghilev had been lent the Hermitage Theater, and there it was we began to rehearse. During the rests, court lackeys would hand round chocolate and tea. Suddenly the rehearsals came to an end!" [6]

Difficulties with the Court and with Kshesinskaya

What had happened? Why were the rehearsals so suddenly canceled? Because, on the one hand, Diaghilev's great patron, the Grand Duke Vladimir Alexandrovitch, had died, and on the other, Diaghilev had managed to offend Kshesinskaya, to whom, more than anyone, he was indebted for his subsidy. Serge Pavlovitch wished to revive *Giselle* with Anna Pavlova in the part, and had offered Kshesinskaya only the rather insignificant *Le Pavillon d'Armide*. Whereupon a stormy interview took place, in which not only arguments, but missiles too were exchanged. Diaghilev's subsidy was withdrawn, and with it the support of his exalted patron. This irked him but little, however, for he knew there were sound friends in Paris on whom he could count. A far greater blow was the news that he could no longer use the Hermitage Theater for rehearsals, nor the sets and costumes of the Mariinsky Theater.

Plots and counterplots were set into motion, and some idea of them may be gained from the following letter. It is addressed by one of the Grand Dukes to the Tsar:

"Dear Nicky,

"As was to be expected, your telegram wrought havoc in the whole Diaghilev business, and now in his attempt to save his beastly affair, he is resorting to every subterfuge, from the vilest flatteries to absolute falsehoods. According to information given me, Boris, who will be in attendance on you tomorrow, has been got at on behalf of Diaghilev, and sympathizes with his grievances. He therefore means to request you not to restore your patronage, for that the latter no longer desires, but to allow him to continue to use the Hermitage for rehearsals, and to borrow the décor and costumes used in the Mariinsky Theater for the season in Paris. We very much hope that you will not take the bait,

[6] Karsavina, *Theatre Street*, pp. 230, 232-3.

which, let me warn you, will be cast very cleverly, nor grant permission for either the use of the Hermitage or the settings. It would only be conniving at a most unsavory business which sullies the memory of dear Father.

"18th March, 1909."

This feud between Kshesinskaya and Diaghilev continued until 1911, when a reconciliation took place in Bezobrazov's house. Meanwhile d'André, Pavlova's husband, had made an effort to bring them together, spurred on by the need of Kshesinskaya's help in the matter of a lawsuit. In return, he offered to arrange matters with Diaghilev, an offer, however, which the famous ballerina rejected. Later, peace was established, and Kshesinskaya made her début for Diaghilev in London in 1911, with Nijinsky, the *ci-devant* dancer of the Imperial Ballet, as her partner. Her success in *Le Lac des Cygnes* during the 1912 Covent Garden season, was tremendous, and special encores of her variations were demanded. Such, however, was Nijinsky's jealousy, that he began to tear off his costume, and refused to continue dancing. Only with the greatest difficulty was Diaghilev able to persuade him to continue.

Thereafter, and until his death, Diaghilev's relations with her—she was to become Princess Krasinska—and her husband, the Grand Duke Andrei Vladimirovitch, were of the utmost friendliness. It always delighted Serge Pavlovitch to enjoy their great hospitality, and they themselves followed the fortunes of the ballet with the most sympathetic interest. I well remember how much Serge Pavlovitch desired I should dance with Kshesinskaya, and his keen disappointment when nothing came of the idea.

But to turn from the "havoc" wrought in "the whole Diaghilev business" to Karsavina's reminiscences of the man.

"All of a sudden there was a break in our rehearsals. After a few days of anxious apprehension and persistent rumors predicting ruin for the enterprise, we resumed our work, this time in the small theater of 'The Crooked Mirror' by the Ekaterinsky Canal. In the interval the *régisseur* of our troupe announced that Serge Pavlovitch asked the artists to pass into the foyer to partake of refreshments. During this collation Diaghilev made a brief speech. Though the high patronage had been withdrawn, the destiny of the enterprise would not suffer. He trusted to the good sense and loyalty of the troupe to carry on their work unaffected by malevolent rumors."[7]

None but a man of Diaghilev's undaunted courage could have withstood so terrible a blow. Naturally enough, the rumor began to run that the whole scheme was doomed, that all thought of a Paris season must be abandoned. And indeed, that would have been so, had anyone but Diaghilev been in control. Nothing, however, could prevail against

[7] Karsavina. *Theatre Street*, p. 234.

his determination, and his feverish preparations in no wise slackened. Neverthless, it was to Misia that he owed his salvation, for she, with other Paris friends, opened a subscription list which proved so successful, that soon a sum sufficient to rent the Châtelet Theater was collected. At the same time, the Comtesse de Greffulhe appointed M. Astruc, then but a little-known theatrical promoter, to be sole business manager to the whole undertaking. Work was resumed with redoubled energy, and the repertoire was duly established. It consisted of the following items: Tcherepnine's *Le Pavillon d'Armide;* Borodin's *Polovtsian Dances* from *Prince Igor; Le Festin* on music from Rimsky-Korsakov, Tchaikovsky, Mussorgsky, Glinka and Glazunov; Arensky's *Cléopâtra* known in the Mariinsky Theater production as *Une Nuit d'Egypte; Les Sylphides* after Chopin; Mussorgsky's *Boris Godunov;* Rimsky-Korsakov's *Pskovitianka* (but renamed *Ivan the Terrible*), and separate acts from Glinka's *Russlan and Ludmila* and Serov's *Judith.*

For *Le Pavillon d'Armide* and *Les Sylphides,* the costumes and décor were entrusted to A. Benois, and for *Polovtsian Dances* to N. Roehrich. For *Le Festin,* it was decided to use the décor of the second act in *Russlan and Ludmila* by Korovin, and for *Pskovitianka* designs by Golovin while for *Boris Godunov,* Golovin and Jouon were the artists. The heaviest share of the work, however, undoubtedly fell on Fokine, for he was responsible for producing five of the ballets: *Le Pavillon d'Armide, Polovtsian Dances, Les Sylphides, Cléopâtra* and *Le Festin.* This last, however, was hardly a ballet, but rather a pretext for exhibiting a sequence of Russian dances in Petipa's arrangement.

The mainstay of the company were the four dancers, Anna Pavlova, Karsavina, Fokine and Nijinsky. All played important parts in Diaghilev's life, and contributed greatly to his creative activity. Thus, we shall need to refer to them each in detail. But of these four "whales" in the Diaghilev ballet, one only, Karsavina, remained faithful to the end. The others, sooner or later, abandoned the company, and thus "betrayed" him who was both its inspirer and creator.

Tamara Karsavina and her Reminiscences

It was at the very first performance of Diaghilev's first season in Paris on May 17th, 1909, that Karsavina made her début in his ballet. In 1920 and 1926 she was still dancing for him. In 1929, shortly before his death, Diaghilev was counting on her for his 1930 season, but it was a season he did not live to see.

In 1931 Karsavina published her memoirs, and very interesting they are. Many of her references to Diaghilev and the Ballet might well have been echoed by the other members of the company. Especially interesting are her reminiscences of the period of Diaghilev's first interest in the ballet, of his "call," at a time when he was more vitally, more intimately preoccupied with dancing than ever again, for it was an enthusiasm which was to go on diminishing, and prove eventually, as I have said, but an unusually protracted episode in that intensely active life of his. Let me quote a few passages:

"A young man then, he already had that grasp of the absolute, an unmistakable attribute of genius. He distinguished between transient and eternal truth in art. When I knew him, he was unerring in his judgment: artists believed implicitly in his opinion. It pleased him to divine a seed of genius where a lesser intuition would see eccentricity only. 'Mark him well,' Diaghilev pointed to Stravinsky. 'He is a man on the eve of celebrity.' This remark was made on the stage of the Paris Opéra while we were rehearsing L'Oiseau de Feu. In the winter preceding our second season abroad, we spoke of Stravinsky as Serge Pavlovitch's new discovery. Ida Rubinstein was numbered among his early ones. Diaghilev unhesitatingly defined the promise of her remarkable countenance. In the roll of celebrities his hand has written many names. Diaghilev's exploration for new talents did not exclude his respect for those fully recognized; but he could not help seeing a potential gem. That search for any new manifestation of beauty accorded so well with his temperament; for, hardly his task accomplished, the impetuous spirit shifted it off to press forward towards a new one.

"A link had been forged between Diaghilev and me by our first collaboration. To suit his purposes he had need of a young, receptive personality, of a clay unhardened in a final shape. He had need of me, and I had implicit belief in him. He enlarged the scope of my artistic emotions; he educated and formed me, not by ostentatious methods, not by preaching or philosophizing. A few casual words fetched a lucid conception, an image to be, out of the dark. Often did I sadly ruminate as to what he could have done for me had he but tried systematically to educate my mind. Who knows, perhaps these peripatetic lessons were what I needed most. Reasoning, logical conclusions never helped me, the more I reasoned, the fainter grew the image I tried to focus. My imagination would set to work only by the action of some hidden spring. I had but a slender luggage of real experience. The emotions called forth in embodying the tragic of which my parts had a large share could not but be potential ones. By uncanny intuition, Diaghilev could set in motion these hidden springs, of which I had no key as yet.

"On his way from the stalls, where he had been watching the rehearsal, Diaghilev stopped to say a few words as to my interpretation of 'Echo.' 'Don't trip lightly as a graceful nymph; I see rather a monumental figure, a tragic mask, Niobe.' He scanned the last word and went his way. And in my vision the heavy metric structure of the tragic name became the mournful tread of sleepless Echo.

"And Thamar, that I had almost given up in despair. My original misconception called for a special visit of the Master.

"'Omission is the essence of art.' That and 'livid face—eyebrows in a single line.' Nothing more, yet that was enough to touch the spring that made me see all Thamar in a flash.

"To have known him I consider a favor of destiny, but not an unmixed blessing. For, if Diaghilev was a spirit that moved the greatest difficulties out of the way, he was also a very erratic organizer. Casting in my lot with his was to bid farewell to my peace of mind." [8]

Yes, many a time was Karsavina to be reft of her peace of mind, and be forced to submit to Diaghilev's indomitable will. Again she writes:

"I dreaded the telephone, as it was not easy to resist Diaghilev's pressure. He would wear out his opponent, not by the logic of his arguments, but by sheer stress of his own will, by tenacity incredible. It seemed natural to him that everything should give way before his progress" [9]..."we became constantly engaged in unequal struggles. Exhortations from him ineffectual arguments from me—he would win at the end." [10]

Anna Pavlova

Anna Pavlova's connection with the Diaghilev ballet was possibly the shortest of any, for though Diaghilev had hastened to sign her up for fifteen performances in London and Paris during 1910, after her 1909 Parisian triumphs in *Cléopâtra* and *Les Sylphides,* it was in 1910 that nevertheless she left him. The reasons were many and various, perhaps the most important being jealousy of the immense prestige enjoyed by Nijinsky, for Pavlova was determined to be the Ballet's one and only glory. Another was her interpretation of Diaghilev's refusal to intercede with his uncle, an important magistrate in Russia, in a lawsuit in which her husband, d'André was involved, as due to personal enmity on his part. A third was Stravinsky.

Meanwhile Diaghilev was going forward with plans for a production of *l'Oiseau de Feu* with Pavlova as *prima ballerina*. When, however, the music was played to her, she thought it so complicated, so utterly meaningless, that at once she declared:

"I shall never dance to such nonsense."

Diaghilev had been one of the first to realize the genius in Pavlova's dancing, at a time when legend had not yet begun to busy itself with her reputation, when she was unknown and just beginning to make her mark among the ballerinas of the Mariinsky Theater. It therefore pained him greatly when she deserted his company, especially as he was unable to compete with the fees she could obtain in America. Yet he, better than most, realized that, with all her divine gifts, there were serious

[8] Karsavina. *Theatre Street,* pp. 256-8.
[9] Karsavina. *Theatre Street,* p. 259.
[10] Ibid., p. 269.

Mathilde Felixovna Kshesinskaya   Anna Pavlova

Tamara Platonovna   Olga Spessiva
Karsavina

faults in her dancing, as, for instance, her addiction to cheap effects, what Diaghilev called her *cabotinage,* and a certain inadequacy in technique, musical sense and rhythmic feeling. For all these reasons Spessiva seemed to him the greater dancer. Such an opinion, and especially one critical of her far-famed virtuosity, may seem to many pure profanation, or to reflect on Diaghilev's judgment. Professionals, however, think otherwise, for all, beginning with her teacher Gerdt, were perfectly aware of the fact, and in no wise ascribed the divine beauty of her dancing to a faultless technique. I venture, once more, to quote from Karsavina's reminiscences of a time when she herself was comparatively a novice at the Theater School, while Pavlova was just about to complete her training.

"Three pupils of great promise were about to finish school this year, Anna Pavlova amongst them. She was so frail as to seem, in our opinion, much weaker than the other two. The pupils' undiscerning admiration was all for virtuosity: our ideals shaped after a robust, compact figure of Legnani's type. Pavlova at that time hardly realized that in her lithe shape and in her technical limitations lay the greatest strength of her charming personality."[11] And again: "Meagerness being considered an enemy of good looks, the opinion prevailed that Anna Pavlova needed feeding up. She must have thought it, too, as she swallowed conscientiously cod-liver oil, the school doctor's panacea, and the aversion of us all. But, like the rest of us, she strove to emulate the paragon of virtuosity, Legnani. Luckily for her, Gerdt fully divined the quality of her talent. It pained him to see executed by the delicate limbs of Pavlova what seemed consistent only with the hard set musculature of the Italian dancer. He advised her not to strive after effects that seemed to endanger her frail structure.

"At the time of her début she suffered acutely from what appeared to be her short-comings. 'Leave the acrobatic effects to others. It positively hurts me to see the pressure such steps put on your delicate instep. What you imagine to be your short-comings are the rare qualities that single you out of thousands,' Gerdt would say to her."[12]

How just was Diaghilev's opinion, I had many an opportunity of assuring myself, for in 1929 I often practiced with this dancer, whom I reverently adored. At such times I would see her going through her monstrous, hardly believable exercises, when, rising on her points at the *barre,* she would ask me to support her while she sought her balance. Whereupon she would say "now go," remain motionless until she overbalanced, and once more repeat the exercise with tireless repetition. Music, the orchestra, were for her merely the thumping of a piano to some silent film, for neither the rhythm nor music meant anything to her: she would indicate to the conductor by a nod the end of a figure. Actually,

[11] Karsavina. *Theatre Street,* p. 83.
[12] Ibid., p. 84.

she simply ignored the music, and behaved much like a tenor who ex-
pects the orchestra always to follow his singing, and adapt itself to all
his rhythmic vagaries. In *The Dying Swan,* her star part, she would die
in a different manner at each performance, completely oblivious of the
orchestra, and rejoining it only with the final chords. To me, it seemed
as though the music actually ran counter to her dancing, for she possessed
her own dance rhythms and music, which in no wise corresponded to
the written accompaniment. She was a dancer of genius, but an inadequate interpreter of the musical image. Anna Pavlova had many faults,
and one of the greatest was an almost total unreceptiveness; nevertheless, she was in her way incomparable and unique, and thus her faults
were forgotten and the legend created. On the stage, in *Giselle,* or *The
Dying Swan,* she became something translucent, intangible, incorporeal.
...It was no longer the dancer Pavlova; it was Giselle eternally dying
and eternally resuscitated, ghostly and imponderable, merging into and
out of the loveliness of the white swan. Such was her dying, there on the
stage, that one always seemed to be bidding her a last farewell. It was
as though only the merest film separated life from death, the woman-
dancer from the ghost of a vision. The dream, the fairy legend, were
made real by her, and when the film vanished altogether away it was
like some natural transition in which her own reality faded into the
land of legend. And still her life seems to go on among us, lovely and
translucent as ever.

The last occasion on which I ever met her was in 1930, at the Golder's
Green Hippodrome, where she was appearing in fulfillment of Diaghilev's
English stage contracts, the whole of which she had taken over. With me
was Lady Eleanor Smith, her sister Pamela, and some other friends of
Serge Pavlovitch, and we sat on the floor, in the front row of the stalls,
for the house was sold out (or so, at least, d'André told us).

Pavlova danced. Her body, her legs, her very knees seemed palpitating with some divine energy, and her arabesques were sublime. Yet
her success was but mediocre, when compared with the applause won
by her partners in their Russian step dance. I alone, the only person in
the theater possibly, applauded frantically, and threw her a rose which
she caught in midair, smiling her thanks. The performance over, I led
my friends to her dressing room, and, when they had gone, remained
for a while alone with her and her dresser. Whereupon the following
conversation took place; our last, as it proved.

"Annushka, why do you do all this, why all these performances in
which so little of the real thing is left?"

At which, reclining there on the sofa, with a sort of dreamy playful-
ness, as though some spoiled provincial actress, she replied:

"I love to give beauty...to spread it among the people...one has
to sow beauty...to sow it whole-heartedly in smiles of beauty."

"But they don't understand you any more, Annushka."

Whereupon silence fell, and I changed the conversation.

"Is it true what the papers say, that this is your last season?"

"What nonsense, what a stupid *canard!* But tell me, Lifar, when are we going to dance together? I haven't by any means given up the idea. I should like to dance with you very much, though you really aren't worth it!"

"Anna Pavlova, I must tell you, that nothing would give me greater happiness. You, your genius, have my completest devotion. When I see you in your divine moments, I value them so highly and enter so deeply into them, and into your art which I consider unsurpassingly lovely, that I would even be prepared to kill you to make you stop dancing.... Then I should be sure my vision of you would be the last, and that you could never impair it by one of those moments in which you are unworthy of your genius."

Pavlova turned pale. I thought she would have me thrust from the room, but suddenly she seized my head and impetuously kissed me. I kissed her leg...the leg of the "Dying Swan" and Pavlova seemed moved.

"Now go away, leave me to myself. I must be alone...."

"Give me something to remember this by."

"Yes, yes, I'll send it to you. But now go...."

I went, and never saw her again. Nothing came, but her image will always remain in my heart, lovely, true, and...dual.

M. M. *Fokine and the influence on him of Diaghilev, Benois, and Bakst*

The second to abandon Diaghilev was M. M. Fokine, the most talented chore-author of the twentieth century. Yet, though a genius of dancing like Karsavina was able to admit her immense debt to Diaghilev, and regret she could not owe more to him, Fokine, with offended pride, would never admit he was anything but an accomplished chore-author on his entry into Diaghilev's Ballet, and could therefore owe him nothing.

This perverse repudiation, however, conceals an error which it would be well to correct. Actually, Fokine had made the acquaintance of Diaghilev and his circle long before the beginning of the Russian season in Paris and his appointment as ballet master. But more surprising still is Fokine's claim to be already the "accomplished choreographer," for in that case Fokine would have remained as he was, and no future development would have been possible, a conclusion but little to his credit. Fortunately, the facts prove otherwise, when we see the immense distance traveled between *Petrouchka* and *Daphnis and Chloë*, created under the direct influence of Diaghilev, Benois and Bakst, and his early productions of *Eunice* and *La Vigne*.

This, however, we may concede to Fokine, that other influences were at work in addition to that of Diaghilev. As powerful, perhaps, was that of Isadora Duncan, to whom *Eunice,* a "dramatic" ballet, raised on a foundation of purely classical academic dancing, stands as a permanent memorial. This ballet is an exemplification of the purest "duncanism," yet similar elements may be traced all through his work. Diaghilev was certainly right when he wrote: "Duncan's influence on him was the very foundation of all his creative activity."

Throughout the whole of his creative activity, based as it was on the traditions of academic ballet as taught in the Imperial Theater schools, a tradition which Diaghilev greatly respected, though welcoming the most daring innovations so long as they linked up with that tradition, Fokine depended enormously on music and the art of the painter. From the very opening of the century, Fokine the reformer, in whom the spirit of protest and reform at times attained an almost schismatic violence, ready to overturn the very bases of his art, was uninterruptedly preaching that music was no mere accompaniment to some rhythmic *pas,* but in fact its very essence, for it alone determined the choreographer's inspiration. Thus the quality of the music was of paramount importance. This, indeed, was the basic principle which brought both him and Diaghilev together. Yet, if any reasonable doubt could possibly exist as to Diaghilev's influence in establishing a new relation between the ballet and music, a relation illustrated so vividly and with such freshness in Fokine's best ballets, ballets which marked an era in the art of dancing, there can be none whatever when we regard that other characteristic of his ballets, the new relation established between ballet and painting, for which he stood so clearly indebted to Diaghilev's co-workers, Bakst and Benois. The analysis of any of the ballets produced by Fokine for Diaghilev must prove this beyond the slightest doubt. In any case, much independent testimony supports my viewpoint, as, for instance, these words by Henri Prunières, already quoted by me, to Fokine's annoyance, in my book *Ballet, Traditional to Modern:*

"I once expressed my astonishment at the lack of originality shown by such an eminent technician as Fokine, after he had left the company. Whereupon, with his invariable smile, Bakst replied: 'You know, they are all the same—no imagination...I had to show him scene by scene what needed to be done. Then finally he worked out the dance steps....In exactly the same way Alexandre Benois inspired the choreography of many of the ballets.'"

True, these words are somewhat cruel, and harshly stated, and I am willing, therefore, to quote others of a milder nature. In this case it is A. Benois who corroborates my statement as to the degree in which Diaghilev and his group of painters influenced Fokine. "Once more the part played by the painters was of the greatest significance, for it would be understating matters to say that painters such as Bakst, A. Benois, Serov, Korovin, and Golovin merely created a frame within which Fokine, Nijinsky, Pavlova, Karsavina, Feodorova and many another, could perform, when in fact the whole idea of these performances was inspired by them, too. It was we, the painters—not the professional stage decorators, but the real painters—who, profoundly attracted by the stage, took up stage-design and so *helped to mold the art of dancing along new lines,* and, indeed, the whole of the production. It was this unofficial, unprofessional influence which imparted a specific character to all our productions, and to it we may venture, without undue presumption, to assert that they owed the major part of their immense success."

V. J. Svetlov, the well-known ballet critic and friend of Diaghilev, refers in much the same terms to the part played by these painters in the development of the ballet. Somewhat earlier I quoted his description of the collective manner in which the ballets were created, and all I would add is the following: "To my mind our painters have played an all-important part in the revolution of the ballet, now taking place in front of our very eyes. It is they who are the true authors of its renaissance, and it seems to me that both historic accuracy and mere justice demand that this fact should at last be admitted and loudly acclaimed."

It is generally admitted, and would indeed be difficult to deny, that Fokine earned his pre-eminence by the magnificent way in which he succeeded in stylizing various historical periods, his most successful efforts being *Schéhérazade* (moresque), *Cléopâtra* (ancient Egypt), and *Daphnis and Chloë* (early Greek). Each of these ballets reveals Fokine as endowed with a knowledge and erudition far superior to anything found in a Russian (or any other) choreographer before. Yet it would be the greatest injustice to Diaghilev, Benois and Bakst to contend that this erudition was Fokine's alone, and not that also of these others. Is it possible to believe, for instance, that Fokine alone created *Cléopâtra* and *Daphnis and Chloë,* when it was Bakst who reconstructed each pose from works of art of the period, and who, with the choreographer, worked out each in detail, so that all that remained for Fokine was to complete the motions appropriate to each? Nevertheless, it was Fokine who first transformed the *corps de ballet* from a sort of generalized and indispensable background, the "ballabile," against which the soloists' dance pattern might stand sharply out, into a definite entity which even at times filled up the foreground. Before Fokine our ballet masters had, as it were, subordinated everything to soloists, the ballerinas in particular, instead of demanding their subordination to their rôles in terms of dancing. Fokine subordinated the individual performer to the ensemble, and utterly set himself against the stage cult of the "inner personality." It is sufficient to recall Diaghilev's articles in *The World of Art* on the Moscow Art Theater to perceive how greatly Fokine's new principles derived from him. As far as I am concerned, Serge Pavlovitch's own words to me, twenty years after, completely decide the matter, when he said, "in the days when Fokine as producer and Nijinsky as dancer, *both decided to carry out my artistic ideas.*" I shall have to return to these words when I come to discuss how that promise was kept.

Diaghilev greatly admired Fokine's talent, his flexibility and impetuosity, not to mention his capacity for enthusiasm. Nevertheless, there were constant quarrels, for the most part revolving round Nijinsky, the pretext of so many of Diaghilev's quarrels, and also because of a certain similarity in their natures. As Karsavina says of him: "What he could not stand was the obviousness of difficulty, an exhibition of technical tricks.

"In the course of the same rehearsal Fokine would be moved to transports, alternately of admiration and fury. Because of his earnestness, of his demanding of the best one could give, we his followers were devoted to him, though he was extremely irritable, and had no control of his temper. At the beginning it used to upset us; in time we grew used to chairs thrown about, to his leaving rehearsals in the middle, to his vehement harangues. At theater rehearsals he sat in the stalls to see the effect of his staging. Over the heads of the orchestra, his voice, hoarse with shouting, opened at intervals a machine-gun fire of imprecations. 'Putrid execution. Loose, untidy. I won't stand carelessness.'

"In time, when not only a comparatively small group was at his command, but the whole of our company abroad respected a leader in his person, he grew even more dictatorial. I remember an incident at Monte Carlo. He was taking the rehearsal of *Giselle*. The same evening I had to dance the part and naturally spared myself, only marking the steps and the chief moments of the acting. The ensemble lagged; Fokine waxed wroth; suddenly he flew at me. 'How can I blame the *corps de ballet,* if the star herself gives a bad example? Yes! your example is corrupting, shameful, scandalous.' He rushed off. The same night he fondly hovered round me, giving a touch to my make-up. He smiled blandly when I poured out my grievance against the morning scene, and commented on my last act of *Giselle*. 'You seemed to float in the air....' " [13]

I shall have more to say about Fokine as chore-author when I come to deal separately with his ballets. Here I would only point out one particular quality of his, as invaluable in a chore-author as in a ballet master, producer or teacher; namely, his capacity for being swept out of himself, a capacity which worked wonders with both dancers and audiences. Though Fokine may not have revealed a remarkable inventiveness in the originating of dance patterns, nevertheless, everything he produced in his first years as ballet master was extraordinarily vivid, astonishingly new and original, and charged with his fiery spirit. One example from his masterpiece *The Polovtsian Dances,* in *Prince Igor,* will suffice us. Solely as a dance creation it cannot be said to differ greatly from the earlier production by Lev Ivanov. But while the latter

[13] Karsavina. *Theatre Street,* p. 212.

seemed drab and insignificant, Fokine's arrangements, by their impetuosity and fire, drew cries of frenzied enthusiasm from all who beheld them. It was this fire in him which made him so admirable a ballet master and producer. The performers themselves became as inspired as he was and would go on working till they dropped.

In 1912, however, soon after the production of *L'Après-Midi d'un Faune,* Fokine abandoned Diaghilev's company, or rather, was sacrificed to the latter's new chore-author, Nijinsky. Serge Pavlovitch was hoping for marvels and made no secret of the fact, and this Fokine found it impossible to stomach. But two years later, the Russian Ballet being then in the throes of its first ballet-master crisis, Diaghilev was forced once more to turn to Fokine. Though he returned, however, it was only temporarily, for Serge Pavlovitch still dreamed of conquering new worlds, while Fokine remained unaltered. As he had been in 1914, so he was still, even though at that date he was already declining. Of the later productions only *Le Coq d'Or* can be said to have been truly successful, and even that cannot compare with his triumphs of 1911-12. Diaghilev realized that nothing new was to be hoped for from Fokine, and fortunately, at just that moment, a new chore-author was revealed in the Ballet...Massine. Thus the matter was finally decided. Diaghilev had no further use for Fokine, and Fokine had no use for the Russian Ballet, upon which the two men parted conclusively.

Vaslav Nijinsky

But the real pride of Diaghilev's life, the joy of his heart, a joy too often poisoned, alas! and the cause of his acutest anguish, was—Nijinsky.

Only a year after passing out of the Imperial Dancing School in 1908, Nijinsky was already being hailed as a very phenomenon of dancing. It must be said, however, that, even while a student, St. Petersburg hummed with rumors of an extraordinary dancer, unique in the annals of the Imperial Theaters and the ballet. Strangely enough, when Jacques Rouché visited Russia in 1914, and there declared how much it astonished him to think that the Theater School could have parted so easily with such a dancer, he was informed that, since the Mariinsky Theater possessed great numbers of first-rate dancers, there was no point in attaching particular importance to any one of them; that, in fact, "they had as many as they wanted," all every whit as accomplished as Nijinsky.

Thus, having abandoned his connection with the Imperial Theaters, Nijinsky linked his fate with that of Diaghilev. And since the whole future of his Ballet, for Diaghilev, was bound up with this ardent friendship of his, Diaghilev felt it incumbent upon him to establish a permanent company.

Also, he began to surround his "Vatza" with infinite attentions, and even provided a bodyguard for him in the person of his own valet, the faithful Vassili, to keep him segregated from the world. As a result Nijinsky never really succeeded in being at home in it.

For instance, during our London season in 1911, a supper was given for Diaghilev by Lady de Grey, afterwards Marchioness of Ripon, one of the Queen's ladies-in-waiting, who, in London, stood much in the same relation to us as the Comtesse de Greffuhle in Paris. Queen Alexandra was present, and the hostess placed Nijinsky on her right, a gesture which English society accepted without a murmur. Nijinsky, however, unable to speak any foreign language, uttered no word, and consequently earned a reputation for being an incomprehensible, "mysterious" creature.

Indeed, Nijinsky had so little direct contact with others and even with the company of the Russian Ballet, before becoming its chore-author, and the tour to America, that hardly anybody realized the kind of person he was. But those who did, knew that in Nijinsky a great dancer had been born: one who, living only for dancing, and possessed of the dancer's instinctive *élan,* was bound to surpass them all. Nature, however, having lavishly endowed him with one gift, denied him every other. He was weak, and could offer no resistance to alien influences; he was unable to think for himself, and besides lacked musical sense. Indeed, his only form of expression lay in dancing.

When Nijinsky became ballet master, his inability to put his ideas into words made rehearsals a perpetual torment to the company. Karsavina, his constant partner, describes them thus: "Nijinsky had no gift of precise thought, still less that of expressing his ideas in adequate words. Were he called upon to issue a manifesto of his new creed, for his dear life he could not have given a clearer statement than the one he had given to explain his wonderful capacity for soaring in the air.[14] . . . Certainly at the rehearsals of *Jeux* he was at a loss to explain what he wanted of me. And it was far from easy to learn the part by a mechanical process of imitating the postures as demonstrated by him. As I had to keep my head screwed on one side, both hands curled as one maimed from birth, it would have helped me to know what it was for. In ignorance of my purpose I occasionally lapsed into my normal shape and Nijinsky began to nourish a suspicion of my unwillingness to obey him. Best of friends on and off the stage, we often fought during the preparation of our parts. On this occasion our collisions were worse and more ludicrous than ever. Unaided by understanding, I had to learn by heart the sequence of movements and once asked: 'What comes after . . .' 'You should have known by now, I won't tell you.' 'Then I will give up my part.' After two days' strike a big bunch of flowers was laid at my door and in the evening a complete reconciliation was brought about by Diaghilev."[15]

---

[14] "It's very simple," he had said; "you jump and just stop in the air for a moment."
[15] Karsavina. *Theatre Street,* pp. 290-1.

Vaslav Nijinsky in *Pavillon d'Armide*

Is it to be wondered at, therefore, that, given Nijinsky's intellectual incapacity, Diaghilev sought to segregate him from society, and the company in particular, lest anyone should suspect that "the King is naked"?

Romola Nijinsky, in her biography of the great dancer,[16] talks of Nijinsky's quite amazing musical sense, but perhaps Stravinsky can better enlighten us as to its actual nature. According to Stravinsky's account, Nijinsky, though possessed of a remarkable feeling for plastic beauty, was absolutely ignorant of the first principles of music. He had never learned to play an instrument and could not even understand musical notation. Worse still, he seemed incapable of any genuine appreciation of music. His comments on what he heard were either *clichés* or derived directly from the criticism of others. He had, apparently, no musical judgment of his own.

Nijinsky's ignorance of music caused great difficulties when he and Stravinsky were working together. It was soon clear to Stravinsky that nothing would be achieved until he had made Nijinsky understand the elementary grammar of music. But Nijinsky did not find it easy to remember what he was taught. In particular, he never thoroughly grasped the significance of tempo and the time values of different notes. Left to himself, he would construct dance-movements that had little relation, rhythmically, to the music which accompanied them. Stravinsky had always to be pointing out his mistakes.

Naturally progress was slow and Stravinsky's patience was hard-pressed. It was all the more discouraging because—partly from inexperience, partly because of the complication of the work he had undertaken—Nijinsky elaborated his dances to an absurd degree and thus imposed on the dancers difficulties which, in some cases, were beyond the scope of the human body.

I repeat, Nijinsky was an exceptional dancer, but only a dancer. Nevertheless, Diaghilev was determined to endow him with greatness, and to turn him into a great creative artist. It was not enough for him merely to mold Nijinsky's genius for dancing, or rather that uniqueness, that phenomenal natural aptitude for dancing of his. This statement may seem strange, but it is well supported by the testimony of practically all his contemporaries. In his last years at the dancing school of the Imperial Theaters, marvelous things were said of his *sauts,* but he himself gave the impression of being on the whole "rather surly and stupid," and no one suspected what he would prove in the end. "In later years," writes his ex-pupil Karsavina, "Diaghilev, with that clear conception of his that was almost uncanny, revealed to the world and to the artist himself the latter's true shape. At the expense of his better self, Nijinsky valiantly tried

[16] It is regrettable that this interesting and abundantly documented book should contain so many unverified statements that one hardly dare quote from it. The fault of the work may in part be explained by the author's ignorance of the Russian language which involves her in a number of serious errors, such as translating Nijinsky's signature, to a document relating to the period of his insanity, as "God and Nijinsky" when clearly "God Nijinsky" was written. Even more fantastic is the tale of Diaghilev's "revenge."

to answer the requirements of the traditional type till Diaghilev the wizard touched him with his magic wand. The guise of a plain, unprepossessing boy fell off—a creature, exotic, feline, elfin, completely eclipsed the respectable comeliness, the dignified commonplace of conventional virility." [17]

The part played by Diaghilev in the development of Nijinsky's personality as a dancer, the glories revealed to the world in discovering its greatest genius of the dance, might well have made him dispense with all further activity in the furtherance of male dancing.

However, urged by his desire to provide Nijinsky with an artistic education, he traveled with him through Italy, and together they visited the art sanctuaries of Venice, Milan, Rome and Florence. But even Florence only brushed him by: there was no impact, and though Serge Pavlovitch sedulously led his "Vatza" to concerts, Nijinsky continued to remain musically deaf.

Not for a moment would Nijinsky stray from Diaghilev's side, and that colossal figure screened and sheltered him from the world. Nevertheless, he lacked the intellect to profit from constant association with so exceptional a man. All he derived were a few stock phrases, more often repeated wrongly than rightly. Then in a flash of inspiration, Diaghilev decided that the moment was ripe for Nijinsky to make his début as chore-author and ballet master. The two men were sitting in the Piazza San Marco, it was 1911, when suddenly the whole outline of a future ballet, *Faune,* appeared to Diaghilev. Leaping to his feet there and then, between two pillars, he began to depict the dense angular plastic movements of this ballet, and so enthused Nijinsky that for a time all else was ousted from his mind. Thereafter, hour upon hour would be spent in museums, studying the plastic forms of the past, in efforts to establish their dynamic motion. Immediately after the return to Monte Carlo the production was put in hand.

This first creative effort of Nijinsky's entailed immense and arduous effort on the part of everyone, chiefly because of his inexperience, one result being that Bakst and Diaghilev needed to be constantly at his side. Stravinsky himself tells us, in his *Chronicle of My Life,* that Bakst, more than anyone else, was responsible for the production of *L'Après-Midi d'un Faune.* Not only did he create the décor and costumes—both of remarkable beauty—but, according to Stravinsky, he inspired the choreography, down to the smallest details.

Diaghilev was present at every rehearsal, of which there were more than a hundred. Nijinsky worked at each bar of the music separately, and after each, turning to Diaghilev, would ask:

"Is that right, Serge Pavlovitch? And now, what next?"

In spite of the agonies undergone by everyone connected with the ballet, to which I shall return, in spite of the fact that Nijinsky revealed

[17] Karsavina. *Theatre Street,* p. 182.

not one ounce of creative talent, and that everyone round Diaghilev constantly reiterated that Nijinsky could never prove himself a creative choreographer, Diaghilev, whether through obstinacy and unwillingness to admit failure, or sincere conviction, the following season entrusted Vaslav with the production of two more ballets, Stravinsky's *Sacre du Printemps* and *Jeux* by Debussy. True, the *Sacre* was eventually brought to a successful conclusion, but what untold torments this choreographical effort cost Nijinsky, Diaghilev, Stravinsky, Roehrich and the whole company, only to be completely recast seven years later by Massine. On the other hand *Jeux* never really entered the repertoire, and was never revived. Hereupon Nijinsky's experiments in choreography came to an end, except for his American production, pushed through in spite of everyone and everything, of Richard Strauss's *Tyl Eulenspiegel,* which even Diaghilev himself disapproved of. I say "even Diaghilev," for obstinately and persistently he would assert that Nijinsky was not only a great dancer, but endowed with immense creative talent. Even as late as the last year of his life he wrote: "His genius was equally at home whether in dancing or choreography. He hated all dancing which he himself had not created,[18] and proved himself remarkably fertile in devising dances for everyone but himself."

One concession and one only does Diaghilev make: namely, that Nijinsky's tragedy lay in the fact that he could not invent dances for himself, that his choreography and inventiveness were at cross purposes with his legs. Nijinsky the choreographer, where Nijinsky the dancer was concerned, forced upon himself steps totally unsuited to the nature of his gifts, and particularly unsuited to his "elevation."

Estrangement between Nijinsky and Diaghilev

From 1913 an estrangement between the two men begins to appear. He who would never allow Nijinsky out of his sight, he who had so jealously guarded and protected him from the outer world, as though with a foreboding of danger, a knowledge that Nijinsky would lose himself in that world, now allowed him to undertake the distant journey to America *out of his hands;* and that world overwhelmed him and crushed his soul.

First Romola Pulszky, who made him marry her, and then the "Tolstoyans" of the troupe, the two N. N.'s, took possession of him. In the matter of his unexpected marriage, Nijinsky manifested an attitude of such passivity, that even then it verged on the abnormal. It was as though anyone who cared might dispose of his life and mind! In her book Romola Nijinsky tells in detail how she made the great dancer marry her, and of the vegetarian, ascetic and Tolstoyan sermonizing that descended on his unhappy head. It is obvious enough from her tale that,

---

[18] Is not this why Fokine was forced to go?

much as she disapproved, she could do nothing to withstand the Tolstoyism expounded by the converts in the ballet. Nijinsky was unable to cope with (or, for that matter, understand), or master, the contradictions in which he was involved by the new creed, the creed of a harsh morality in conflict with his dancer's nature. No one can read the pages relating to his Tolstoyism, which hastened the progress of his mental disease, without emotion and dread.[19] I often felt haunted by the image of the wretched Nijinsky walking down the street of his Swiss village wearing his big gold cross, and stopping the passers-by to preach his Christianity, a dread as intense as that produced by Romola Nijinsky's account of how she caused him to marry her.

Nijinsky betrayed Diaghilev for another, but can one speak of betrayal when the betrayer lacks any real will power, and is, in addition, hardly responsible for his actions? Given the lead, Nijinsky would follow no matter whom, and thus it was that his master, his "demigod," was supplanted by a mistress who brought him many misfortunes. Not a word of the marriage did Nijinsky convey to the man with whom his life had been linked so closely, and Diaghilev heard of it only from that faithful servant Vassili, whom he had sent with Nijinsky to America. On receiving the news he burst into a fit of ungovernable fury, a lion's madness, smashed chairs and tables, and, raging, hurled himself round the room.

This marriage bludgeoned Diaghilev. Nothing had ever caused him such anguish. True, there had been the beginnings of an estrangement, but the blow and its irrevocable nature revealed how deeply Nijinsky had entered into his soul, how impossible it was to tear him out of it. To his last breath Nijinsky remained dear to him, however much the latter might have hurt or outraged him, however utterly he had died to dancing and the world. Thus, life always repeated itself for Diaghilev: his attraction to his friends would wane, his affections cool, he too would even "betray"; and yet some link remained in his soul. Then a day would come, soon or late (though generally late), when, confessed or unconfessed, he would once more assume that allegiance which he had appeared to cast away with such ease.

About to start back from America, Nijinsky received the following telegram: *"Le Ballet Russe n'a plus besoin de vos services. Ne nous rejoignez pas. Serge de Diaghilev."* Thus it seemed that the breach was complete and final. During the war, however, Nijinsky was interned in Austria under conditions impossible to describe, whereupon Diaghilev, who still kept a watchful eye over him, was moved to come to his help. The "demigod" still ruled over some corner of the dancer's unhappy soul, and he was cruel enough to confess the fact to his wife: "I do not regret my relations with Serge Pavlovitch, whatever morality may say."

On a number of occasions the two men, for Nijinsky still remained

[19] Nijinsky had a hereditary predisposition to mental abnormality. Even in the St. Petersburg days, Diaghilev had already had him treated by Dr. Botkin, who saw threatening symptoms in the fact that Nijinsky suffered from glandular defect.

under the sway of his former master and friend, were on the point of reconciliation, but on each occasion Romola stood in the way. Finally, after considerable effort, Diaghilev succeeded in obtaining Nijinsky's release, and permission was given for him to leave for America. There, Diaghilev welcomed them both in all friendship, and placed Nijinsky in charge of the artistic side of the ballet for the forthcoming season. In spite of the fact that this was unwelcome to the company, for we know how intolerable he made rehearsals, even Romola Nijinsky admits that the dancers treated Vaslav with the most perfect courtesy. In her own words: "Great courtesy was shown to me, more even than in the old days." And adds in explanation: "Diaghilev must have given his orders." [20]

Just, however, as Diaghilev was taking steps to effect a complete reconciliation with Nijinsky, the latter's wife saw fit to embark on a lawsuit against him, and at the same time did all in her power to instill into the impressionable, unresisting mind of her poor husband the absurd and pernicious idea, now an obsession, that Diaghilev was determined to encompass his utter destruction. She even suspected him of having instigated an attempt on her husband's life in Buenos Aires.

Nevertheless, Diaghilev received the couple with the utmost cordiality when they next met, in Madrid. To quote Mme. Nijinsky yet again: "At that time Diaghilev affected a fatherly, protective, and kind manner towards me. Vaslav triumphantly declared:

" 'There, you see, Femmka, I always told you he would be our friend!'

"And Vaslav told me again how Diaghilev had helped a former great friend when he got into difficulties, years after his marriage, and his wife sought Serge Pavlovitch's aid. Vaslav was so happy that he would have done anything to please Diaghilev, and the matter of the contract was not brought up. 'Serge Pavlovitch is the same as ever; there is no need of discussion. He will be fair to me—let us give him a chance to prove it.'

"Every day Diaghilev thought of some place of interest to take us to. He was very friendly to me during these days in Madrid. His amazing hypnotic power did not seem to have lessened with the years." [21]

With open hearts Nijinsky and Diaghilev went out to meet each other, but once more the figure of the dancer's wife was to rise between them. As a result, Diaghilev found himself compelled to resort to the police to force Nijinsky into fulfilling his side of the contract. No alternative was possible, for he himself had contracted to present Nijinsky. For several days after, Nijinsky kept to his room, and then, acting on the advice of certain "friends," instead of going to the theater, packed his trunks and left for the station.

These performances under duress, presented in 1917 in Spain, were the last in which Diaghilev saw Nijinsky dance. Soon after, the latter,

[20] Romola Nijinsky. *Nijinsky,* p. 316.
[21] Romola Nijinsky. *Nijinsky.* pp. 358-9.

with the whole company, though not Diaghilev, left on a South American tour after which Nijinsky settled in Switzerland. Here his mental disease became more pronounced, and soon all intercourse with the outer world was necessarily interrupted.

Diaghilev was grievously afflicted by the calamity which had overtaken the great dancer. Cruelly inevitable though it was, had not life's hazards removed him from Diaghilev's beneficent influence, that breakdown would certainly have been delayed.

To his last breath Diaghilev refused to reconcile himself to his friend's misfortune, and never abandoned the hope that some shock might restore to the world the old Nijinsky. He himself, on several occasions, sought to provoke such a shock. I remember, for instance, how, in the spring of 1924, Nijinsky, accompanied by his sister-in-law, Tessa Pulszky, was taken to a rehearsal of *Les Fâcheux,* where his appearance greatly distressed our dancers. It was impossible to look at him without an obscure feeling of dread, for he went on gazing intently over their heads, while a senseless half-smile played on his lips, the terrifying, unearthly half-smile of a human creature, *oblivious to all things.* There we stood with hanging heads, both newcomers and long-established members of the ballet, once his familiars, when his fame had resounded through the world, while sad thoughts and bitter memories passed through our minds and were reflected in every motion of our dancing. Every *pas* we danced was slow, solemn and unwilling, as though fearful we might offend; while he, the King of Dancers, looked on as one who would *never dance again.*

But no beneficial shock resulted, in spite of the familiar surroundings, and when, five years later, Diaghilev repeated the same experiment at the Paris Opera House, only a few months before his own death, the effect was equally negative.[22]

Other collaborators in the Ballet

If I have perhaps devoted overmuch space to Nijinsky, the reason must be looked for more in the part he played in Diaghilev's life than in his importance to the Ballet, great though that was. Such was the intimacy of the bond which bound these men together that any omission must have produced an equivalent impoverishment in my account of the life of Diaghilev.

Among those who accompanied the latter to Paris none was of equal importance, and I shall therefore limit myself to mentioning but few. And first, those by right of seniority: Bolm, to whom is due the chief credit for the success of the *Polovtsian Dances* and who produced *Sadko* in America, and Kremnev, for whom Diaghilev felt greater sympathy and fondness than for any member of the company. Often he would relate

[22] For the most recent account of Nijinsky's condition see Appendix A.

how he and Rosay came to the rescue and "saved" *Le Pavillon d'Armide* during the Coronation festivities of 1911.

Nor must we forget Grigoriev, who, as producer, was associated with the Ballet from its first days to the last, duties which, in 1901, he shared with Satin. Though he had passed through both the Dramatic and Ballet Schools, Grigoriev never revealed creative imagination or initiative. As Diaghilev bid, so did he do. But orders were always transmitted with the utmost fidelity, and the discipline, the general order of the company, were admirably watched over. He was one of the most faithful of Diaghilev's collaborators, and the latter had implicit faith in him, though always keeping him at a certain distance.

Closest to Diaghilev was the valet who had been in his employ ever since his undergraduate days. This Vassili, surnamed Zuiev (which, with Diaghilev's permission, he changed to Zuikov, became also the ballet's "costumier." In many ways his position resembled that of the nanny Dunia, and except for one occasion, that on which Diaghilev entrusted Nijinsky to his care during the journey to South America, he was never absent from his master. Nijinsky was very fond of Vassili, for when nervous and depressed none but Vassili could soothe or reason with him. To his master, Vassili was slavishly devoted. All through the period when Diaghilev was scouring Russia for paintings for his exhibitions, and later, in Europe, always Vassili accompanied him. From him, more than from anyone else, Diaghilev knew everything that went on in the company. Though he himself remained aloof from his dancers, Diaghilev nevertheless enjoyed listening to tales and gossip about the inner life of the company. Simple peasant though he might be, Vassili's influence in the troupe was immense. To me he was always the soul of kindness, though he could never refrain from having his little joke at my expense, always reminding me I was "a greenhorn." But again, he was the first to see me for what I was, for "You are a real one," he one day declared, from which moment everyone in the company began to think similarly.[23]

One of the friends of *The World of Art* days, V. F. Nouvel, became, as it were, the business manager, and as such was constantly mislaying the files which contained the contracts. Nevertheless, his position in the Ballet was far less important than it had been on *The World of Art*. However highly Diaghilev had esteemed his opinions, that estimation sank

[23] In her *Theatre Street*, p. 262, Karsavina quotes the following anecdote about him, which I, too, have heard from Diaghilev's lips: "His valet, as was indeed natural to Russian servants, would come unbidden constantly in and out of the rooms. Diaghilev and his friends being practically staggered under a recent blow, there was much talk of intriguing and intrigues. When the suggestion crystallized in Vassili's mind, he suggested direct action.

" 'Barin, shall we do away with the villainess?' 'What do you mean?' The hand moved in dumb show, brushing something aside. 'What can one do, Vassili?' 'Shall I, Barin ... ?' Another dumb show demonstrated the action. 'Just a little powder.' No common hireling, Vassili had towards his master the unquestioning devotion of an old retainer. When crossing to America, Diaghilev daily ordered Vassili to kneel down and pray for the safety of their voyage. And while the valet performed religious exercises his master paced up and down the deck in better spirit."

greatly after Valetchka had "seen no music" in Stravinsky's *l'Oiseau de Feu* at a moment when Diaghilev was proclaiming Stravinsky's genius from the housetops. It was an error from which his prestige never recovered.

In the early years of the ballet, N. N. Tcherepnine enjoyed a position of some importance. Serge Pavlovitch, in 1909, included this composer's *Le Pavillon d'Armide* in his repertory, though it had already been produced at the Mariinsky Theater, while in 1911 he also produced Tcherepnine's *Narcisse,* which had been specially composed for him. It was a short-lived collaboration, however, for shortly after, the talented though somewhat humdrum Tcherepnine was superseded by a composer of genius: one more modern, more suited to Diaghilev's tastes—Stravinsky.

Bakst and his estrangement from Diaghilev

Throughout the whole of the early years of the Russian Ballet we find the painters associated with *The World of Art,* Bakst, Benois, Golovin, Korovin and Roehrich, playing an all-important part in it, and in particular the two first-named, as is testified by the fact that I have been forced so often to refer to them when writing of Fokine and Nijinsky. I shall have to revert to them yet again in my next chapter, and shall therefore confine myself now to the main facts of their relation to Diaghilev.

From 1909 to 1914 Bakst painted the scenery for twelve ballets, after which came a break owing to the war. But in 1917 their collaboration was resumed, though it proved but short-lived. Bakst provided the sets and costumes for *Les Femmes de Bonne Humeur,* and the following year set energetically to work on a new version of the same ballet, besides preparing *La Boutique Fantasque.* In a letter to Diaghilev, dated July 18th, 1918, we find him saying:

"Dear Seriozha,

"Here is my new sketch, the second, and also as yet unpaid (the price is 2000 francs), for the *'Donne di bon umore.'* Although it disgusts me to produce tidy little houses, I make a concession to your need to curry your audience's favor. But one thing only I implore you not to do: do not make the color of the sky any lighter, for that would *ruin* everything, because no concentration on the artists *below it* would be possible, and instead of Goldoni and Italy, as seen through Hogarth, we should have nothing but Werther and Massenet; in fact something that would just suit Gunsburg. Please remember this, and most important, that the public will instinctively have less liking for it. The scenery is unbelievably simple, the houses pure Italian, though unfortunately I did them on the table where the sketch looks miles better than on the easel. Enfin! On the spectator's left we have the Marquise's 'Piccolo Casino,' then a

Vassili Zuikov

sort of Hôtel de Ville, 'the Casa del Capitano' as they were called, a typically Venetian mixture of 12th century romanesque and 14th century gothic, with an arch leading to a second inner square, out of which all the entrances into the street will be made. Next comes a typical 18th century tavern, with its doorway making a corner, over which there hangs the inn sign, visible from every part of the house, and very much finer than before. Then, at the back there comes a monastery wall and finally, at the right, that deaf devil Cecchetti's 'casino.' The exits for the dancers are very simple, an opening into the inner square, and another into the tavern; nothing in fact could be simpler, but the monastery wall will have to disappear into the distance to fill up the space to the right. My advice would be not to make Cecchetti's casino symmetrical with that of the Marquise's, but to move it back a bit, so that only her casino *really stands out*. . . . I am comfortably busy, working on the costumes for *La Boutique Fantasque*. It will be a *very resurrection of Naples in* 1858."

And while Bakst was resurrecting "Naples, 1858" . . . at that very moment Derain, commissioned by Diaghilev, was preparing the scenery and costumes for the same ballet. Whereupon the two men quarreled, as they had done Heaven alone knows how often in the course of their twenty-five years' friendship, though only to be reconciled later.

In 1922, however, this ancient, tried and tested friendship did really end, for in that year Diaghilev produced *The Sleeping Beauty,* the sets for which were provided by Bakst. At the same time Bakst was at work on the scenery for Stravinsky's *Mavra.* In spite of this, however, Diaghilev commissioned Survage to provide the same sets, and since Bakst had not even been paid for his work on *The Sleeping Beauty,* the two friends quarreled for good. In 1923 Bakst brought an action for the recovery of his fees, and obtained an injunction restraining the Ballet from the use of his scenery.

It was a breach which profoundly affected Diaghilev, for though, where his artist's ideals were involved, he would unhesitatingly remove his dearest friends from his path, their pride or feelings counting as nothing, any personal quarrel or dispute disturbed him greatly. This complete rupture was therefore a fearful blow. Indeed, it was felt equally by both, such was the underlying depth of their long friendship. Anonymously, Bakst would send Diaghilev cuttings referring to that "genius Bakst" to recall to his friend the irreparable loss he had brought on himself, though indeed his absent friend was never far from Diaghilev's mind. When, in London, in 1924, Serge Pavlovitch heard of his old friend's death, I shall never forget the bitterness of his tears as he fell into Vassili's arms, or his hysterical collapse at the Coliseum. I remember, too, how, not long before Bakst's death, Serge Pavlovitch sought to make his peace, and bowed as he saw him sitting at the Café de la Paix, and how Bakst ignored it. Never before had such an insult been offered to his pride, he who till then had only met with indulgence, he who had always been forgiven. And now the proffered hand was rejected. So, too, it had been with Ravel, whom he had commissioned to compose *La Valse,* which he had then refused. Happening to meet, Ravel ignored him completely.

Importance of Benois and Bakst

It was no real quarrel or rupture which severed Diaghilev and Alexander Benois, but a certain divergence of views felt by each in regard to the aims of the Ballet. Though artistically in charge of the whole of the first Russian seasons, and, in spite of the triumphant success of *Le Pavillon d'Armide* and *Les Sylphides* (1909), *Giselle* (1910) and *Petrouchka* (1911), Benois, from 1914 on, when he designed the sets for Stravinsky's opera *Rossignol,* ceased altogether to paint for the ballet. Only ten years later, in 1924, did he paint the scenery for two operas, *Le Médecin malgré Lui* and *Philémon et Baucis.*

All these quarrels, divergences, and open ruptures, date, of course, from a period long after that of the early years of the Ballet, namely 1909, but these digressions have to some extent been inevitable. Before I return to that period, however, I shall allow myself yet another question, and ask whether, from 1913-14 on, Bakst and Benois really appreciated the manner in which Diaghilev's artistic tendencies were developing, tendencies they could have never approved, though often as not the results may even have disappointed Diaghilev himself. But, did they realize that not for a moment was Diaghilev in any way seeking to minimize the achievement of the Ballet's splendid beginnings, when Bakst and Benois played such outstanding parts in providing both décor and inspiration for some of its greatest productions?

The first epoch of the Russian Ballet derived immediately and directly from The World of Art, *being in fact only a fresh phase of it.* But by 1913-14 that phase had been so brilliantly lived through and expressed that nothing remained to be added to it. It was not so much that Diaghilev was now drawn towards new experiments, but that he was firmly resolved not to spoil a great artistic achievement by inferior repetitions, and by recurrent self-limitations. In order to "be taken up living into the heavens," Diaghilev, while determined to follow new paths, felt it his sacred duty to preserve inviolate, and to the very end of the Ballet's existence, the immense artistic achievement it owed to Benois and Bakst. Thus, we find him, in 1929, reviving Bakst's *Schéhérazade* and Benois' *Petrouchka.* Indubitably, Bakst and Benois played an exceedingly important part in the early period of Diaghilev's Ballet. Indeed, they greatly influenced the general and, at times, the main lines along which dancing developed. Fortunately they were not only great artists, but also men devoted to the theater.

I should have been guilty of an important omission in my account of the preparations for the Paris season of 1909, and of the Russian Ballet in general, had I not mentioned the name of a once renowned dancer, at that moment the most reputed of dancing masters, and custodian of every academic tradition of the Ballet, the man who was mainly responsible for the actual performances, Maestro Enrico Cecchetti. Through Cecchetti, who had taught practically every outstanding dancer in the Russian Ballet, and who periodically continued to work with Diaghilev's troupe, a link with the traditions of academic ballet, a link immensely valued by Diaghilev, was kept permanently alive.

The Russian Ballet arrives in Paris

As April, 1909, was ending, the Russian "barbarians" arrived in Paris, and at once set feverishly to work. Russian barbarians indeed! . . . for soon after their arrival that devoted admirer of Diaghilev and Russian art the Comtesse de Greffuhle (together with Mme. Sert) gave a dinner at the Hotel Crillon for the Russian artists. Her heart sank, she told me, when she saw how drably provincial and uncultivated they seemed; almost she regretted having allowed herself to be so swept off her feet by Diaghilev's aristocratic and European charm as to believe all his wondrous tales of their capacities. But at the dress rehearsal of May 18th she fell completely under the sway of those "drab provincials" in whom she had been so disappointed, and once and for all became a firm believer in the "miracle of Russian art. . . ."

Now work began at the Châtelet Theater, to a general background of fearful hammering and terrific uproar. Ill-adapted for performances such as those of the Russian Opera and Ballet, the Theater, because of its generally neglected appearance, provided a most unsatisfactory setting for productions where every detail was of account. The stage also proved too small, and the floor unsatisfactory for dancing. However, by Diaghilev's orders, it was replaced by a pine-wood floor, provided with a trap door for Armida's couch, and the stage enlarged by extending the new floor to cover the space originally reserved for the orchestra. But now it became necessary to do away with five rows of stalls to make room for the musicians. Dissatisfied, however, with the look of the *parterre* Diaghilev had the remaining stalls replaced by boxes, the whole being covered with new velvet. After which plants were placed about, the corridors redecorated, and the old Châtelet began to assume quite a festive air.

Amidst all this bustle of reconstruction, amid fearful sounds of hammering, sawing, and the deafening cries of workmen, rehearsals continued, while Fokine shouted himself hoarse in vain efforts to be heard. So much needed to be done, and so little time remained before the première of May 19th, that the lunch hour was canceled, and food was sent in from Larue's. All day the company remained in the theater.

Frantically, Diaghilev rushed hither and thither, torn between workmen, actors, painters, musicians and visitors, the latter mainly critics and journalists, who now began to arrive in ever greater numbers. Whole columns appeared in the newspapers recording the doings of the company, and these immensely stimulated public interest in the approaching opening night. Most assiduous of the visitors were Jean Cocteau, Jacques Emile Blanche, Vaudoyer, Reynaldo Hahn, Robert Brussel and Calvocoressi, all from the first stout friends of the Russian Ballet, and faithful supporters of Diaghilev and Russian art. Later, all these men, and in particular, Cocteau, wielded great influence in the Ballet, and did much to ensure the triumphant success of that first season of Opera and Ballet. Of the greatest importance, too, were the articles R. Brussel contributed to *Le Figaro,* for from the very first Russian season of 1906, he had become an enthusiastic admirer of our national art. As a result, he made the journey to Russia, and there became acquainted with Diaghilev. To his pen we owe one of the most important contributions to the history of Diaghilev's life, an article published in the *Revue Musicale,* which in 1930, issued a special number dedicated to *Les Ballets Russes de Serge Diaghilev.* In this article, entitled *Avant la Féerie,* Brussel very concisely states Diaghilev's artistic problems:

"What did he wish? Stated simply, these three things. To reveal Russia to itself, to reveal Russia to the world, to reveal the new world to itself. And that in the simplest, most direct and easiest manner, through painting and music, and only later did he dare to say, 'and through the dance.'

"What did he not wish? That Russia should be deemed something exotic, with nothing to offer Western eyes but the contrasts of some picturesque bazaar. Nothing exasperated him more. Indeed, he would almost rather have preferred to have its real beauty misprised, than to have them admired merely as something Eastern. There is not the least bit of an 'Asiatic' under the skin of a true Russian, except perhaps for the poet's or musician's daydreams of seeking the sun. Even authentic Russian relics of the past were for him almost so much bric-à-brac, good at best for some dead-and-alive museum.

"This national pride and threefold aim inspired his every act, and explains both his aesthetic deviations, and his fluctuating ideals.

"Better than most, he had realized that one must go forward breakneck, to make sure of not being out-distanced; that it was of the utmost importance to hurry forward.

"He had, therefore, to move fast, and having recalled Russia to the Russians, and the new Russia to the world, to exchange his Russian clothing for clothing that was European, turn polyglot, dominate all discussion, and become the arbiter of the artistic destinies of two continents. The first version of the *Sacre* was profoundly pagan and Russian; the second, only by its motley of stage props."

No one could have expressed more concisely the very essence of Diaghilev's artistic ideas. But it is the conclusion of this article which is of especial interest in revealing Diaghilev's own dissatisfactions with the last epoch of the Russian Ballet.

"'One must move fast,' but life moved faster, and yet the ageing Diaghilev was still demanding his way. And now I am sure, he was no longer certain which path to take.

"The last time I saw him—we were lunching with V. F. Nouvel in a big restaurant—he asked me to act as mediator with a great musician whose collaboration he wanted, but whom he had somewhat neglected of late. This return to his old enthusiasms struck me. Once more, this man who had been a visionary and who now seemed to be walking like a somnambulist, was turning back to the ancient truths. He questioned me about what was being written, about the composers. As in the past, we began remembering old names, and evoking the phantoms of old ballets.

"In passing I reminded him, in all innocence I may say, of certain of his creations which had been hallowed by his sacred imprimatur, and about which we had each felt so differently. Whereupon the huge, sagging, worn and saddened face turned to me, the monocle was screwed into the lack-lustre eye, a bitter grimace twisted his lips, and he said: 'That's enough of all that *musiquette*,' and left me on that slashing retort. I was never to see him again."

Finally, after interminable preparation, endless fears and anxieties, the dress rehearsal of the first production took place, the program being *Le Pavillon d'Armide, The Polovtsian Dances* and *Festin*.

All artistic Paris was present, and so enthusiastically were the ballets received that no doubt could possibly remain as to their future success with the Paris public. And indeed the performance proved a veritable triumph, a revelation, besides being the most important artistic event of the first decade of the twentieth century.

CHAPTER IX

THE FIRST RUSSIAN SEASONS

1909: the great success of the first Festivals of Russian Art

ON MAY 19th, 1909, the Russian Ballet made its début at the Châtelet Theater with a program including *Le Pavillon d'Armide, Prince Igor* (*Scenes* and *Polovtsian Dances*) and the dance-suite *Le Festin*. The cast for each of these ballets was as follows: *Pavillon d'Armide,* Karsavina, Coralli, Baldina, Alexandra Feodorova, Smirnova, Dobroliubova, Nijinsky, Mordkin, Bulgakov, Grigoriev and A. Petrov; for *Prince Igor,* Sharonov as Prince Igor, Petrenko as Konchakovna, Smirnov as Vladimir, Zaporozhetz as Kontchak, d'Ariel as Ovlur, Sofia Feodorova as a Polovtsian maiden, Smirnova as a slave, Kozlov, Kremnev, Leontiev, Noviko, Orlov and Rosay as Polovtsian youths, and Bolm as a warrior; for *Le Festin,* Karsavina, Fokine, Sofia and Olga Feodorova, Coralli, Baldina, Nijinska, Shollar, Smirnova, Dobroliubova, Nijinsky, Monakhov, Mordkin, Bolm, Kozlov, Novikov, Rosay, etc.

In the memory of every spectator, this performance stands out as a veritable miracle of dancing, and the Comtesse de Noailles was to write twenty years later:

"When I entered the box to which I had been invited, I arrived slightly late, not altogether believing in the revelation certain initiates had promised me; but I realized at once that something miraculous was happening, that I was witnessing something absolutely unique. Everything that could strike the imagination, intoxicate, enchant, and win one over, seemed to have been assembled on that stage, to be luxuriating there as naturally, as beautifully, as vegetation responds to a beneficent climate."

Words cannot describe the reception given to this first night. Success? Triumph? The words convey nothing of the exaltation, the religious fervor and ecstasy which took possession of the audience. "Success" or "triumph" may be appropriate in describing the reception according to some remarkable, unusual performance, better than most; but here no comparison was possible, for nothing like it had ever been seen. Suddenly, unexpectedly, a new, marvelous and totally unknown world was revealed: a world, whose existence not one of these Parisian spectators had even suspected and which so intoxicated, so overwhelmed them that for a time all else was blotted out completely. A sort of psychosis, a mass delirium, seemed to sweep over the spectators which the Press re-echoed the following and many a succeeding day.

"The Elders of Troy," wrote Reynaldo Hahn, "were content to accept all the horrors of war without a murmur, because theirs had been the joy of seeing Helen. So, I too, find consolation for what is happening round us, since I have seen *Cléopâtre* on the stage." Not for a day, but for six weeks this frenzy continued unabated: six enchanted weeks in which opera and ballet alternated. The first miracle had come to pass on May 19th; it was succeeded by that of the 24th, when Rimsky-Korsakov's *Pskovitianka,* renamed *Ivan the Terrible,* was presented, and in which Chaliapin, Lydia Lipkovska, Petrenko, Pavlova, Kastorsky, Sharonov, Damaev, and Davidov all appeared. The third miracle was the performance dedicated to the first act of Glinka's *Russlan and Ludmila,* in which Lipkovska, Zbrueva, Sharonov, Davidov, Kastorsky and Zaporozhetz appeared; the one-act *rêverie romantique* entitled *Les Sylphides,* in which for the first time Paris audiences saw Anna Pavlova, side by side with Karsavina and Nijinsky, and the dramatic ballet *Cléopâtre* presented by Pavlova, Ida Rubinstein, Karsavina, Nijinsky, Fokine and Bulgakov. ...In addition, an act from Serov's *Judith* was given with Chaliapin and Felia Litvin.

All through these six weeks, both audiences and artists seemed to be living in an atmosphere not of this world, an atmosphere and existence which Diaghilev himself described "as though enchanted in the gardens of Armida. The very air round us seems as though it were drugged."

Even a quarter of a century later, we find Jean Cocteau writing: "The red curtain rises on performances instinct with such joy that they will revolutionize France, and ecstatic crowds will follow the chariot of Dionysos."

Even as recently as September, 1938, i.e., thirty years after, we find the Academician, Louis Gillet, remembering the performances.

"The Russian Ballets mark one of the great epochs in my life. I am speaking of those first, veritable and memorable productions of 1909-1912. Those Russians! How explain the conviction their mirages created?

"The advent of the 'Ballet Russe' was an event in the truest sense of the word, a shock of surprise, a whirlwind, a new impact. . . . *Schéhérazade! Prince Igor! L'Oiseau de Feu! Le Lac des Cygnes! Le Spectre de la Rose!* In a word, I may say without exaggeration that my life is split into two epochs: before and after the Russian Ballet! All our ideas underwent a change. It was as though the scales had fallen from our eyes."

Critics, Russian and French

Thus, without the slightest hesitation, Paris took this revelation to its bosom, and welcomed it as a portent of the new era. As the excitement faded, attempts at a critical evaluation began to appear. But there were no bounds to the enthusiasm accorded to Benois' scenery and costumes for

Les Sylphides and *Le Pavillon d'Armide,* Bakst's *Cléopâtra,* Roehrich's *Prince Igor,* Korovin's *Le Festin* and Golovin's *Pskovitianka.* This, however, was due not so much to the decorative effect—even though Bakst's orgies of color created almost a furore—as to the new vision they manifested of the art of the stage.

But, indeed, how could the public, the critics, have reacted otherwise, since, for the first time in the history of the stage, the sets were painted by artists of distinction instead of by the usual hack scene-painter? Further a mortal blow was dealt to the time-honored principles of stage perspective, whose sovereignty now at last began to be disputed. Thenceforth, its place was to be taken by that riot of color, that feast of the senses, which the spectator seeks in the theater, since he cannot find it in life.

"It was almost a sense of stupefaction that now took possession of the audience," we find A. Warnod writing, "and even before the actual dancing began, the design on the curtain, the first bars of the music, had already created the propitious atmosphere.

"The sets for *Le Pavillon d'Armide* were the work of Benois, and wonderfully they evoked the magnificence of that great age, miraculously designed to dazzle eyes accustomed to Versailles. As for Bakst, we saw his genius in all its brightness in *Cléopâtra,* when the huge lapis lazuli carpet was little by little buried beneath roses, flung into the air by slaves clad in topaz and emerald.

"It was Egypt revealed under an entirely new aspect; but it was also the East, Russia; it was a trifle, and yet it was everything; something immense and infinitely moving, as much in itself as in its novelty. It was impossible not to be moved by such a revelation. Some acclaimed it a miracle, others pure barbarism—but all without exception were deeply, profoundly moved by it.

"But of course it must be borne in mind to what our public had grown accustomed. . . . A dinginess, a half-light, a vagueness, and the malaise of twilight, was the stage's highest achievement, and *Pelléas et Mélisande* its pinnacle; mustiness, melancholy, listlessness and dim color, delighted the most exacting, while no one spoke with more authority than Gambon, lord of the scene-painting of the Opéra Comique.

"It is easy enough to imagine, therefore, the impact on all this flabby sweetness, these papier-mâché stage-props, of the sets brought by the Russians. They were a rock dropped into a puddle; a bullet fired at a mirror."

Thus, by way of the Ballet's décors the Parisian public came to admire the Russian Ballet, and indeed these décors were undubitably its most original feature. But the artists too were incomparable, and Pavlova, Karsavina, Rubinstein (as Cléopâtra), Nijinsky and Chaliapin all soon had their devotees. Mme. de Noailles, for instance, says of Nijinsky:

Les Sylphides, 1909

Petrouchka, 1910

"That angel, genius, triumphant god of the performance and divinest of dancers, Nijinsky, took possession of our souls, till our hearts overflowed with love, while the suave, the harsh sonorities of the Asiatic music, enveloped us ever more deeply, lulling us into a stupor.

"Whoever has once seen Nijinsky dance, must forever feel the poorer by his absence, and cannot but ponder upon that overwhelming departure of his towards those infernal regions of melancholy madness where he now lives: he, whose corporeal body dwelt in space, unaided, unsupported, and as has been so picturesquely said, as though *painted on the ceiling*. Those who never saw him will never know what youth may mean in all the intoxication of its rhythmic strength, or the terror that lies in steely muscles, a fear akin to that felt by some child alone in the fields, when it sees the grasshopper shoot upwards on its long limbs of steel."

Nijinsky's impact upon the Parisian public was all the more startling, in that they had, as it were, almost forgotten that there could be such a thing as male dancing, that one might find delight not only in the grace of the ballerina's art, but in the "elevation," the divine inspiration of the male dancer. Yet besides the genius Nijinsky, the Russian Ballet numbered several outstanding dancers, among them Bolm, Rosay, Mordkin, Monakhov and Bulgakov.

Of the ballerinas, Karsavina and Pavlova were soon prime favorites with the public. When, for instance, Karsavina and Nijinsky appeared together, veritable dithyrambs would be chanted in their praise, for how else can be described notes such as this, by R. Brussel in the pages of *Le Figaro?*

"Karsavina's beauty is perfect, incomparable: substance itself seems bewildered at being the adorable veil of so much grace.

"She remembers the *Lac des Cygnes* when, with such exquisite slowness her neck delicately droops. And when the dark, dark eyes open in the dead whiteness of her face, how delicious is the vision of poetry and grace she evokes." Or again:

"Long ago in the past, orphic hymns sang her praises twixt the 'perfume of the clouds,' which is myrrh, and the 'perfume of Aphrodite' for which there is no name. And when she droops it is only under the weight of all her ineffable grace."

So, too, praises were sung of the *corps de ballet* which, traditionally static, had now become as it were a single being, with its own organic part in the ballet, and its own psychological justification. Thus, we find M. Henri Ghéon, in 1910, writing in *La Nouvelle Revue Française,* "No longer is the ballet a mere setting for some star, for the reign of the star is ended like that of the tenor. To do true justice to the Russian company, one should avoid making the slightest individual reference, for the collective result by far outweighs the sum of the individual talents which compose it. Its supreme quality is that of seeming indivisible, of being one with the work it represents, even to the point of seeming to issue from the very music itself before melting back into the colors of the settings."

Thus, painting (the sets and costumes) and the dancers (ballerinas, dancers and *corps de ballet*), sublimely united, absorbed the interest of the public. Therewith, however, went a new-born enthusiasm for Russian music: an enthusiasm which finally was to establish the empire of that Russian music which Diaghilev had done so much to familiarize in the past two years, and to which the excellence of his conductor E. R. Kuper —it must be said—largely contributed. Names such as Glinka, Tchaikovsky, Borodin, Rimsky-Korsakov, Mussorgsky, Glazunov, were to be heard on every lip. But not all criticism was enthusiastic, for we find J. Tugendhold writing of *Le Festin* "conveying a painful impression as of some Court entertainment, though certain features cannot be denied a very real interest." On the other hand, V. Svetlov claims that "the Paris public and critics have been deeply interested in the artistry and ensemble of the production." *Le Festin* was put together from Rimsky-Korsakov's march in *Le Coq d'Or,* Glinka's *Lesginka,* Tchaikovsky's *Bird,* Glazunov's *Czardas,* and the finale from the second symphony by Tchaikovsky.

Much less understood and appreciated was the choreography of the Russian Ballet, and the Press found little to say of this aspect. No doubt the reasons were many, but clearly the spectators, as well as the critics, were so carried away by the beauty of the spectacle, the excellence of the performers, and the enchantment of the music, that they did not realize the extent to which the beauty of the dance pattern contributed to the perfection of what they were seeing. But further, so low had the French Ballet sunk by the beginning of the twentieth century, that ballet criticism had become a lost art. There was a complete dearth of really competent choreographic criticism. Since, however, no self-respecting newspaper could afford to ignore something to which all Paris was flocking, the Press was forced to resort to what was said by the Russian Ballet critics, material which it then adapted to its own use, and, heaven knows, "inspired" was the last word which could be applied to it. Again, and this was the more usual practice, they would seek the opinions of painters, and particularly, musicians, who, naturally, gazed at the ballet through their own spectacles. And here it may be said that it is just this very approach which continues to prevail even to our day, so that all too frequently ballets, though conceived in terms of dancing, are, alas! valued only for their music.

Now that twenty years of Russian Ballet have brought about a rebirth in the French Ballet, which today may justifiably claim a world-wide pre-eminence, it is difficult to picture to oneself the decay of dancing in France some thirty years ago. In those days the ballet was treated as a survival from some dim past: meaningless and sterile, it seemed to have abandoned all hope of resuscitation. Thus, although the public responded with particular enthusiasm to the Russians, their appeal lay, it was said, in their barbaric, exotic and other qualities hardly to be found in a civilized community. No one could object to crowning it with laurels, for the national pride was in no way involved. However, in 1911, we find a salutary change beginning to take place.

And indeed what could be more characteristic than these two articles, from the hands of Abel Bonnard and Marcel Prévost, both written in 1910?

Says the former: "Really, we no longer know what dancing is. We are not savage enough. As a community, we are too civilized, too polished, too prone to self-effacement. We have lost the knowledge of how to express feeling with the whole of our bodies: why, we are almost afraid to let it transpire in our features, or in the words we utter, so that all that remains is for it to seek refuge in our eyes. Our very gestures have become impoverished, restricted, tight, and fall from us like branches from lopped trees. We all live in our heads. Our bodies, so to speak, have been abandoned and we no longer exist in them: they have become, as it were, impoverished and foreign to us, and have lost that palpitating sincerity which makes savages and the beasts of the wild so magnificent in our eyes. Thus it is only too comprehensible that that art which lives by reproducing man, sculpture, should be fading away at the same rate.

"Think then, how great must be one's joy at recapturing through this dancing, all the bewildering modalities of the human body and its richness of gesture, for no longer do we find ourselves merely gazing at those drear gymnastics, so characteristic of our ballerinas. Here, once more, in the vivacity of this miming, we see feeling expressed, not merely upon the narrow stage of the features, but as a living force from the crown of the head to the toes, and so molding the material it inspires that, for an instant, the whole body is joy or sadness to the very tips of the fingers; a clear hieroglyph of rage, hatred or desire."

The attitude expressed by Marcel Prévost is very similar:

"What reassurance such a renaissance conveys to the ancient lovers of this delightful art, childlike and venerable both, rare *dilettanti,* their ranks cruelly thinned by death, now standing on the threshold of the 20th century. One of these, as we left the theater yesterday, after seeing *Schéhérazade* bore witness to his happiness, his enthusiasm, in moving lyrical terms. He was ready to chant his *Nunc Dimittis:* yet he was leaving an Opera House in which the *élite* of the city had acclaimed a ballet.

"'After so long an eclipse,' he cried, tears of joy on his lashes, 'the dance will once more reign over Paris.'

"Old balletomane, my friend, do not rejoice too soon. I see indeed that the 'Russian Season' in Paris is enjoying a brilliant success. But to collect such a company would be impossible in Paris. It could not be got together in any democratic country.

"For, in the first place, who would form these young priestesses of the dance, needing as they do a hundred times the care, the growth, the flowering that some rare orchid, some exquisite chrysanthemum demands? Yes, I know....Ballerinas too are trained in Paris....And we applaud them when we see them in our Opera House. No matter! The truth is, that among us, this most moving of all arts, in which the female body is both the substance and the instrument, is utterly decadent. Yet how many neophytes devote themselves seriously to study in hopes of winning fame, fortune and glory...? Yes, our little French girls would need the most imperious of vocations to win through. How little our usual ballets compel the interest of real lovers of dancing! A sort of convention, a free and easy relation, has been established between the artists and the public. Priestesses without faith run through their outworn rites in front of skeptical, inattentive devotees.

"The pleasure which, this season, has been given to us by the Russian dancers, is therefore exclusively a pleasure for *the happy few*. We are incapable of preparing it for ourselves. They have come from afar expressly for our delight, and some few of us relish their archaic and subtle flavor; but the crowds that rush to the music halls will not follow us there....Old devotee, my friend, do not therefore shed pious tears of joy over the renaissance of your cherished art: this art is dead among us, utterly dead, and nothing will ever resuscitate it....Let us content ourselves with applauding it, and delighting when it is here. A courtly pleasure, a royal entertainment, let us reserve for the dance the welcome Paris reserves for queens."

During the seasons of 1910-1911, however, the Paris critics began to manifest a greater competence where choreography was concerned, and did not hesitate to express a qualified enthusiasm for *Les Sylphides,* very different from the triumph accorded to both *Prince Igor* and *Cléopâtra*. This, it is true, might have been expected, for *Les Sylphides* was conceived in a European and romantic manner, to music by Chopin, with which all were familiar, by a Russian chore-author, whose vision of the "romantic movement" differed greatly from that of his European compeers, much to the confusion of Paris audiences. The same phenomenon took place a year later with Schumann's *Carnaval*. But what, in fact, were the critics expecting of the Russian Ballet? Only that it should be *exotic,* an exoticism admirably represented by the whirling dances and bacchanalian color of *Prince Igor* and *Le Festin*. For the same reasons, *Le Pavillon d'Armide* was only moderately well received, if we except the pictorial side of the ballet and the fame of the dancers, since there was but little which was typically Russian in either the music or dances, and Fokine was still clinging to the traditions of the academic ballet.

If the French Press, however, gave but little space to choreography, because the music and decorative aspects of the Ballet forced the choreography into the background and because critics of choreography were lacking, another reason also existed, and one inherent in the Ballet, namely, the apparent absence of any unifying trend. For this Fokine's choreography must be held responsible, since all the onlooker saw were widely diverging trends, ranging from a *divertissement, Le Festin,* through a dance poem, *Les Sylphides,* and a full ballet, conceived almost in Petipa's tradition, *Le Pavillon d'Armide,* to the exaltation and bacchanalian riot of *Prince Igor* and the dramatic action of *Cléopâtra*—and from which, taken as an *ensemble,* no clear indication of the young chore-author's creative abilities could be gathered. The permanent critic of the Russian Ballet, himself a member of its unofficial artistic committee, V. Svetlov, did indeed make some attempt to expound Fokine's choreography, but even this sworn ballet critic's appreciations reveal themselves as inadequate and vague. Though admitting certain defects in *Le Pavillon d'Armide,* he limits himself to the statement that it represents "a transitional step in Fokine's creative progress from the old forms to the new." His remarks on the magnificent dance scene, it can hardly be called a ballet, in *Prince Igor,* seem somewhat more to the point, but once he has praised the *Polovtsian Dances,* which, in his words, "had become the talk of all artistic Paris, and proved a veritable eye opener to the painters, artists and impresarios as to the quality of our choreographic art," Svetlov abstains from proceeding further, and contents himself with saying that "Fokine has even managed to establish a choreographic design for the counterpoint of Borodin's score."

In another place, this chronicler of the Russian Ballet affirms that *Les Sylphides* and *Cléopâtra* are, as it were, the "twin poles of choreography." The first for him was a "white ballet," a "memory of Taglioni," "pure and aerial classicism": whereas *Cléopâtra* represents "a break with all the old tradition."

"*Cléopâtra,*" he wrote, "is an overturning of all the old standards, a negation of classical technique, of traditional canons. *Cléopâtra* is the 'new factor,' a vitally interesting excursus into the realms of archaeological iconography and ethnographical dancing."

This phrase "archaeological iconography" seems admirably appropriate. The inspiration for this ballet did indeed issue from such a source, and for that very reason Bakst's part in it was all important. This critic of the Russian Ballet is entirely justified in speaking of the "twin poles of choreography" represented by Fokine's ballets. All that it was necessary to add, was the fact that these poles are a permanent characteristic of all Fokine's work, which, turn and turn about, accepted and rejected the "classic" tradition of the Ballet.

Preparations for the 1910 season

This first season had proved immensely successful, and as a result the fame of the Ballet spread far beyond the confines of Paris, proof being the offers which flooded in on the leading dancers from all parts of the world. London was eager to have Pavlova, Karsavina, Rosay, and Schollar, America was eager for Pavlova, Karsavina and Fokine, and Italy too made tempting offers to the latter.

The season ended, Diaghilev returned to St. Petersburg and set about preparing his next season, that of 1910. It was a task of peculiar difficulty, for the immense success of the last made it incumbent on him not only to ensure the maintenance of the same high standard, but even to see it surpassed. Again, there was the question of finance: but this was satisfactorily dealt with by including Baron Dmitri Gunsburg as co-director. It proved an admirable choice, and such was the latter's faith in Diaghilev, that Serge Pavlovitch was left with entire freedom of action, while he himself limited his activities to producing his checkbook as occasion demanded, an operation that needed to be frequently repeated, for in spite of often very considerable takings, swollen by packed houses and increased prices, Diaghilev's wildly expensive productions always outran his budget. In his passion to present the world with magnificent productions, Diaghilev neglected all other considerations. It was his one problem, and no other could make the least impression upon him. A perfect friendship united the two men, save for a period between 1913 and 1914, when Diaghilev, who deemed the Baron in part responsible for Nijinsky's marriage, was anxious to oust him from the company, though it was found impossible owing to the Ballet's financial obligations. The war interrupted Gunsburg's connection with the ballet, and he perished in 1919, in Russia, during the civil war.

Thus we find Diaghilev actively engaged in trying to strengthen his troupe, and successfully enrolling Lydia Lopokova from the Mariinsky Theater, the Muscovite *diva* Ekaterina Geltzer, prima ballerina to the Imperial Grand Theater, and the male dancer Volinin. But the painters, as before, were Bakst, Golovin and Benois, for their worth had been proved, and Serge Pavlovitch owed much of his success to their efforts. Meanwhile a new conductor was engaged, in the person of Gabriel Pierné. What, however, absorbed Diaghilev's greatest efforts was the choice of his forthcoming programs, and the infinity of detail necessitated by that choice. In the upshot we see the strong opposition of two distinct tendencies in Diaghilev's mind: on the one hand, a constant urge towards the classic ballet of the past; on the other, a modernistic and even iconoclastic trend. Thus, we find him wishing to render unto Paris, that which France had herself created and long forgotten, though still preserved inviolate in Russia. But, at the same time, he wished to repeat the great success enjoyed by *The Polovtsian Dances,* the Russian Ballet's most recent creation.

No ballet, therefore, seemed more appropriate to the first of these aims, than *Giselle,* Diaghilev's best-loved ballet, which, for one reason or another, had not been ready in time for the previous season. Accordingly

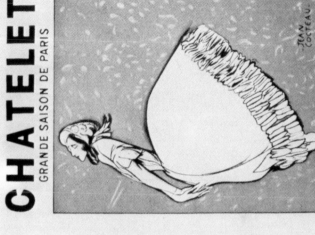

Karsavina, by Jean Cocteau, 1911

Ballet Russe Posters

Pavlova, by Serov, 1909

it was arranged that Pavlova, incomparable in the part, should dance in it, with Nijinsky as her partner. As it happened, however, Pavlova broke her contract, and Giselle was danced by Karsavina.

A second ballet in the classical tradition was found in a work but lately produced by Fokine for the ball held by the review *Satiricon*—Schumann's *Carnaval*. Moved to enthusiasm, Diaghilev arranged to include it in his 1910 program.

More difficult to discover, however, was a ballet that should be both Russian and original, and next to find an appropriate score for it. A choice had already been made of *Schéhérazade*, to a slightly altered score of Rimsky-Korsakov's symphonic poem of that name. Thematically, however, this music had never been intended for dancing, and in addition the story itself differed considerably from that of the proposed ballet. Contemplated also was another ballet, *L'Oiseau de Feu*, for which it was necessary to find music of a purely Russian nature, and consequently an appropriate composer. Whereupon Diaghilev appealed to A. K. Liadov the composer of *Baba-Yaga* and a well-known collector of Russian folk songs. Liadov's capacity for procrastination, unfortunately, was almost mythical, with the result that, when Benois, three months after he had accepted the commission, asked casually how the music was progressing, Liadov replied with the utmost simplicity:

"Oh, excellently. I've already bought the music-paper...."

Some other composer had therefore to be found. Luckily Serge Pavlovitch already knew what he wanted, for, during a pupils' concert in the Conservatoire at St. Petersburg, he had heard a short symphonic poem by a youthful musician composed in honor of his professor's[1] daughter, by which Diaghilev had been greatly impressed. This work was entitled *Feu d'Artifice,* and the composer's name was Igor Stravinsky. Solely on the strength of this work, Diaghilev was convinced—and throughout his life would boast of the fact—that Igor Stravinsky was indubitably a genius, and the future leader of modern music. This event took place in 1909, and there and then Diaghilev commissioned Stravinsky to orchestrate two excerpts from *Les Sylphides,* after which he commissioned the score of *L'Oiseau de Feu.* In Stravinsky, he recognized a new trend in Russian music, original and contemporary—the absolute subordination to rhythm of the broad melody that was essentially characteristic of his predecessors, the "Big Five."

Nevertheless it does not appear that Diaghilev asked himself whether this new rhythmic form would prove appropriate to dancing. Had he done so we may feel sure that dancing would willingly have been sacrificed to music, for what mattered to him and those about him was the intrinsic quality of the music rather than its greater or less suitability to the dance. It must also be remembered that dancing was then being subordinated more and more to music, and that chore-authors had begun

[1] N. Rimsky-Korsakov.

to claim an ability to make their dancers render no matter what score, provided the music was of good enough quality.

R. Brussel tells how, visiting St. Petersburg in 1909, he was invited by Diaghilev to come and hear a new and unperformed ballet read by a young friend of his, the composer.

"At the appointed hour, we all met in the little ground-floor room on Zamiatine Pereulok, which saw the beginnings of so many magnificent productions.

"The author, young, slim, and uncommunicative, with vague meditative eyes, and lips set firm in an energetic-looking face, was at the piano. But the moment he began to play, the modest and dimly lit dwelling glowed with a dazzling radiance. By the end of the first scene, I was conquered; by the last, I was lost in admiration. The manuscript on the music rest, scored over with fine pencilings, revealed a masterpiece. The musician was Igor Stravinsky, the ballet *L'Oiseau de Feu*.

"And now Diaghilev possessed the talisman able to open all those secret doors which hid and closed the future. The influence he wished to wield, the battle he was determined to wage was now his to choose or renounce, for the predestined being had entered his life."

Igor Stravinsky and the Ballet

Thus, with Stravinsky, a new force entered Diaghilev's creative existence, and a man with whom the fate of the Russian Ballet was henceforth inexorably to be linked. Diaghilev had not the slightest doubt of Stravinsky's genius, and did all in his power to gain it world-wide acceptance. His whole life bore testimony to this single conviction. Stravinsky's name on a score so vouched for its excellence in his eyes, that even when he felt it to be quite unsuitable, as in the case of the oratorio *Oedipus Rex,* in 1927, or disliked it frankly, he would not hesitate to present it, or to consider he lacked understanding. It was impossible, and that he was convinced of, for Stravinsky to write anything unworthy of himself. Only, it must be added that, towards the end of his life, Diaghilev began to doubt whether all Stravinsky's work revealed the same genius.

A lasting friendship united the two men, echoes of which we find in Stravinsky's *Chronicle of My Life*. Stravinsky had the highest admiration for his friend, an admiration all the more genuine in that it had not the faintest tinge of sycophancy. Stravinsky worked intimately with Diaghilev over a considerable period. For men of such dissimilar temperaments their collaboration was astonishingly harmonious. That is not to say that they did not have disagreements. Once he had determined on a course of action, Diaghilev would pursue it with a strength and perseverance that was almost frightening. To maintain against him a difference of opinion, even on matters of detail, was to provoke violent resistance.

But whatever the disagreements on questions of means, the collaborator had always the consolation, that once preliminary difficulties were settled, the common end was certain to be achieved.

Stravinsky admired Diaghilev's pertinacity; he admired no less his astonishing *flair*. Diaghilev was capable, he admits, of the most exact rational thinking. But that was not his natural medium. What he valued most highly was freshness and originality. These qualities, wherever he found them—and he could find them in the most unlikely places—would excite him to unreasoning enthusiasm. Sometimes, of course, his passionate temperament would lead him to disaster. But his intuitive judgment was seldom at fault, and once his decision was made, nothing could prevent its fulfilment.

Such were the main features of Diaghilev as Stravinsky saw them. But there was nothing in Diaghilev that was not characteristic. Like many others who came into close contact with him, Stravinsky was struck by the strange streak of ingenuousness in Diaghilev's character. Being himself highly competent—shrewd almost—in practical matters, Diaghilev could not tolerate inefficiency in others. He was horrified by ignorance of the world. He never seemed to resent, even in those nearest to him, what can only be described as doubtful honesty, provided he found in them other compensating qualities. Even when he was himself the victim, he would display no indignation, but remark, ingenuously, "Well, what of it? He's looking after himself."

In the twenty years of its existence, the Russian Ballet presented eight ballets to music by Stravinsky: *L'Oiseau de Feu, Petrouchka, Le Sacre du Printemps, Le Chant du Rossignol, Pulcinella* (Pergolesi-Stravinsky), *Le Renard, Les Noces, Apollon Musagète,* in addition to two operas, *Mavra* and *Rossignol,* an oratorio, *Oedipus Rex,* and a symphonic tableau, *Feu d'Artifice.* Incontestibly, Stravinsky was one of the main driving forces of the ballet and in the years 1910 to 1913 exerted as much influence upon it, as did its other art directors, Bakst and Benois. As they, by their painting, decided the nature, and often the very design of the dancing, so Stravinsky, with his scores, mapped the outlines of the dance pattern, and so determined the character of the whole ballet. The ballet was thus compelled to illustrate the music, and the ballet master, obliged to engage in a perpetual struggle with often insurmountable difficulties, had no alternative but to abandon his own conceptions, and frequently "fake" the dancing. Here is what I myself have written in my book, *Ballet, Traditional to Modern:* "M. Stravinsky's music, richly and fundamentally rhythmic, was by a curious misunderstanding, taken for dance music. Not everything rhythmic is necessarily danceable, not all that makes our muscles contract is necessarily dancing. I shall even go further—nothing is more opposed to dancing than M. Stravinsky's music of the first period with the exception of *Petrouchka,* in which popular dance music is largely used, and that is because of its *non-dancing* rhythms and above all on account of its changes of rhythm, truly opposed to dancing....A score by M. Stravinsky enfeebles dancing and weighs it down, and enslaves it rather than serves to embellish it; on the other hand dancing never enhances M. Stravinsky's music, as it does that of Weber or Adam. Stravinsky's music is so beautiful in itself that it is all sufficient: it has no need of any dancing addition, and dancing only serves to distract the listener's attention: here we touch on an important point—Why are the best ballets never those arranged to the most beautiful music?" [2]

To this we may add that the *terre-a-terre* quality which in time became so characteristic of Diaghilev's ballets was, to a considerable degree, the result of its association with Stravinsky's music and, in particular, with that especial favorite of Diaghilev's *Le Sacre du Printemps.*

Stravinsky himself was always at odds with the chore-authors for overloading their ballets with dances. In *L'Oiseau de Feu*—and his criticism in this case is typical of his general attitude—he felt that Fokine's choreography was so elaborate, so burdened with details of movement and pose, that it was impossible for the artists to co-ordinate properly dance and music. It is important not to misrepresent Stravinsky's argument. He is far from arrogating to himself chief credit for the success of *L'Oiseau de Feu.* He does not underrate the part played by Golovin's décors and by the dancers themselves. Above all he does not deny the importance of the choreography; for Fokine as a choreographer he had indeed the highest respect. What he deplored was an unharmonic relation between the *pas* of the dance and the measures of the music.

In a sense, Stravinsky is perfectly right, for to avoid "this unpleasant discordance between the movements of the dance and the imperative demands which the music imposed" it was necessary to reduce all gesture to a minimum and not, as he states, overburden the ballet with it.

But, needless to say, no choreographer could agree to such an impoverishment of the ballet.

Stravinsky and Diaghilev

With 1914, however, the connection between Stravinsky and the Russian Ballet for a time ceased, and no new contribution was made by him. Some indication that all was not well between Diaghilev and the latter, reaches us through Romola Nijinsky's book on her husband, in the part which deals with their halt at Lausanne on their way to America:

"He [Stravinsky] spoke to Vaslav for hours of his plans, his compositions, the ideas of Diaghilev, his injustices: the torrent of his words never seemed to stop. He tried to assure himself he was independent of him.

"I'm a composer, and sooner or later people will realize the value of my music. Of course, Serge Pavlovitch is a great help, and especially now

[2] Lifar. *Ballet, Traditional to Modern,* p. 168.

that the war is on. In Russia, anyhow, it is impossible to be played when one has modern ideas. He can't crush me.'

"One evening he came to us in a frightful temper. This time Diaghilev really had played him a dirty trick. It was arranged that as soon as Serge Pavlovitch arrived in New York, he should arrange that an official invitation should be extended to Stravinsky, who was to go and conduct his own ballets at the Metropolitan. This would be an appropriate occasion to present himself to the American public. But as soon as in New York, Serge Pavlovitch forgot his promise.[3] Naturally Stravinsky was hurt at this lack of attention. He insisted that if Vaslav was a real friend, he would make it a condition to go to America only if Stravinsky was asked also. I thought this was rather stretching the bounds of friendship. Stravinsky talked, raged, and cried: he paced up and down the room, cursing Diaghilev.

"'He thinks he is the Russian Ballet himself. Our success went to his head. What would he be without us, without Bakst, Benois, you and myself? Vaslav, I count upon you.'"[4]

Stravinsky's "real friend," however, left without him, and later we find Vaslav's "real friend" in his *Chronicle of My Life* writing of his friend in a way no one could consider even friendly or well meaning....

Nevertheless, in 1920, Stravinsky once more returned to the Ballet, though only for a period of three years. Then, in 1923 (with the single, though fortunate, exception of *Apollon Musagète*—1928) we find him finally repudiating the ballet, his religious convictions no longer permitting him to employ his art in anything so base as theatrical ballet. (Indeed a letter to Diaghilev at this time speaks of the ballet as *"l'anathème du Christ."*) Thus, Diaghilev felt it the more bitterly, when he learned that Stravinsky had "taken service under Ida Rubinstein" in her competing ballet.

In the course of time, a close friendship had grown up between the two men, and it was only towards the very end that their friendship was troubled. The misunderstandings began with the rehearsals for *Apollon,* Serge Pavlovitch considering the "Terpsichore Variation" far too long, tedious, and generally unsatisfactory. He therefore advised Stravinsky, either to omit it completely, or to make a number of cuts; but these suggestions the latter repudiated completely. Diaghilev then, on his own initiative, had the variation omitted at the second performance, on the pretext of the ballerina's indisposition.

"But of course it will be put back at the third performance?" To which, Diaghilev somewhat vaguely replied, "Of course, of course." The "of course" however failed to materialize, and a somewhat amusing episode resulted, for the "audience" then protested. Since I was dancing the part of Apollo, and knew that the variation was being omitted, I had

---

[3] Actually he had not forgotten, he did his best but without success.
[4] Romola Nijinsky. *Nijinsky,* pp. 307-9.

left my pedestal, and was preparing to dance, when three scattered voices in the audience began shouting:

"*Variation de* Terpsichore! *Variation!*"

It was the musician's relatives voicing the "general" protest! ...

After the production of *Apollon* in London, Diaghilev organized a gala performance in Stravinsky's honor, consisting entirely of ballets to the latter's music, at which, in the name of all, a crown of bays was presented to him. This, however, was to prove his last act of homage to his friend.

Apollon had always meant very much to Serge Pavlovitch, who, in the course of time, had come to consider it the property of the Russian Ballet, and so it greatly annoyed and distressed him when rumors began to be heard that Stravinsky was offering the work to Ida Rubinstein for her own ballet.

As a result Diaghilev asked Stravinsky directly whether there was any truth in the rumors that he had suggested *Apollon* to Ida Rubinstein. Stravinsky in a letter denied categorically that the story had any foundation whatsoever; he denied that he ever offered his works to anyone. What, apparently, had given rise to the rumors—and this Stravinsky admits—was that Ida Rubinstein, among many others, had approached Stravinsky's publishers, Paichadze, about the possibility of a production of *Apollon*. For the time being Diaghilev was satisfied.

This letter of Stravinsky to Diaghilev is, from another point of view, of the highest significance, especially the concluding paragraph, in that it vividly reveals the paths, opposite though they were, by which, in 1928, both Diaghilev and Stravinsky were withdrawing from the arts; Diaghilev through his passion for book-collecting, Stravinsky through mysticism and religion.

In this case the two men had, so to speak, common ground in Diaghilev's intended visit to Mount Athos. Diaghilev was attracted chiefly by the magnificent books and manuscripts for which the monasteries of Mount Athos have been famous since the Middle Ages. For Stravinsky Mount Athos was a holy shrine, the traditional treasure house of Greek theology and learning. It is typical that in his letter Stravinsky asks Diaghilev to bring back for him a number of oleographs of sacred pictures and a wooden cross, which he begs Diaghilev to have blessed for him there, on Mount Athos. He asks too, perhaps as a concession to Diaghilev's tastes, for a catalogue of all works in Russian and church-Slavonic that were for sale.

Shortly after, Diaghilev learned that Stravinsky had indeed, as he put it, "sold himself" to Ida Rubinstein, and was composing ballets for her, ballets which made him "shudder with disgust." ("I have just got back from the theater with a severe headache caused by sheer horror of what I saw and heard, particularly of Stravinsky's," he wrote to me later.) In

his letters about this ballet season of hers, he goes on to wish that someone "would blow up these old barracks with their audiences, their redheaded...who imagine themselves artists because of the millions they
can squander and the composers they can buy." So great was Serge Pavlovitch's disappointment in Stravinsky that he even wished to doom him
also to the same destruction. With what satisfaction he accuses Stravinsky of hypocrisy, as, in another letter, he relates how Stravinsky had
expressed his admiration for one of Ida Rubinstein's performances: "Delightful, I say it from the bottom of my heart...delightful..." contrast-
ing it with a telephone message to himself next morning, in which
Stravinsky said he had felt nothing but regret, mingled with disgust. Full
of bitterness, Diaghilev notes: "Stravinsky, our famous Igor, my first
son, has given himself up entirely to the love of God and cash."
(Diaghilev always considered Stravinsky his first, Prokofiev his second,
and Dukelsky his third, son.)

By 1928 Diaghilev had lost all further interest in Stravinsky. But how
very different had been the sacred springtime of their friendship in
1909-10!

1910: *The triumph of "Schéhérazade" and "L'Oiseau de Feu"*

The spring of 1910 once more welcomed Diaghilev in Paris, but now
he had with him the very pick of what he had found in Russia, in addition to the repertoire of the preceding season. He brought new productions, *Schéhérazade, L'Oiseau de Feu, Carnaval, Les Orientals* and
Giselle. Generally speaking, the new program followed the lines laid
down in 1909: indeed, there was in many ways an exact parallel between
the two seasons. The orientalism of *Cléopâtra* found its equivalent in
Schéhérazade, the *divertissement* of *Le Festin* in *Les Orientales*—a ballet,
by the way, which was never revived—the romantic *Sylphides* in *Carnaval,* while even *Giselle* linked up through Théophile Gautier with *Le
Pavillon d'Armide*. It was a parallelism which threw into relief the
manner in which the Russian Ballet had developed, and the full extent
of its ambitions. No one could doubt that *Schéhérazade* showed immense progress when compared with *Cléopâtra,* and the coruscating
L'Oiseau de Feu lost nothing in comparison with *The Polovtsian Dances*.

Diaghilev's ambitions were fully gratified, and the new season in truth
exceeded in splendor all that had gone before. With justice, the Paris
correspondent of the review *Apollon* could write that, "although barely
a week has elapsed since the Russian performances began, they have
achieved a tremendous success in spite of Pavlova's absence."

Nevertheless, though this season met with greater success than its
predecessor, that success expressed itself more temperately. Originally, the
audience had, as it were, been swept away by so great a profusion of
riches, whereas now its appreciation, though deeper, was far less boister-

ous. The public was beginning to know and understand better what Diaghilev was seeking.

The season made its début with *Carnaval, Schéhérazade* and a *divertissement,* all of which were received with an acclamation that left no doubt as to the success of future performances. Later, additional novelties were introduced into the program, of which *Giselle* and *Carnaval* proved the least successful, the time evidently *not being ripe* to return to Paris what France had created. I italicize "not being ripe" for eventually *Giselle* was revived for the Paris Opéra where it became, and is, one of the most successful ballets in the repertoire. In addition, the public had come to expect works specifically Russian, and for that reason experienced some disappointment. European romanticism, as refracted through Russian prisms, could hardly satisfy the French taste, as we see by the following quotation from Jean Louis Vaudoyer:

"There is already a sufficient tendency to daydreaming in the tender irony, the fragile smiles which one finds in Schumann's *Carnaval,* for one to regret seeing, superimposed on these sound-images, the somewhat less satisfactory materializations of the decorator and costumier....Let us therefore ignore Schumann's contribution, and gazing at the green stage-cloth, allow the eternal marionettes to lay at callous feet their tiny, wooden, painted hearts.

"Bergamo and Gavarni, it may be, have not revealed to these Russians the inner secrets of their grace. Their nonchalance perhaps seems somewhat forced, their interpretations perhaps too obvious, the sparkle overdone, and the whole perhaps too heavy. Perhaps it is all too reminiscent of a German champagne. Asti, swimming with Como's flowers, or the wines of our France, produces a headier intoxication. This Pierrot darts too heavily over the stage, and Pantaloon's walk in a goose-step. Miming is a question of latitude, and it is a mistake to exile it from its own country. Eusebius, in Naples, may perhaps find some healing for his melancholy, but Harlequin, beneath northern skies, languishes and softens to mere sweetness; even his dazzling clothes, here, under our skies, become sad diamonds, faded like the petals of the 'little blue flower.'

"That divine simplicity, which is the essence of the great Watteau, as also of the lesser Guardi, which impregnates both *Fantasio* and *Il Barbiere,* is a Latin treasure which, with Mozart, we alone know how to utilize. We were better pleased with the first act of *La Fête chez Thérèse* than with this *Carnaval,* which may be appreciated nevertheless for a certain harmony, frank and sober, and lovely details, such as Chiarina's robe with its blue flounces—when bearing her two roses, she so strangely resembles those shapes one guesses beneath the dark waters of some daguerreotype."

First and foremost among the Ballet's triumphs was undoubtedly *Schéhérazade,* but it was largely Bakst to whom that success was due. With the very rising of the curtain, storms of thunderous applause rang out in recognition of the painter's genius. Indeed, the public went quite mad about Bakst's sets and costumes, and their success eclipsed everything Diaghilev had so far presented. Later, the designs were bought by the Musée des Arts Décoratifs with the Press's universal approval. Somewhat different, however, was the reception accorded to the music, and many a critic thundered against the manner in which, according to them, Rimsky-Korsakov's music had been maltreated and distorted. As a result a spirited polemic ensued, maintained to some extent by the indignant protests of the composer's widow. One section of the critics, it is true, found the procedure entirely legitimate, but another, with Pierre Lalo at its head, attacked Diaghilev for desecration, and for condoning a "criminal" practice. Nevertheless, even Pierre Lalo, in spite of his indignation, could find nothing but praise for this production:

"And yet, ridiculous and shocking as this falsification of the meaning, the expression of the music may be, one almost forgets it when one sees *Schéhérazade,* so overwhelming is the magnificence, the originality of the spectacle presented to our eyes. On the stage, the very simplest of décors, reduced to its basic forms, represents the interior of the Shah's harem, a sort of enormous tent of the intensest, most dazzling green, extraordinary in its richness and impact. There is no other color, to all intents and purposes, and only dimly does one perceive, on these huge green surfaces, a few vast outlines, Persian in origin, black or orange-red. The ground is covered by a similar orange-red carpet of a paler tone. On the ballet-cloth, blue doors that verge on blackness. The clothes worn by the men and women, for the most part, are in colors complementary to the décor, different shades of reds and a few greens. And against this background glitters and moves the golds and silvers of the amorous negroes. Here and there, deeper touches of color, like the Shah's robes, in which blues and somber violets strike the dominant note, and make one think of the loveliest Persian miniatures. The whole creates an ensemble miraculously harmonious and compelling; an enchantment that continually dazzles the eyes. M. Bakst, the Russian painter, who has composed this remarkable painting, linked up the colors of this décor and the costumes, is, in truth, a very great artist. And the spectator's delight is all the keener because, against this background of immobile fixed beauty, all is activity and constant variety. The groups of dancers and ballerinas come together and break up, and always there is the contrast, the merging of the differently colored costumes. All this movement, this billowing and flowing of color, has been worked out and developed with the most exquisite daring and assured art.

"*Schéhérazade* is without doubt one of the loveliest, perhaps the loveliest, of all the productions the Russians have offered us yet....

"See the amorous orgy of the negroes and the Shah's women, see the voluptuousness of the dances, the passion and frenzy of the gestures, the attitudes, the embraces; compare it with various scenes of orgy in our own ballets, and then you will realize which deserves pre-eminence."

It must be said, however, that *L'Oiseau de Feu* participated in this success. Certain critics, for instance, including R. Brussel and A. Bruneau, even expressed a greater admiration for the latter, in which they claimed to see a completer renunciation of tradition in favor of newer concepts of plastic design and motion. Thus we find M. Henri Ghéon writing: "*L'Oiseau de Feu,* being the result of an intimate collaboration between choreography, music and painting, presents us with the most exquisite miracle of harmony imaginable, of sound and form and movement. The old-gold vermiculation of the fantastic back-cloth seems to have been invented to a formula identical with that of the shimmering web of the orchestra. And as one listens, there issues forth the very sound of the wizard shrieking, of swarming sorcerers and gnomes running amuck. When the bird passes, it is truly the music that bears it aloft. Stravinsky, Fokine, Golovin, in my eyes, are but one name."

Thus we see the French critics more and more beginning to understand the real nature of what the Russians were trying to show them. So, too, we find M. Ghéon writing of *Schéhérazade:*

"It was inevitable that the day would come, when the organic and basic law which transformed opera into lyric drama, by suppressing all hors d'œuvres and acrobatics, and demanding utter obedience to basic principles, would need to be applied to the ballet. The honor of making the attempt must rest with the Russians, as must their successful accomplishment of it. Thus the ballet has become dancing. The moment it is no longer a simple *divertissement,* ballet asserts the privilege of pure dancing and imperiously calls to its aid the sublime art of music—an art from which it should never have been separated."

"Fœmina," in *Le Figaro,* addresses an imaginary interlocutor: "After all, these ballets are surely similar to others, though the décors are more charming and the costumes of a surer artistic taste...? They are *not* similar!

"The Russian dancers are possibly unaware of the mystic nature of their frenzy...? But it communicated itself to us, and that is why these productions are the revelation they have proved to me. Those who witnessed them boast of having observed this or that detail, this or that step, the lighting, grouping; then they part, feeling they have not really said what they wanted to say, left out the most essential....

"It is impossible. In the rapture one experiences at these performances, there is something too original, too new. It is as though something had happened which affected us deeply. We have seen dancing, and now see it for what it should be. Dancing, the faithful custodian of all our long and forgotten history, the holy dance! The dance before the altar, of the lover before his beloved, of the child before hope; the dance pious or fierce, commanded to the body by the soul, in which, for a moment, a god reigns."

Schéhérazade, 1910

How little this resembles the words of A. Bonnard, or M. Prévost, who speak of dancing as an exotic art, incapable of rebirth in a civilized country. A timid dream begins to arise of resuscitating the French Ballet. Camille Mauclair has put it into words in *La Revue,* in an article entitled "What We May Learn from the Russian Ballet": "Dancing, too, has no less brought its surprises, but in a very different way. On this occasion it has surprised us greatly to recognize, in Russian choreography, the principles of our ancient French choreography, absolutely forgotten today, but exported to Russia at the end of the 18th and the beginning of the 19th century by our own ballet masters. When it was said of Mlle. Salle or of Camargo that 'every step was an emotion,' it was as though Pavlova or Karsavina were already being spoken of; and the mimed dance of Nijinsky can alone restore to us some idea of what Vestris meant to our ancestors."

After which the author of this article sets his reader a number of questions.

"Where is there any indication of that measured, noble art in our *corps de ballet,* which hurls itself feverishly about in a fictitious Italian *furia,* in the livid illumination of a last judgment, and whose unbridled sensuality marks the limits of its capacity for expression? Where find an equivalent to that Dance of the Bowmen, in *Prince Igor,* sustained by that masterpiece of Borodin's, and lovely as a Persian miniature come to life? Where find that dance of *L'Oiseau de Feu,* in which Karsavina seems to defy the very laws of gravity, and is metamorphosed into a fairy? What theater of ours has ever put on dancing equal to that of the bacchanal in *Cléopâtre,* or the orgy of *Schéhérazade,* or beaten out a measure instinct with a melancholy, a fury, a languor so oriental and nostalgic as Rimsky-Korsakov's rhythms? Alas! how distant all this is from our own *coryphées* and *corps de ballets!*

"Among such troupes of dancers, discipline and good taste are *de rigueur,* and each in turn moves on from some unimportant rôle to that of a star, each in his turn and without an atom of jealousy....A Fokine inventing a ballet, to music by Debussy, and decorations by Maurice Denis, with a Karsavina on the stage, and a Messager to conduct, what a magnificent evening that would make...if it could ever be anything but a dream! But who will remake, from top to bottom, our own dancers and ballerinas? Who will deliver us from the ridicule of our own traditional ballet?"

Renaissance of ballet criticism

All this may seem very rhetorical, for the French Ballet could certainly have been resuscitated had it but followed Diaghilev's example, which demonstrated how necessary it was to break through the routine and convention that hamper all progress. Nevertheless, merely by the fact of having given Paris his two seasons in 1909-10, Diaghilev had already done much to solve the difficulties of the French Ballet, for he had cleared a path, greatly stimulated public interest, and set certain problems, connected with the aesthetics of dancing and ballet, which demanded immediate answers. And here I make a distinction between dancing and ballet, for in the latter the elements of the dance are inseparable from the arts which are associated with it. Last, but not least, Diaghilev helped to bring into existence a real criticism of the ballet, which at the turn of the century did not even exist.

In Russia, too, ballet criticism began to appear,—a fact which must be attributed entirely to Diaghilev's efforts, accompanied by many critical and philosophical articles, among the authors of which must be mentioned A. Volynsky and his disciple A. Levinson. That celebrated writer on dancing, A. A. Pleshcheyev, was always more the historian than the critic of the ballet, whereas others, like V. Svetlov and Prince S. M. Volkonsky, restricted themselves to its theory. Not for nothing does A. Levinson begin his long article, *On the New Ballet,* with the following words:

"...It is only recently, and by chance, that the history, the aesthetics, of the ballet have begun to exercise us. By chance, because, recent adepts of an ancient tradition, we have come to the Russian Ballet only after making an immense detour through Paris and Berlin. Meanwhile 'classical ballet' has meant nothing to us except as seen through the innovations of Fokine, and his protestant and reforming spirit."

Nevertheless, though he wrote in defense of the academic ballet, and attacked both Fokine and Diaghilev, it was to them that Levinson chiefly owed his love of the dance.

"Neophytes of the cult of Terpsichore, but recently indifferent, and perhaps antagonistic to this miraculous art, which today delights us so profoundly, it is not for us to talk of it categorically or dogmatically, or to define its aesthetic or trace out its paths...."

I shall have to revert to this article, dealing as it does with the seasons of 1909-10-11, and so shall confine myself now to one simple question. Why were these critical neophytes "but recently indifferent" and today "so profoundly delighted," when the only ballet in existence at that "today" was Diaghilev's ballet, which was then being so fiercely attacked?

The Russian Ballet permanently established

Triumphant as was the result of the 1910 season, it had, in one respect, the same unfortunate consequences as that of 1909, in that several of Diaghilev's artists abandoned him to accept excellent offers from many parts of the world. Thus it was necessary to find others to fill their places. But to this problem another and far more onerous problem was added, namely, that of establishing a permanent company. Thus far, Diaghilev's seasons had lasted but six weeks at a time, a period short enough to offer no difficulty to the artists of the Imperial Theaters in obtaining leave of absence, since it was really their "holidays" they were spending in this manner. But early in 1911 a drastic change took place, for he who had borne away such triumphs in Paris; he, who had revealed so vast a talent for organization; he, who had returned in a blaze of world-wide publicity, began to seem dreadfully dangerous to the administrators of the Imperial Theaters. An additional irritant was the fact that Diaghilev found it necessary, for his projects, to remain in constant contact with the best artists attached to the Imperial Theaters, singers, ballerinas and dancers, and this too made him an object of apprehension to the Grand Duke Serge Mikhailovitch, who was anxious to reinstate Teliakovsky as Principal Director of the Imperial Theaters. Whereupon an obscure struggle was engaged, which ended in the bitter destruction of all Diaghilev's hopes, consequent on Nijinsky's forced resignation.

This new fact made it necessary to think no longer in terms of a short six weeks' season, but in those of a permanent theater and established company. Alternately, he might manage to get Nijinsky attached to a great metropolitan theater, abandon all thought of an enterprise of his own, and find a post as artistic director for himself. The latter solution would perhaps have been easier, but was entirely unacceptable to Diaghilev's nature. Such difficulties as encumbered his path not only did not weaken his energy, but seemed to increase it tenfold. Eventually, Diaghilev was able to enlist some of the most brilliant artists in the Imperial Theaters who, like Bolm and Feodorova, were willing to resign their positions to join him. Even such splendid stars of the Mariinsky Theater as Kshesinskaya and Karsavina, while continuing to belong to the Imperial Theaters, were willing to lend their services to his company. Mastro Cecchetti, then a professor at the Theater School, and ballet master to the Mariinsky Theater, also agreed to join the new enterprise.

The year 1911 opened favorably. An international exhibition was about to be held in Rome, and London was preparing a series of Coronation festivities. Thereupon, Serge Pavlovitch determined to embark on a grand tour which would embrace Rome, Paris and London. Its organization, however, offered considerable difficulty, necessitating as it did numerous journeys across the length and breadth of Europe, the supervision of innumerable details, and all the effort associated with winning fresh support and establishing new connections.

In addition, it was necessary to establish the company in some permanent European center, where the needed preparatory work might be brought to completion. Such a center was eventually decided upon at Monte Carlo—and so it remained to the last day of the Russian Ballet's existence.

Now the feverish activities begun in St. Petersburg were resumed in Monte Carlo. The new creations for the forthcoming season were numer-

ous, and considerable difficulties attended them. These included the Stra-
vinsky-Benois-Fokine *Petrouchka,* continuing the tradition of *Prince Igor*
and *L'Oiseau de Feu;* the Vaudoyer-Weber-Bakst-Fokine *Spectre de la
Rose,* following the "romantic" *Sylphides* and *Carnaval;* a new ballet by
Tcherepnine-Bakst-Fokine, entitled *Narcissus;* the "submarine kingdom"
scene from *Sadko,* with sets designed by Anisfeldt; and the Dukas-Bakst-
Fokine ballet *La Péri,* in which Trukhanova was to star. But though her
appearance was announced, she and Diaghilev quarreled, and as a result
it was never presented. In addition, work went busily forward on the
London productions, these being *Le Lac des Cygnes* and an extract from
The Sleeping Beauty, entitled *Aurora and the Prince.* The moderate success of *Giselle* in 1910 had convinced Diaghilev that any production of a
nineteenth-century classical ballet in Paris would still be premature.

Creation of "Petrouchka" and "Le Spectre de la Rose"

The most important item of this season was undoubtedly the Stravin-
sky-Benois-Fokine *Petrouchka.* This year also saw Diaghilev's engagement of Pierre Monteux as conductor, an association which was to
continue for many years.

In his *Chronicle of My Life* Stravinsky gives, at length, an account of
his part in the creation of *Petrouchka.*

Stravinsky was staying at Clarens in Switzerland, a small town on the
Lake of Geneva. His immediate task, it seems, was to compose the music
for *Sacre du Printemps.* Before embarking on this formidable and arduous undertaking, he decided, by way of diversion, to write a work for
piano and orchestra. While he was composing it, he tells us, he had
clearly before his mind the image of a puppet miraculously come to life.

From Stravinsky's account it is a little difficult to understand precisely what part the puppet played. It appears that the music developed
as a quarrel between the puppet and the orchestra, in which the puppet
is defeated. The climax was a violent outburst of noise from the orchestra and the "death" of the puppet.

When the piece was finished Stravinsky searched for a title, a title
that would express precisely the character of the music, or rather of its
protagonist, the puppet.

At last the title came to him—Petrouchka, the traditional puppet hero
of every Russian carnival, and indeed, under different names, of every
fair in the world. It was inevitably right, and Stravinsky was overjoyed.

Not long afterwards Diaghilev arrived at Clarens, anxious to hear the
first sketches for *Sacre du Printemps.* Instead Stravinsky played to him
the work he had just finished. Diaghilev was enthusiastic. Relegating, for
the moment, *Sacre du Printemps,* he begged Stravinsky to expand the
idea of the puppet come to life into a whole ballet.

Stravinsky agreed and suggested, he tells us, the main lines on which the theme should be developed. During the rest of Diaghilev's visit, the two men worked together over the plot of the ballet.

Before Diaghilev left, the essential shape of the ballet *Petrouchka* was decided—the fair, the puppet theater, the conjuror, the characters of the three puppets, and Petrouchka's short tragic enjoyment of life. The music already written was allotted to the second scene—in which Petrouchka, passionate, frustrated, tries vainly to escape from his cell—and Stravinsky sets to work at once to compose the rest.

Such is the account given by Stravinsky of the origins of the ballet *Petrouchka*. The most important fact about it is that Stravinsky claims that it was he who first realized the significance of his "piano-concerto" as portraying the life of an animated Petrouchka.

Diaghilev himself tells the ctory very differently. According to him, Igor Stravinsky played him a "concert-piece" for piano, with no thought in his mind of *Petrouchka* or any ballet whatsoever, whereupon Diaghilev, in a burst of enthusiasm, suddenly cried:

"But that's a ballet! Why, that's *Petrouchka!*" [5]

The whole décor of the ballet, both scenery and costumes, was entrusted to Benois, the choreography to Fokine. Stravinsky has nothing but praise for Fokine's treatment of the *ensembles* and solo dances, but complains, in his *Chronicle of My Life,* that the crowd scenes were not worked with sufficient care. He makes the criticism—similar in principle to his criticism of the production of *L'Oiseau de Feu*—that details of movement were left to the whim of the individual artists, instead of being determined by the structure and character of the music.

Diaghilev's idea was to use the brothers Molozov in this ballet, but, to his great regret, he could conclude no satisfactory arrangement with them.

I now quote what J. L. Vaudoyer, author of the "argument" to *Le Spectre de la Rose* says about the origin of this ballet.

"It was performed for the first time in Paris, during the third ballet season. The idea of this *pas de deux* came to us, as we were writing some notes for *La Revue de Paris* on the first productions of the Russian Ballet, those of 1909 and 1910. By a sudden impulse, we had placed the

[5] The same story is repeated in the fine obituary notice on Diaghilev from the pen of one of his last collaborators, N. Nabokov, the composer of the music for the ballet *Ode:* "Sometime in the first decade of the present century, Stravinsky, then living in Switzerland, played over his piano-concerto to Diaghilev. The latter listened to it with extreme attention, and at the end exclaimed: 'But that is *Petrouchka!*' Thus it was that with his exceptional sensibility, his phenomenal artistic flair, he sensed the characteristics of a whole future epoch. The piano-concerto became *Petrouchka,* Stravinsky's greatest creation, and the most original ballet created by Fokine and Benois; possibly the best in the repertory of the Russian Ballet. It is important to note here that, at the time, *Petrouchka* was an absolutely new departure in music, that it became the forebear of a whole epoch, and revolutionized orchestral treatment. No less important is the fact that the composer himself did not realize the true importance of his 'piano-concerto'; that Diaghilev's prophetic insight was alone responsible for ..."

following lines from Gautier at the head of one such item dealing with Schumann's *Carnaval*:

> *'Je suis le spectre de la rose*
> *Que tu portais hier au bal.'* [6]

"When these pages appeared, in July, the Russian dancers were no longer in Paris, but our fresh and fervent memory still, in imagination, perpetuated their radiant presence. Again, we had not forgotten that Gautier had a particular predilection for Weber's music, and particularly for *L'Invitation à la Valse*. For that reason it occurred to us to associate that famous piano piece, orchestrated by Berlioz, and the romantic 'white reverie' in rhyme. Whereupon we immediately wrote to Bakst, suggesting the idea to him for a ballet. Summer, autumn, winter passed, but no reply was forthcoming. We were no longer thinking of *Le Spectre* when, in May, we received a note from Diaghilev requesting us to appear without delay in Monte Carlo, there to witness the final rehearsals of this trifling divertissement. Thus our letter, which we had imagined lost, had yet sufficed; and all was ready. Fokine had worked out the choreography, and Bakst had designed his décor and the costumes for the two parts: the specter would be Nijinsky and the girl, Karsavina. Unfortunately, it was not possible for us to go to Monte Carlo, with the result that the following month we made acquaintance with a *Spectre* complete in every detail, lovelier than anything we could have imagined, and divested of all that laborious groping, that experimentation, seeking and trial, which inevitably accompany any theatrical production, and which, like the somber wrappings of the chrysalis, swathe the butterfly with still shut wings."

In Rome, as in Paris, the Russian Ballet enjoyed an immense success, fully comparable with that in Paris, and, as was to be expected, *Petrouchka* was the keynote of that success. Indeed, this ballet must be considered one of the peak-points, if not the peak, of the Ballet's first epoch. But having attained such heights, the Ballet had now to choose between two alternatives, either to decline or seek further. It was not difficult to guess the choice made by Diaghilev. Meanwhile, *Petrouchka* was stimulating an immense amount of enthusiastic and critical writing, but, as in 1909 and 1910, attention was mainly concentrated on the scenery and costumes designed by Benois, the music composed by Stravinsky, and, least of all, on the "choreography." Even Veuillemin, who called this ballet "a miracle of choreographic art," saw the "miracle" as existing chiefly in the richness of Stravinsky's orchestration, whereas the critic for *Gil Blas* admired it as "a feast for the senses."

Jean Chantavoine, in a long article in *Comœdia*, provides perhaps the

---

[6] I am the spirit of the rose
You wore at last night's ball.

warmest tribute to this ballet: but here, too, one fails to discover any reference to the choreography.

Interesting and enthusiastic as such articles may be, one cannot help wondering what it all has to do with dancing.

Be that as it may, *Le Spectre de la Rose* fared somewhat better in this respect, being in fact one of Fokine's simplest, most perfect choreographic efforts, though hardly ambitious enough to be termed a ballet. Nevertheless, for over a quarter of a century it has held the stage with invariable and permanent success. The following remarks by R. Brussel are in the highest degree deserved by it:

"In the whole of this program one work stands out particularly for its charm and utter perfection, *Le Spectre de la Rose*. It is no concern of mine whether Gautier's fable, the materialization of the perfume of the rose to a young girl who has returned from a ball, is perfectly wedded to Weber's intention in the writing of *L'Invitation à la Valse*. One sole object only remains to be considered, the spectacle, and that spectacle is an exquisite one. To realize the overwhelming charm that choreography may attain, one must have seen this exquisite tableau. *Le Spectre de la Rose,* short as it is, and barren of every 'picturesque detail,' with its accompaniment of old and hackneyed music, is a sort of masterpiece."

Possibly less enthusiastically received than *Petrouchka* and *Le Spectre de la Rose,* though indubitably successful, was the submarine scene from *Sadko,* in which the vocal parts had been retained. Nevertheless, it contributed nothing especially original after *Cléopâtra, Schéhérazade,* and *L'Oiseau de Feu.* Tcherepnine's *Narcisse* proved even less popular.

First Appearance of the Russian Ballet in London

Meanwhile, Diaghilev was contemplating his approaching début in London with no little apprehension, a record of which has come down to us in his article written in French, dated 1926 and entitled *Les Quinze Ans.*

"In 1909, the Russian Ballet having made its début in Paris, a great and revered friend, the Marchioness of Ripon, wrote to me as follows:

"'I thought I had experienced everything life could offer—but you have brought a new joy into my life, the greatest and last—and you must come to London, for King Edward would simply adore your productions.' I saw Mr. George Edwardes in London, the successful manager of a number of London theaters, who immediately made me an offer, and it was arranged we should open at the Aldwych Theater in 1910. But the King died and we did not go. A year later Sir Joseph Beecham, encouraged by his son, Sir Thomas, arranged for us to appear at Covent Garden for the coronation of King George. But our dancers were so nervous that they could hardly dance. The auditorium was even more magnificent than the stage, the walls were hung with over a hundred thousand roses, and the boxes contained almost as many maharajahs. Our reception was icy, and neither Karsavina's variations, nor even those of Nijinsky in *Armide,* received the slightest applause. It was only after the dance of the buffoons that the strangest of sounds came to us: the public was gently clapping its kid-gloved hands.

"The next evening, however, came our real opening, which proved an immense success, though during the last ballet *The Prince Igor Dances,* half the public went home. At least a hundred old ladies, covered with diamonds as though they were icons, went out and past me, with a look of disgust on their faces. The business manager came running up, crying: 'You've spoiled your magnificent opening by this barbarian horror at the end—it isn't dancing—it's just savages prancing about.' The Press was of the same opinion! And it was only fifteen years ago!

"From then on, until the war, Beecham became our patron, and made an arrangement with me, which I confess worried me somewhat, for it was merely a letter, authorizing me to produce the finest ballets I could, and to engage the best artists—the whole of Russia—while he himself footed the bill. When, on one occasion, he wanted Chaliapin, Smirnov, Kusnetzova, Nijinsky and Karsavina all to appear in the same program, and I modestly protested, saying that the expense of such a production would be unheard of, he merely said it was none of my business."

So remarkable was the Russian Ballet's success in London that Diaghilev returned again in October for a season of almost three months. From that moment Monte Carlo, Paris and London became the three main centers of the Ballet's activities.

André Levinson as critic of the Russian Ballet

I have already said that there appeared in *Apollo* in 1911, a first long article, *On the New Ballet,* by the critic, A. Levinson. With this article, a brilliantly intelligent, talented and highly cultured critic of the ballet inaugurated a career, which, in books and articles, was to prove how fundamental and universal was his knowledge of the subject. For years, his articles appeared in *Comœdia,* and though at times one might dispute their conclusions, they never failed to be of the greatest interest. It almost appeared as though a most dangerous adversary of the ballet had sprung up—"appeared," I say, because in effect, however destructive that criticism may have seemed, the reader was nevertheless inspired to visit the theater, where, to his surprise, he would find himself enthusiastically applauding.

From the very first, A. Levinson declared himself an implacable, and at times prejudiced, adversary of the Russian Ballet and its chore-authors, beginning with Fokine. But though his criticism was brilliant, and only too often justified, more positive significance would have attached to it,

Pierre Monteux   Ansermet

Sir Thomas Beecham   Desormières

had it not been based on preconceptions of, at times, doubtful validity.

Having proclaimed himself champion and defender of "classical" ballet and dancing, and against the incursion of elements foreign to its nature, Levinson, though he drew attention to a number of abuses, which, as he claimed, had deformed and distorted the very nature of the dance, unfortunately made no real distinction between the primitive basis of the perpetually changing edifice of academic dancing, and certain precise moments in its history, as for instance, the condition in which he found it at the beginning of the twentieth century, in the Mariinsky Theater. His assumption that what was ephemeral in the art, was its eternal principle, and his defense of the latter in opposition to all that might foster evolution and progress in the perdurable but necessarily protean shape of the academic ballet and dancing, was the fundamental error which vitiated the foundations of all his reasoning.

Thus too, his view of Fokine, the first chore-author of the Russian Ballet was of necessity distorted, since he held him to be both revolutionary and one who sought to break down and destroy academic tradition; whereas, in fact, Fokine was merely a protestant, a reformer (I admit, I am here using Levinson's own epithets), one who, though forever swept away by his own enthusiasms, and often at fault, did, nevertheless, base all his creative work on purely academic principles.

When Levinson reverts to the errors and mistakes of Fokine and his successors, it is impossible not, at times, to agree; but the moment he begins to generalize and then to draw his erroneous conclusions, his prejudices vitiate everything he says. Indeed, so powerful did these prejudices prove, that practically no production met with his approval. Articles such as the following, consecrated to *Schéhérazade,* are but the exception and even then we see him attempting to minimize his praise:

"The women surround their incorruptible guard, the chief eunuch, with suppliant or imperious gestures; they murmur their secret desires in his ears, and when he turns indifferently away they seek to soften him by that lissome and languorous dance with which the orange-clad odalisques strive to distract the sovereign tedium of the Shah. This repetition, by three soloists, of the theme entrusted earlier to a whole crowd of dancers, is one of the most appealing inventions of the choreographer. Nevertheless, one must admit that, once the figure has been danced, practically the whole choreographic content of the ballet has been expended." [7]

Again, in *L'Oiseau de Feu,* Levinson is in error when he states that it lacks any element of real dancing. He is correct, however, in his observation of a certain tendency in Fokine, formulated as follows:

"Even in *L'Oiseau de Feu,* M. Fokine has had to suppress a number of his dances, but what was retained, is justified by him with an ardor only equaled by its hypocrisy. Thus, the dance of the bird is supposed to

---

[7] "Practically the whole" cannot but mean that something is left. Nevertheless he *is* careful to omit any mention of such other virtues as this ballet possesses.

represent the moment in which it takes to flight, that of the princesses a game at ball, that of Kastchei himself is justified by the spell cast over him by *L'Oiseau de Feu.*"

Again he manages to praise *Les Sylphides,* but here too this "lovely romantic dream"—according to the reviewer—"lacks pantomimic action." Clearly, the critic has taken refuge in "pantomime" and "literary approach" only to evade an expression of unqualified approval.

Yet, if it be possible to agree with certain of Levinson's remarks, it is impossible to accept the principles on which they are based. For instance, I would have agreed with him when he attacks Fokine for attaching too much importance to "ethnography and archaeology," had he been basing his attitude on the consideration that their possibilities must soon be exhausted, and therefore lead to the dead end of repetition. And again, I would agree when he attacks Fokine for his physical realism, carried over from the traditions of the Moscow Art Theater, since, because of them, Fokine was only able to permit a dance when and where it was dramatically justified. Nevertheless, I cannot accept the viewpoint from which the accusation is made, as when he says "he does all he possibly can, to prevent the onlooker imagining that a scene is being danced just because it forms part of the ballet. If, however, we were to enumerate the dance themes which exist today, and which have existed in the past, we should have to reduce to nothing the part played by the ballet masters and choreographers."

I am entirely in agreement too with Levinson, in his shattering criticism of that most dangerous dramatic tendency in the ballet, the introduction of dances only where they would naturally occur, and their prohibition —again in deference to dramatic realism—wherever no such motive can be assigned. In ballet, every dance always has its *raison d'être,* because the very foundation of the art of ballet lies in the fact that, in contradiction to everyday life, it expresses in dancing, and dancing alone, every possible human emotion, and therefore, from this point of view, *there is nothing which cannot be danced.*

But when Levinson girds against *dramatic action expressed in dancing,* then I can only protest, and accuse him, in his turn, of wanting to thrust us back into the *divertissement* of the nineteenth century.

A similar error is perpetrated by him, when he speaks of the mutual relation of music and dancing, and painting and dancing, in these same productions of Fokine's. But here I am unable to follow him, for why should a non-picturesque setting be in any way preferable to some truly artistic achievement?

When Levinson states that "painting being in two dimensions is static," we may concur, but he forgets that, for Diaghilev and his friends, the painters of *The World of Art* group, the chief attraction and delight of a ballet lay in the opportunity it gave for transposing a painting into a third dimension of volume and action. Thus, they were able to make painting dynamic, and this development worked to the mutual advantage of both painting and ballet. Indeed, it is in just such instances that Levinson's prejudices redound most to his discredit, for though in earlier criticisms, we find him declaring a preference for the simplest of décors and costumes, later, when the process of simplification has set in, we find him regretting past splendors.

But there were other sore points which much exercised this critic, though he did little to mend them, no doubt because of the same inherent disability in himself. Thus, we find him accepting the new relation between music and the dance, in which the former dominates the latter, and in consequence, forces it to subjugate itself to motions and patterns which do not arise spontaneously, and yet at the same time complaining that a symphonic suite is hardly a suitable medium for the structure of a *ballet-divertissement* of the kind to which he is partial. Thus he demands that the music shall be both lovely and self-justificatory.

This is the fashion in which Levinson refers to the innovating zeal of Fokine, "a gradual development from the ambiguity of the old ballets towards a new unity, and from choreography towards pure miming, in the name of a realist fiction: after which the dramatic movement will be subjugated to the static principle of painting, the musical rhythm become more elaborate, and the 'symphonic suite' replace the ballet score." As a formulation it cannot be considered particularly happy, and its acceptance would need so many qualifying clauses that little indeed would remain. Much more just, though cruel, were the words of his article dealing with the creator of *The Polovtsian Dances*. "More and more frequently he imitates his own discoveries. Less than three or four years have passed since we first saw his productions, and already his style seems both petrified and derivative." But that Diaghilev also was already beginning to feel. The end of Fokine's association with the Russian ballet was hurrying near.

CHAPTER X

THE RUSSIAN BALLET 1912-22

The three periods in the history of the Russian Ballet

IN SPLITTING up the history of the Russian Ballet into three periods, 1909-1911, 1912-1922, and 1923 to the year of Diaghilev's death, I am aware that my method may arouse doubt, and possibly some disagreement because of the disparity between the periods and, even more, by the fact that I have combined into single periods tendencies which can only be called disparate, while dividing others manifesting a certain similarity. In both the first and second periods, we meet the names of Bakst and Fokine, but, in the 1912-1922 period we find the colorful exuberance of Bakst set off by the simplifying cubism of Picasso, the impetuous dynamism of Fokine and the sculptural designs of Nijinsky set off by the *burlesquerie* of Massine, whose ideology was so different from that of his two predecessors. A similar relation might be found between the two latter periods, for though many things unite them, they also contain much that is difficult to reconcile.

It is, of course, true, that any cross-section of an organic living process —and the Diaghilev enterprise as such was intensely vital and active— must of necessity be accepted conditionally at the risk of destroying, to some extent, its integrity, and, in some measure, falsifying it. Nevertheless, the method is a convenient one, and even I would say indispensable, when important and complicated events are to be studied. Yet, we must remember always, that this division is to be accepted only conditionally, and with a proviso that the lines of demarcation are necessarily vague, for the periods almost imperceptibly merge into each other. Thus, though the names of Bakst and Fokine, for instance, intimately link up 1911 and 1912, each, nevertheless, belongs to a different epoch.

Yet, if the years 1911 and 1912 have much in common, no less great are the differences. Indeed, 1912 might be treated, and justly, not only as a fresh epoch, but as a fresh epoch inaugurated by Diaghilev in that year.

Diaghilev's inspiring influence during the second period

What made this fundamental, this basic difference between the preceding years and that year of combat, 1912, heralding the second epoch of the Russian Seasons, was the fact that, whereas before, Diaghilev had been content merely to reveal the *achievements* of Russian art, thereafter he was to begin his searchings for *new forms in art*. Already, however, the first Russian Seasons had revealed to the world what had so far been achieved in Russian art, either by the Imperial Theaters throughout the nineteenth century, or later, in protest against established canons, or again as the result of the artistic ferment caused by *The World of Art* in a summing up that was both brilliant and comprehensive! Yet even in the very last years preceding the war, a feeling was abroad that the finest manifestations of contemporary art, though barely in bloom, were already doomed to decay; doomed to make way for a new art sprung from a new culture, a new conception of life. Then came the war years, and their aftermath: culture declined, and the over-simplification of all things soon swept out of existence an art which had seemed so young, so rich in beautiful promise. To the new man, the glittering oceans of sound, color and movement, the complexity of the orchestra, the indescribable perfection of the *fouettés,* the blinding riot of color, the bewildering and fantastic beauty of the spectacle, all meant nothing.

One of the first to realize this change was Diaghilev—the inspired architect of the splendors which formed so notable a feature of the first years of the new century. Nevertheless, he did not mourn the past, now useless and inaccessible to the new generation, nor did he try to galvanize it into new life. Instead, he united with those who sought a new culture, a new art, and the creation of new beauty. Diaghilev, one felt, sensed and knew better than his compeers that beauty, in art, did not necessarily derive from form, and that men were only able to perceive that beauty in terms of their epoch. Eclectic and subtle, he was able, not only to sense and make contact with every new trend, but even to lead in its van, thus exactly paralleling his activities during the first years of the twentieth century, however different artistically and organically the present might be. Thus, in 1912, the first portents of his changing viewpoint appear in the production of the *Prélude à l'Après-Midi d'un Faune,* which marks a new milestone in the history of the Russian Ballet. Yet, steeped in an ancient culture as he was, and fervent admirer of impressionism, it was not possible for Diaghilev wholly and completely to break with the past. And it was because he strove to link the old and the new, to save what might be saved of the lovely past, that Diaghilev produced that remarkable new ballet, *Faune,* to the impressionist music of Debussy, and the impressionist décors of Bakst.

Perhaps the most striking proof of coming change was Diaghilev's decision to cease concentrating exclusively on the series of "national" ballets, so remarkably evocative of ancient Russia. Hitherto, everyone of his ballets, with *Le Spectre de la Rose* as virtually the sole exception, had been purely national in character.

It may, of course, be argued that long before this, Diaghilev had produced ballets to music by various foreign composers such as Chopin,

Les Sylphides; Schumann, *Carnaval;* Weber, *Le Spectre de la Rose;* and even that wholly French ballet, *Giselle.* To this I must perforce agree, but with one proviso, that this was music of universal importance, long part of our musical consciousness and tradition, and already merged with our national art. From 1912, however, while continuing to avail himself of the services of his Russian collaborators, Diaghilev begins more and more to have recourse to foreigners. In Fokine's ballet *Le Dieu Bleu,* for example, we find the librettist, Jean Cocteau, and the composer, Reynaldo Hahn; *Faune* is created around Debussy's music, and *Daphnis and Chloë* to that of Ravel. No doubt, his long acquaintance with France contributed greatly to Diaghilev's predilection for French collaborators.

This second period of the Russian Ballet may seem to cover a period almost inordinately protracted, actually eleven years, but it must be remembered that war and revolution are both included, periods which, from any creative standpoint, must be considered entirely negative. Years of the greatest difficulty they proved, spent in erratic wanderings, or quasi-internment in Italy, Portugal and Spain. Thus, if we only take into account the years of productive activity, the third and final epoch will be found the longest.

Fokine, Nijinsky, Massine—can we consider it justifiable to include all three in one and the same epoch? In fact, however, Fokine's importance relates only to the earliest of the "Russian seasons." For, in 1912 and 1914, he is little more than an "extra," a guest ballet master, and his productions bear no real relation to the new path of the ballet. Thus, all his three ballets of 1912, *Le Dieu Bleu* to music by Reynaldo Hahn, libretto by Cocteau; *Thamar* to music by Balakirev, and *Daphnis and Chloë* to that of Ravel, were, in spite of Bakst's lovely décors, and some remarkable inventions in the sphere of dancing, completely overshadowed by the *clou* of the season, that "new word" of the Russian Ballet, the *Prélude à l'Après-Midi d'un Faune,* in the production of which Diaghilev, Debussy, Bakst and Nijinsky all collaborated. Fokine cannot really be considered, therefore, to have played any part in the development of the second period, the predominant factors in which were Nijinsky and Massine. Massine, it is true, disavowed Nijinsky, not only by word of mouth, but in his acts and even his being; nevertheless, his choreography, like that of Nijinsky, belongs to a similar epoch, the dance-ideology of which was "fixed" by Diaghilev's choreographic researches: that same Diaghilev who formed Nijinsky, and later the youthful Massine. This all-determining influence of Diaghilev, on the painting, music and dancing of the Ballet, is what is most characteristic of the second period, and what differentiates it utterly from the third and last, in which he more and more withdrew from the Ballet. So great indeed was Diaghilev's creative influence on the Ballet, in this second period of its existence, that one may even describe him as the arbiter of all its artistic tenets, and even as prime ballet master.

1912 came to an end in an atmosphere of classic antiquity, with the creation of two new ballets: *Prélude à l'Après-Midi d'un Faune* by Debussy and Nijinsky; and *Daphnis and Chloë* by Fokine and Ravel. That the researches into antiquity of such painters as Benois and Bakst greatly influenced ·the stylized ballets of Fokine, we already know. *Daphnis and Chloë* proved no exception, the only change being the more arduous effort demanded of Bakst to make it possible for Fokine to recapture and dynamically express the form and image of the ancient dancing depicted in red and black on Attic vases. It was Bakst, too, whose duty it was to familiarize Nijinsky with the plastic forms of the past, and help him bring the *Prélude à l'Après-Midi d'un Faune* to fruition. That is why these ballets present so great a similarity, fundamentally different though the two choreographers might be. What made this similitude particularly striking was the frequent recurrence, too frequent perhaps, of movements in profile. But whereas, with Nijinsky, these movements seemed cumbersome and set, Fokine, with his vaster experience, was able to communicate the ease and grace and upsurge of pure dancing, and thus wed Bakst's plastic sense to the technical perfection of *The Polovtsian Dances*. Indeed, there is many a reminiscence of *Prince Igor* in *Daphnis and Chloë*. Yet, great as was Bakst's influence on the *Faune,* it was *Diaghilev who actually inspired and created* this ballet, for he it was who persuaded the unwilling Debussy to allow his music to be used in this manner. Indeed, only Diaghilev's determination could have prevailed against Debussy's resistance. To repeat myself, therefore, it was in Venice, in 1911, that the idea of the *Faune* first came to Diaghilev, and it was he *who first* demonstrated its angular forms to Nijinsky, and envisaged it in all its completeness, from the moment the nymphs appear, living images from ancient vases, to the closing gestures and utter immobility on the final crescendo. Diaghilev it was, too, who spent long hours studying sculpture, bas-reliefs and antique vases in an effort to resuscitate the ancient poses, and translate them into a new dynamic. These discoveries he communicated to Nijinsky, for final expression in terms of dancing. Thus, Nijinsky was in fact interpreting Diaghilev's inspiration, and no surprise need therefore be felt because, in his uncertainty how to continue, Nijinsky was constantly forced to resort to his mentor. I shall have to revert yet again to Diaghilev's choreography, for the *Faune,* though his first, was by no means his last effort in choreography.

Diaghilev and Ravel

Daphnis and Chloë, that masterpiece of Ravel's, was only created after an interminable succession of delays, which led to many complications, difficulties and misunderstandings with the composer. For instance, we find Ravel in his biographical sketch writing:

"*Daphnis and Chloë,* a choreographic symphony in three parts, was commissioned from me by the director of the Russian Ballet.... In writing it, my intention was to compose a vast musical fresco, concerning itself less with archaic fidelity, than with fidelity to the Greece of my dreams, which in many ways, resembled that imagined and depicted by the French artists of the latter end of the 18th century.

"The work is constructed symphonically, but the tonal plan is kept severely in check by the employment of a very few themes, whose elaboration ensures that the work shall be homogeneous.

"Sketched out in 1907, *Daphnis* was put back on the loom a number of times, and especially the finale."

If M. Ravel is not mistaken in the date, it would appear that Diaghilev commissioned him to compose *Daphnis and Chloë* as early as 1907, during the concerts of Russian historical music then held in Paris. By 1909, the work had progressed so far, that Diaghilev, certain of being able to present it during his season the following year, ventured to include a clause in his contract with Karsavina, stipulating her appearance as *Chloë* in alternation with Pavlova. Nevertheless, the ballet was not presented either the next or the following year, owing to delays on the part of Ravel. Finally, in 1912, the score was sent to Diaghilev, who though positive of its exceptional merit, had begun to doubt the advisability of producing the work at all, given the many difficulties which had already attended its preparation. Then again, this Greece of Ravel's seemed to have nothing in common with the archaic Greece of the Isles, pictured by Bakst. However, one would be hard put to it to say which of the two, painter or musician, was more in the spirit of Longus, taking into account the fact that the action takes place on Lesbos. Bakst wished to return to an archaic Greece, but it is possible that Ravel and the French painters of the eighteenth century, were nearer to Longus, and the decadence of his epoch.

Another difficulty was the composer's refusal to accept the libretto, or "choreography" as interpreted by Fokine, on the grounds that it failed to render either his ideas, or the musical structure. Thus Ravel was constantly demanding fresh changes, which often ended in compromises painful to all.

On the other hand the chore-author himself had reasonable grounds for dissatisfaction, in spite of the excellence of the work as music, and even as a background for dancing. For eminently "danceable" though it was, and this is true of all Ravel's music, seeing how much of it derives from Spanish and Basque dance tunes, the musical structure of this work was particularly unsuited to the ballet form, so that the choreographer found his difficulties all but insurmountable. Indeed, Ravel might, with far more justice, have called his composition a "*symphonie musicale,*" rather than a "*symphonie choréographique.*"

A glimpse of the many difficulties which arose in connection with

Claude Debussy

Maurice Ravel

Erik Satie

G. Auric

this production are afforded by Ravel's publisher, J. Durand, whom we find writing:

"...We were all ready to start rehearsing at the Châtelet, when, one day, at my office, I was informed that Diaghilev had come to see me. M. de Diaghilev gave me to understand that he was not wholly satisfied with the composition, that in fact he was in some doubt as to whether to proceed with the ballet. I used all my powers of persuasion to bring him back to his original feeling about the work....After thinking a bit ...M. de Diaghilev said simply, 'I'll put it on!'

"During rehearsals, violent discussions went on between the author of the 'argument,' the choreographer, and the soloist in the main part, Nijinsky, in which Diaghilev naturally participated. As everything took place in Russian, all I could hear was the sound of somewhat violent voices. They were discussing the choreography, and the opinions seemed diametrically opposed. I do not know who finally prevailed. They must have reached some compromise, but a certain amount of resentment evidently persisted, and from that moment the break between Fokine and Diaghilev began, a break which became official once the Russian Ballet season was ended."

Rehearsals were conducted with difficulty, and in an atmosphere charged with ill-feeling, the finale, in particular, giving endless trouble to the *corps de ballet,* written, as it was, in five-four time. However, by omitting actual counting, and substituting the syllables "Ser—ge—Dia—ghi—lev" in its place, the *corps de ballet,* after humming it over an infinity of times, finally succeeded in getting it right.

This ballet was dedicated by Ravel to Diaghilev. It did not, it is true, lead to any open rupture, but their relations certainly became perceptibly cooler, and a long time was to elapse before they collaborated afresh. Yet, so greatly had Diaghilev admired the genius of Ravel, so near his heart were his hopes for the closest collaboration, that he was profoundly disappointed when, as he thought, the latter's music proved unsatisfactory in terms of dancing, and even, in some degree, alien to what he himself and his ballet masters were seeking. The following spring, however, we find Ravel collaborating with Stravinsky on the re-orchestration of *Khovantchina.* Later, in January, 1917, Diaghilev invited Ravel to compose the music for a ballet-libretto by the Italian poet Canguillo, an offer which was accepted, though its subsequent history is unknown. For all we know, the work may never have been begun. Then, in 1919-20, Ravel, commissioned by Diaghilev, composed the music for a new ballet —*La Valse.* This proved a remarkably beautiful and eminently danceable score, and (with *Bolero*) became Ravel's most popular item, first in France and later throughout the world. In spite of all this, Diaghilev refused to accept *La Valse* for the Ballet, and thereby mortally offended the composer. It is hardly necessary to enter into the moral aspects of this *"affaire* Ravel-Diaghilev," for where art was concerned Diaghilev cared nothing for moral obligations or wounded pride. But all he had seen in this remarkable score was... merely a delightful *valse*. As ballet he considered it lacked scenic action, and so paralyzed every possibility of choreographic development. As a result Ravel broke off all relations with him, though the rupture was felt with equal keenness by both. Later, in 1925, at a time when Gunsburg was helping the company to produce *L'Enfant et les Sortilèges* at Monte Carlo, the two men happened to meet. Diaghilev put out his hand, but it was ignored, and the affront all but led to a duel. I well remember how wretched the whole episode made Diaghilev. Shortly before his death, in 1929, Diaghilev wished that a reconciliation might take place, and that Ravel might once more work with the Ballet. He begged R. Brussel to do what he could in the matter, but, alas, Diaghilev died before anything was accomplished.

However, to return to the 1912 season, continuing its progress amid thunderous applause and no less vociferous catcalls. *Thamar* proved somewhat dim, and received but little notice, but Balakirev's music and Bakst's décors got their fair share of appreciation. The ballet itself, however, created but moderate interest, for as the critic of *Apollo* put it: "To be frank, apart from certain national Caucasian dances, presented as a *divertissement*, plastic rhythm is hardly the outstanding feature of this ballet." *Le Dieu Bleu*, too, scored only a moderate success. In this ballet, which was profoundly influenced by Siamese dancing (possibly because, in 1900, Fokine had seen the Siamese Dancers performing in St. Petersburg, where they created a furore), the *corps de ballet* was pushed completely into the background, much to the disgust of Parisian ballet-goers, who had come to love the ensemble of the Russian Ballet as much as they loved the Russian choirs. Even Nijinsky could not save this ballet, and his "dance of the hands" fell far short of his usual triumphant success. We find the same Russian critic of *Apollo* writing: "The dance of the Bayadères with which it opens, was hardly noticed, and was treated as a slight *divertissement*. As for the rest of the ballet, it would seem to consist in several new poses (I insist on the word 'poses,' for the whole effect is one of monotony) by Nijinsky, and a number of precious and angular gestures, derived from Indian sculpture and admirably stylized, by Mlle. Nelidova, wonderfully helped by her amazingly flexible, snakelike arms."

"Prélude à l'Après-Midi d'un Faune" and the resulting controversy

No substantial success can be recorded for the third of Fokine's ballets, *Daphnis and Chloë*—notwithstanding the magnificence of the music, and its, at times, extreme originality—due possibly to a particularly flagrant lack of artistic unity, but more probably to its complete eclipse by the outstanding feature of the season, the *Prélude à l'Après-Midi d'un Faune*

—the performance of which raised a veritable storm. This outcry was concerned, not so much with problems of art, as with certain moral aspects of the performance, for what roused the spectators to shocked protest was not its daring and originality as dancing, but Nijinsky's final gesture with the nymph's veil. The first shot was fired by an article by G. Calmette in *Figaro* entitled "Un Faux Pas":

"Our readers will not find, in its accustomed place under 'Theater,' the criticism of my worthy collaborator, Robert Brussel, upon the first performance of *L'Après-Midi d'un Faune,* choreographic scene by Nijinsky, directed and danced by that astonishing artist.

"I have eliminated that review.

"There is no necessity for me to judge Debussy's music, which, besides, does not in itself constitute a novelty, as it is nearly ten years old, and my incompetence is too complete for me to be able to discuss the transcriptions of these subtleties with the eminent critics or with the younger amateurs who tax Mallarmé's masterpiece with the interpretation arbitrarily imposed on it by a dancer.

"But I am persuaded that none of the readers of *Figaro* who were at the Châtelet yesterday will object if I protest against the most extraordinary exhibition which they arrogantly presented to us as a profound production, perfumed with a precious art and a harmonious lyricism.

"Those who speak of art and poetry apropos of this spectacle make fun of us. It is neither a gracious eclogue, nor a profound production. We saw a faun, incontinent, vile—his gestures of erotic bestiality and heavy shamelessness. That is all. And well-deserved boos greeted this too expressive pantomime of the body of an ill-made beast, hideous from the front, even more hideous in profile.

"These animal realities the true public will never accept.

"M. Nijinsky, little accustomed to such a reception, badly prepared likewise for such a rôle, took his revenge a quarter of an hour afterwards with an exquisite interpretation of the *Spectre de la Rose,* so prettily written by M. J. L. Vaudoyer."

Calmette's, however, was not the only pen to attack *Le Faune,* for we find Pierre Lalo in *Le Temps* dealing with the same ballet in the following terms: "The production of the *Faune* is a great error in itself: nothing can relieve the glaring contradiction between the slavish archaism and hardcast rigidity of the choreography and the flexible flow of Debussy's prelude or Mallarmé's poem—both so alien and distant in their attempt to interpret antiquity."

He then goes on to attack the Russian Ballet in general, ending with the words: "The stigma of the Barbarian is common to them all!"

Meanwhile the Press had split into two camps, part hardly able to find words strong enough to express an indignation and opprobrium that almost reached the point of calling for action by the police, the rest overflowing with enraptured panegyrics. Worth noting here is the fact that, while its detractors were mainly musicians, artists expressed the greatest enthusiasm for it! *La Guerre Sociale,* for instance, glorified Nijinsky and *"l'âme slave,"* while Odilon Redon declared it inconceivable that anyone could have interpreted Mallarmé more perfectly than did this animated frieze of the Russians. The greatest impression of all, however, was produced by a long article from the pen of A. Rodin in *Le Matin,* which, after stating that "Loie Fuller and Isadora Duncan had taught us to love the beauty of body, movement and gesture," went on: "The last of them, Nijinsky, possesses the distinct advantage of physical perfection, harmony of proportions, and a most extraordinary power to bend his body so as to interpret the most diverse sentiments. The sad mime in *Petrouchka* seems, in the last bound of *Le Spectre de la Rose,* to fly into infinite space. But in no part is Nijinsky so marvelous and admirable as in *L'Après-Midi d'un Faune.* No jumps, no bounds, nothing but attitudes and gestures of a half-conscious animal-creature. He stretches himself, bends, stoops, crouches, straightens himself up, goes forward and retreats, with movement now slow, now jerky, nervous, angular; his eyes spy, his arms extend, his hands open and close, his head turns away and turns back. The harmony between his mimicry and his plasticity is perfect. His whole body expresses what his mind dictates. He possesses the beauty of the antique frescoes and statues: he is the ideal model for whom every painter and sculptor has longed.

"You would think Nijinsky were a statue when he lies full length on the rock, with one leg bent, and with the flute at his lips, as the curtain rises, and nothing could be more soul-stirring than his movement when, at the close of the act, he throws himself down and passionately kisses the discarded veil.

"I wish that every artist who truly loves his art might see this perfect personification of the ideals of the beauty of the old Greeks."[1]

This panegyric, however, earned a lively rejoinder from Calmette:

"...I admire Rodin deeply as one of our most illustrious and able sculptors, but I must decline to accept his judgment on the question of theatrical morality." After which, he went on to urge, that the Hotel Biron, presented to Rodin by the State, should be withdrawn since "it was inconceivable that the State—in other words, the French taxpayers —should have purchased the Hotel Biron for five million francs simply to allow the richest of our sculptors to live there."

Indeed, so bitterly did the controversy rage that the attention of the Russian Embassy was drawn to the matter, for it was feared that the Franco-Russian Entente might be imperiled. Whereupon the police intervened, and though the ballet was permitted to continue, the condition made was that Nijinsky should modify the particular gesture at the root of the bother. During his subsequent London season, Diaghilev felt

[1] Romola Nijinsky. *Nijinsky,* pp. 175-6.

it unwise to risk presenting the *Faune,* and only did so in the following year, with *Le Sacre du Printemps* in the same program.

It is interesting to compare the heat and passion of this controversy with A. Levinson's calm detachment, for to him this "archaeological experiment" seemed of no particular significance.

The Russian critics, on the other hand, were far more concerned with the ballet as dancing than with any social aspect. Thus we find J. Tugendhold writing in a Russian paper: "If, in the classical ballet, there was an abyss between the dramatic element and the *divertissement,* and if Fokine has striven to eradicate these two conflicting principles (which one feels at times, as I say in *Thamar* and *Le Dieu Bleu*) and if he has even been able to dramatize dancing in his finest creations such as Thaôr in *Cléopâtra,* and Columbine in *Petrouchka:* in the *Faune* movement becomes posture, dance gesture, mimicry an 'archaic' smile, the dynamic static, and the theater a sort of decorative fresco or *tableau vivant.* The spectacle, I agree, is lovely, but it is also a blind alley. Actually, the very basis of the theater is the rhythm of its movement, its three dimensions, the soaring of the soul, the flesh, the blood."

Such views may be justified, but they do not take into account the quite exceptional historic importance of the *Faune,* and its effects on the Russian Ballet, for this "archaeological experiment" was to prove of very particular significance.

Nijinsky's choreography, behind which stood Diaghilev, and to such an extent that "Nijinsky" is almost in this case a pseudonym for Diaghilev, marked the turning point in the whole future evolution of the ballet's dancing ideology, since it determined *Le Sacre du Printemps,* as well as Massine's artistic development and that of subsequent choreographers of the Ballet.

Diaghilev was particularly grateful to Rodin for his defense of Nijinsky. Nevertheless, if we are to believe Romola Nijinsky, that joy was soon to be poisoned, and to bring all relations with the French sculptor to a close. I quote her story as it stands, but without accepting any responsibility for it.

Rodin had expressed the desire to sculpt Nijinsky and the sittings had begun: "Serge Pavlovitch was rather alarmed by the intimacy which developed so quickly between the aged sculptor and the young dancer.... He became jealous, but he controlled himself. The statue of Nijinsky was unfortunately never finished, for Diaghilev found continual excuses to prevent the sittings. His jealousy now became uncontrollable. One day he arrived at the atelier sooner than expected. It was a heavy, storm-laden, suffocating afternoon, as only Paris can have in July. Serge Pavlovitch went through the house, and found both artists in Rodin's sanctuary, Nijinsky sleeping peacefully on a couch, covered by a shawl, and Rodin also asleep at his feet. The intense heat, the hours of posing, the heavy wine, had fatigued the aged sculptor as well as Nijinsky, who was not used to drinking. Diaghilev did not wake them. He left without being noticed and only confided in Bakst. The incident was never mentioned, but he energetically hindered any further sittings, and because of this he undoubtedly robbed the world of a masterpiece." [2]

Tours in London and Central Europe

This season, which had begun so stormily in Paris, pursued an uneventful course when continued in London at Covent Garden, though it established the Ballet once and for all on the British stage. Queen Alexandra and the Empress Maria Feodorovna both took it under their august patronage, and their common enthusiasm contributed greatly to establishing its success. The season ended, Diaghilev for the first time transported his company to Germany and Austro-Hungary, and thus extended his empire to Central Europe.

The most notable success of the Berlin season proved to be *Cléopâtre*, a performance of which (with *Petrouchka*) was attended by both the German Emperor and Empress, the former telling Diaghilev that there was more real Egypt in Bakst's reconstruction than in all the works of the archaeologists put together. Indeed, he went so far as to say that he intended compelling every German scientist and archaeologist to go and learn from the Russian Ballet. He also expressed a wish to go back-stage, much to Diaghilev's discomfiture, who was thus forced to steer a way backwards through innumerable gangways, far too narrow for him, while the Kaiser plied him with endless questions.

Here, and in Budapest, the Russian Ballet gained a well-deserved triumph. Their reception in Vienna was very different.

It is true that, for political reasons, Russians were not notably popular in Austria at the time; but that is not sufficient reason to account for the antagonism of the officials of the Vienna Opera, the members of the orchestra and the Imperial Viennese Ballet. Stravinsky, who was present at the rehearsals of *Petrouchka* at the Hofoper, says, in his *Chronicle of My Life*, that the musicians displayed open hostility. One must remember that the Viennese orchestra of the immediately pre-war period was conservative in its tastes and that the music of *Petrouchka* was unlike anything heard in Vienna before. But that scarcely justifies frank sabotage of rehearsals or their interruption by such audible insults as *"schmutzige Musik."*

If *Petrouchka* was the *casus belli*, the brunt of the attack was borne by the Prussian Director of the Hofoper, who was responsible for bringing Diaghilev and his Ballet to Vienna. It was against him particularly that the members of the Imperial Viennese Ballet directed their jealous indignation.

[2] Romola Nijinsky. *Nijinsky*, pp. 184-5.

Léon Bakst
(L. S. Rosenberg)

Alexandre N. Benois
"Shura"

Larionov

Pablo Picasso

But now Diaghilev was beginning to think of an expedition to America.

"Le Sacre du Printemps," its historical importance in relation to the Russian Ballet and Diaghilev's part in it

It was now 1913, a year of extreme importance in the history of the Ballet, as it was also to prove in the life of Diaghilev, for in this year *Le Sacre du Printemps* was first produced, the first South American tour was undertaken, Nijinsky married, and the friendship between the two men came to an end.

With Fokine's departure two new ballet masters took his place, Nijinsky and Diaghilev; but, since the work proved too much for them alone, it was found necessary to engage a third in the person of Romanov, after which it was possible to split up the work. Diaghilev and Nijinsky made themselves responsible for the Stravinsky-Roehrich *Sacre du Printemps* and the Debussy-Bakst *Jeux*, while Romanov was entrusted with *La Tragédie de Salomé* by Florent Schmitt and Sudeikine.

But here we must stop a moment to deal with *Le Sacre du Printemps* which, because of its historic importance in the evolution of the ballet, deserves some special mention.

About this time Diaghilev was passing through a phase of great enthusiasm for Gauguin, the primitive and pictorial qualities of whose painting interested him deeply. Thus, he made a point of visiting each of the painter's exhibitions from the very first—held soon after the latter's return from Tahiti—to the last. Meanwhile, he had himself conceived the idea of producing a primitive ballet, but decided on a Russian setting, and to this end called on Roehrich and Stravinsky, the painter and musician most familiar with our ancient folklore, to join hands with him. Eventually, they produced the libretto and score of *Le Sacre du Printemps*.

Thus Diaghilev received his libretto, and with it the most magnificent and greatest of all Stravinsky's scores. Fired with enthusiasm himself, and communicating it to Nijinsky, the men set to work. After his first experiments in choreography with *Le Faune*, which he might with justice consider a success, as indeed he did, Diaghilev, although, strictly speaking, not really competent to produce a ballet, nevertheless attacked the *Sacre du Printemps* with confidence. The fact that Stravinsky's music was "non-danceable" failed to discourage him, for had not the same been true of Debussy's lovely, though diffuse and spineless, music for that other novelty of 1913, *Jeux?* In the new choreography, with its statuesqueness, its predilection for posed gestures, adumbrated action and angularity, all this mattered nothing.

Among Diaghilev's papers [3] I find the following letter addressed to

[3] Now in my possession.

him by Roehrich: "In the ballet of the *Sacre du Printemps* conceived by myself and Stravinsky, my object was to present a number of pictures of earthly joy and celestial triumph, as understood by the Slavs. I don't propose to set down a list of all the items in the ballet; such a list hardly matters when we are dealing with sets and groupings. My intention, therefore, stated simply, is that the first set should transport us to the foot of a sacred hill, in a lush plain, where Slavonic tribes are gathered together to celebrate the spring rites. In this scene there is an old witch, who predicts the future, a marriage by capture, round dances. Then comes the most solemn moment. The wisest ancient is brought from the village to imprint his sacred kiss on the new-flowering earth. During this rite the crowd is seized with a mystic terror, and this our excellent Nijinsky has stylized for us admirably well.

"After this uprush of terrestrial joy, the second scene sets a celestial mystery before us. Young virgins dance in circles on the sacred hill, amid enchanted rocks, then they choose the victim they intend to honor. In a moment she will dance her last dance, before the ancient old men, wrapped in bearskins, to show that the bear was man's ancestor. Then the graybeards dedicate the victim to the god Yarilo. I love antiquity, for its sublime happiness, and its deep thoughts.

"I don't know what Paris will think of my sets. So far my memories of Paris could not be better. The camp of the Polovtsians (*Prince Igor*), the tent of Ivan the Terrible in *Pskovitianka,* as well as my work for the exhibitions, have all been appreciated there."

Upon Nijinsky the dancer, however, fell the task of informing the ballet with its dynamic impulse, each element of which Diaghilev had carefully to explain to him. But it was a task which proved too difficult, since a still more difficult problem remained to be tackled; that of transposing the movement on to a musical canvas but little suited to dancing. Whereupon Stravinsky came to the dancer's rescue, backed by Diaghilev and Mme. Rambert, an expert in eurhythmics. Stravinsky, writing of these difficulties in his *Chronicle of My Life,* says that Nijinsky's plastic conceptions were sometimes superb, but how much of this vision is to be attributed to Nijinsky and how much to Diaghilev?

In spite of Stravinsky's help, work on the ballet was continued in an atmosphere that was very far from peaceful. To Stravinsky it seemed that the rôle of choreographer to the Russian Ballet was beyond the scope of Nijinsky's abilities, especially in the case of a work so full of technical difficulties as *Sacre du Printemps.* Nijinsky, he says, unconscious of his own incapacity, relied on the firm support of Diaghilev to protect him against growing criticism from the company and so became increasingly difficult to work with.

Had Stravinsky, one wonders, any notion why Nijinsky had become so difficult to work with? Did he know that Diaghilev, in the privacy of his room, demonstrated every step to Nijinsky, which explains why he was forced to turn deaf ears to every criticism, and maintain and defend a creation, not his own, but Diaghilev's.

Eventually, after immense efforts on the part of all three, the *Sacre* was completed and produced in the spring of 1913, only to be rearranged seven years later by another collaborator of genius—Massine—to which it owes its present, and richer, qualities as dancing.

Le Sacre du Printemps, to his last day, remained Diaghilev's most beloved creation, and he would claim that in the twenty years of its existence no work produced by the Russian Ballet could be considered of greater significance. It pained him greatly when others failed to understand or accept the work; and again, any kind word or critical appreciation gave him delight. It was a long time before London accepted the *Sacre,* though in 1929 that event did come to pass. Less than a month before his death we find Diaghilev writing to one of his new friends:

"Yesterday *Le Sacre du Printemps* proved a tremendous success. At last these fools have got to understanding it. *The Times* says that the *Sacre* is to the XXth century, what Beethoven's 9th was to the XIXth! At last! Yes, one has to learn to be patient and philosophical, even to rise above the obstacles that puny, narrow-minded men set in the way of whatever seeks to depart from mediocrity. Heavens, all this is as trite as can be—but what's one to do? One can't go on living without some hope of seeing 'in the dawn the rays of tomorrow's sun.' "

An interesting record of this moment is provided in an article by G. Auric in *Gringoire,* for during the performance he had been watching Diaghilev's face: "His somewhat puffy face now looked incredibly kind, almost childlike.... Suddenly he bent forward, his opera glasses to his eyes, watching for faults, observing the public. But when the scene ended, he stood up without even a moment's hesitation. What applause when Sokolova reappeared once, twice, thrice, and innumerable times, to bow to this auditorium metamorphosed by the *Sacre.*...I did not dare to say a word to Diaghilev, so profoundly did the happiness on his face touch me. When I think of his death, some weeks after, and of that which was broken around him because of it, it is this vision of him which my memory always conjures up...."

It is a picture of a man rejoicing in his creation.

In the production of *Jeux,* however, Diaghilev's part was much more limited, and the ballet proved a comparative failure and was never revived.

In addition to his three new ballets, Diaghilev brought three operas with him from Monte Carlo: *Boris Godunov,* Mussorgsky's *Khovantchina,* and Rimsky-Korsakov's *Nuit de Mai,* the décors for the two latter being by Fedorovsky. Earlier seasons had always been presented at the Châtelet or Opera House, but now G. Astruc offered him the Théâtre des Champs-Elysées, and was ever after to remember the event as one of the main causes of his subsequent financial difficulties. In his *Pavillon des Fantômes* we find him referring to this episode in the following words: "Eventually the Russians arrived with their operas and ballets. Meanwhile I had told Diaghilev, 'This year no more Châtelet, no more Opera House. You're coming to my theater.'

" 'But as a matter of fact, old friend, the directors of the Opera House want me there.'

" 'Well, and what then? I suppose they're offering you your usual price, 12,000 francs.'

" 'Yes, but don't you see, people have been saying for six years now that Astruc invented the Russian Ballet. And that sort of thing, old friend, comes expensive.'

" 'How much?'

" 'At least 25,000 francs a night.'

" 'Even for twenty performances?'

" 'Even for twenty.'

"It meant half a million! But both my honor and pride were involved. I signed. But it was my death warrant. For in addition to those 25,000 francs, another 20,000 had to be added for supplementary expenses, the orchestra having to be paid for morning and afternoon rehearsals, besides stage hands, electricians, coiffeurs, costumiers and a thousand more— without taking into account Stravinsky's ukases, demanding, in that sad delightful Slav voice of his, a score of extra musicians, or the re- moval of the whole front row of the stalls, though they had already been sold.

" 'You know, old friend, it's done with the utmost ease nowadays by that powerful machine they have for cutting steel and reinforced con- crete. And the upholsterers will patch up the damage very quickly.'

"And then that 'enfant terrible' Stravinsky, that dear genius Igor, who wanted me to pull down all my partitions. But I do not regret my madness."

Uproar at the First Night of "Le Sacre du Printemps"

The first night of the *Sacre* created a riot—a violence of applause and catcalls unparalleled since the production of *Hernani*. Many accounts are available, but I choose that of Romola Nijinsky because she was present both in the auditorium and the wings. She begins by quoting another eyewitness, Carl van Vechten: " 'A certain part of the audience was thrilled by what it considered to be a blasphemous attempt to de- stroy music as an art, and, swept away with wrath, began, very soon after the rise of the curtain, to make catcalls and to offer audible sug- gestions as to how the performance should proceed. The orchestra played unheard, except occasionally, when a slight lull occurred. The young man seated behind me in the box stood up during the course of the ballet to enable himself to see more clearly. The intense excitement under which he was laboring betrayed itself presently when he began to beat rhythmically on the top of my head with his fists. My emotion was so great that I did not feel the blows 'for some time.' " [4]

"Yes, indeed, the excitement, the shouting was extreme," continues Mme. Nijinsky. "People whistled, insulted the performers and the composer, shouted, laughed. Monteux threw desperate glances towards Diaghilev, who sat in Astruc's box and made signs to him to keep on playing. Astruc in this indescribable noise ordered the lights to be turned on, and the fights and controversy did not remain in the domain of sound, but actually culminated in bodily conflict. One beautifully dressed lady in an orchestra box stood up and slapped the face of a young man who was hissing in the next box. Her escort rose and cards were exchanged between the two men. A duel followed next day. Another Society lady spat in the face of one of the demonstrators. La Princesse de P. left her box saying: 'I am sixty years old, but this is the first time anyone has dared to make a fool of me.'

"At this moment Diaghilev, who was standing livid in his box, shouted *'Je vous en prie, laissez achever le spectacle.'* And a temporary quieting down followed, but only temporary. As soon as the first tableau was finished the fight was resumed. I was deafened by this indescribable noise, and rushed backstage as fast as I could. There it was as bad as in the auditorium. The dancers were trembling, almost crying. They did not even return to their dressing rooms.

"The second tableau began, but it was still impossible to hear the music. I could not return to my stall, and as the excitement was so great among the artists watching in the wings, I could not reach the stage door. I was pushed more and more forward in the left wing. Grigoriev, Kremnev, were powerless to clear this part of the stage. Opposite me there was a similar mob in the back of the scenery, and Vassili had to fight a way through for Nijinsky. He was in his practice costume. His face was as white as his crêpe-de-chine dancing shirt....

"Everybody, at the end of the performance, was exhausted. The month's long work on the composition, the endless rehearsals, and finally this riot.... Once more Vassili's guard broke down and Nijinsky's dressing room was stormed, Diaghilev, surrounded by his friends and the balletomanes explaining, discussing.... But they all agreed and knew that their creation was good, and that it would one day be accepted. They were so excited that they could not go and have supper right away, so somebody suggested a drive *autour du lac*. And Diaghilev, with Nijinsky, Stravinsky, and Cocteau, drove around in the Bois to quiet down, and only towards the morning did they return home."

[4] Romola Nijinsky. *Nijinsky,* p. 199.

André Levinson on Nijinsky's ballets

Neither the Press nor the public, however, showed any real awareness of the significance of this ballet, all the resentment being concentrated on Stravinsky's music. Daring and new as was the choreography,
it was practically ignored, as was also the less original choreography of
Jeux. André Levinson proved himself the most competent of the critics
on this occasion, for he had glimpsed the choreographic dualism of *Le
Sacre,* though with no suspicion that it was upon just this dualism that
the ballet was based. Levinson, of course, had no inkling that the former
stood for Diaghilev and the latter for Nijinsky and Rambert. But as
he put it, there was a fatal falsehood inherent in the ballet masters' conception of Stravinsky's "intensely refined Hottentot" music, with its "ear-
splitting intolerable discords, its ponderous, imperious rhythms..." for
"the ballet master had concentrated solely on movement designed to embody and express those rhythms." Continuing, he says:

"The dancers translate into bodily motions the beat, the volume of
the sounds, and express its acceleration, its retardation by a systematized
series of gymnastic movements, bending and straightening the knees,
raising and dropping the heels, and forcefully emphasizing each accentua-
tion of the music. This is indeed the complete Dalcrozian pedagogical
arsenal, as employed in the teaching of rhythmic gymnastics. Rational
and expedient in their proper place, these systematized motions have no
utilitarian value on the stage!

"By reason of some aberration of artistic taste and understanding, inexplicable to the writer, a number of secondary pedagogical formulae,
have here ousted the plastic, symbolical and psychological content of the
dance.

"Nijinsky, with blind infatuation, appears to have lost sight of the fact
that rhythm itself is but the bones of a formula, a measure of action in
time, but with no particular validity. Nevertheless, he has sacrificed the
plastic side of his art to it, the result being that a whirling frenzy of
savages maddened by the earth's vernal rebirth, is reduced to a
tedious demonstration of rhythmic gymnastics in which 'wizards' and
'possessed' begin to 'pace their notes,' 'follow the syncopation,' and thus
wreck the whole psychological conception, while provoking a somewhat
humorous perplexity in the spectator.... To my mind, any attempt to oust
the plastic forms of the dance by the new *rhythmic formalism* cannot be
justified, and the latter should be relegated to the insignificant place to
which it belongs."

Levinson then goes on to describe the second scene "as too, too lyrical."
In this scene, maidens in red garments move shoulder to shoulder in a
round dance, with the angelic and prim gestures we have seen in icons.
They disperse in search of a mystic trail, then elect, and worship, with

leaps and dances, the chosen victim. Elders, bowed with age, in animal masks and hides, surround her. Immobile, until this moment, her face white beneath the white kerchief, she begins her last dance, the death dance of the consecrated. Her knees are joined: her feet turned inwards. A sudden convulsion sends her body sideways, leaving it bent rigid at a sharp angle. Propelled by the urge of a ferocious rhythm, deafened by the strident discords of the orchestra, she flings herself hither and thither, her tense form contracted and squirming in the ecstasy of this angular dance. The dance grows faster and more violent, until, at last, she who has been chosen, falls inanimate into the arms of the elders. "At which point, this nightmare, compact of primitive lyricism and primal terror, where these have not been obliterated by the purely sterile mechanism, comes to an abrupt end, bringing with it, for the spectator, a feeling very akin to relief...."

In comparison with Igor Stravinsky's cyclopean poem, continues Levinson, "Debussy's *Feux* charms with its fragile cobwebs of shifting harmonies. The weaving of its rhythms is elastic and infinitely varied, but the achievement is characterized by much that is strange.

"In this ballet Nijinsky, even more determinedly than Fokine, sets aside the traditional concept of the dance. Fokine, the eclectic, compromises by seeking to justify it on grounds of emotional expression. But Nijinsky disrupts and splits it into a sequence of distinct movements, kept apart by pauses, and linked only by the continued flow of the music."

To Fokine, the mechanical, the aesthetic value and significance of angularity and turned-outness, "mean nothing," and he rejects them for the sake of a natural position of the legs and feet. But Nijinsky, in a plastic paradox, makes his ballerinas join their toes and turn their heels outwards.

"For him the plasticity of motion lies in a mechanical schematization. Every pose, every motion of the dancer might be graphically rendered— in straight lines. Both maidens hold their knees unbendingly rigid, their torsos erect, their wrists and elbows bent at right angles. With faces turned to the audience, they move down the stage in sudden angular jerks on half-raised toes. The single and solitary motion in which there is any freedom, a broad leap over a flower bed, comes as a pleasant relief to a tension of the utmost discomfort to the spectator.

"This symbolism of split-up, of angular motions, fails to convey conviction: a scenic event, almost unintelligible in itself, and lacking variety, seems tediously long in spite of its actual shortness."

Very unexpected, however, from the pen of so conservative, so constant an adversary of the Russian Ballet, is the conclusion of this article. "There can be no doubt that *Jeux* is but one more failure...for it met with no particular approval. Yet this ballet, in its conception, is characterized by a certain novelty, by no means sterile, however colorless, rigid and affected it may seem. Indeed, the impersonal, architectural background, the rudimentary and materialistic symbols of sport and sports gear, are sufficiently representative of certain aspects of contemporary life. Again, in the angular groupings of tensed bodies, one feels something in common with the most modern tendencies in painting, seeking as it does a greater depth, a more elaborate synthesis on the path to geometrical simplification: a process which the work of the Swiss master Hodler excellently exemplifies. In the work of Nijinsky there is something of this purposeful and noteworthy approach to the abstract in art. His inspiration is by no means commonplace, but his approach to the problem [how one longs to explain 'to Diaghilev's problem'] is shallow, devoid of creative plentitude and forcefulness."

In particular, one is tempted to emphasize Levinson's words that "in the angular groupings of tensed bodies one feels something in common with the most modern tendencies in painting, seeking as it does a greater depth, a more elaborate synthesis on the path to geometrical simplification." No doubt can be felt that, after the *Sacre* and *Jeux*, Diaghilev definitely pursued this new road in his efforts to develop a new ballet form, more representative of contemporary trends in art and life.

Of Romanov's *Tragédie de Salomé,* Levinson speaks cautiously and diffidently: "Romanov's choreography," he says, "struck me as lacking in definition, purpose and style. In the form of its movements it closely approaches the methods of Fokine, but a tendency to revive a decoratively symmetrical arrangement of the dancing groups is especially noticeable: yet this symmetry is an exclusive characteristic of the classic ballet. In its content, Salomé's broken, and mosaic-like dance seemed singularly unexpressive, possibly because we could find no faintest trace of tragic experience in the 'fussiness' of Mme. Karsavina's dancing. This ballet evoked no kind of reaction, either way, from the audience. All in all, it proved most sketchy."

Diaghilev's participation in "Khovantchina"

The opera season, as was to be expected, proved very successful, the repertoire consisting of *Boris Godunov,* Mussorgsky's *Khovantchina* and Rimsky-Korsakov's *Nuit de Mai.* Some idea of Diaghilev's activities in connection with these productions may be guessed from what we know of his efforts in regard to *Khovantchina.* Dissatisfied with Rimsky-Korsakov's general treatment of the work, in any case incomplete, he began a careful study of the original manuscript, with the view to making a new version. It was necessary, he decided, to orchestrate certain parts, to re-orchestrate others and to have a new chorus for the finale. Mussorgsky, in the case of the finale, had merely sketched in a theme, the melody of a Russian song, and Diaghilev was dissatisfied with Rimsky-Korsakov's version of it.

The work of reconstruction was divided between Stravinsky and Ravel.

Stravinsky undertook to write the new chorus for the finale and to deal with two other numbers. The rest of the opera was allotted to Ravel.

The new version, as it turned out, apart from the new finale, did not differ substantially from Rimsky-Korsakov's. Occasional cuts were made and various alterations in the order of scenes, but the result, says Stravinsky in his *Chronicle of My Life,* was an incongruous mixture of different styles.

After this London season of April, 1913, the Russian Ballet sailed for South America. Both the directors, Diaghilev and Gunsburg, were to accompany the troupe, but soon after sailing, the cabin booked by Diaghilev (No. 60) which adjoined that of Nijinsky, was discovered to be empty, Diaghilev having been unable to overcome his dread of the sea.

Benois, the artistic manager, also remained behind, his place being taken by Bakst.

In September, the Ballet made its début in Buenos Aires, Pierre Monteux conducting, and received a tremendous ovation. The stars were Nijinsky, Karsavina and Feodorova. One other dancer came to the fore, A. Gavrilov, and since he frequently deputized for Nijinsky, was often mistaken for him and rewarded with the same frantic applause.

Massine as ballet master

Nineteen-fourteen opened inauspiciously for the Russian Ballet, since after Diaghilev's telegram to Nijinsky, stating that the Russian Ballet had no further need for his services, the Company was left without a ballet master.

Meanwhile, the former had returned to Russia. In St. Petersburg he met Jacques Rouché, former director of the Théâtre des Arts, who played so great a part in the reform of the French stage. Rouché, preparatory to assuming his duties as Director of the Paris Opera, in 1914, was visiting Europe and Russia. The stage of the latter was particularly interesting to him. He was Diaghilev's friend, he never missed a rehearsal or performance of the Russian Ballet in Paris. Serge Pavlovitch was accustomed to say that of all his colleagues (the theater managers) he respected Rouché alone for his outstanding merits. It was during this stay in St. Petersburg that Diaghilev engaged the artist of the Imperial Theater, Vladimirov.

In Moscow he met Massine, then a youth and strikingly handsome, who, recently graduated from the Imperial Theater Schools, was abandoning the ballet, in order to take up a dramatic career. Meanwhile, he continued to figure in the *corps de ballet* of the Moscow Grand Theater, and Diaghilev was able to persuade him to join his company in Monte Carlo.

For seven years he was the Russian Ballet's sole ballet master, and was never entirely to break his connection with it. Though Diaghilev freely admitted Massine's great talent, yet there were times when he

found the results frankly disappointing. All the same, he sought his collaboration time and again.

Massine had not been long in Europe, before Diaghilev and Larionov
set themselves the task of completing his artistic and choreographic education, Larionov being his professor of ballet (in this second epoch, the
influence of the painters was particularly preponderant) while Diaghilev
took him to study under Cecchetti, and to visit the museums. This double
influence of Cecchetti the traditionalist, and Larionov the dilettante-mod-
ernist, has meant that Massine is always oscillating between two opposed
tendencies which, often in the same ballet, predominate turn and turn
about.

According to Diaghilev, it was in Florence, during the war, that he
at last succeeded in fanning into flame "that essential though indefinable
something which made the creator in Massine," adding, however, "for
all too short a time, alas!" These words he wrote in 1924, at a moment
of profound disillusionment with Massine the creator; for now his work
seemed to him mechanical, obvious, cold and uninspired, as did the man.
Indeed, he was ready to place all his misfortunes at Massine's door, from
his poverty in Portugal and Spain, to the diabetes which was finally to
prove his destruction.

Of all the friends Diaghilev had known and loved, there were but
few to whom he owed such moments of happiness or anguish as to
Massine. Those near Diaghilev remember still, how in 1917, in Rome,
during a stormy scene with Massine, he tore the telephone from the
wall and shattered it on the ground, and how, in his uncontrollable rages,
he would smash the furniture in his room....

But this aspect of their relationship only developed very much later,
and in 1914-15 Diaghilev was still awaiting miracles of art from his
friend.

Expectations or no expectations, it became clear on Massine's arrival
in Monte Carlo, that he was as yet far too young and inexperienced to be
able, even with Diaghilev's immediate help, to work out the choreography of a whole ballet. The result was that the dance numbers in Stravinsky's *Rossignol,* the scenery and costumes of which had been designed by
Benois, were entrusted to Romanov. Since, however, it was obvious that
the Russian Ballet could hardly bolster itself up with this single opera,
Diaghilev saw himself forced to turn once more to Fokine.

Working at full speed, Fokine planned out the choreography of four
new ballets: the dim *Midas,* with music by Steinberg and scenery and
costumes by Dobuzhinsky (never revived, and soon forgotten), a revival
of Schumann's *Papillons,* orchestrated by N. N. Tcherepnine, the scenery
by Dobuzhinsky and costumes by Bakst, *La Légende de Joseph,* this too
never revived, and *Le Coq d'Or.*

La Légende de Joseph, to a libretto by Hugo von Hofmannsthal and
Count Kessler, with music by Richard Strauss (Diaghilev paid a hun-

M. M. Fokine   Leonid Massine

Bronislava Nijinska   Georges Balanchine
                             (Balanchevadze)

dred thousand gold francs for it), décors by Sert and costumes by Bakst, was especially produced to exhibit the young Massine to the best advantage, but it was more his beauty than his art to which he owed his success. As ballet, however, the *Légende* lacked distinction, being restricted to a sort of miming of the libretto, accompanied by Strauss's dynamic music. Indeed, in Paris, the leading part, that of Potiphar's wife, was in fact taken by a singer—Maria Kusnetzova. This season, therefore, in Paris as in London, proved somewhat colorless and dim, for Fokine had failed to reveal the least spark of originality, and Diaghilev thus lost all further interest in him.

The one success, though even that did not pass uncriticized, a success which cost Diaghilev a lawsuit with Rimsky-Korsakov's heirs, was *Le Coq d'Or,* which may justly be said to have saved the season. This production, inspired by Benois, contained a number of original features, from the décors and costumes by N. Goncharova, very different from Bakst's orgies of color (with Goncharova and Sert new decorative trends began to appear in the Ballet), to the double cast of dancers and singers. Thus, the vocalists stood motionless on the stage, while the "mimes and dancers" rendered the dramatic action.

This wedding of the dance to vocal music (and choral singing in particular) had already been employed very successfully by the Russian Ballet in the production of *Daphnis and Chloë,* and was to be freely resorted to in after years, perhaps most happily in Milhaud's *Salade.* I myself have observed that dancing always goes better to choral singing, possibly because the chorus itself was once a mass of singing dancers.

In *Le Coq d'Or* we see Fokine drawing the major part of his inspiration from the principles worked out by Diaghilev and Nijinsky, and applying them to the rhythmic gymnastics developed by Dalcroze. The whole rendering is therefore rather a form of miming than actual dancing. Indeed, the dancing in this ballet was perhaps its least interesting feature. Prince Volkonsky, for instance, though a fervent admirer of Dalcroze's eurhythmics, could not but admit to some disillusion on seeing this experiment of Fokine's, who, he thought, had failed to utilize the possibilities of the score's basic rhythms, whereas the miming exactly followed the pattern of the music.

In this way, dancing began more and more to subjugate itself to music, and with the advent of Massine, that subjection became complete. Not idly did he state, during his first choreographic efforts, that dancing must be considered the visual counterpoint of music.

The War Years

Suddenly war broke out, and the Russian Ballet all but ceased to exist. In those awful years, Europe had no use for the Ballet, and neither London nor Paris saw the Ballet during 1915 and 1916. The company scattered to the four winds, and there was every doubt whether the members could ever be reassembled. Thus, in 1915, when Diaghilev signed his contract with the Metropolitan Opera House for a New York season, and committed himself to presenting the whole of his company, Fokine, Karsavina, Nijinsky included, it proved impossible to procure either Karsavina or Fokine, both of whom were retained in Russia, Fokine for military service. After endless trouble, however, he did finally manage to "borrow" Nijinsky, held at the time in Austria as a civil prisoner of war, and eventually succeeded in gathering together not only a company, but such magnificent new dancers as Nemchinova, Sokolova, Makletzov, Idzikowsky, Woizikowsky, etc. Lydia Lopokova was engaged as prima ballerina, ably supported by Tchernicheva, and Diaghilev's friend, Ansermet, became the Ballet's new conductor.

We know little of Diaghilev's life in Florence and Rome at this time, but that it was a difficult time both emotionally and financially, we know from what Stravinsky has told us, in his *Chronicle of My Life,* of his visits to him during this period.

The war and the consequent dispersal of nearly all the members of his company, had thoroughly disturbed Diaghilev's plans. He felt the vital need of comfort, encouragement and advice. Diaghilev would never listen to advice in artistic matters from his friends, but, in times of profound depression such as these, demanded the presence of friends and relied absolutely on their support.

By the time that Stravinsky visited Rome, in the winter of 1914, Diaghilev had created for himself a wide circle of friends and acquaintances—a protection, in a sense, against the difficulties of the world and a new basis for his existence. There was Gerald Tyrwhitt, later Lord Berners, who became a great friend of Diaghilev and was commissioned by him in 1926 to write the music for *The Triumph of Neptune.* Diaghilev indeed had the highest admiration for his work. Another new figure was Prokofiev. He had come from Russia—at Diaghilev's command—to discuss the composition of a new ballet. This was the ballet *Chout,* which I shall discuss more fully later on.

From Rome, Diaghilev went to Ouchy, still in the same year. There, he began his negotiations with America, and set about preparing his forthcoming season.

About this time, a charity performance in aid of the Red Cross was presented by the Ballet in Geneva, the program consisting of *Carnaval, L'Oiseau de Feu,* and a new ballet, adapted from Rimsky-Korsakov's *Snow-Maiden,* entitled *Soleil de Nuit.* The décor and costumes by Larionov were markedly Russian and futurist, and in this ballet Massine made his début as chore-author. Another ballet, *Liturgie,* sketched out by Massine at this time, was never produced.

Diaghilev also organized a gala charity performance in Paris, on December 29th, which was opened by Felia Litvin singing the Russian national anthem, followed by songs by Mussorgsky and Rachmaninov. Stravinsky conducted his own *L'Oiseau de Feu,* while the other ballets, consisting of *Schéhérazade, La Princesse Enchantée,* the *pas de deux* from *La Belle au Bois Dormant, Soleil de Nuit,* in which Massine enjoyed a deservedly great success, and *Prince Igor,* were conducted by Ansermat. Four hundred thousand gold francs were taken, a remarkable total.

Tours in America

Bad times, however, were in store for Diaghilev, and it was not without much apprehension that he eventually left Bordeaux, en route for America.

His situation was now such that it was absolutely *indispensable* for him to sail—and so he sailed. It may be wondered how, with his mortal dread of the sea, he eventually landed safe and sound, for the crossing was nothing but a long martyrdom, since all through the voyage he remained shut, for the most part, in his cabin, wearing his overcoat and hat, with three life-belts strapped to his body—such was his fear of German submarines—and moaning the whole time in a voice that was scarcely human. His only moments of relief were when the faithful Vassili sank to his knees and prayed for a happy ending to their journey. Throughout the voyage Diaghilev was able neither to eat, to drink, to sleep or even talk.... Indeed, the first day at sea saw him a complete nervous wreck, and yet day followed day till the crossing seemed endless! Look where he might, there was never anything but the illimitable ocean, with not a ship, not a reassuring speck of land in sight. His whole being yearned for terra firma, now and at once, yet every moment drew him farther from it. Yes, indeed, it may be wondered how he landed safe and sound!

This New York season prolonged itself from January until May, 1916, and was received with an enthusiasm quite unique in the annals of the American stage. That enthusiasm grew even greater when Nijinsky arrived in April, but the meeting of the two friends left much to be desired. Serge Pavlovitch made every effort to restore the old friendly footing with his Vaslav, but the dancer's wife was forever present, setting them by the ears, inventing idiotic lawsuits, treating Diaghilev with intentional rudeness, and doing all in her power to poison his American visit. It was a moment when Nijinsky was all on fire to produce *his* ballets (and indeed, they were entirely *his*), *Tyl Eulenspiegel* to the music of Strauss, and *Mephisto* to the music of Lizst. Romola Nijinsky describes this moment in the following words:

"Then Vaslav began to speak to him about his new compositions, *Tyl* and *Mephisto,* but Diaghilev showed no interest. 'It can't be worth much if it's German music.'

" 'But it's Richard Strauss, whose music you yourself produced a year

and a half ago,' I ventured. 'Well, times have changed; the war is on
and in any case Strauss, *c'est du cabotinage.'* "

Whatever the truth about Diaghilev's opinion of Strauss, one thing
is certain, namely that Diaghilev showed no interest whatever in these
new productions of one whom he himself admittedly considered a
choreographer of genius. From his point of view, doubtless, this genius
could only manifest itself when Diaghilev and Bakst were present to
shore him up: lacking such support, it could "not be worth much." In
any case, Diaghilev never saw this ballet, which was put on, and passed
almost unnoticed, during the following year, while Nijinsky was acting
as artistic manager to the company in America. During this period his
partners were Spessiva, who had come from Russia as a great artist, and
a new Cleopatra, who won golden opinions, the Swiss ballerina, Mlle.
Revalles.

Meanwhile, Diaghilev and Massine had gone off to Italy and to Spain,
where the whole latter part of the year was spent, save for rare excur-
sions to Italy. By this time, the new artistic trends were firmly ensconced
in the Ballet, and after 1916 Diaghilev entrusted every new décor to
Goncharova, Larionov and Sert. At this moment he was all for simplifying both scenery and costumes. Goncharova began work on the décors
for *Triana* and *España,* while Massine began to sketch out the dances.
Nevertheless, neither of these ballets was ever completed, and only the
former's décor for *Sadko* eventually saw the footlights. Meanwhile, Larionov was busily engaged on the décor for Ravel's *Histoires Naturelles,*
the whole being presented against moving scenery, but without dances.
One single ballet was created in the course of this season, *Las Meniñas*
to music by Fauré, décor by Socrate and costumes by Sert. This ballet
made its début at San Sebastián in 1916, but was not shown in Paris
until the year after. In 1918, considerably amplified by the addition of
excerpts from Chabrier and Ravel, it was renamed *The Gardens of
Aranjuez,* and presented again in Paris. During part of 1917, Diaghilev
was in Spain, while his company toured the United States. This tour
covered an immense amount of territory and lasted from October, 1916,
until February, 1917.

The Spaniard, Felix

Among the patrons, and even fervent admirers, of his Ballet, Diaghilev
numbered King Alfonso, who almost deemed it a point of honor to be
present at every performance, and often, at times, attended rehearsals.
Two cultures, one Russian, the other Spanish, dissimilar though they
were, but impregnated with the very soul of dancing, now came together
to their mutual benefit. The creative, the educative influence of Spain on
Massine is particularly noticeable. As I have already stated, two opposing

tendencies ruled in Massine, one the academism of Cecchetti, the other the dilettante-modernism of Larionov. But to these must be added a third, and no less important: that of the Spaniard, Felix.

"During the Ballet's Spanish season Massine had been taking lessons from Felix, an expert performer of national dances," writes Karsavina. "Felix had been brought over to London to continue these lessons,[5] and Diaghilev wishing to give me inspiration for my novel role, asked me to come and see Felix dance at the Savoy. It was fairly late when, after supper, we went downstairs to the ballroom and Felix began. I followed him with amazed admiration, breathless at his outward reserve when I could feel the impetuous half-savage instincts within him. He needed no begging, he gave us dance after dance, and sang the guttural nostalgic songs of his country, accompanying himself on the guitar. I was completely carried away, forgetful that I was sitting in an ornate hotel ballroom till I noticed a whispering group of waiters around us. It was late, very late. The performances must cease, or they would be compelled to put the lights out.... A warning flicker, and the lights went out. Felix continued like one possessed. The rhythm of his steps, now staccato, now languorous, for a time faint, and then seeming to fill the large room with thunder, made the unseen performance all the more dramatic. Against such possession all hotel officials were powerless. We listened to the dancing enthralled."[6]

To these interesting and moving reminiscences, I can add Diaghilev's no less moving account of Felix's first and last days with the Russian Ballet. No epilogue could be more tragic, and Serge Pavlovitch would never allude to it without the profoundest sadness.

Some time in 1917, Diaghilev and Massine happened to be witnessing a competition for Spanish dancers in one of the squares of Seville. A number of dancers were present, many of them highly accomplished, for Spain is full of excellent dancers. Their picturesque clothing, haughty bearing and distinctive carriage, their marvelous *pas,* all elicited stormy expressions of delight from the crowd and *cognoscenti.* Suddenly a youthful, wild-looking Andalusian pushed his way to the front, rolled up his shirt-sleeves and the legs of his trousers and—turning pale as death and clenching his teeth—began to dance the farrucca. It was Felix, and, such was his performance, that there and then the verdict acclaimed him the best dancer in Spain.

Whereupon Diaghilev ravished him from Spain, and enlisted him in the Russian Ballet. Alas! his brilliant victory in that Seville square was to be his first and last triumph in life, for soon he was absorbed in the *corps de ballet,* dancing what he was told, and teaching Spanish dances to Massine. The end of his ballet career was particularly tragic. It hap-

[5] 1919.
[6] Karsavina. *Theatre Street,* pp. 301-2.

pened in London, soon after the episode Karsavina describes. Massine and
Felix were collaborating together on the production of *The Three-Cornered Hat,* in which the Spaniard was to dance his famous farrucca.
The posters, however, bore only Massine's name as the ballet's creator,
and such was the impression this made upon Felix's mind that, having
arrived at the theater for the première, he then rushed wildly away,
pushed himself through one of the windows of St. Martin's-in-the-Fields,
which he had mistaken for a cabaret because of the red light over the
porch, and there, in front of the altar, began to dance his farrucca. Serge
Pavlovitch could never recall the episode without the same terror and
dismay, and always reproached himself for allowing himself to pass the
wording of that poster. To the very day of his death, he went on visiting
Felix in the asylum.

The 1917 Paris Season: the Cocteau-Picasso "Parade"

Nineteen-seventeen was to prove a year full of activity in the Russian
Ballet, for, beginning with Rome, Naples and Florence, it moved on,
after a rest of some months, to Paris, thence to Barcelona and Madrid,
and later to South America.

Meanwhile, helped by Diaghilev, Massine prepared three new ballets,
to which Diaghilev added a symphonic tableau by Stravinsky, *Feu
d'Artifice,* with scenery by Balla. These new ballets were *Les Femmes
de Bonne Humeur* by Scarlatti-Tommasini (adapted from Goldoni's
comedy), *Contes Russes* by Liadov, and *Parade* by Cocteau-Picasso-Satie,
all manifesting the new directions in which Diaghilev was moving. *Les
Femmes de Bonne Humeur* and *Contes Russes* were created in Rome and
Naples, and comic and gay as they were, enjoyed a great reception in
Italy.

The main attraction of the Paris season, however, was the Cocteau-Satie
Parade, the scenery and costumes being by a new genius in the art of
simplification, Pablo Picasso. A close friendship developed between the
two men, and thenceforth Picasso's influence on the Ballet assumed an
importance only comparable with that of his predecessors, Benois and
Bakst. Jean Cocteau, the author of the argument, was one of the earliest
of the Ballet's collaborators in France, and composed literally hundreds
of the Ballet's first posters and program articles. It was he, too, who invented the story of *Le Dieu Blue.*

With *Parade,* Cocteau's influence over Diaghilev was established firmly
(the former was then the moving spirit in *"Les Six"* [7])—and Diaghilev
was persuaded to ask Satie for the score. In a little, Cocteau's position was
unassailable, and, as one of the "inner circle," he managed to wield great
influence over the choreography of the new ballets.

Diaghilev, from the very beginning of their friendship, realized the

[7] A group of young, advanced French musicians. (Ed.)

Jean Cocteau

Jean Louis Vaudoyer

Boris E. Kokhno

Sacheverell Sitwell

genius in Cocteau, and was perpetually seeking some new, some surprising revelation. Thus, he would ever and again urge his poet:

"*Jean, étonne moi.*"

And Jean would oblige, and "amaze" Diaghilev. Indeed, this constant urge from Diaghilev towards new and original discoveries kept Cocteau stimulated, and prevented his lingering over what was already discovered.

Massine's "finds" in *Parade,* and in the ballets which succeeded it, derive directly from Cocteau, as does its literariness and circus stylization. The time had come for literature, too, to have its say in the ballet, since painting and music had each had their turn. All this, which is now the usual currency of the ballet, was invented by Cocteau for *Parade,* every *pas* of which he suggested and knew by heart.

The Moscow Imperial Ballet, Diaghilev, Larionov, Cecchetti, Felix, Picasso and Cocteau are the varied influences which went to create the ideology of Massine's dancing, and helped to develop his undoubtedly most individual talent.

Meanwhile, Guillaume Apollinaire had made himself responsible for converting the Paris public to *Parade.* The result was an article published in the program, entitled *"Parade* and the New Spirit." I cannot do better than quote some excerpts:

"It is a scenic poem, for which Erik Satie has written music exceedingly clear, simple and expressive, music which it would be impossible not to recognize as the pure transparent air of our France.

"The cubist painter, Picasso, and the most audacious of choreographers, Massine, have made that music concrete, by bringing about, for the first time, that union of painting and dancing, of plastic form and miming, which establishes the precursive signs of a yet completer art....

"This new union, for so far the décors and costumes on one hand, the choreography on the other, have been linked only superficially, gives to *Parade* a semblance of surrealism, in which I see the beginnings of that New Spirit which, having now found an opportunity of expressing itself, cannot fail to tempt the elect, or radically change the arts and costumes of humanity, since reason demands that they at least must keep pace with scientific and industrial progress....

"All in all, *Parade* must modify the ideas of many of its spectators. They will be surprised, but in the most agreeable of fashions, and, charmed, will learn to love the grace of these new movements, a grace they have never suspected...."

But though the ballet was entering a new phase, Diaghilev was careful not to break too suddenly with everything on which the Russian Ballet had been built. Thus, in the same program as *Parade* we see him producing Liadov's *Contes Russes* with scenery and costumes by Larionov, who certainly aspired, however unsuccessfully, to be a Russian Picasso, and *Les Femmes de Bonne Humeur* with scenery by Bakst.

Thus, without repudiating his ancient path, now fully explored, Diaghilev courageously sought out newer and more modern forms of expression, in the conviction that it was futile to go on repeating himself. Thus *Cléopâtra, Schéhérazade, Petrouchka,* might be said to be fundamental to the ballet, while any echo of them would certainly not be.... We even find him, in 1928, wanting to modernize *Schéhérazade* by introducing new décors by Matisse.

Effects of the Russian Revolution

But now occurred an event which swept off its feet, not only the whole of the advanced Russian intelligentsia, but Diaghilev himself, conservative though he was in politics, and revolutionary only in the mind: the Russian Revolution. In consequence, the red flag made its appearance on the French stage, in *L'Oiseau de Feu.*

Whereupon Léon Bailby wrote to Serge Pavlovitch, on May 12th, as follows:

"Dear M. Diaghilev,

"Will you allow me to call your attention to the trifling incident of yesterday, anent the changes introduced into the setting of *L'Oiseau de Feu* and the apparition of the red flag, symbolizing the Russian Revolution. Believe me, I write on no personal grounds, since it is no longer a question of a charity performance in which my friends were interested, and since, in the same charity performance you are giving next Friday on behalf of the same cause, *L'Oiseau de Feu* does not appear in the program. I believe, however, that you intend giving this same ballet as a commercial production, and so I must warn you that a considerable portion of French society, in the person of its upper classes, were, at yesterday's matinée, disagreeably impressed by an exhibition, which at best they deemed pointless, since it seemed quite out of place in a ballet, and could only appear to challenge their most honorable feelings.

"They are perfectly ready, they say, to acclaim the tricolor Russian flag, representing the Russian Republic. It is not therefore any reactionary motive which makes them feel thus, but they deem it unnecessary to glorify a popular revolution on the French stage, at a moment when it threatens to lead Russia into paths which, without perhaps helping it, may prove, to Frenchmen, definitely hostile.

"The people who, yesterday, scrupulously refrained from protesting, in order to avoid any turmoil which might have involved those respected figures under whose patronage the performance was given are of a mind, when the production is public and commercial, to express their feelings with the utmost clarity, should the red flag again appear on the stage.

"Allow me to state in all frankness, that I do not believe that the newspaper reports which are likely to follow will be in your favor. And does it not seem rather dangerous to you, to affront all the many difficulties which such an action may create, even to the point, possibly, of further performances being prohibited? It is not that I mean to exaggerate anything, but merely wish to point out some very real dangers. I add that, on every occasion when you have come to France, such favor as was shown you has come from above: it was Society which made your success, and spread it little by little among a wider public. It is that same Society from which the greater part of your large takings come. Will you, from your point of view, as a free and independent artist, yet one bound to consider matters from a businesslike view—will you deem it to your interest to quarrel definitely with those who constitute the majority of your clients?

"Please believe me to be your cordial admirer,

"Léon Bailby."

The only result of this incident, therefore, was this unpleasant letter; but soon Diaghilev, like all Russians living abroad in 1917-18, was to be subjected to infinitely worse, for after the peace of Brest-Litovsk, signed by the Bolsheviks, all sorts of accusations were hurled at the Russians, who, without exception, were now the objects of a common hatred. Every sacrifice made by the Russians, not omitting that disastrous offensive against East Prussia, when Russia so willingly offered herself to the German thrust to relieve the pressure on Paris, all the three long years of war in a common cause, were forgotten in an instant: and there were even those who spat in the faces of Russian officers who had fought in the ranks of the French. Thus, though material obstacles made it impossible for Diaghilev to bring his ballet to Paris in the spring of 1918, morally too it was equally impossible for one who from 1906 to 1914 had come to it as a conqueror.

Success of "Les Femmes de Bonne Humeur"

Nevertheless, the Ballet continued to enjoy a certain degree of artistic success, but a success infinitely more subdued, and far removed from the frantic enthusiasm which had greeted the first productions. Most successful of all was Les Femmes de Bonne Humeur, and even so rabid an adversary of the ballet as Levinson, wrote of it:

"... The inspiration of this humorous ballet is so fundamentally adroit, the execution so homogeneous and free from constraint, the whole so well composed that I freely surrendered myself to the sweetness of living that exquisite hour of forgetfulness. Did one wish to resist, one is seized from the first notes of Scarlatti's music, hustled along by the agile and sly rhythm which draws us within its magic circle. You drink deeply of that music, which resembles distilled sunshine. It froths, dazzles, and intoxicates; it is a fine vintage. For imaginary background, that great setting sun of the 18th century in which Venice is drowsily expiring.

"Doubtless Lawyer Goldoni would have accepted the authorship of the mimed scenes devised by Massine, and Théophile Gautier would have added some stanzas in his honor to his *Variations sur le Carnaval:* these are the natural, spiritual fathers of this fleeting vision. But do not imagine this to be a reconstruction, a *pastiche* of the inimitable past: quite the contrary, it is a living and original work, where the past only appears in the form of a distant suggestion, an echo softened by the passing of centuries.

"The choreography combines a sense of delicacy with a feeling of fitness in which the laws of the classic dance are only rarely abrogated, its normal movements distorted and parodied, heightened and dispersed by the rhythm. Because all the varied, hurried episodes of this comedy, so full and so gay, are realized in music, are *misurati* as Salvatore Vigano, the master of *choreo drama,* would have said. And one feels what a source of humorous surprises can spring from the rhythmic execution of the trivial and realistic movements of everyday life. As to the conformation of gesture, that paradox of players juggling with imaginary properties is really most enjoyable.

"The execution is full of go: you see artists who yesterday clumped in the *Sacre* happy to dance *Les Femmes de Bonne Humeur:* they are as much amused as we are."

A note in the program to the same ballet added:

"The painter, Bakst, and Leonid Massine, have together created a production which though ultra-modern, nevertheless derives directly from the 18th century. With these décors, Bakst the painter has taken the first steps towards annihilating stage perspective." [8]

Captivity in Spain

The Paris season ended, the Russian Ballet returned to Spain, and thence left for a tour in South America, though without Diaghilev and Massine, who were enjoying an Italian holiday. Towards the end of the year the whole company reassembled in Brussels, after which it left for Barcelona and Madrid, and again for Lisbon. This final season began with the greatest hopes, but was soon brought to a close by the Portuguese Revolution. Diaghilev and the company were caught in a trap, and were soon in an intolerable moral, and worse material situation. Soon funds came utterly to an end, and they were often the vicitims of real and pressing hunger. Serge Pavlovitch would never recall this epoch without reluctance and, when he did, spoke of it as the most disastrous period of his life. His fighting energy was ebbing fast, he was often on the verge of complete despair, and seemed to be living in a perpetual

[8] Lifar. *Ballet, Traditional to Modern,* p. 172.

stupor. Somehow or other Diaghilev finally managed to scramble out of it all into Spain. Here the general position remained much as before, except that at least a gleam of daylight began to appear. Work was resumed with Massine, and at last *Les Jardins d'Aranjuez* was produced in Madrid.

A year in London

Fortunately, the London Coliseum invited Diaghilev to open an autumn season, but some time was still to elapse before Serge Pavlovitch could manage to extricate himself from Spain. In an article he wrote for this London season, we find him saying:

"The war has put an end to those wonderful seasons, and after the separate peace of Brest-Litovsk, we Russians were wanted so little that we were shut up for almost a year in Spain.

"The King of Spain, godfather of the Russian Ballet, as he has so named himself, went to considerable personal trouble to get permission for us to appear in England. But it was necessary for us to have a London contract. Beecham was dead. I have accepted the invitation of Sir Oswald Stoll, and though I have never found that music halls provided a *favorable setting* for my productions, nevertheless I am grateful to Sir Oswald for having come to our aid at a time when politics had put such serious obstacles in the path of an institution as unimportant politically as a company of dancers.

Thus, after an infinity of complications, the company found itself in London, and was able, in September, to begin presenting a number of ballets, among which may be mentioned *Cléopâtra,* for which new décors and costumes were designed by R. Delaunoy, Bakst's sets being destroyed by fire in the course of the South American tour.

Here the Ballet remained a whole year, at first appearing in the London Coliseum with Defosse and Ansermat conducting, and then leaving for a few performances in Manchester. In April they were back again in London at the Alhambra, and after September at the Empire. But now the Russian Ballet, which had almost seemed on the point of expiring in Portugal and Spain, seemed to take on a new lease of life, and even to change its character. Work went feverishly forward. Massine was busy with *La Boutique Fantasque,* to music by Rossini, orchestrated by Respighi, which, based on academic dancing, was perhaps his most successful comic ballet. In collaboration with his professor, Felix, he was also at work on a ballet with a Spanish setting, *The Three-Cornered Hat.*[9] Meanwhile, Bakst was making the maquettes and costumes for the *pas de deux* taken from the Tchaikovsky-Petipa *The Sleeping Beauty,* and those for *L'Oiseau et le Prince,* Derain was preparing the décors, etc., for *La Boutique Fantasque,* and Picasso those for *The Three-Cornered Hat.* Karsavina had also returned to the company and was instilling it with

[9] *Le Tricorne.*

new life. New vitality flowed into the Ballet—and into Diaghilev...and he no longer remembered how near he had come to abandoning it altogether.

All these ballets made their début in London, where they were received with the greatest appreciation, and later, all, with the exception of the fragment from *The Sleeping Beauty,* were again presented at the Opera House in Paris, a season which continued through December, 1919, and January and February, 1920. During this period a new production, created by Massine, *Le Chant du Rossignol,* adapted from Stravinsky's opera *Le Rossignol,* was also presented, with décors by Matisse, those originally provided by Bakst for the operatic work having gone astray during the war. This, with *La Boutique Fantasque* and *The Three-Cornered Hat,* were the only novelties presented in Paris that season. Later, the Ballet departed for the Teatro Costanzi in Rome, and there presented a number of performances.

In 1920 regular and orderly work was resumed in Monte Carlo, as were those dazzling London and Paris seasons, which, in 1917, had almost ended forever. Various new ballets were put into rehearsal for the forthcoming spring season in Paris. These included *Pulcinella,* a ballet with vocal parts after Pergolesi, adapted by Stravinsky, choreography by Massine and décors by Picasso; the opera *Le Astuzie Feminili* (orchestrated by Respighi), choreography by Massine, and décors by Sert, and a new version by Massine of *Le Sacre du Printemps,* suaver, and more danceable, though less interesting, and, it must also be said, less original than the first.

The creation of *Pulcinella* and *Le Astuzie Feminili* proves clearly the relentlessness of Diaghilev's activity, even at a time when he seemed forced to be idle, since it was no light matter to collect the necessary material for his ballets and adapt it to his needs. Most of this work was done in Italy, in days and weeks spent rummaging through musty archives.

Le Astuzie Feminili is of great interest in many ways, for it was composed by Cimarosa—late in the eighteenth century—on his return from Russia to his native Naples. The result is a profusion of Russian themes in an otherwise Italian opera.Though presented in Naples it soon fell into oblivion, the last performance having taken place in 1794. Diaghilev discovered the score, and got it re-orchestrated by Respighi, after which, some years later, it was converted into the ballet *Cimarosiana.*

Even greater was the part played by Diaghilev in the creation of *Pulcinella.* The successful use of Domenico Scarlatti's music in *Les Femmes de Bonne Humeur,* encouraged Diaghilev to attempt a similar adaptation of the music of Pergolesi. Pergolesi, though as fertile a composer as any Italian of the eighteenth century, died prematurely at the age of thirty, and it was perhaps for this reason that a relatively small proportion of his works saw the light. Diaghilev, however, during his frequent visits to Italy had discovered and examined a large number of Pergolesi manuscripts, many unfinished and all unpublished. These he had had copied. In London he found further material. The result was a magnificent collection of the music of Pergolesi, which he handed over to Stravinsky to sift and adapt.

The plot of the ballet was based on various traditional adventures of Pulcinella, one of the most famous of characters of the *Commedia dell'Arte*. The décors and costumes were entrusted to Picasso, the choreography to Massine.

The production was worked out in Paris by Diaghilev, Picasso and Massine together. Stravinsky meanwhile was writing the score. As the music was to fit an elaborate, exact scenario, it proved necessary for him to go frequently to Paris for conferences with his three collaborators. These conferences, Stravinsky tells us in his *Chronicle of My Life,* often ended in passionate and stormy disagreement.

From time to time, as was inevitable, there were misunderstandings that caused delay and irritation. In order to prevent unnecessary waste of time Stravinsky would send Massine a piano version of each part of the full score as he completed it. The plan was that once the shape and design of each scene had been determined, Stravinsky should compose the music, then Massine work out the details of the choreography from the installments of the piano arrangement sent by Stravinsky.

This method of work had the most unfortunate result. His severest critics would not deny Stravinsky's brilliance and originality in his use of the orchestra; but the more effective the scoring, the more difficult to transcribe for the piano. Stravinsky himself considered it as difficult to transcribe a work for different instruments as to orchestrate it in its original form. In the case of *Pulcinella,* it frequently happened that Massine's choreography, based on a hurriedly constructed piano arrangement, proved completely beyond the capacity of the modest chamber orchestra for which the work was scored.

There was only one solution. The choreography had to be modified to suit the character and scope of the music. But one can imagine the effect on the protagonists of such a *contretemps*.

As in all his ballets, so in *Pulcinella* and *Le Astuzie Feminili,* it was Massine's talents as a comedian that won him his greatest success. A character-part dancer himself, he severely excluded from his ballets that restrained and severe "elevation," that lyricism, of the old-time academic ballet. If one may talk of Massine's "academism," one might say that it consisted chiefly in his predilection for ballets of the pre-romantic epoch and that he restrained, and attenuated, his modernism, by dissecting both action and movement. In this respect, one cannot but concur with A. Levinson, when, writing of *Pulcinella* he said, very truly, that what characterized Massine was his "ironic approach to classicism."

Diaghilev's breach with Massine

In spite of the important part played by Massine in the life of the Ballet, it was this very year, 1920, which saw his severance from it, after a terrible scene with Diaghilev. Thus, Massine, escaped at last from Diaghilev's "golden cage" and *the Russian Ballet lost its ballet master*. This "terrible scene," as the words indicate, was an emotional one, and Massine was the prime mover in the quarrel. Apart from this, however, Diaghilev was already beginning to weary of Massine, whose inspiration appeared to him to be drying up, and who tended to repeat himself. For six years Massine had been choreographer to the Ballet, a period all too long in Serge Pavlovitch's eyes, for he now feared that the Russian Ballet, after taking this fresh step forward, might again suffer a sort of petrifaction. It was of the utmost importance, therefore, for him to find someone to succeed Massine, though such a successor seemed impossible to discover. But when Massine left, no one at all seemed available to replace him, unless one excepts the painter Larionov.

The year 1921 opened with an important season in Spain, after which, the company having in the interim repaired to Monte Carlo, a number of gala performances was given in Paris at the Gaîté Lyrique. More important, however, were the spring and winter London seasons, that of June at the Prince's Theatre, and that of November at the Alhambra.

Of interest among the Paris productions was the *Cuadro Flamenco,* a suite of Andalusian dances, the décors by Picasso, and Prokofiev's *Le Bouffon*. The former consisted of eight separate numbers—"La Malagueña," "Tango Gitano," "La Farruca," two "Alegrias," "Carrotin Grotesco," "Carrotin Cómico," and "La Jota Aragonesa" performed by Spanish dancers of both sexes. Choreographically, therefore, it cannot be said to have been created by the Russian Ballet.

S. S. Prokofiev and "Le Bouffon"

The case of Prokofiev's *Bouffon,* however, was very different. Long before the war and revolution there had been much talk in the best musical circles of a new *Wunderkind,* Serge Prokofiev, then aged ten, whose praises were tirelessly sung by his professor, R. M. Glière. This period of "wunderkindism" has left marked traces on all Prokofiev's work, and no doubt it is responsible for the fact that, magnificent musician though he is, his creative capacity has failed to keep pace with the promise shown by his early compositions. His *Love of the Three Oranges,* for instance, won the highest approval in a certain circle of Russian musicians, but nevertheless in Russia, as in Western Europe, his name was unknown to the general public.

Diaghilev was perfectly justified, therefore, in claiming to have "dis-

Serge Prokofiev

Igor Stravinsky

covered" Prokofiev, who, after infinite difficulties, succeeded in escaping to Paris. Later on, his attitude to Bolshevik Russia changed, and he made every effort to convert Diaghilev to sympathy for the new regime. Diaghilev was inordinately proud of this "second" son of his, and of the fact that, thanks to his efforts, Europe had begun to admit his genius.

Thus, from 1921, it is Prokofiev's influence which begins to influence the Ballet, an influence which marches parallel with that of Stravinsky, less determinant though it was.

Le Bouffon, therefore, had always greatly interested Diaghilev, though much time was to elapse before it was finally decided to put it on. Indeed, the first discussions of the matter actually went back to 1915, when Diaghilev commissioned Prokofiev to compose the music for a ballet. In 1917 this music was completed, and in 1918 we find him writing to Serge Pavlovitch that from something hinted by Bolm he had got the impression that neither Diaghilev nor anyone else had understood in the least what he was driving at in his story about a buffoon.

Even so, another three years were to elapse before this score left the darkness of Diaghilev's portfolio. Indeed, it might never have done so, perhaps, but for Massine's resignation, and the former's need for a new ballet. Thereupon, so enthused was the painter Larionov by this score that he succeeded in persuading Diaghilev to entrust him, not only with the scenery and costumes, but also with the choreography, trusting only to the sole aid of the dancer Slavinsky for assistance. Naturally, this sort of dilettante choreography was unlikely to prove successful, but strange to say the production was not wholly and entirely a failure, for what saved it was the excellence of its music.

"The Sleeping Beauty" in London and resulting complications

While Larionov was busy with Le Bouffon, Diaghilev, with the utmost energy and devotion, was working at the production of that lovely and old-fashioned Tchaikovsky ballet—Petipa's The Sleeping Beauty, a ballet which, it may be said in passing, was shown only in London, and never in Paris, and which Diaghilev always considered his favorite ballet. In his determination to stage it as magnificently and as fully as possible, various themes were added from the Nutcracker Suite, together with new variations invented by Nijinska. Finally, after infinite discussions, Bakst began to design the décors and costumes,[10] while Stravinsky in part re-orchestrated the score. This collaboration of Nijinsky's sister, Bronislava, was made possible by her recent appearance in London, after a hazardous escape, in 1921, from Kiev. Having failed to make any satisfactory arrangement with Romanov in Bucharest, she met V. F. Nouvel

[10] Originally Diaghilev had intended to entrust this ballet to A. Benois, but the latter was unable to leave Soviet Russia.

in Paris, who brought her to London to see Diaghilev. In this manner the crisis was solved, and a new ballet master found. It may be remembered that she had formed part of the company in the earliest years of the Ballet's existence.

In spite, however, of the fact that Mme. Brianza-Carabosse and Spessiva both appeared in this ballet, the latter being an especial favorite of London audiences, that Trefilova, Lopokova, Egorova and Nemchinova alternated in the part of Aurora, that their partners were dancers as excellent as Vladimirov and Vilzak, the ballet did not prove the immense success Diaghilev had hoped. Indeed, certain portions proved unduly tedious and prolix, and it became clear that the day of the full-blown transformation-scene ballet was definitely ended. At the same time, Diaghilev had alienated the critics by his disrespectful references to Beethoven. Certain individual performances were as enthusiastically received as he could have wished, but that alone could not make good the colossal expense of so insanely lavish a production. The result was that Diaghilev found himself completely bankrupt, and in the midst of a financial crisis remarkable even in the annals of the Russian Ballet. The London season ended in a complete fiasco, the company broke up, and Diaghilev was convinced that the days of the Ballet were finally ended.

It was at this moment, exactly as at other grave moments in his life, that Misia Sert came to his rescue by introducing Gabrielle Chanel, that poet of women's fashions. Whereupon "Coco" Chanel manifested so much enthusiasm and faith in the Ballet's world-wide artistic significance, that she herself advanced money sufficient, not only to support the Ballet, but to revive and develop it also. As a result, Diaghilev, who had been in the habit of recruiting his perpetually thinning ranks from English dancers such as Sokolova, Savina, etc., who then assumed Russian names, now decided to procure new dancers from Russia. But how was that to be managed? For him to go to Soviet Russia in 1921-22 on such an errand was quite out of the question. Though he might possibly have entered it, leaving would have been a different matter.... "Lasciate ogni speranza voi ch'entrata." Whereupon Nijinska (the new ballet master) began urging Diaghilev to send for some of her Kiev pupils, among whom was the present writer. Indeed, so eloquent was her praise that Diaghilev began to await the arrival of these extraordinary dancers with the greatest impatience. But almost a year was still to elapse before their arrival, it being no easy matter to step over the Soviet barbed wire...and then Diaghilev was to find himself cruelly disappointed.

B. E. Kokhno and his connection with the Russian Ballet

This same year a new personality, destined to play an important part in the life of the Ballet, entered Diaghilev's existence. He again was one of Serge Pavlovitch's discoveries—though hardly of the same order as Stravinsky or Prokofiev—his connection with the Ballet having begun as a result of his collaboration with Stravinsky in the composition of the libretto for the opera *Mavra*. I refer to Boris Kokhno, whose acquaintance Diaghilev made, through Sudeikine, some months after his break with Massine. For a time Diaghilev pinned great faith to Kokhno's literary talent, took him to Rome to see Vyacheslav Ivanov, intended to publish his verses, and established him as regular librettist to the Ballet. Soon Kokhno had become one of the inner circle, and a member of Diaghilev's "family." For the rest of his life Kokhno remained deeply attached to Diaghilev, an attachment very precious to the latter, and in many ways reciprocated.

As I have said, Kokhno was the Ballet's librettist, but he was also Diaghilev's assistant and secretary, to whom was entrusted the general supervision of the Ballet's productions, Serge Pavlovitch attaching much importance to his opinion. Kokhno's influence on Balanchine was a very real one. Profiting by the fact that he had composed the librettos for most of the ballets presented between 1923 and 1929, he would even lay down the law to the dancers and *corps de ballet* in regard to choreography. Kokhno's permanent attendance at rehearsals, his authoritarian suggestions and categorical demands, his somewhat haughty manner towards the members of the company, and his obvious intimacy with Diaghilev (he would "thou" him in public, and call him Seriozha), gave birth to many rumors that Kokhno was designated to succeed Serge Pavlovitch. And as the artists were, on the whole, somewhat afraid of Kokhno, and did not like him, considering that his influence contributed to Diaghilev's aloofness, it was with some anxiety that they watched the "young sapling" preparing to take the place of the mighty old oak.

The following year another collaborator appeared in the person of Prince Shervashidze, originally one of the stage designers to the Mariinsky Theater in St. Petersburg, but now to be permanently attached to the Russian Ballet.

Before this period the Ballet had never possessed its own stage designers, all its sets being painted from rough designs provided by various painters. Thus, among the many painters who had worked for the ballet may be cited Allegri, Anisfeldt, the Polunins, Sapunov, Socrate (responsible for the décors of the new production *Sylphides*), Charbé and Yaramitch. But frequently the final result would differ considerably from the artist's designs, since each scene-painter had his own method of working. Prince Shervashidze, however, "our dear little Prince," as Diaghilev, who was very fond of him, would often call him, would go to the greatest pains to reproduce the artists' designs with the utmost fidelity.

Summary of the 1922 season

This year there is nothing particularly spectacular to relate in the history of the Ballet. Monte Carlo, some productions at the Théâtre Mogador in Paris, a protracted tour in France and Belgium, make up the tale of the year's achievements. Also, painful as Diaghilev found it, *The Sleeping Beauty* was abandoned for good, an injunction having been obtained forbidding the use of the scenery. Nevertheless, realizing all the risks attendant upon so lengthy and cumbrous a production, of a kind no longer suited to the taste of Western audiences, a change for which his other productions were partly responsible, he resolved to remodel the whole ballet as the one-act *Mariage d'Aurore,* and to employ the scenery designed by Benois for *Le Pavillon d'Armide.* Still in my possession is a shortened version of the piano score of *The Sleeping Beauty* showing the part played by Diaghilev in shortening it for his production. In its new form the ballet was exceedingly well received by the Parisian public, and became a permanent feature in the repertoire.

Very different was the fate reserved for the two "real" novelties of the season, Stravinsky's opera *Mavra,* with sets and costumes by Survage, and Stravinsky's ballet *Le Renard,* with sets and costumes by Larionov, for both met with little success, were never revived (except for my own production of *Le Renard* in a quite different version) and were soon forgotten. Stravinsky alone remembered the first version of *Le Renard,* and was completely satisfied with Nijinska's interpretation of his score. Objectively speaking, however, this first effort of hers cannot be considered very successful, since Nijinska's talents as ballet master only reached their full development in the two succeeding years, 1923-24.

CHAPTER XI

THE LAST EPOCH

1923-24: *Nijinska as choreographer*

I HAVE now brought this history of the Russian Ballet, necessarily so abridged that at times it appears to be merely a dry compilation of dates, tables and events, to the year 1923, which marks the beginning of its third and last epoch. In what has gone before, I have had the advantage of being able to utilize material gathered from Serge Pavlovitch's own reminiscences and conversation, a copious literature, and what I myself found still surviving in the repertoire; for, though he sought restlessly for novelty, Diaghilev held to the ancient acquisitions, with the result that the Ballet's heritage was perpetually growing. In this year, on January 13th, I first reached Paris and "moved in" at Diaghilev's, from which moment I was a constant witness of, and participant in, the life of the Ballet. Subsequently, my life became so closely bound up with that of the Ballet, and of Diaghilev, that it is no longer possible for me to treat these matters objectively. I have therefore preferred to deal with the years 1923-29 in a separate section, in the form of my own reminiscences. Only a summary account of the main events of these years, therefore, seems necessary here.

In 1923, the peak-points reached by the Ballet were the Stravinsky-Goncharova-Nijinska production of *Les Noces* and the gala performance at Versailles, *Les Noces* being particularly interesting for the manner in which it reveals Nijinska's neo-realistic trends, and her efforts to eliminate all "elevation," all the charming conventions of "classical dancing," from the ballet, in order to replace them by a modernist dancing vernacular based on sport and "jazz." In *Les Noces* it is as though Nijinska is seeking to bind her new choreography to the tradition laid down by her brother, though softening its harshness and angularity. As in all her succeeding ballets, one sees academic dancing turned wrongside out in exactly the same way, and posture dominant in place of the dance pattern. Thus the new ballet was not so much dancing, as a Botticellian fresco expressed in motion: an incarnation of the Italian Renaissance seen through Russian eyes. Yet the mass movements of the *corps de ballet* were of the greatest beauty, and were immensely popular with the public. Eminently successful also was the Versailles gala.

Les Noces was the single novelty of this season, after which Diaghilev toured France, Spain and Holland, but omitted his usual appearance in London. In 1924, however, the London performances were resumed, with a veritable cornucopia of new creations: two operas by Gounod, produced at Monte Carlo, with décors and costumes by Benois; *Le Médecin malgré Lui,* and *Philémon et Baucis,* not to mention *Colombe* by the same composer; Chabrier's *L'Education Manquée* to décors by Juan Gris; a series of ballets designed by Nijinska, i.e., *Les Biches,* music by Poulenc, décors by Marie Laurencin; *Les Fâcheux,* music by Auric, décors by Braque; *Les Tentations de la Bergère,* music by Montéclair, décors by Gris (rehearsed for the Versailles gala but not ready); *Le Train Bleu,* music by Milhaud, costumes by Chanel and décor by Laurens, and the ballet version of *Le Astuzie Feminili,* to be known thereafter as *Cimarosiana.* In addition there was a host of ambitious schemes which came to nothing.

The most successful of Nijinska's ballets was undoubtedly *Les Biches,* and the most modern *Le Train Bleu,* the movement of the former, however, being too markedly frenzied, as though the dancers were determined to plow up the earth with their feet, as indeed Nijinska herself seemed to do in her ragtime mazurka. But many of the variations were highly successful, and her original and whimsical humor joined to an intimate lyricism reached its highest point in this ballet.

Diaghilev himself was much more interested in *Les Fâcheux, Les Tentations de la Bergère,* and *Le Train Bleu* than in *Les Biches,* but none of the former ballets really came up to what he expected of them, one proof being that four years later he asked Massine to re-create *Les Fâcheux;* and another, that *Le Train Bleu,* whose music he so much admired, was never even revived. Indeed, Diaghilev hardly considered the latter work a ballet, and had it described on the program as an *"operette dansée."*

That untiring admirer of the ballet, Louis Laloy, warmly appreciated *Les Tentations de la Bergère,* and we find him writing: "With his great sensitiveness to all that is most remarkable, most finished in every epoch, Diaghilev has succeeded in bringing together a number of works chosen from among those presented on the stage by French composers from the time of Louis XV unto our own day and, if the expression be permitted, unto tomorrow."

In a very different manner, A. Levinson found a number of undeservedly cruel and cutting things to say about this ballet.

"Mme. Nijinska's choreography is cast in a style which evokes very faintly the dances of other days—ceremonious *pas de menuet* for the courtiers, quick *pas de bourrée* for the peasants. Mme. Nijinska rejected a documentary reconstruction of the *pas* of Pecourt's day, which would, I agree with her, possess no real theatrical value. But I believe her extreme timidity in the choice of steps to be due rather to an incomplete knowledge of eighteenth-century choreography. All the *petite batterie* was at her disposal, both historically and without any offense against correctness of style. Montéclair was still living when Camargo beat her first *entrechats cinq*.... There is another error in respect to the character of the King. He appears through a trap, facing the public, and walks down the stage without departing from that frontal aspect.... And the *grands changements de pieds* which raise the living statue would not have been so comical if the King had been allowed to make use of an *épaulement* or to place himself at an oblique angle to the audience. This is both an historical error and an aesthetic one. In art, symmetry cannot be absolute: it would petrify the masterpiece." [1]

Naturally, Diaghilev found these lines somewhat painful, particularly as, deep down, he could not but agree, severe as was the verdict. Himself, a devoted and profoundly understanding admirer of that classicism, which, for him, held the keys to all further experiment, however daring and uncharted: he, who with his Louis XIV fête at Versailles had so recently demonstrated his unique sense of the past, and even more, his ability to revivify it, could not but realize how unsatisfactory were Nijinska's re-creations of the seventeenth century in Molière's *Les Fâcheux*, and of the eighteenth, in *Les Tentations de la Bergère*. They had proved infinitely dimmer than any of the visions dreamed by Diaghilev...and this was mainly why Nijinska soon left the Ballet.

Meanwhile, Diaghilev had begun work on the production of *Le Train Bleu* with the greatest enthusiasm. This ballet, according to him, was to inaugurate a new epoch of modernist realism in dancing, a modernism, however, which was to prove very superficial. Nijinska borrowed largely (but poorly from the viewpoint of dancing) from the music hall and the cinema (slow-motion effects) and from sport. Modern as it was, dancing played no real part in it. Indeed, sports gear assumed such importance in this ballet that had Nijinska, for example, appeared on the stage minus her racket, no one would have guessed she was meant to be playing tennis.

Again, *Le Train Bleu* owed infinitely more to literature and music than to choreography. But though the architectural décor designed by Laurens, representing a beach dotted with bathing huts and parasols, was very beautiful, and though all Cocteau's inspiration found full expression, he and Nijinska seemed to be pulling in different directions, and the result was often tedious. There were frequent moments when the action seemed to stop completely, or the dancers would consult imaginary wrist watches, or begin to move in slow motion, as in a film, or raise their eyes to convey the idea that an aeroplane was flying overhead. These incidents held back, slowed down, and even completely arrested, at times, the whole rhythm of the ballet. True, Nijinska made admirable use of the acrobatic gifts of Anton Dolin (through opportunism rather than her own invention), an excellent dancer, who walked on his hands,

[1] Lifar. *Ballet, Traditional to Modern*, p. 157.

turned somersaults, made dangerous leaps, rolled on the ground, rose
to his knees, then to his feet, and fell heavily. It was all so adroit, full
of such youthful enthusiasm, that the applause rang out immediately
and spontaneously. Nevertheless the ballet itself was so crammed with.
different sports and athletics, that it was quite impossible for an audience
to take it all in.

Diaghilev's notebooks

A number of Diaghilev's more ambitious projects for 1923-24, however,
were never to reach fruition. But we have a record of their existence,
because of two notebooks, now in my possession. These are of the
greatest importance, in that they reveal the whole of Diaghilev's effer-
vescent activity, concealed even from those with whom he collaborated
most closely. They provide much insight into his methods, and reveal
how nothing was too small or insignificant to be given his attention.

Only too vividly do these notebooks reveal how restless and troubled
was that spirit of his, a spirit never content with what it could give, but
ever dreaming of greater achievement.

For his 1923-24 season, Diaghilev contemplated a festival in Monte
Carlo, another in honor of Stravinsky, another in Austria, another in
Italy and Spain, a series of symphony and chamber music concerts, the
production of various operas, and a number of painting exhibitions. Swept
away by his plans, ever more elaborate, Diaghilev nevertheless began
to see that he could not realize them all in a single season, and so spread
them over a number of seasons planned to finish in 1928. These plans
would spring to mind quite spontaneously, as is shown by the fact that
often some ambitious plan follows immediately after the laundry list, to
be followed again by hastily scribbled notes, revealing both his impatience and his enthusiasm. A complete lack of any system was combined
in him with the mind of an extraordinarily methodical organizer. In
these books, we find as many as fifteen programs for the Monte Carlo
festival continually revised and altered.

As an example, I quote the first of these programs (the words in
square brackets denoting what Diaghilev crossed out). This whole program, apart from a few corrections, is in ink, but the names of the
painters he had thought of employing, occur in pencil in the right-hand
column.

I.	*Adam*—Giselle	DERAIN
	Montéclair—Les Plaisirs champêtres	GRIS
	Poulenc—Les Biches	M. LAURENCIN
II.	1. *Méhul*—La Dansomanie	VLAMINCK
	4. *Godard*—Les Contes de Perrault	GRIS
	3. *Mouret*—Le Jardin des Amours	BRAQUE
	2. *Milhaud*—	LEGER?

III. [*Ravel*]—[Daphnis and Chloë]—Lalo	?
[*Monsigny*]—Le Ballet de la Royanne	
Dalayrac	MATISSE
Satie—Parade—DERAIN	PICASSO
	DERAIN
Delibes—La Fête de la cloche	GONCHAROVA
IV. *Lesueur*—La Cour des Miracles	LARIONOV
	[TAIROFF]
Debussy—l'Après-Midi d'un Faune	PICASSO
Auric—Les Fâcheux	?
Bizet—Jeux d'Enfants	KISLING
(Here the note N.B. "orchestration Dukas")	
V. *Auber*—La Flûte Magique [Naples, 1830]	UTRILLO
(Note: "arrang. Ansermet")	
[*Dalayrac*] *Monsigny*—Sérénade à	
l'Infante	SERT
Satie—[Parade—Derain]—*Ravel*	
Chabrier—Valses—Bourrée—Espagna	PICASSO
(Note for Bourrée: "Orches. Stravinsky")	

In the following programs, various other ballets appear, such as Lalo's *Namouna* (intended by Diaghilev for Karsavina), Ravel's *Ma Mère l'Oye*, Debussy's *Pan* (décors by Laurens), Naudot-Satie's *Paul et Virginie*, etc., etc. All these programs demanded an enormous amount of preparatory work, in connection with which Serge Pavlovitch had many pages copied from old music books in the Opéra library, as, for instance, Auber's *Marco Spada* and *Cheval de Bronze*, and Méhul's *Daphnis et Pandrose*, *Persée et Andromède* and *Le Jugement de Paris*. He too spent much of his time there, studying old scores by Méhul, Herold, Auber, Halévy, Lefèvre, Rameau, Mouret, Mondonville, Destouches, etc., etc., ordered music catalogues, saw innumerable people, consulted authorities, etc.

For the three performances of the Stravinsky Festival the repertory drawn up by Diaghilev was as follows: *Les Noces Villageoises, L'Oiseau de Feu, Pulcinella, Le Chant du Rossignol, Le Sacre du Printemps, Le Renard* and *Petrouchka*. It was his intention, too, to provide *L'Oiseau de Feu* with an entirely new setting, and to use Russian singers for *Le Renard*.

The Austrian festival was intended to comprise items by Haydn, Mozart, Schubert, Johann Strauss, Liszt, Schönberg, Bartok and—under a question mark—Richard Strauss and Brahms. Even more interesting was the plan for the Italo-Spanish festival which was to include Scarlatti's *Les Femmes de Bonne Humeur*, Pergolesi's *Pulcinella*, Rossini's *La Boutique Fantasque*, Cimarosa's *Le Astuzie Feminili*, Paisiello's *La Serva Padrona*, Falla's *Le Tricorne*, Albeniz's *Triana*, Berners' *Caprice Espagnol*, Ravel's *Rhapsodie Espagnole*, and *Alborada del Grazioso*, Rimsky-

Korsakov's *Capriccio Espagnol*, Glinka's *Jota Argonesa*, Bordes' *Danses Basques*, Stravinsky's *España*, Falla's *Seville*, Berners' *La Carosse du St-Sacrament* (this last work being much in Diaghilev's thoughts at the time) and works by Breton and Donizetti.

In addition, Diaghilev planned a cycle of six or eight symphony concerts entirely, or almost entirely, devoted to the works of some thirty distinguished French composers, a series of chamber-music concerts, and a Russian festival devoted to works by Aliabiev, Varlamov, Glinka, Dargomirsky, together with operatic works by Bortniansky, Berezovsky; Tchaikovsky—*Eugen Onegin*, Prokofiev—*Tsar Dodon*, and Stravinsky—*Mavra*.

Earlier, and before the decision not to include opera in the Russian seasons, Diaghilev had compiled a long list of comic operas, pride of place being allotted to Delibes. He had also drawn up the following strange and interesting "grand project," for ·so we find it named in the notebooks.

(1) *Carmen*—Bizet; (2) *Le Prince Igor*—Borodin; (3) *Pskovitianka* —Rimsky-Korsakov; (4) *La Dame de Pique*—Tchaikovsky; (5) *Eugen Onegin*—Tchaikovsky; (6) *Le Coq d'Or*—Rimsky-Korsakov; (7) *Mavra* —Stravinsky; (8) *Les Maîtres Chanteurs*—Wagner; (9) *Étoiles*—Chabrier; (10) *Le Roi l'a Dit*—Delibes; (11) *Djamileh*—Bizet; (12) *L'Italiana in Algeri*—Rossini; (13) *Cambiale del Matrimonio*—Rossini; (14) *Snegourochka*—Rimsky-Korsakov; (15) *Don Juan*—Mozart; (16) *Le Barbier de Seville*—Rossini; (17) *Paul et Virginie*—Satie [*Paul et Virginie* occurs very frequently in Diaghilev's lists]; (18) *Falstaff*—Verdi; (19) *Elixir d'Amore*—Donizetti; (20) *Don Pasquale*—Donizetti; (21) *Philidor;* (22) *Servante-Maîtresse*—Paisiello; (23) *L'Omelette à la Follembuche*—Delibes; (24) *Le Roi Dodon*—Prokofiev; (25) *Lakmé*—Delibes.

During this period, we find Diaghilev as interested in plans for exhibitions of painting as in his projects for ballets and operas. His first conception is limited to the three following exhibitions: (1) An exhibition of French landscape painters including Rousseau; (2) An exhibition of Spanish painters, and works by Cézanne; (3) An exhibition of works for the theater. The first of these (which soon assumed a more ambitious shape in his mind, and no longer limited itself exclusively to landscape painters) was intended to comprise a representative collection of works by Poussin, 'Claude Lorrain, Hubert Robert, Corot, Rousseau, Gauguin, Manet, Monet, Pissarro, Matisse, Marquet, Dufy, Vlaminck, Derain, Lhôte, Laurencin, Delaunoy, Seurat, Courbet, Signac, Gleizes, Fragonard, Blanche, etc. The Spanish exhibition was to show works by Larionov, Goncharova, Survage, Picasso, Gris, Derain, Matisse, Benois, Laurencin, Leger, Gordon Craig, Lovat Fraser, Zak, Fedorovsky, Stellezky, Hugo Rumbold, Toulouse-Lautrec, Seurat, Gonzaga, Ribera, Pannini, Chirico, etc.

Another plan was devoted to a portrait exhibition (Ingres, Manet, Monet, Renoir, Derain, Picasso, Modigliani and *le douanier* Rousseau), another to a "Dress" exhibition, and there were still others for which the very dates had been fixed:

January 1st to 21st—Exhibition of French Painters.
January 24th to February 13th—Exhibition of Spanish Art.
February 16th to March 1st—Retrospective exhibition of works by painters of the Independent Group.
March 4th to March 17th—Dress and Jewelry Exhibition.
March 20th to April 2nd—Russian Ballet Exhibition.

Such projects were no fleeting notions, for much work had already been done on them, and we actually find many references to the ownership and whereabouts of numbers of the paintings he had in mind to exhibit. Indeed, negotiations for them were already in progress with the management of the Monte Carlo Theater, and matters were so far advanced that a form of agreement had already been drafted.

Understood though it was, that Diaghilev was to assume the place left empty by Gunsburg in the life of Monte Carlo, it was clear that he would never be content to play the part of a mere operatic impresario. What he wanted, what he dreamed of, was the creation of a new artistic center in that city, something immense and representative of all that was greatest and best in the arts. Given his excellent relations with the young Prince Peter of Monaco—his constant protector and most enlightened patron—he had every reason to believe that his many proposals in connection with classical ballet, Russian ballet, *opéra-bouffe,* festivals, concerts, exhibitions, and recitals of chamber music, to be held in the Monte Carlo Palais des Beaux-Arts, would be accepted. This same notebook from which I have quoted, also contains details of every matter relating to expenditure connected with the ballets, operettas, and new productions for the Palais des Beaux-Arts. No mention however is made of the Puppet Theater, this idea only occurring to Diaghilev much later. Nevertheless, in this same year, 1923, he outlines a program of such performances.

I. The forces of love and magic in French literature of the seventeenth century. 3 Acts (1 hour). Dances, songs, readings.
II. The Episode of D... Music by Falla.
III. Turkish theater—shadow show in original colors as in eighteenth century (30 minutes).
IV. The Mysteries (6-8 scenes) with prologue. Scenes from the New Testament—Italian figures of the seventeenth century (20 minutes).

None of these plans materialized, however, a fact to which may perhaps be attributed Diaghilev's discontent with things in general, and the Ballet in particular.

I am not suggesting that these still-born conceptions only occurred to Serge Pavlovitch in 1923-24. The likelihood is that Diaghilev was always tormented by his immense schemes, and indeed it would be difficult to imagine him otherwise than in a fever of activity. It is simply that, by some hazard, these two notebooks happen to be preserved, while those which preceded them are now lost to us. But what we do see is that after 1925 plans for ballet productions became increasingly rarer. Whether this was due to his many disappointments, his incipient disease—diabetes —or the fact that circumstances linked him inseparably to *one and the same* enterprise, it is clear that, in spite of his great mental activity, Diaghilev having passed into his fifth decade, was beginning to lose interest in that "enterprise." At the same time an enormous amount of detail needed to be seen to, and these notebooks reveal how meticulously Diaghilev fulfilled that task. We see him noting available dates for performances, probable outlays, the names of singers, male and female throughout the world, likely to suit him for such and such parts, ideas for décors, the whereabouts of scores and piano parts, and even managing to keep an eye on doors needing to be painted, velvet for the boxes, small tables in the buffet, publicity, advertising—not to mention the infinity of props needed for each performance....

The assiduous and painstaking care with which Diaghilev worked out the minutest details of his productions is beautifully demonstrated by the notes we find in the second of these notebooks, all devoted to the same production, *The Triumph of Neptune*. I cannot do better than quote it fully as an example.

Scene I. (Bridge.) At the end of the scene, spotlight on a telescope surrounded by a crowd of people.

Weights for the telescope legs, dust cover, platforms and railings round it.

Two straw cylinders.

Posy, Victorian style, for sailor's wife.

Boots for workmen.

Artist painting bridge.

Five professors uncovering telescope. In frock coats, spectacles, bald wigs, white buttonholes, ribbons and decorations, tophats.

Scene II. (Skies.) Arrange wings behind backcloth (as in "Polka").

Narrow black velvet ribbons round necks—with medallions.

Winglets.

Black gloves.

Loose swinging sides to backcloth.

Scene III. (Departure.) Big colored handkerchiefs.

Scene IV. (Shipwreck.) *Noises* to begin *immediately* after departure and continue until Scene V. T. Hoir's costume to be American cloth ... or a mannequin.

Scene V. (Fleet Street.) Cut score in first part, and lengthen "jig."
Add Evene—girl flower seller, dancing "jig."
Journalists have quill pens behind ears.
Sailor's wife to have Victorian posy.
Two large shawls for both women.
Umbrellas—black, gray and green.
N.B. Sky on set to be *gray* with *rain* painted in.
All artites under open umbrellas except beggar, who covers his head
with paper.
Paper boys with bill boards—"Sailor meets Fairy."
Telescope covered to protect from rain.

Scene VI. (Snow.) Long gloves—white silk.
Pale Green foil flowers.
Tu-tu's covered with down.
Have snow falling after adagio.
Delete Petrova's variation.
Add two wings and introduce six flying fairies (two new costumes),
sprinkling snow.
Oval mirrors for ladies.

Scene VII. (Dance of goddess.) Cut music.

Scene VIII. (Polka.) Cage hanging on wall between windows?
Coffee-pot and cups for journalists, served by waiter.
Pipes for journalists.
See to finale with policemen.

Scene IX. (Cannibals.) Gibbet, Journalist; white makeup before the
hanging.
Green spotlight for clowns and later white—stronger—for journalist
and sailor.
Décor of grotto; grotto music to be cut in first part up to allegretto.
New choreography for 2nd cannibal scene.
Blue cooking pots and *black* devils. King black, too.
Hang journalist.
Masks more terrifying, little caps inside, hair stuck down.

Scene X. (The nigger.) Second telescope—*breakable*.
Rearrange dance—more virtuosity.

Scene XI. (Neptune.) Musical cuts at the end of the *pas d'action?*
New arrangements for harlequins.
New variation for Amor—Idzikowsky.
Cuts in "Matelotte."
Inclusion of Idzikowsky in finale.
Pedestals *painted* by nigger to look like marine stalactites.
Danilova appears through trap door in front of backcloth in a shell;

shell to be stuffed and embroidered in different colored silks, frogged and sequined.

Neptune's body stuffed and costume jeweled.

Pages to wear white and yellow plumed turbans and yellow gloves.

Women to have diamond necklaces.

For niggers—turbans?

Costumes and headgear for sea-gods.

Ladies to carry Victorian fans.

Sequins and "frogs" for harlequins.

Amor's costume with *tin-foil* flowers and winglets.

N.B. Dancing to start from the very beginning of scene.

A few pages further we find Diaghilev noting other "additions to Neptune," but even that does not complete the preliminary work, for again we find more changes later.

A considerable amount of work also devolved upon Diaghilev for the budgeting of his enterprises, the notebooks being littered with figures, additions, subtractions and multiplications. : . . . Expenses were colossal and somehow had to be balanced. It is true that the returns were considerable also (for instance, the six weeks' London season of 1926 brought in £25,000).

Diaghilev's articles on the Russian Ballet

These notebooks also contain the rough drafts of two articles contributed by Diaghilev to English papers, one in 1926, the other in 1929. The former is in French, and entitled "Les Quinze Ans" (though originally "Après Quinze Ans"), and presents a concise and lyrical account of the Russian Ballet in London, from its début in 1911. I have already quoted from this article in dealing with the Coronation Gala of 1911, and the Spanish epic of 1918, the last paragraph of which is a tribute to Lord Rothermere and the London public.

"After this time of trial, we entered upon our third period. This same year we concluded our second Ballet season, thanks entirely to the assistance of an eminent Englishman, who might object if I said who he was, for his personal modesty is only equaled by the lavishness of his generosity. He it was who came to our assistance, and without the slightest degree of self-interest, for the ballet to him meant what music and painting mean to others, placed us where it was necessary for us to be. To that powerful and animating spirit I would like to express here the deep, the infinitely deep and sincere gratitude I feel. People of such quality, believe me, are rare.

"My letter would be incomplete, if I omitted one most important matter. It was my habit to leave the theater generally at 7, when rehearsals were over. Though it rained as it can only in London, with blasts that tore the hair from one's head, I would pass huge queues of people hidden beneath their umbrellas with their feet squelching in water. It was the public waiting for the doors to open to see and judge what I had done, and my heart would expand with surprise, with gratitude. Yes, one must indeed love, and be fired by the keenest interest to overcome such unpleasantness on the path to joy. Good public, if we have not always managed to please you, know at least that we too, on our side, have passed interminable hours anxiously waiting for the doors to open, to permit us too to glimpse some tiny corner of that new beauty, which we have striven to submit to your critical or admiring judgment."

His second article, dated 1929, is of greater interest. It begins and ends with the following phrase: "The longer the earth turns, the deader it gets." This article was written at a moment when, being ill, he could only jot down some stray lines and thoughts. The first part was therefore dictated to P. G. Koribut-Kubitovitch, and the second part to myself. Its purpose was to present a new composer to the London public, the youthful Igor Markevitch, as well as a new chore-author whom London already knew and loved as a star, namely, myself. But the significance and interest of this article goes far beyond the limits set it by its author.

In particular, this article draws up the balance sheet of the third period of the Ballet, "mine," and demonstrates the manner in which Serge Pavlovitch envisaged its future development. In this final period, Diaghilev's one preoccupation was the search for new forms of scenic art, a preoccupation from which, alarming though others might find his perpetual experimenting, he refused to allow himself to be diverted. Diaghilev wrote: "Our epoch has devoted itself almost wholly to mechanical problems of motion, but yet, whenever a new *artistic* movement appears, humanity's fear of being crushed by it is greater even than its fear of being run over by some motorcar. For twenty-five years now I have sought to find new movements in the theater, and society should therefore accept once and for all these experiments of mine which today seem so dangerous to it, but which tomorrow will form part and parcel of its life."

"Constructivism" as applied to décor, modernist "simplification" of music, the literary approach, contemporaneity and choreographic "acrobatics," were the predominant trends in this third period of the Russian Ballet, during which its constructivist trend found its most complete expression in the ballets *La Chatte* and *Le Pas d'Acier,* presented in 1927.

Thereafter, the trend changes towards a scenic and neorealistic dramatization, typical of which was the production of *Le Fils Prodigue* in 1929. But, though Diaghilev had been one of the first to realize the constructivist trends of the new epoch, a trend soon to be reflected in his ballets, he was also one of the first to realize just how ephemeral it was, and how quickly destined to fade. "Constructivism in painting, décor, music, choreography," he wrote, "is what will, and does, lead our generation away." Very typical is this "will and does" of his, for though the present generation wears what was fashionable yesterday, that fact mattered nothing to Diaghilev. Nevertheless, though he might bury away this constructivism in the painting and décor, this constructivism so typical of our times, very differently does he judge the part played by it in music and choreography. "Its reign, both in painting and décor, is now approaching its end, yet it is still remarkably vital in music, which only lately overwhelmed us with impressionism and neo-sentimentalism, as it is in choreography, whose classicism we have so blandly accepted."

However that may be, Diaghilev completely abandoned constructivism in his décors, as altogether out of date, and in addition pronounced cruel sentence on that music which, in the third period of the Russian Ballet, influenced it so greatly: that *"musiquette"* of which he talked to R. Brussel in this same spring of 1929. In his article we find him writing: "In Paris, we have just passed through a scandalous period of sentimental and debauched 'simplification' where creation in music is concerned. It began with the cult of Gounod, Tchaikovsky and Donizetti, only to end with a pastiche of Godard and Lecoq. Melody and simplicity were considered obligatory and as though its inevitable principle, with the result that the wretched music reached such a dead level of banality as was not even attained by the sentimental romances of the late 19th century. That is why I acclaim to such a degree whatever may help us to forget, even for a moment, the fatal error of the international mart of Paris." These errors Diaghilev wished to forget by returning to his "old loyalties," real music such as that of Ravel, and by going forward with Hindemith and Markevitch. About the latter we find him writing:

"His music is dear to me, because I see in it just that rebirth of this new generation which might set itself against the Parisian orgies of these last years. True, Markevitch and those who think like him fall involuntarily into the opposite extreme, all romantic melody being their enemy. Markevitch's début is characterized by an exaggeratedly dry and formal constructivism, for he is unable to admit of any compromise. But if we remember his youth, the intensity of the rhythmic movement is quite astonishing, although the counterpoint masks his themes. To our contemporary ears, his music proceeds *'parallel with the pleasure* it is meant to give,' but how much more agreeable that is, than music written *'to give* pleasure.' Besides, Markevitch will not always be merely sixteen, and again, our ear in time will discover the key to a new 'order' of artistic joys. [Originally Diaghilev had dictated our "ears will discover the key 'to its thematic structure so timidly hidden.'"]

In spite of the fact that the majority of Diaghilev's articles are dedicated to choreography, to elucidating and defending acrobatics and constructivism, his evaluation of the dancing aspects of the ballet, and his prognoses of the choreography of the future, are much less clear and definite. It must be admitted that, to the very end of his life, he remained a far more competent judge of painting and music than of dancing. "The new appreciation of my 'Spectacles' of today," wrote Diaghilev [*The Times*, July 13th, 1929], "is a series of exclamations: what an 'Etrange' [sic], 'Extravagant,' 'Repellent' show; and the new definitions of the choreography are 'Athletics' and 'Acrobatics'.... But a production must first and foremost be 'Etrange.' I can well imagine the amazement of those who saw the first electric bulb, or heard the first telephone. Yet that first 'extravagant' electric bell offered the London public was the inoffensive production of *The Polovtsian Dances* which I presented in *Prince Igor*. [Earlier, Diaghilev had dictated: "My grandfather hated the first trains to such a degree that he gave orders for his carriage to be driven along by the railway lines so that he might drive those monstrous railway trains out of his way. And when his grandson merely wished to push out of his path the traditional classical ballet, he began with a most inoffensive production entitled *The Polovtsian Dances* from *Prince Igor*."] The elegant spectators could not endure such wild and brutal acrobatics and everyone fled. This happened in Covent Garden in 1911. And according to the critics, in the same theater and in 1929, my dancers became athletes, and my groupings pure acrobatics.

"I have no room here to discuss this grave question in detail, but, in a few words. The classical dance has never been and is not today the Russian Ballet. Its birthplace was France; it grew up in Italy, and has only been conserved in Russia. Side by side with the classical dance there has always existed the national or character dance, which has given the evolution of the Russian Ballet. In such rare countries as Spain, where the national dances have reached their highest point of development, it is obvious what an important part is played by character dancing. I do not know of a single classical movement which was born of the Russian folk dance. Why have we got to take our inspiration from the minuet of the French Court, and not from the Russian village festival? That which appears to you acrobatic is a dilettante terminology for our national dance step. The mistake really, in fact, goes much deeper, because it is undoubtedly the Italian classical school which has introduced into the dance the acrobatic elements. The *double tours en l'air*, next to the classical *pirouettes en dehors*, and the hateful 32 *fouettés*, that is when acrobatics should be attacked. In the plastic efforts of Balanchine in *The Prodigal Son* there are far less acrobatics than in any classical *pas de deux* in *Aurora's Wedding*." [2]

Is it still possible to believe that in so-called classical dancing, there is not a constant infiltration of the elements of character dancing and acrobatics? Diaghilev is certainly correct in his affirmation, but his opinion that in Balanchine's ballets there is less acrobatics than in *Aurora's Wedding* must certainly be considered paradoxical, especially as the acrobatism

[2] Lifar, *Ballet, Traditional to Modern*, p. 159.

of the classical ballet is of quite a different order. Nor is his defense of the "athleticism," "acrobatics" and "extravagance" of this period made more convincing by his appeal to character and classical dancing, for though acrobatics may have been employed, that does not in any way justify its general utilization, in principle, in the ballet. In any case, Diaghilev understood all this perfectly, and for that reason dictated the following phrase, the first portion of which was scored out: *"Acrobatics are intolerable when they become theory."* Yet those very acrobatics contained many of the elements of that constructivism which was "at the bottom of everything contemporary." Defending the honor of constructivism in his ballets, Diaghilev wipes from his mind the fact that acrobatism, in principle, is intolerable. This same dubiety concerning acrobatics is characteristic of the last years of the Russian Ballet.

While denying the acrobatics of Balanchine, Diaghilev considered that only after my *Renard* did it become possible at last to talk of the "ballet acrobatic." But the next lines seem to suggest that this "acrobatism" is not characteristic of all my choreographic creativity, but only of my *Renard*. "On the cover of the score for *Renard* Stravinsky noted 'Le Renard to be represented by buffoons, acrobats, or dancers.' Lifar produced it with dancers and acrobats, real circus acrobats. In this union of the plastic art of the circus and choreographic invention lay the very crux of the choreographic problem. When, in *Le Renard,* Stravinsky causes the bass to sing with a womanly voice, and when the sentimentality of the Fox expresses itself by the clanging restaurant cymbals, we must realize that in this work no other visual expression is needed than that invented by Lifar." In the following sentence, however, we see Diaghilev stating quite clearly that this acrobatism of mine is only a particular instance *"and not at all a principle with Lifar,* for it was merely that he saw no other way of expressing Stravinsky's music choreographically. Stravinsky himself is often clearly the acrobat of sound, just as Picasso is the acrobat of line." But if acrobatism is not at all a principle with Lifar, true though it is, is one justified in that case in stating that from the moment I became ballet master to the Russian Ballet, that is, in the last year of its existence, "one could at last begin to talk of the 'ballet acrobatic' "? If this be true, then all that remains of Diaghilev's statement about myself is that "constructivism" and "an absolute horror of all compromise" were marked features of my work. But Serge Pavlovitch had once had immeasurable faith in me as a choreographer, as a result of which we find him saying in his article: "When he [Lifar] appeared for the first rehearsal, it was as though the only thing he had ever done was producing ballets. He knew exactly what he wanted; it can be felt in his little acrobatic ballet...." Without a moment's hesitation, Diaghilev confided the future of the Russian Ballet to my care, but the choreographic principles of the new era in the Ballet, *which Diaghilev foresaw,* were never entirely clear to him.

Last years of the Russian Ballet

But to return to 1924. Nijinska had parted company with the Ballet, and once more the company was left without a ballet master. It is exceedingly probable that at that moment the company might have ceased to exist, but for two new discoveries of Diaghilev's: namely, that of his "third son" in the realm of music, Dukelsky, and that of a dancer—myself. In after days, Diaghilev once told me that what played an important part in deciding him to continue was largely curiosity to see whether I would fulfill all the promise he imagined he had detected in me. This year Dukelsky composed the music for the ballet *Flore et Zéphyre,* with which Diaghilev was frankly delighted. I have a letter dated August 13th, in which he writes to me: "Dukelsky came yesterday and played me the music for *Flore et Zéphyre* which I like enormously. I made such comments as I thought fit, and he very nicely said he would take note of it all, and go on working at it in Monte Carlo, under my eye: all of which pleases me greatly. For his twenty years he's extremely gifted and developed." But Dukelsky's reign was soon ended, and *Flore et Zéphyre* proved not only his first but his last ballet.

For the time being, however, the ballet-master difficulty was settled by Diaghilev's inviting Massine first to put on *Flore et Zéphyre* and then Auric's *Les Matelots,* but there was no pretense that the invitation was anything but temporary, or that it would contribute in any way to resolve perhaps the most difficult and unpleasant problem which always confronted the Ballet: namely, its almost perpetual difficulties with its choreographers. About this particular crisis of 1925, A. Levinson has some particularly pointed things to say:

"Today, after six performances and two first nights, it is more difficult than ever to make out the views and define the policy of the company. The theory and practice of the 'Ballets Russes' have changed twice in three years. The schemes and constructions of Mme. Nijinska, which caused such a stir at the time of *Les Noces,* have been brushed away with an iron hand. The return to the choreographic methods of Massine has the air of being a temporary truce only. Despite the success of G. Auric's *Les Matelots,* Diaghilev's collaboration with Stravinsky's French followers is doomed to a speedy end. It may very well be that everything which at this moment represents the artistic ballast, whether it be inspired by Mihaud or Poulenc, will in its turn be thrown overboard. As though in an enchanted maze, the company of the 'Ballets Russes' finds itself where it began, at the crossroads where it has struggled so many years in search of a way out.

"Fokine's departure, in 1912, was the origin of a crisis which Diaghilev so far has been unable to resolve. Massine, who was to be used as an antidote to Mme. Nijinska's methods, has himself become subject to their influence. His production of *Flore et Zéphyre* was no longer thought to be good after it had been performed in Paris. He himself is going to return to his English music-hall activities. What is to be done? The question is just as acute as ever. What is to be done to fit choreographic movement to music? What is to be done to harmonize the dancer's *plastique,* a formal element, with the problems of expression and of symbolic gesture? Should the traditions of the classic dance be frankly employed, or should they be relegated to second place, and only used surreptitiously? These various problems receive a different solution each season. Only the orgy of color, the archaeological ornament and impassioned pathos of M. Fokine seem to be banished forever...." [3]

In regard to this article, two remarks need to be made. In the first place, Levinson is perfectly justified in claiming that Massine succumbed to Nijinska's influence. Nevertheless, he does not explain how Massine, who had never worked with Nijinska, could have come under her influence, nor does he mention the fact that Nijinska herself had already been influenced by Massine, and Massine himself in his first period, by Fokine, Nijinsky, etc., etc. Yet, this was something that might have been underlined, for, once the constant and reciprocal effects of these influences had been explained, the phrase, "the theory and practice of the 'Ballets Russes' have changed twice in three years," might well have been softened. This reciprocal influence upon each other of the Ballet's chore-authors is explained, not only by the fact that old ballets continued to remain in the repertoire, but principally by the permanent influence wielded over everything connected with the Ballet by its chief guiding spirit, Diaghilev. Thus, it was not so much Nijinska influencing Massine, or Massine influencing Nijinska, as Diaghilev influencing them both; and so a certain continuity was assured, in spite of evolutionary processes, and the diverse trends and doctrines which marked the progress of the Ballet. Indeed, so powerful and determinant was Diaghilev's influence, that J. Sazonova is perfectly justified in asserting that the choreography of the various ballet masters to the Ballet was, in fact, the choreography of Diaghilev. Thus, in *La Revue Musicale,* we find her writing: "Diaghilev left no school, his enterprise died with him, and those who worked with him are now dispersed, each working in isolation. But the seal of Diaghilev remains engraved upon them, and though each is absorbed in his own creations they still continue to propagate the new choreographic conception, a concept which, whatever one may say, can, in the widest sense of the word, be called 'The School of Diaghilev.' "

Again, the period in which Levinson wrote his article (July, 1925) happened to coincide with the very apogee of the Paris season at the Gaîeté Lyrique, a moment when there were actually no complications in regard to ballet masters, for a new choreographer, Georges Balanchine, was already working on the new ballets.

---

[3] Lifar, *Ballet, Traditional to Modern,* pp. 179-80.

The two novelties of the season, *Flore et Zéphyre,* by Dukelsky-Braque-Massine, and *Les Matelots,* by Auric-Pruna-Massine, both enjoyed the greatest success in Paris (as also in London at the Coliseum), but were received more critically by the Press, that of Paris unanimously praising the dancers, while objecting that the ballets themselves could not be compared with its original productions, the very glory of the Russian Ballet.

As for the musical qualities of the new ballets, there was obvious diversity of opinion, though all agreed it was unsuitable for dancing. It was added further that as a result the ballet master had been compelled to resort to "stunts" and technical feats of considerable difficulty, which still further urged the ballet along the path of clowning, circus tricks, the music hall and the physical culture. In these music-hall trends the critics saw the signs of a new epoch, and it was said of Diaghilev that he was "hurrying in advance of the times."

Balanchine as choreographer

The première of the next new ballet, by Balanchine, *Barabau,* took place in London, and proved immensely successful. Balanchine, who had completed his studies at the Imperial Theater Schools of St. Petersburg, was a disciple of the Moscow fanatic Gailizovsky, a ballet master who cultivated acrobatism on an academic foundation. Acrobatics and humor were Balanchine's two great resources, though he was now to pass through a new school, that of Fokine, Massine and Nijinska, for not only did the old ballets continue to remain in the repertoire, but Massine and Nijinska continued to be employed at intervals, since Diaghilev hardly dared to deliver the fate of the Ballet completely into Balanchine's hands. Thus in 1926 we find Nijinska creating *Roméo et Juliette,* which, plastically speaking, was one of the best, and a choreographic poem *Une Nuit sur le Mont-Chauve* by Mussorgsky; while in 1927-28 it was the pre-revolutionary Massine and not the Soviet Balanchine who produced Prokofiev's *Le Pas d' Acier* and Nabokov's *Ode.*[4]

Balanchine, while creating his own ballets, continued to learn much from the productions of his predecessors, and to assimilate their spirit, thanks to which he was able happily to combine his "sovietism" with the main trends of Diaghilev's Ballet. Indeed, remarkable progress is revealed, if we trace his development from the first comic ballets, through the delightful and frankly amusing *Barabau* (1925), *La Pastorale, The Triumph of Neptune,* with its roots in English folk song, *Jack in the Box* and its naïve "darky" themes (1926), to his most perfect, most personal creation *La Chatte* (1927), the genuinely inspired and important *Apollon* and *Les Dieux Mendiants* (1928) and the tragic miming of *Le Fils Prodigue* and *Le Bal* (1929), the latter an utterly insignificant ballet

---

[4] Again in 1927, Diaghilev included in his repertoire *Mercure* created by Massine in 1924.

which anyone might have created. And in addition to these, there was the new version of *Le Chant du Rossignol* presented by him in 1927.

Balanchine's inventiveness was particularly rich in the devising of tricks and parodies. If Mme. Nijinska and Massine brought the ballet back to earth and deprived it of all "elevation," Balanchine's creations, inspired by the circus, and the most realistic trends, had, so to speak, no connection with academic ballet. "Nevertheless, Balanchine enriched the 'Ballets Russes' and the academic dance with new methods, but above all, alas, with possibilities no more than hinted at and unfulfilled, a fact which left Diaghilev with a profound sense of dissatisfaction." [5] It must be admitted, however, that the problem confronting him was infinitely more difficult than that faced by his predecessors, for Fokine, Massine and Nijinska had always co-operated closely with Diaghilev and those about him—painters, musicians and poets—a collaboration which often enabled them to produce works amazing in their unity. Balanchine, however, was working practically in isolation, with Diaghilev helping him less and less, and was thus forced into trying to guess the desires of his employer. No longer was there the least effective collaboration with painters and musicians, and their names follow each other in endless succession: Utrillo, Pruna, Derain, Mirò, Ernst, Jakovlev, Gabo, Pevsner, Tchelitchev, Charbonnier, Bauchant, Gris, Rouault, Chirico, Auric, Rieti, Satie, Poulenc, Milhaud, Lambert, Berners, Sauguet, Nabokov ... they received their orders and carried them out, without taking any real part in the life of the Ballet, while Soviet producers like Meyerhold and Tairov began to assume an ever greater importance in Diaghilev's eyes and to exert an ever strengthening influence, clearly discernible in Balanchine's work. Meanwhile the old fire in Diaghilev was beginning to burn low, and he who had once been all things to the Ballet had now, as it were, become its conscientious manager, who, though supervising each new production with efficient interest yet remained indifferent to them all. From this period date the *Roméo et Juliette* (1926), of Lambert-Mirô-Ernst-Nijinska; *The Triumph of Neptune* (1926), of Lord Berners-Prince Shervashidze-Balanchine; *Le Pas d'Acier* (1927), Prokofiev-Jakovlev-Massine; *La Chatte* (1927), of Sauguet-Gabo-Pevsner-Balanchine; *Apollon Musagète* (1928), of Stravinsky-Bauchant-Balanchine; *Le Fils Prodigue* (1928), of Prokofiev-Rouault-Balanchine, and finally a new version, created by myself, *Le Renard* (1929), with Stravinsky and Larionov. Serge Pavlovitch took great interest in this, my first production, and often came to rehearsals, but he gave no advice and took *no* creative part in the realization of my ballet.

Diaghilev's bibliophilia

Had the creative fire died out in Diaghilev, had he lost all interest in sponsoring the newest developments in art? I do not think so. Diaghilev

[5] Lifar, *Ballet, Traditional to Modern*, p. 182.

Gerald Tyrwhitt, Lord Berners

Constant Lambert

remained Diaghilev, and the weakening of his interest in the Ballet merely confirms the unchanging nature of his character, for what constituted its very basis was an utter inability to content himself with past achievement, and problems already solved.

Then in 1927, a new passion, capable of absorbing every energy, took possession of him—his bibliomania. For a time, the old and the new were at grips and it seemed that the old, the Ballet, must be defeated and go to the wall. That struggle continued until 1929, his love of the Ballet and his passion for book hunting alternately predominant. Yet, the more furiously this passion flared up in him, and the more colossal grew the plans he conceived in the *true Diaghilev spirit,* the clearer it became that rebirth and not death awaited the Russian Ballet.

Diaghilev's original idea had been merely to build for himself a private collection of important books and musical manuscripts. By degrees, however, his plans grew vaster, until we find him contemplating an immense Russian Library in Europe, somewhat similar to the Pushkin Museum in Russia, which would centralize everything relating to Russian culture abroad. This bibliomania ate greatly into his time, for not content with buying books, he also went in for "mounting books" himself, confecting rarities by completing missing, or imperfect, signatures or pages, from other imperfect copies of the same book. But what more than anything took up his time, was the compilation of his catalogue, when, lying on his bed in his boots, he would spend hours and days, concentrating, not, as once, on where he might seek new dancing talent, or what new contracts might be signed for the Ballet, but on his catalogues and bibliographies, in the hope of discovering something that would throw new light on his rare, his precious, and even occasionally, unique finds.

Among other valuable items, he could number three from the presses of Ivan Feodorov, the Gutenberg of Russia, The Acts of the Apostles, A Book of Hours, and the first Russian Grammar, which latter, before Diaghilev's discovery, was unknown; rare editions published in Prague and Venice during the sixteenth century, and some superb seventeenth-century volumes. The epoch of Peter the Great and Catherine the Great were also represented with rare completeness, and there were besides some magnificent editions of the nineteenth century. A special section was devoted to manuscripts and numbered works by Pushkin, Jukovsky, Gogol, Turgeniev, Glinka, Wagner, etc.

All this necessitated considerable expenditure, and where was the money to be found if not in the Russian Ballet? Willy-nilly, Diaghilev was forced to continue working with the Ballet, but incapable of doing so passively and inertly, he began to dream of new worlds to conquer, of immense reforms to be made. These reforms were to operate in two directions: on the one hand, new researches into ballet worked out in the rehearsal room by the ballet master found by himself; and on the other, the reorganization of the actual composition of the Ballet, which in

Diaghilev's opinion, now seemed inadequate. Both these changes involved the foundation of a real school of classical dancing, and that school Diaghilev contemplated establishing in Monte Carlo.

Death of Diaghilev

Thus, once more we find Diaghilev conceiving his vast projects, but alas, he was now at grips with his illness, borne down by it, all that was left being an immense apathy, indifference and weariness. To the last day of his life, August 19th, 1929, that creative spirit of his went on struggling, refusing to submit. But death conquered at last, and left us with the host of unsolved problems with which we have been wrestling all these years, and which we are still seeking to resolve.

Let us be thankful to the fates, that they at least have permitted us to know Diaghilev, to work with him, and be infected by the burning flame of that spirit to which we owe so much beauty, such unsuspected artistic joys.

Diaghilev's creative achievement, the edifice he created, must always remain. They have become part and parcel of the very lifeblood of contemporary art, which to all eternity will transmit them through the arts to come.

The miracle of Diaghilev remains eternal.

BOOK II: WITH DIAGHILEV

TO

MADAME MISIA SERT

CHAPTER I

IN THE *CORPS DE BALLET*

IT WAS early and cold that morning of January 13th, 1923, as we, Unger, the brothers Khoer, Lapitzky and I, refugees from Kiev, approached Paris. Slowly the train crawled under the sooty arches of the Gare du Nord. Someone from Diaghilev would be there to meet us on the platform. But barely had we had time to alight, before we were surrounded by such tender, such touching attentions, that the tears started to our eyes. Everything was so stirringly joyful and new after Soviet Russia, with all its wolfishness; after foppish, inhospitable Warsaw, where we suffered from hunger and deadly cold.

From the railway station, we were driven to the Hôtel St. Georges and left to ourselves until five o'clock that afternoon, at which hour we were expected to present ourselves punctually in the hall of the Hôtel Continental, there to meet Serge Pavlovitch Diaghilev. Paris, five o'clock in the afternoon, January 13th, 1923: an unforgettable moment!

It was exactly 5 P.M. The Continental! Never before had I seen such regal splendor as that of this hall, crammed with tropical plants.

V. F. Nouvel met us and, solicitous, ingratiating, asked us to sit down: "Kindly wait a moment, gentlemen; Serge Pavlovitch will be here very soon."

I was unable to sit still, I was in a fever, my hands and feet trembling, and shaking all over:

"Is it possible that Diaghilev will really be here in a moment? That I shall see him, talk to him?"

And then suddenly, a small group began to walk straight over to us, led by a tall bulky man, carrying a walking stick, and who looked a veritable colossus in his fur coat. I saw a large head, a pink, slightly puffy face, big shining eyes full of sadness, yet endlessly mellow and kind, a Peter-the-Great mustache, a gray lock in the black hair.... Then he sat down at our side and began talking, and immediately we were enveloped, subjugated, irresistibly charmed by his luminous soft warmth.

It seemed to radiate from the very man, from the slight lisp, the lazy gentlemanly voice, the expression in his dark, young eyes.

Then, an imposing *maître d'hôtel* bowed obsequiously, and Diaghilev in a resounding baritone voice ordered tea. After which, with an engaging smile, he thus addressed us:

"Gentlemen, you have just arrived from over there—from Russia. Your impressions are still so fresh, and I feel so homesick for our dear country.

... Tell me everything, everything.... Unburden yourselves of all that you, in your youth, have suffered—has it been very dreadful?"

Sadly his voice faded into silence. One could guess how infinitely he loved our country, and all the sharp burning pain he felt. Everything we tell him seems to interest him intensely: it is as though he has completely forgotten the business side of our meeting, has forgotten everything save what we have left far, far behind us, beyond the thousand-mile barbed-wire barrier of the Soviet frontier. But suddenly he becomes a different man. His sad eyes sparkle, his voice grows firmer, drier.... Before us sits our future manager.

"Gentlemen, I am very glad you have arrived at last, for I really need you.... I hope our work together will surpass all expectations; nevertheless, I expect great things from you all.... You must see Europe—and I am sure I shall be proud of you.... Bronia [Nijinska], for instance, has told me a great deal about you all.... Now, what can you do?" Then, turning to the eldest of us all, Khoer, a young man of about five and twenty, Serge Pavlovitch asked:

"You, for example—are you quite ready? Can you do *two tours?*"

"Oh yes, yes.... Certainly!" the answer came with assurance. Just as assured were the three next answers he got. And now the kind velvety eyes rest on me. I feel my very soul slipping away....

"And you, young man, what can you do? To me you are a question mark. I have heard nothing about you from Mme. Nijinska...." I feel so small, so weak and helpless, so alone. My lips open and shut, a tearful spasm catches me by my throat, and tears begin to well into my eyes....

"Oh, Lifar has worked a lot! He can do everything!" So say my friends, and Heaven be praised, I am saved....

Now Diaghilev comes down to business:

"Gentlemen, we shall sign the contract today, tomorrow you all start for Monte Carlo, and I shall join you there in a few days.... I am sorry to say that, of late, things have not been as one would have liked them to be.... For that reason I can offer you not 1,500 francs a month as I had intended, but 1,300. However, there is no need to repay the advance I sent you in Warsaw—that will be my present to you...."

Whereupon my colleagues risk a protest:

"But how is that, Serge Pavlovitch? We agreed to come for 1,500 francs a month. Mme. Nijinska mentioned that figure in her letter?"

But Diaghilev, always with the same charming smile, accompanied by a flowing motion of the hand, says:

"Gentlemen, you must have confidence in me.... You won't come to any harm," and rising adds: "very well then, we shall meet again in Monte Carlo, and there sign the contracts.... Pleasant journey!"

And so he leaves, accompanied by his suite, while I—for a long time I seem to be still dreaming....

Then came festive, gleaming, snow-white Monte Carlo. Life in that

gay city, however, began by no means festively for us. From the beginning, Diaghilev's ballet was hostile to us: we were interlopers imposed
on them from the distant "beyond"—a thing *emigrés* always dislike. In
this hostile atmosphere, while awaiting Diaghilev's arrival, we began to
work under Nijinska's direction. Our exercises were conducted behind
closed doors, for we had asked Nijinska to arrange that no one should
watch us during rehearsals.

When, the day following our arrival, we all met at her house, she said
to me:

"And you, Lifar, can you dance?"

That question almost robbed me of breath. If even Mme. Nijinska did
not know I could dance, and had her doubts—what could I possibly expect from the rest, from all those other hostile, searching eyes?

After the first lesson, my despair was even greater, for I myself realized
that I was not ready at all, and that six months of wandering and more,
had robbed me of all control over my body.

"Where have I come? Why did I come at all?"

Terror gripped me in gleaming Monte Carlo. Feeling even lonelier,
and more unwanted than before, I mingled with the cheerful, rejoicing
crowds that were filling the streets to watch the fireworks.[1] As I sauntered
along the walks of the fairylike tropical gardens, I wondered, in deep
dejection, how to escape from this glittering loveliness in order to return
to grim and distant Russia!

But by degrees, with every further lesson, this dark mood began to
fade, and when, three weeks later, on February 6th, S. P. Diaghilev
eventually arrived, I no longer felt completely useless.

Immediately on arrival, that very same day in fact, Diaghilev appointed a time for a general examination.

Now Diaghilev appears with his entourage, followed by the whole
company, who have been given permission to see us put through our
paces.

The examination begins. . . .

The exercises at the *barre* go off more than smoothly, and Diaghilev
is obviously pleased. Leaning back in his seat, Serge Pavlovitch nods his
head in approval.

But the *allegro* out in the center of the studio, turns out to be not nearly
so good. I, however, avoid taking part and remain only a spectator. I
see Diaghilev frown and turn pale, while malevolent sneers begin to
appear on the faces of some of the cast. . . . Suddenly Serge Pavlovitch
jumps to his feet, and his seat slaps up with a terrific bang. . . . Then,
silence—a quiet that presages the storm. . . . All faces, ours, the company's, look haggard and drawn. Then, like a hurricane, Diaghilev
rushes off to his study, followed hastily by Nijinska, pale and dismayed.

[1] January 17th is the national Monegasque holiday.

Presently his baritone voice is heard thundering forth, but now it is neither charming nor kind, but threatening, terrifying:

"Bronia, you have deceived me! Why, they are absolutely no good at all...are you not ashamed of having praised them so highly to me? I cannot, I will not and I am not going to work with them...I'll send them back to Russia...! Grigoriev! Producer! You are to send to London for Woizikowsky and Idzikowsky! Immediately!"

Mme. Nijinska's answers are inaudible, but what can she say? It means the shattering of all our hopes....

Fortunately, Diaghilev, whose fits of temper disappeared as quickly as they arose, decided to repeat the trials some few days later in response to Mme. Nijinska's persistent entreaties:

"Serge Pavlovitch, they've had no time to get properly rested or get used to the place....I agree that technique is not my pupils' strong point, but their *sauts* I assure you, aren't bad at all.... You see for yourself.... We'll put out a few small tables. You see...."

And indeed, although my colleague's *sauts* over tables were more of the athletic than the ballet kind, and somewhat clumsy, one had to admit that as a beginning, as a base, they could not be called entirely hopeless.

Diaghilev watched them without approval, but without, at least, the gloomy frown I had last seen on his face.

Then came my turn.

It seems that my *sauts* were better than those of my colleagues, lighter, more plastic, without effort, for Diaghilev's face lit up, and a pleased expression began to sparkle in his eyes....

Then, thinking a moment, he said:

"I ought to be sending you all back to Kiev, but I'm sorry for this boy, the more so as something can be made of him. *Il sera danseur.*" [2]

And so I stayed on in Monte Carlo, a tiny miserable chick of a boy.

Thus ended my childhood, such an unchildish one, and adolescence began, and a new epoch in my life, in which I found my true place under Diaghilev's tutelage. When I compare the seven years of my life spent with the Diaghilev Ballet (1923-29) with the preceding seven (1916-22), it becomes clear that all the adventurousness was beginning to go out of my life, and that I was becoming, for a time at least, more obedient, more humble, more the *youthful novice* and less independent, less daring: I was being born to a new life, but this new birth was different from the first. Then I had been left to shift for myself, to make my own way in life. But now, I myself, and my education, in preparation for an artist's life, were being guided; but such was that guidance, that most of the time there was nothing for me to do but follow my impulse,

[2] These pages are taken from the last chapter of *The Years of Suffering*, or rather in that book, I make use of the first portion of my reminiscences of S. P. Diaghilev.

and hold on to the hand that led me on to the goal I had set myself at the end of my first, my childish life. Yet, the end of my adolescence culminated in an inner revolt, though at the time I hardly realized it, against the man who was thus helping me find myself, against him who, superficially, appeared to be trying to suppress my independence. Youth is always ungrateful, and fearful of losing its independence, is ready to revolt against any spiritual father, however loving and careful that guidance may be.

Both my lives (and I mean lives and not periods in my life, for they are organically distinct) before and after 1922, were stamped by the domination over my soul of two, and only two people. Before 1923 there reigned over it and held sway, *she,* the woman from Kiev, who had cast a spell over my childhood. But after 1923 it was *he,* Serge Pavlovitch Diaghilev, the great Diaghilev, with whom my spiritual adolescence is inseparably united. It was not, however, the woman who molded me, it was I, or rather it was my vision, that created her. Diaghilev was no dream or vision of mine, he was reality unattainable, pure—to which everything in me yearned. Thus Diaghilev did indeed become part of my life, and though he did not create me in his image and likeness, he nevertheless helped me to find, to re-create, myself. Of others, save for this *she* and *he,* there have been none in my life (I speak here of the now distant past), and when as sometimes happened, my contact with them was broken, I was lonely and abandoned; and that I only too often was.

Diaghilev, however, did not immediately enter my life: not at once were our lives linked together, and before the connection became close, I very seldom even saw my divinity.

To the whole company he was a distant, unapproachable deity, sometimes gracious, sometimes and more often formidable, before whom one trembled, and whom one feared. He would come to rehearsal surrounded by his suite, would sit down and watch, express dissatisfaction—how difficult it was to earn his praise—and then leave. No artistic contact existed between him and the company, and all his orders were communicated through his secretary, B. E. Kokhno or S. L. Grigoriev or, and this but seldom, through the senior member of the company, N. V. Kremnev.

To me, as well as to the rest of the company, Diaghilev and his inner circle were immeasurably remote and unattainable, so that I dared not even think of approaching them, but could only gaze on them from a distance, and remain fixed in timid veneration: such timidity indeed, that Serge Pavlovitch could certainly have had no idea of the reverent tremors he inspired in me. If I did happen to meet him, every limb began to tremble in my fear lest he might look at me. But I could not merge myself in the Ballet in the same way as the rest of the group from Kiev, the brothers Khoer, Lapitzky and Unger.

Yet if Diaghilev and his suite were too far above, and inaccessible to me, the company itself attracted me but little, owing to its, as it seemed to me then, lack of culture. Technically, professionally—in everything, in fact, which related to our craft—the company stood exceptionally high and beyond all doubt it was, at the time, the best of its kind in the world: but outside the sphere of its art, it was not at all what I had imagined when still in Kiev. Survivals of serfdom still seemed to cling to its frame, and the artists, for instance, would send out the boys in the *corps de ballet* for cigarettes or beer, just as though they were still tied apprentices! This whole immense community seemed to be stewing in its juice, and apart from performances and rehearsals, spent its time in gossip and trifling primitive flirtations. Fortunately, owing perhaps to the inaccessibility of the artistic management, intrigues and underhand schemings had no place in its make-up. It was a great event when a ballerina managed to secure a husband for herself and left the company. But even more sensational was the entry of some new ballerina or dancer, for then one had to discover everything about the newcomer, he or she was discussed from every angle and thoroughly cross-examined while one strove, not very delicately it must be admitted, to pry open his or her innermost being. I had quite a different idea of the priests and priestesses of my beloved art. Only much later did I realize that our frequent tours through all sorts of countries, and the distant, though nevertheless effective influence of our artistic management, lent our company a distinction which raised it above all others. Nor was it, after all, as devoid of culture as I had imagined, while still obsessed by my Kiev dreams of a quite unique "Diaghilev" ballet.

This new world, which was henceforth to be mine, proved to be not at all what I had dreamed it, and I felt lonely and apart. Nowhere was there any support. Serge Pavlovitch appeared to take no notice of me while Bronislava Nijinska now turned her back on us, and ceased to count us as "her own." Grigoriev, the producer, had no particular liking for me, the company was prejudiced against and suspicious of the interlopers, inadequately trained as they were and newly arrived from Soviet Russia, and I, having in spirit already rejected my new family, could less than any contribute to dispel this instinctive distrust. Constant underfeeding, coupled with two painfully difficult attempts to escape from Kiev to the charmed, promised land of "Diaghilev," had undermined my health, and weakened me considerably. I suffered from headaches, my head often swam, and black circles kept zigzagging in front of my eyes. My heart either beat so feebly as to bring me to the verge of fainting, or began to thud with dreadful, loud, uneven strokes. It was difficult indeed to adapt oneself to this new life, so different from the Soviet life: difficult to be in a foreign land, ignorant of the language. All was new, unaccustomed, alien....

In this condition of bitter solitude, and utter neglect, my dreams of my Marina in Kiev began to flare up afresh. They burned within me, forcing me back to Kiev, so different was the life abroad and in "Diaghilev's ballet" from what I had imagined it when confined in the frontier O.G.P.U. station amid people dying of typhus.

From this heart-rending anguish of youthful loneliness, from this temptation to return to Russia, but also too, prompted by an irresistible urge to dance, I sought refuge in work, living in it and it alone. I was determined to justify my arrival in Diaghilev's eyes and earn his approval. Besides, the first production we began to rehearse was Stravinsky's *Les Noces*. The work proved fearfully hard. Fortunately rhythm was my strong point, and this made it possible for me, imperceptibly, to find my place in the ensemble. Grigoriev approved of my work, and my first joy in Monte Carlo was the knowledge that at last I had "passed" and would be called to participate in the performance.

But what was most terrifying at rehearsals was Diaghilev's presence. It is impossible to convey any idea of how exacting he was. Ballerinas and dancers would sometimes be made to repeat a single gesture a score of times. I would tremble with terror lest he should see me, notice my work, grow angry, and make me repeat it all over again. So panicky with fear did I become that I worked, not only at rehearsals, but alone and at night on the jetty. In that fantastic setting I would practice for hours, not noticing how time slipped by, while the two colored harbor beacons gleamed strangely over the sea, and silhouetted the dark outlines of the sleeping rock-citadel. These exercises strengthened my dancer's take-off, and fixed the work done at rehearsal, with the result that next day I would be quite sure of my part, whereas many of my colleagues had already forgotten what it was they had been so assiduously practicing the previous day. Thus, for them, it had all to be repeated, and new efforts made to achieve what had already been acquired.

In the same way, on Monte Carlo jetty, I worked at *Aurora's Wedding* and all the things we were rehearsing at that time.

Every rehearsal of *Les Noces* was attended by the composer, Igor Stravinsky, but not by any means as a simple spectator, for nothing could exceed his eager interest. To begin, he would only indicate roughly what was meant, but soon he was angrily gesticulating, and then, thoroughly aroused, would take off his coat, sit down to the piano and, reproducing all the symphonic sonority of the work, begin singing in a kind of ecstatic, but terrible voice, which carried so much conviction that no one could have thought it comical. Often he would go on in this way till he was completely exhausted. But still, a new life would have been infused into the rehearsal, and the whole company would start dancing for all it was worth. Practice ended, he would put on his coat, raise the collar, and walk off to the bar, a weak and puny little man. And it seemed strange that this all-but-common-place-looking mortal (though his individual and striking features distinguished him from all others) had, a moment before, been a composer of genius.

Stravinsky, like everyone else, was delighted with the choreography and setting in which Nijinska and Goncharova were attempting to capture something of the Russian popular print. Because it was first to employ mass movement in the dance, the Russian Ballet, through *Les Noces,* was brought closer, though in slight degree, to the Russia of the Soviets, with its deification of the masses and its oppression of the individual. Choreographically, the aesthetic basis of this ballet was a combining of sharp angular movements with the soft harmonious flowings of the groups. This was particularly apparent in the first female tableau, the robing of the bride, where the hands and feet were held in normal but intentionally ungainly positions (though for some reason this ungainliness appeared as a hunch). Here the dancers, with their accomplished technique, excelled themselves as successfully as they conveyed the underlying mysticism of the ballet by the expression of their faces and movements. The *leitmotiv,* and possibly the best moment in the ballet, is the *pas de bourrée* which the women dance on their toes, thus producing a harmonious silhouette, while the men dance accenting the beat. The slow, flowing movement of the groups is very beautiful.

Diaghilev soon began to pay attention to my work at rehearsals. Even in February, 1923, he had praised me and uttered words which filled me with joy and pride:

"This is good, young man, quite good. Go on working hard."

And I began to work harder than ever, spending innumerable hours in our long, low, basement rehearsal hall, with its vaulted ceiling.

On March 13th I made two *tours* in front of Serge Pavlovitch, on March 22nd an *entrechat-six*—and noticed in his eyes an expression of gentle approval.

I now found myself in a very different mood from that succeeding my arrival when, in moments of despair, I thought of returning to Kiev, for anyway "nothing would come of it." Now a hope, though faint at first, had begun to wake in my heart that nevertheless something might still "come of it." Then, soon after, I almost got a part.

At one of the rehearsals of *Schéhérazade* Diaghilev turned to Grigoriev and said, the whole company being present:

"Put Lifar as the boy dying on the stairs, he seems to suit the part."

Grigoriev gave me the part, but now my teacher, Bronislava Nijinska, intervened:

"No, Serge Pavlovitch, Lifar is still too inexperienced for a part of his own, he has still a lot to see and learn. Give the part to Slavinsky, who has more experience and talent."

"Very well," said Diaghilev, "let Slavinsky do the part, and let Lifar watch: but he will soon be dancing on his own. He's still young and inexperienced, it's true, but you'll see, Bronia, when he grows up, he'll be a second Nijinsky."

Bronia pursed up her lips, but did not answer, while I ... I seemed to sprout wings, and my heart fluttered like a joyful bird. On wings of joy, as though the leading part were now my own instead of the trifling part I had almost been given, I walked about Monte Carlo like a victor, and threw myself into my work with tripled energy, determined to prove myself worthy of Diaghilev's confidence.

On April 17th, 1923, our first performance took place and I made my début in the back ranks of the *corps de ballet* in *Le Mariage d'Aurore*. So terrified was I of coming out on the stage, that I grew numb and unable to move a single step, whereupon my colleagues thrust me forcibly out. The instant I found myself on the stage, however, another strange feeling at once possessed me, as though some other person had been put in my place, as though I had become a wholly different being, no longer myself, but someone springy, thrilled, heroic.... Suddenly I forgot to think. But I forgot nothing of my movements.

Then began the thorny path of Monte Carlo: rehearsals by day, performances at night. Often the Prince and Princess of Monaco were present, often they came to rehearsals, and then they would send champagne to the whole company, half a bottle per person. We found it immensely stimulating, but still I lost strength daily, and suffered greatly from dizziness as a result of too strenuous work and insufficient sleep.

During that spring at Monte Carlo I went to bed late, rose with the dawn, and, all alone, hurried into the mountains to see the sun rise from La Turbie. There was something so precious and near to me in these gradually unveiling immensities that I could not tear myself away, could not move.... Then, suddenly, I would be seized with terror lest I should be late, and rush panting down, only to arrive long before anyone had reached the theater. At rehearsal after my lesson, black zigzag circles would float in front of my eyes, my head reeled, and such weariness overcame me that everything dropped from my hands, and it was all I could do to keep myself from falling.

At one such rehearsal, *Schéhérazade,* when I could barely stand on my feet, and nothing I did would go right, Diaghilev, in a fury, began shouting:

"What's the matter? Don't you understand what you're expected to do, or can't you dance?"

After rehearsal, Serge Pavlovitch called me over and I went up to him, feeling more dead than alive, so great was the fear with which he inspired me: "What's the matter with you, young man? You look desperately ill. What are you doing about it?"

Such was my embarrassment in Diaghilev's presence that I always lost the power of speaking, and here he was talking to me personally, point blank! Like a sheep, I began to peer helplessly in all directions, though still unable to utter a word.

"How old are you?" Diaghilev went on.

"Eighteen," I replied at last, like a schoolboy who has omitted to do his homework.

"The best years! And with your eighteen years you probably imagine yourself grown-up, and go whoring with women. Well, in that case, young man, you'll soon philander your talent away, and never be a dancer. Shame on you, I had put such hopes in you."

"Serge Pavlovitch, I . . . I don't . . . philander."

"No? What is it, then? Why do you look so ill?"

"I'm not ill."

"But what is it? Tell me a little about yourself, your life."

Tell Serge Pavlovitch about my life, my dreams! My tongue utterly refused to obey me, and I continued to maintain my ridiculous, my desperate silence.

"Well, come on, young man. You're not dumb, I hope? When do you get up?"

"At five."

"Five? What do you do at five, when everyone else is asleep?"

"I do nothing . . . I . . . I go for a walk in the hills. . . ."

Serge Pavlovitch burst out laughing, a merry, loud, pleased laugh.

"Why, you must be crazy! Can a dancer lead such a life? A dancer should work and rest, not exhaust himself with walks, either during the day or night. I forbid you to go on with them, do you hear? I forbid you, and you must promise to obey me, and not do anything so idiotic again."

I promised Diaghilev not to go to La Turbie again, and soon after we left for Paris, via Lyons and Montreux. On my arrival I rented a room, in a small hotel, in the rue de l'Ours. That year there were so many people in Paris that it was almost impossible to find a room, and for the first night we dancers had to sleep in the rehearsal room at the theater. I had to lead a modest, very modest life, and I could only allow myself half a cigarette after each meal, for my monthly wages amounted to no more than 800 francs, from which were deducted sums I had borrowed in advance for the purchase of sundry small necessities and my uniform. We, the "boys" of the company, wore a uniform, consisting of black breeches with five buttons at the knees, white shirts with rolled sleeves, white stockings and black shoes. The shoes were distributed by the management, not very regularly, once a fortnight.

Life in small, shady hotels, first in the rue de l'Ours, then in the rue de Lappe, hid from me that other real and most dazzling Paris; indeed, the capital of the world hardly seemed to exist for me in that June of 1923. Meanwhile, rehearsals and performances went forward in the Gaîeté Lyrique, where Stravinsky's *Les Noces* proved an immense success. But about this time our company went on strike for higher wages, and though we all gathered in the Gaîeté Lyrique, not one of us would begin rehearsing. A little later Diaghilev appeared, easy and confident as ever, and in the presence of us all listened patiently to our collective demands through the mouth of a spokesman, after which, very calmly (though one might guess at a certain nervousness by his pallor) he said:

"Ladies and gentlemen, you demand the impossible. I take good care of you, you know that, and I do the utmost I can. I know your wages are not sufficient, and should like to be able to increase them, because I value your work: but there are limits that can't be overstepped, if one wishes to preserve our great common cause, which you should love and cherish as much as I do. Calm yourselves, ladies and gentlemen, think it all over and, I beg of you, begin working, we can't afford to miss even a day or an hour." Then, as though detecting some indication of "persuasion" in his words, he stopped short, and ending somewhat dryly, added: "Of course, you are at liberty to do as you please, so whoever feels loath to work may leave the Russian Ballet. Good-by, ladies and gentlemen."

Whereupon the whole company became aware that it had entered into collision with the wall of Diaghilev's immutable will, impregnable to any of their futile, petty assaults, and immediately began rehearsing. The strike ended in a general disturbance of quite another kind, for Tchernicheva's bag, with a diamond clasp, proved to have been stolen.

Here, in Paris, our company was increased by one very important member; for, from Romanov's Romantic Theater in Berlin, arrived Alice Nikitina, my colleague in the ballet school and permanent partner, who later acquired an outstanding position in the ballet. She was a gifted dancer, who more than anything (save trinkets) loved dancing, but she often antagonized Diaghilev by attempting to get this or that other part by pulling all sorts of strings.

Now, an immense exhilarating travail began at the Gaîeté Lyrique, and in the Princesse de Polignac's large salon, where we held our first musical rehearsal of *Les Noces*.

Stravinsky was conducting. Round Diaghilev were Nijinska, all our leading artists, and the whole musical world of Paris. I sat on the floor, absorbing the music and rhythms, and floating away, as it were, into the inner world of this ballet. The powerful sounds enthralled me, swept me on, thrilled me with their mystery, their timelessness and illimitable space, their wild Russian upsurge. Both body and soul seemed as though shattered by the Russian dance tunes, the sad music of the ritual folk songs sent a pang through the heart, and the church bells of mysterious old Asiatic Russia sounded prenatally familiar and moving, as I wondered what could have made the ancient Russia of Boris Godunov so well known and so familiar to me. Did ancestors pass on these memories with their blood? Which took precedence in my soul, Pushkin's verse or Mussorgsky's music? ...I seem to be afire with all that this music has brought me, with the knowledge that now it is mine, that now it is deep in my soul. Diaghilev looks at us kindly and smiles the smile of a great, loving, omniscient father. Princess de Polignac embraces Stravinsky, and loads us all with attentions. We, Diaghilev, Stravinsky, the leading actors, the *corps de ballet,* are all overwhelmed with a happiness which brings us close to each other, and we know our success is assured.

And so it happens. *Les Noces, Petrouchka, Prince Igor* are produced at the Gaîeté Lyrique on the 13th of July. After *Les Noces* some of the audience begin hissing, but only to be drowned by the applause, which goes on increasing until it becomes a veritable ovation.

At one of the rehearsals of *Petrouchka,* I had improvised the part of a boy playing a concertina, and must obviously have done well, for A. N. Benois came up to me afterwards, saying: "My heartiest compliments and congratulations on your part."

Then, in June of the same year, Diaghilev gave a performance in the Hall of Mirrors at Versailles, in the presence of Poincaré, various ministers, and many French notables.

Perhaps the very solemnity attaching to this magnificent palace made an impression on the company, but we danced as never before, ending to a burst of stupendous, deafening applause, unique in the theatrical annals of France, and comparable only with our London triumphs. A talk with Diaghilev, which belongs to this time, moved me deeply.

Though our work at Versailles was hard, there was no doubt that Diaghilev worked considerably harder, for he was present at every rehearsal and remained behind after we left. And all this despite the incredible heat, for June that year was unimaginably hot.

Thus, after we had had our last rehearsal, Diaghilev dismissed the company for lunch, and was left alone in the Hall of Mirrors. I crossed the square to a small restaurant, but as I was eating, the thought flashed through my mind that though we were lunching, poor Serge Pavlovitch must be overcome with hunger, thirst and the heat, while completely exhausted with work. So I thought ... and with my few poor pennies went and got him some sandwiches and a bottle of beer. Then I returned to the Hall of Mirrors, placed the beer and sandwiches in front of him, and then and then only realized how bold I had been, and blushed with confusion. Serge Pavlovitch looked at me intently, his eyes seemed to jump over the monocle, while I turned pale under his glance.

"How nice of you, young man! I'm very much touched that you should have thought of me," Diaghilev was saying, as a hot maiden flush dyed my cheeks. What frightened me most was the thought that Diaghilev might ask me to stay and so I might have to talk. I, therefore, turned quickly away, and doing my best not to listen, though even so I could not help hearing his "Where are you running away to?" dashed through the Hall of Mirrors.

On the 30th of June we did our *Louis XIV* in the Theater of the Palace, at which for the first time, and especially for Diaghilev's ballet, electricity was employed for lighting. The performance began at 10 P.M. and continued with festive music and a fireworks display far into the perfect June night. It was like fairyland. This remarkable ballet closed our season, after which we dispersed in all directions.

When the party was over I summoned up all my courage and, approaching Diaghilev, asked him to allow me to have a program to keep as a souvenir.

"Very well, Lifar, come and see me tomorrow, and I'll give you the program."

I do not myself understand what kept me from going to see Diaghilev next day, and Serge Pavlovitch would often refer to this incident in later days, and say:

"Why didn't you come to fetch your program? It would all have turned out so differently, and you would never have lost a whole year."

Without saying good-by to Diaghilev I left Versailles, and for the next ten weeks established myself in a tiny hamlet near Chartres. There—in this almost Russian village—I spent my summer holiday.

The days flew by unnoticed, calm and blank. Then again came work and travel. All that autumn we were traveling through Switzerland, Belgium, Holland, and finally reached Monte Carlo on October 25th. About this time, too, Pavel Georgievitch Koribut-Kubitovitch arrived from Russia. Active, responsive and with a stately presence, the old gentleman, Diaghilev's cousin, instantly won all our trust and affection. Later, I was to find in him all the qualities of a real "nurse," and in fact throughout all this Diaghilev period of my life, I was never so intimate with anyone as with him.

From the very moment of his arrival Koribut-Kubitovitch entered completely into our life, shared all our joys and sorrows, was inseparable from us, and at Diaghilev's death lived wholly in the memory of him and his ballet, and made our Monte Carlo his home. He was the only man round Diaghilev whom the company loved and treated as one of themselves, and that in spite of his being Diaghilev's cousin. He was its mascot, and was never weary in its defense. Nothing but good did he ever say of us, at which his cousin would angrily cry:

"What's all this hole-and-corner whispering with the artists? Why don't I hear anything? What's the meaning of this familiarity and gossip?"

With Pavel Georgievitch's arrival, a new link was established between Diaghilev and myself, and two pairs of eyes were now watching me, for, as he told me later, he was able thenceforth to watch my every step with the aid of his faithful Vassili. Nevertheless, I continued to avoid any meeting with Diaghilev. But now it was not confusion and timidity which overcame me in his presence, but a strange restlessness. Something within told me (possibly because his monocle and glance were constantly focused on me) that Diaghilev was anxious we should meet and talk together. But, whether through timidity (was it only timidity?), I feared this talk, and strove to stave it off. However, towards the end of October

I found I was caught, for hurrying past the casino after bathing, I ran straight into him.

"Where are you hurrying so fast, young man?"

Completely taken aback, with lowered eyes and faltering heart, I managed to stammer:

"Good morning, Serge Pavlovitch," and made as if to hurry past.

"Why are you so afraid of me, and run away all the time? Do you think I'm a wolf and will gobble you up? Don't be afraid, I'm not as fierce as I look."

I scuffled helplessly with my foot, fearful of glancing at Serge Pavlovitch, fearful of uttering even a word.

"I . . . I'm not afraid . . . I . . . was hurrying home. . . ." And still my feet went on scuffling the ground, till finally there burst from me a timid and desperate:

"Good-by, Serge Pavlovitch."

But now Diaghilev felt some annoyance.

"My stopping you, and wanting to talk to you, is on your account, not mine, and that you don't seem able to understand. I've been interested in you for a long time, you seem to me different from the other boys, more talented, and with a more inquiring nature. But yet you lead just the same colorless, dull, empty, uninteresting life as they do. I want to help you to develop, to improve your talents. But you don't seem to understand any of that, and run away from me as though I were something fierce. Very well! Do as you like, it's your own affair. You think, perhaps, that I'll go down on my knees and beg of you? You're wrong, young man! You are not the only young man in the world, and I'll prove it to you. A treasure indeed! One takes an interest in him, wants to help him, and he just turns up his nose! In that case, go to the devil, I've no further use for you! . . . What are you standing there for? Go home, as you wish."

Heavens! what *have* I done?

The day after this conversation Diaghilev left for Paris, returning on November 3rd, but not alone, for now an Englishman, Anton Dolin, accompanied him. This Dolin was a pupil of Astafieva's, and had danced in Diaghilev's *corps de ballet* during the 1921 London productions of *The Sleeping Beauty,* under the name of Patrikeeff.

And now again Diaghilev ceased to pay me any attention, seemed never to see me or be in my path. Again he had become a distant divinity. . . .

I went on practicing my art, working assiduously, and improving greatly. That winter of 1923-24 marked an important epoch in my life. In spite of the fact that I felt really unwell, that I suffered from continuous headaches, certain ominous stabbing pains in the heart, and a constant feeling of weakness, nevertheless my successes seemed to have lent me wings. By the end of January I could do six *tours* with ease, by the

Adolf Bolm   Lydia Sokolova

Lydia Lopokova   Anton Dolin

end of February seven *pirouettes* and three *tours en l'air*. On New Year's Day I had made a bet with Zverov that I would do six *pirouettes* and two *tours en l'air,* and won it on April 4th. On the 15th, in the presence of the whole company, I performed eight classical *pirouettes* with such perfection and finish that all were amazed. My facility in mastering technique was a great source of joy to me . . . and yet, of great bitterness also. However great my ecstasy at feeling so light, so springy, so wafted away might be, there was always the bitter knowledge that everyone in the company watched these successes with obvious spite and envy. Not only did they give me no support, but they would put themselves out to find faults that did not even exist, and criticize me with the utmost ferocity. Even when I had accomplished three impeccable *tours en l'air*, Vilzak, who had never been able to do as much, said, as he gave a derisive shrug of the shoulder: "You call these *tours en l'air!* Why, anyone can do that kind of thing! It's pure athletics, not dancing!"

My diary for November 30th, 1923, I find, contains the following entry: "I am trying to come to a decision over something of the utmost importance to me. Would it not be better to give up practicing entirely, and simply remain an ordinary member of the *corps de ballet?* The better I dance, the more I learn and work and show promise, the worse they treat me. There is a heavy weight in my heart. Perhaps I should give up dancing altogether?"

Soon after, however, I forgot all my resentment, for meanwhile I had found powerful support. Actually, no jealousy in the world could have stood in the way of my ambitions, for they were stronger than I, and could never have been diverted.

That November, December and January the company was dancing in Monte Carlo. In all, we gave forty performances in the presence of practically all Diaghilev's collaborators—Cocteau, Poulenc, Auric, Braque, Gris, Milhaud, Picasso, Benois, and Trubnikov.

Meanwhile, at the very beginning of the season, I had won praise from Diaghilev for the excellence of my miming in *Petrouchka* and *Prince Igor.* Now, he again began to watch my work at rehearsals. My colleagues congratulated me on my progress, and predicted I should soon be *premier danseur,* with a leading part in a ballet. Then in December came my first part. Diaghilev was beginning to test my capacity, and entrusted me with Slavinsky's part as the dying slave in *Schéhérazade.* Anxious to do my best, I went to the theater before the performance began, and with the Monte Carlo supers, began working on the finale. It was a tiny episode depicting the death of an insignificant boy, but into it I put everything I was capable of, all it meant to me, contempt of death, and a challenge. In this finale I had to dart on the stage, run the gauntlet of men armed with long swords, then, in a long staggering leap, bring myself to the negroes' tent, and unexpectedly appear from the other side, run up the stairs, and there die. At the actual performance I acted my part with joy and enthusiasm, though fearful of being taken to task for so freely interpreting my part. It was with some agitation, therefore, that I awaited the end of the performance. But Diaghilev gave no sign of disapproval or of wishing to remove me from the part, and I took it therefore as approval, and felt stimulated and encouraged. At one performance of this ballet I was bold enough to carry my improvisation even further. Just as Grigoriev and Tchernicheva (his wife) were miming the jealousy scene, in one mad rush I reached the top of the stairs, hung for an instant precariously balanced, and then, with several half-stops, began to hurtle down them to frightened cries of "Oh" from all parts of the audience, and, rolling to the footlights, died to thunderous applause. Curtain, calls! ... But when the footlights had gone out, and I returned to the wings, I was met by the furious Grigoriev: "I will never forgive you," he shouted. "Dare ever again to spoil the artists' parts, and in two twos you'll be thrown out of the company. You forget yourself, you miserable *corps de ballet* boy. You seem to think you're a leading dancer. You wait till Diaghilev's done with you. He's furious with you for your outrageous behavior, and you know very well you can't take liberties with him."

Thereupon Diaghilev appeared, asked everyone to stay, and in front of them all reprimanded me, unmistakably indeed, yet it was kindly too, and in no wise threatening: "What you did, Lifar, was very inartistic and youthful, very green. I can't help regretting seeing you use your talent to the detriment of the ensemble instead of trying to support it by disciplining yourself. The art of an actor with only a minor part consists in performing it with perfect artistry as a minor part, and not in any way trying to eclipse the principals, thereby distracting the audience from the main action on the stage. All artists must take their instructions from the producer and never depart from them in any way: he is responsible for you all to the ballet master, and me." Then followed a short silence, after which, having obviously decided to cut his speech short, Diaghilev ended: "If you intend to go on submitting to every fantasy that comes into your mind, and disobeying orders, I shall have to have you fined!"

I duly absorbed it all, but it was more words like "your talent" and "I shall *have* to have you fined" that stuck in my mind than those expressing disapproval. Meanwhile, I was gazing at his smiling eyes, innocent of any trace of anger, which seemed to be saying, "A good lad, all the same! Better imagination and miming than the dancers dancing the leading rôles (not outstanding artists, but dancers who just happened to have the outstanding rôles)."

During December we put on a season of classical ballet for which Diaghilev specially engaged Mlle. Vera Trefilova. Four times she danced in *Le Lac des Cygnes* with dazzling distinction, grace and technique, giving altogether a most moving performance. Her thirty-two *fouettés* in the second scene, and the brilliant manner of their execution, will remain forever engraved on my memory.

On November 22nd I was sent on in one of Trefilova's performances to dance in the first pair of czardas. Diaghilev praised my performance warmly, and as a result gave me my first real part, that of an officer in a new ballet called *Les Fâcheux*. I rehearsed this ballet for the first time on January 15th, 1924, and at the first night on the nineteenth acquitted myself brilliantly, or so my colleagues earnestly assured me.

This production of *Les Fâcheux* was made notable by the fact that Diaghilev dismissed the ballerina Maikerska for her refusal to dance the part of the naked nymph, and by the unpleasantness caused when Idzikowsky left the ballet just at this time. In him, our company lost one of the most brilliant virtuosi of classical dancing, whose "elevation," as Cecchetti told me, was better than Nijinsky's except in the *grand jeté*.

I was beginning to make my mark among the youngsters of the *corps de ballet,* and as a result Diaghilev's co-workers began to "discover" me. To me, and me alone of all the company, they showed especial attention and sympathy. They would often invite me to the Café de Paris, to restaurants and shows. Diaghilev was not merely displeased, he was positively angry, and would furiously accuse his friends of "depraving and ruining" the company, destroying discipline, and leading young dancers astray.

I remember an occasion when I had been asked to go to the Café de Paris, and we were all sitting at a couple of tables, drinking coffee, when suddenly Diaghilev appeared, accompanied by Kokhno and Dolin. There and then he came up to us, and almost shouting, declared he did not intend to allow such a disgraceful practice to continue, that Lifar needed to work, and not waste his time sitting about in cafés, and that his collaborators were evidently intent on hindering his work and meant to destroy the Ballet which he, with such difficulty, had managed to create through fifteen long years of effort.

On another occasion I had been invited by friends to one of our own performances, although it was against our rules for any of us ever to be seen in front of the curtain. My seat was next that of Cocteau, Auric, Trubnikov and others. Diaghilev came in, and, adjusting his monocle, saw us all: whereupon the right side of his face began nervously twitching, his eyebrows rose, and moving towards us, in a perturbed, irritated voice, he began to address me as follows: "If I am not mistaken, you, young man, are in your second year in the company, and should be aware that the management has forbidden members of the *corps de ballet* to occupy seats intended for the paying public."

During the entr'acte he met me in the foyer, and literally threw me out:

"I forbid you, once and for all, to be seen in a theater. If you don't choose to obey me, you're at liberty to leave the company, and spend all your nights in the front row with Jeanchik.[3] I keep nobody by force in my ballet."

Some few days later, happening to run into these friends in the street, I was made aware that they had decided to cut me, in their fear of Diaghilev's scenes.

What was so puzzling was that Diaghilev was obviously angry with me, while giving me full support on the stage. He also disliked his collaborators' coming to watch me rehearsing alone, in spite of their pleasure in doing so.

January 31st marked the last and forty-first performance (a charity performance) of our winter season in Monte Carlo, and with it departed our honored guests. I was almost glad of the fact.

Next began a short spring season which lasted less than a month. About the time it opened I asked Diaghilev to increase my salary, and was accorded 200 francs. Four of us, boys of the *corps de ballet,* went with a similar request to Gunsburg, manager of the Monte Carlo Opera House, where we were paid fifteen francs a performance, but met with a flat refusal.

The future historian of the theater will linger over this somewhat original, anecdotal figure, while attaching due weight to his propagandist activities in popularizing Russian music and Wagner, for it was he who staged the first performance of *Parsifal* in France.

Since Gunsburg had refused any increase in our salaries, we resolved to bungle our dance at the next performance, a plot made possible by the fact that Diaghilev happened to be in Paris, and thus we should be safe from any consequences. The performance was *Aïda,* in which one of the most successful items is always the ballet number. We began to dance our parts as Arab boys, and keeping my word as arranged, I managed to slip and fall, while my three colleagues continued with the most perfect accuracy. As bad luck would have it, Diaghilev had returned from Paris, was in the auditorium and saw my performance.

Thereupon he sent Kokhno to Grigoriev with an order to assemble the company on the stage after the performance, and then, appearing himself, turned the full blast of his fury on me. "You seem to have absolutely forgotten how to dance, Lifar, and are a disgrace to my company. I am certain there is some disgusting prank at the back of it, but you must take this as your first warning."

Nevertheless, a few days later Diaghilev asked me to have myself photographed as the officer in *Les Fâcheux* in order to have some for his book, and himself ordered three of them.

The season being concluded, we went to Barcelona, where we gave eleven performances in all. It was a busy time, indeed, with performances in the evening and rehearsals for the Paris season by day.

On April 25th we had our first rehearsal of the Cocteau-Milhaud ballet

[3] Cocteau.

Le Train Bleu. Before we started, Diaghilev assembled us all to hear a lecture on Milhaud. Briefly outlining the modernistic music, already known to the troupe, of Stravinsky and Richard Strauss, which ignores thematic melody and strives for color, rhythm, and angularity in order to express the feverish, nervous pulse of our day, Diaghilev went on to tell us how he foresaw the music of the future, which seemed to him exemplified by Milhaud's music with its new thematic material and its still unfamiliar, melodic line, which no longer derived from the school of *bel canto,* but from that of the street.

"You are already acquainted with the poetry of machinery, skyscrapers, transatlantic liners; now you must absorb the poetry of the streets, their tempo, and think seriously about it. You must not let the 'banality' of this new music of the future frighten you off. Diaghilev's Russian Ballet, the first ballet in the world, cannot afford to mark time, cannot be content with yesterday, or even the present alone. It must forestall the future, and predict *tomorrow;* must lead the masses and discover what no one has discovered before. To me, our new ballet seems of the greatest importance, and my wish is that you should treat it as it deserves, and so help to conquer 'tomorrow.' "

Diaghilev had no particular eloquence as a speaker. At times he would omit some word he had obviously intended to use, and substitute another more adapted to his audience; nevertheless he spoke so clearly and with such conviction, his meaning was so clear, that his average and not particularly cultured audience could not fail to be convinced by him. A keen desire to do the new work justice infected us all.

On Diaghilev's insistence Mme. Nijinska agreed to give me a part at the beginning of the ballet. I was the youngest. Need I say I was in the seventh heaven of delight?

In Barcelona I paid frequent visits to the numerous cabarets, and found them a veritable revelation to me. Even in the smallest the dancing would be good, and at night the whole town seemed to be dancing! In places like the Casa Rosso, the Cuadro Flamenco, or the Sevilla, one would find astonishingly gifted dancers. I remember that one day as I was sitting in the Sevilla, with several of our ballerinas, Diaghilev came in with Nijinska, Anton Dolin and Kokhno. He was in an excellent mood, and chatted amiably with us across the tables, expressed entire approval of my frequenting such places, and assured me I should find it of the utmost value to my dancing. It was at the Cuadro Flamenco that I had the privilege of seeing the famous Macarona, Diaghilev's favorite dancer, a huge, fat old woman of about sixty, doing her famous dance with a train. I was so carried away that I immediately began learning Spanish dances, and took several lessons in the use of the castanets.

On May 1st we gave our eleventh and last performance, and next day left for Paris. On the journey, during the halt at Toulouse, I happened to hurt my head badly, and as at the time Diaghilev was sitting in our carriage, I am afraid it proved rather a shock. I had suddenly thought of doing two *tours en l'air* in the carriage. The first were brilliant, but the next smashed the top light to fragments, and I dropped to the floor like a sack, with my head cut open. In the first instant Diaghilev was quite transfixed with terror, thinking I was killed, but when I got up and forced a smile in spite of my pain, his anger went beyond all bounds. Once we had arrived in Paris Diaghilev insisted on my seeing a doctor, but nothing serious was found, and next day I left with the others for a tour in Holland.

Another interesting chance meeting with Diaghilev took place in Amsterdam. In those days I was so intent on self-improvement that the moment we arrived anywhere fresh I would hurry off immediately to the local museums. The very day after our arrival therefore, I hastened to the Rijks Museum to see the Rembrandts. I had only the vaguest acquaintance with Dutch painting: all I knew of it, in fact, being that I had conscientiously studied every one of the Dutch paintings in the Louvre, though I confess they meant little to me, and often frankly bored me.

However, once I was in the enormous museum, I soon found myself utterly lost, and for a long time failed to find what I was seeking. But at last I hit upon the gallery of old masters, and discovered the Rembrandts which I had always yearned to see, the celebrated "Night Watch," the "Cloth Guild" and the "Anatomy Lesson," the last of which especially impressed me.

Then, in this room, in front of a picture by Hals, I suddenly saw a group I so well knew already, Diaghilev, Dolin and Kokhno, and heard Diaghilev analyzing it. He seemed to be discussing the early influence of Hals on Rembrandt, and the later influence of Rembrandt on Hals. I saw him glance swiftly at me in astonishment, even amazement, so puzzled was he to find me there. "What on earth can this lad from the *corps de ballet* be doing here? ..."

On May 13th we returned to Paris. And now Paris enslaved me once and for all. My little hotel room in the rue Victoire was far too small to do any work, and so my rehearsing was done in the street on the bright asphalt, between midnight and two. Round me the windows of "gay houses" would gradually open and faces, astonished at first but gradually serious and interested, would watch me going through my exercises.

Now we rehearsed in the Théâtre de Paris, and before brilliant, highly-enthusiastic onlookers. Mme. Sert and Chanel were often present, and here, for the first time, I saw the women who, with the Princess de Polignac, played so exceedingly important a part in the annals of Diaghilev's ballet.

I remember we were rehearsing *Le Train Bleu* when Mme. Sert and Chanel for the first time saw me, and took an immediate liking to the little dancer in the *corps de ballet*.

"Mais il est charmant, ce petit russe, regarde-le!" Madame Sert said to Diaghilev.

And *"Voilà ton danseur!"* said Chanel.

"Eh ... What? ... You find him a good dancer, your 'godson'?" Diaghilev was saying, with assumed indifference, as he adjusted his monocle, and threw me a sidelong glance as if in doubt as to who exactly I might be, though all the time, by the expression in his smiling luminous eyes I could see how much it delighted him to hear his little dancer praised.

This glance, and what I had heard said by Mme. Sert and Chanel, redoubled my enthusiasm for my work, and encouraged me to greater achievements. I was aflame with ambition to turn myself into a truly great dancer, and just at this point Kremnev, who knew my zeal, uttered the words that set the match to the powder:

"Do you know what, Lifar? You ought to be properly taught by Cecchetti, then something really worth while might come out of you. Have a talk with Diaghilev about it."

Have a talk with Diaghilev? But how could I possibly think of such a thing?

That year the season was a particularly brilliant one, both as regards music and the theater. So far as my modest means would allow, I did not miss a single interesting concert or performance, and greedily absorbed all these new impressions.

One of my most moving and significant experiences during this period in Paris was Anna Pavlova's appearance in her own productions.

The moment she appeared on the stage I felt that I had never before set eyes on anything remotely comparable to such divine beauty and grace. Her airy lightness seemed to defy the very laws of gravity. I was shaken through and through, and completely enslaved by the simplicity, the ease, the plasticity of her art. Not one *fouetté,* not one trick of the virtuoso, but loveliness alone. She seemed to glide through the air without making the least effort, as though it were some divine Mozartian gift, which left her free to add nothing at all. In Anna Pavlova I saw not the dancer, but the very *genius* of the dance, as I prostrated myself before that divine manifestation. For the first moments I had no use for my reason; I could not, and dared not see any fault or imperfection. I was gazing at some divine revelation, I was no longer on this earth.

All through the performance I felt either away up in the clouds or down on the earth. Now a divine gesture, or classical pose would make me tremble in reverent awe, then again a hint of unnecessary skittishness would appear in her miming, a taint of something akin to "stunting," to cheapness even, and then my enthusiasm would suffer a severe blow.

In the interval I met Diaghilev in the *foyer* (wherever I went that spring I was always meeting him) and on his asking how I had liked Pavlova, all I could do was stammer my enthusiasm:

"Divine! Genius! Beautiful!"

But there had been no need for Diaghilev to ask me my opinion, it was so clearly written on my face. Nevertheless, I did not dare to discuss either with Diaghilev or anyone else, the double effect I had experienced, that certain things in her dancing had seemed to me cheap and "faked." I was all too sure I should be laughed at, and told I was blaspheming, or else that it was beyond my understanding. Later, however, I found I was not alone in my "blasphemy." Diaghilev felt so himself, and told me much about Pavlova.

Of the ballets seen that spring, another stands vividly out in my memory, *Mercure,* with Massine as the *premier danseur:* a night when Massine was late for the show, and the crowd tried to attack Picasso, who had designed the beautiful sets (perhaps the only noteworthy ballet in the whole performance, and that, perhaps, due wholly to the painter). I had heard so much about Massine, the late ballet master of the Russian Ballet, that I was in a state of enormous expectation, and no little emotion. But whereas Pavlova had been a genuine revelation, Massine, on the contrary, impressed me but little and was, indeed, almost a disappointment. Agreed, the music was lovely, well suited for dancing, the choreography excellent and technically most accomplished: nevertheless it all seemed so cerebral, so mannered, that I found not the least inspiration in his ballets.

At this performance I once more met Diaghilev, but this time pale, agitated, nervous.

Serge Pavlovitch felt that there was a threat to the Russian Ballet in these evenings of ballet presented by E. Beaumont. He was afraid of his ex-ballet master, now his rival. But the rival proved not to be dangerous, and the performances were clearly a failure, except for *Mercure* alone. Later Diaghilev included *Mercure* in his own repertoire, though the ballet was created without him, by one of the men with whom he had once worked.

Now I often went to concerts, and so heard a great deal of music all through that important significant spring. Particularly I remember the Stravinsky-Koussevitzky concert in the resplendent Opera House. During the interval I was walking timidly about in the mirror-lined pompous foyer, in which one instinctively seeks to muffle one's steps, when yet again I met Diaghilev. I bowed and, as always, wished to pass by, but he approached me and gave me a cheerful greeting. Never before had I seen him so full of joy, or smiling so kindly.

"I never thought, I never dreamed of meeting you here, my dear little flower, on the very day of our own Stravinsky! That means you really adore music and understand it!" And therewith he began to shower me with numberless kind words, such as "little flower," "little berry," "my darling good boy" . . . and all said so tenderly, with such kind simplicity, that my heart began to beat with gratitude and joy. It was the *first kind-*

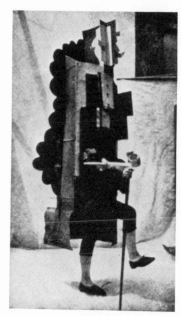

Parade, 1917

Pas d'Acier, 1927

ness I had ever received in my life (except from my mother). *And I had received it from whom?* From Diaghilev, the great Diaghilev, my God, my Divinity!

I have always regretted that I did not, at the time, make a detailed entry in my diary, recording the whole of the ensuing conversation, for I had always had the habit of putting down in it everything that in any way attracted my attention. All I did was merely to note the main outlines. It was about women, and of Serge Pavlovitch's jealousy in regard to them, where I was concerned. . . . Nevertheless, there was something else I noted with great completeness, and that was, that this conversation, so unexpected, so full of kindness and endearing words, did not come altogether as a surprise—as though, deep down at the bottom of my heart, I had for a long time felt that *thus it must come.*

At Stravinsky's concert I rejoiced whole-heartedly in Serge Pavlovitch's kindness, in the charming things he had said and called me, but once I was at home, a sudden sense of fear overcame me, as I remembered all that was said in the company about Diaghilev's unusual life, his favorites and so forth. "Can it be possible," I said to myself, "that I too am to be one of those future favorites of his, that even now he sees me in that light?" Though I was alone the thought flushed my cheeks a glowing crimson. But, immediately, I rejected every thought of such a possibility. "No, whatever you like but that, never! Never shall I become a 'favorite' " . . . And there arose the memory of that faithful promise to my fairy-countess in Kiev, the vow the youthful knight and page had sworn that—for ten whole years even—he would wait. Yet two years only had passed. And now again, her image, with tormenting vividness, rose up in all the ineffable beauty endowed it by love as a result of two long years of separation and passionate longing.

But how was I to keep my troth? The one solution, the only issue that presented itself, was to abandon Diaghilev's Russian Ballet. But then what? For after Diaghilev, away from Diaghilev, there was no other company in the wide world that I could think of joining. . . . So I decided to abandon the dance altogether, to bury deep the greatest dream of my life: that dream for which I had abandoned all—even *her* who had clung to my sleeve, as I said good-by before leaving for Paris . . . and Diaghilev.

But to abandon the dance—was that not abandoning life too? What could life hold for me when that was accomplished? Nothing but emptiness! The world would have lost all its attraction for me. So I decided I would abandon that world for another. Once before, in Kiev, I had gone into retreat, had abandoned this world during fifteen months in order, solitary and alone, to study dancing and books. Now I would choose for myself a final retreat, a monastery cell. And so I, the incorrigible nineteen-year-old dreamer, began to dream of being a *monk* exactly as before I had dreamed of her, of Diaghilev, of his ballet and the dance. But now, it was with a poet's vision of the monastic life, with its lovely devotional seclusion, its rest and contemplation and prayer.

I had made my decision. I would remain with the Ballet a fortnight longer, until the season came to an end, then take leave of Diaghilev and enter a monastery. But yet, that world from which I was about to retire, was spreading its nets, preparing to lure me with all its snares....

Then on the 20th of June the first performance of *Le Train Bleu* took place. It proved an immense personal success for Dolin. Before the dress rehearsal, however, Diaghilev happened to meet me in the Théâtre des Champs Elysées, and started a talk about my future. With excessive praise, and greatly exaggerating my merits, he said he considered me the most talented and capable of the male dancers in his company, and urged me to think of my career, and devote myself assiduously to working and learning.

"I want you to become my leading dancer, and I shall make you my leading dancer. Come on Monday to see me at the Hotel St. James, but meanwhile keep our conversation a secret, and don't mention it to anyone in the company."

On the twenty-fourth I called on Diaghilev as arranged, after a sleepless night, for the more I had pondered his words the more I feared the future he was preparing for me. An immense, intolerable burden of responsibility had seemed suddenly to descend with the words "most talented and capable" male dancer. It had been easy enough to dream in prison in Kiev about dancing, it was easy enough to imagine oneself leading dancer or, greatest dancer of all, when nobody paid the least attention to you, as a lad in the *corps de ballet:* easy enough while it was all far away and inaccessible; but now when, by Diaghilev's will, I was on the threshold of either a great future or a great fall ... my head swam, not with joy or a foretaste of future glory, for that seemed infinitely remote, but with fear, lest my shoulders should never be able to bear the burden of all Diaghilev wished to impose on them. And again, I felt I must leave the Ballet, leave it now, before it became too late, for that distant monastery, by the dream of which I had so often been haunted.

In this mood, I reached the hall of the hotel, where Diaghilev greeted me with the utmost friendliness, and ordered tea for two.

Suddenly I became bold.

"Serge Pavlovitch, I should like to talk to you."

Diaghilev smiled.

"Good, I also want to talk to you, and that's why I asked you to come and see me.... But what is it you want to tell me?" he says with a kind, warm-hearted smile. He is obviously in an excellent mood.

Yet here I become timid again: but, overcoming that feeling, and trying hard not to look at him for fear my courage will fail, I begin stumblingly and shyly to say:

"I ... for a long time ... Serge Pavlovitch ... I have been wanting ... I have been wanting to thank you for the season, and say good-by ... I intend ... I must go away next week ..."

"Why, where do you want to go, where are you thinking of spending your two months' holiday? You know that the whole company has to be back by September 1st, and that I dislike it very much when dancers overstay their leave. Where do you intend going? I have a suggestion to make too. ... However, tell me your plans first."

How am I to tell Diaghilev of my decision?

"Serge Pavlovitch, it isn't for the summer I'm going away; it's for good ... I've decided to leave the company—"

"What, what are you saying?" Diaghilev cries, turning purple and leaping out of his seat, whereupon an incredible thing happens, for he seizes the small table at which we are sitting, crashes everything on it to the floor, and begins to scream out in a choking voice, while the French, English and Americans in the hall sit transfixed:

"What, you dare to say this to me, you ungrateful puppy? Do you realize all the ingratitude, the meanness, the insolence of what you're saying? I brought you from Russia, I supported you for two years, taught you everything, you whipper-snapper, and now, now when I need you, you tell me you're leaving my ballet! The impudence, the indecency of it! I can't believe it's your own idea, someone must have persuaded you, induced you to do it. ... Tell me at once, which of the little sluts you are always running about with is it that is depraving you, teaching you to repay with ingratitude everything I have done to help you? I said I was counting on you in the future as my leading dancer, and so no doubt you imagined you were a first-rate dancer already. You're wrong! At present you're nothing, a nobody, and any other decent ballet company would have thrown you out long ago. I was talking of you as a future dancer, and that future is in my hands; if I want it so, you'll be a first-class dancer, if not, you'll be nothing, a speck of dust, a nonentity. ... Well, if you want to resign, resign and go to the devil, all the devils! I've no use for such ungrateful beasts. To hell with you!"

I said nothing to interrupt Serge Pavlovitch, but could not help looking at him with compassion, until, under the influence of my gaze, and no doubt because he felt he had had his say and was tired of shouting, Diaghilev grew calmer and continued more calmly:

"I've said a lot of harsh things: forget them and let's talk sense. ... You really must understand, Lifar, that it isn't right, that it looks like blackmail, and that all those little girls—I saw you again with some of them at Anna Pavlova's performance, and I very much regret that you should entangle yourself with them—are doing you a disservice? I value your work, Lifar, and I won't let you go to any other company. Now what do you want? Tell me frankly and openly. Your salary isn't sufficient? You want a rise? Very well, you shall have it. ..."

Diaghilev's outburst and the compassion I had felt, helped me to master my own feelings, and I said:

"No, Serge Pavlovitch, it was never my intention to join some other company, and I don't want a rise. I came here, not in order to ask you for something, but to thank you for all you have done for me, and to say good-by, for I am going into a monastery."

And now a new heart-rending scene occurred, for Diaghilev dropped his heavy head on the table, and began to weep with emotion:

"So Russia, the real Russia, the Russia of the God-seekers, of the Karamazovs', still exists. But you are Alyosha Karamazov, my poor boy! Poor children, bereft of your country, but still longing for it, longing for all by which your forefathers lived!"

Then, getting up, he this time threw his arms about me, at which fresh consternation appeared on the faces of those sitting about in the hall. "Those Russians! One minute they're breaking tables and crockery, shouting at the top of their voices, and the next, for no visible reason, they're kissing each other in public!"

"For this mad, irrational impulse, I love you even more, Alyosha! But what's wrong? Why do you wish to bury your talent in a monastery, bury yourself away, commit suicide? It's sheer madness, it's impossible ...I won't allow such an act of self-destruction. What's going on inside you? What can be behind this prompting to abandon a brilliant career, just as it's beginning to open to you?"

As well as I could, I tried to make him understand my spiritual condition, and especially the anxiety which the very brilliance of that future career now inspired in me. I said I felt hardly strong enough, and was afraid of being unable to justify his confidence, or the hopes he was building on me.

Not so long ago you said you were relying on me as your future first dancer, but today, you said I was nothing, a mere nobody, and I can't help wondering whether what you have just said isn't truer than what you said first. It's better to renounce dancing now than to turn into a failure, for that I could never survive...."

"Forget what I said in anger. I have faith in you; I can see—do you hear—I can actually see you one of the world's great dancers with Spessiva as your partner. I cannot be, I am sure I am not mistaken about you. It was not for nothing that you interested me from the first moment I saw you, or that I have been watching you all through. There is real talent in you, and your duty is to develop it to its fullest extent. You must work, overcome all difficulties, not be afraid and try to desert. Everything must be paid for in this world. A man with determination and talent hasn't the right to be a coward, or fold his arms and give up.... You must work, and I, on my side, will do everything I can to lighten your task. And first you must take a long holiday to mend your health, and store up some strength for work, for at present you look like a plucked chicken. Name anywhere you like by the sea, don't worry about the details, I'll see to it all. Leave everything to me, I insist upon it, for you are the only person that matters to me in this ballet and but for you, I should have dispersed it all and retired long ago. I want to see what you develop into, I want to turn you into one of the world's greatest dancers, a second Nijinsky."

These words impressed me profoundly. Never had I suspected that his interest in me was so great, or that he could so exaggerate my capacities. I knew I could never fulfill all he expected of me, yet nevertheless I was conquered, I lost all power to resist, there seemed nothing I could say, and I relinquished myself into his strong, kind hands.

"If you feel so certain, Serge Pavlovitch, that something can be made of me, send me to Italy to study under Cecchetti. Maybe that will help. If not, so much the worse, for then I shall leave the Ballet."

"What an excellent, admirable idea! How on earth did you think of it?"

"Kremnev said I ought to be studying under Cecchetti."

"Fine lad, Kremnev! It really is a most excellent idea, and we must lose no time in acting on it. Come and see me tomorrow at five, bring your passport, we'll talk it over again, and I'll send a telegram to Mussolini." (Mussolini, in the old days, used to write the notices about the Ballet for his paper, and was on friendly terms with Diaghilev.)

Next day found me punctually at the Hotel St. James. Diaghilev was waiting. We left in a taxi to go to the tailor's where we ordered a suit, then went to buy shoes, a hat, and other small necessaries. That evening I went to the theater in the straw hat Diaghilev had bought me, whereupon I was greeted with such a burst of laughter from the whole company ("Look! here comes our own little Maurice Chevalier!") that, hating it myself, I was only too glad to resume my old cap.

Next day I went once more to see Diaghilev, only to be greeted with some irritation.

"Where is your new hat, young man?"

Embarrassed, I blushed, and hardly knew what to say.

"Serge Pavlovitch, I took it off; it did not suit me."

Whereupon Diaghilev completely lost his temper, again in the hall and surrounded by strangers.

"What? It doesn't suit you? You suggest that I haven't any taste, that I don't know my business? You good-for-nothing brat, out of my sight, and don't dare come back. I don't ever want to see you again!"

The whole room seemed to be looking at me; I felt eternally disgraced. And I went, thrown out by Diaghilev....

But I began to wear the straw hat again, though I did not see Diaghilev till June 30th, the date of our last performance.

I happened to run into him before the performance, and now again he was smiling and kind.

"Ah, so you're wearing my hat after all? So, in the end you like it?"
I remained silent....

"Come to Weber's tomorrow at seven!"

The next day, trembling with foreboding, I went to Weber's. Already,
I felt I was Serge Pavlovitch's slave, that I no longer moved by my own
volition, that I was utterly in his hands to be molded to whatever shape
he desired. The moment I entered, Diaghilev paid his bill, and we left
in a taxi for *chez Cabassus*. There, at a table on the terrace, he ordered a
sumptuous champagne supper to celebrate—as he said—the end of the
brilliant season and my approaching visit to Italy: the new life that
was about to open to me. And there, far into the night, we went on
sitting, while Diaghilev drew me out about my life in Soviet Russia,
listening with the greatest attention and asking innumerable questions:
questions which somehow made me see my life in a new light, and
brought back to mind things I had seemingly forgotten forever. When I
told him of all the anguish and torments I had had to suffer, in the
course of my two unsuccessful attempts to escape abroad in order to join
him, tears ever and again stood in his eyes. In particular my tale of how
I had gone into retreat, to study the dance, touched him deeply.

Of my beautiful lady in Kiev, I told him also; how I was, as it were,
enchanted, and of the abnormal repression which then weighed on my
life—as it did now.... But when I came to this point, a sort of jealous
watchfulness leaped out, and Serge Pavlovitch exclaimed abruptly, sharply,
"All this is absurd nonsense, a dreamer's fantasies and imaginings. It
will soon pass, and leave not the least trace."

Later, I accompanied Diaghilev as far as his hotel, where he presented
me with a parcel of books, my railway ticket to Turin and my passport
already complete with visa. After which he embraced me with great
kindness and bade me good-by. It had been arranged that I should
leave for Italy on the 6th of July, and we decided no one should know
I was about to begin studying under Cecchetti. The company was merely
to think that I, like everyone else, had just gone off for my holidays.

The same day Serge Pavlovitch, happening to meet Nijinska, told her
he was sending me to Italy to study with Cecchetti, whereupon, in a
rage, she burst out, "You are absolutely wrong to do it. Nothing will
ever come of Lifar; he not only will never be a *premier danseur,* he will
never even be a soloist."

"You think so? But I think differently, and am utterly convinced that
not only will he become a *premier danseur,* but a choreographer too."

"Never," she replied, "I'll take my bet on it."

The stake was a dozen bottles of champagne, which, however,
Diaghilev was never to see.

July 6th, 1924. At six o'clock that morning I was to leave my little hotel.
The day before, I had taken leave of Diaghilev, but had stayed up all

night, restless because of the coming journey, and because it was necessary to pack. Suddenly, without the least warning, at five (absorbed in packing, I must have ignored his knock), my door opened, and in walked Serge Pavlovitch, his usual fresh, well-groomed self, carrying his heavy cane, and a black overcoat over one arm. So unexpected was his visit, and so taken aback was I by having to receive the scented, well-cared-for Serge Pavlovitch in my small attic room, strewn with papers and all sorts of rubbish, that I hardly knew how to welcome him. It irritated and shamed me to have to reveal the squalor of my life to him, and yet, too, I felt proud and elated. Here was Diaghilev himself, having sacrificed his night's rest.... Then we had coffee very cosily together, and Serge Pavlovitch drove me to the station.

We entered a carriage. "Now concentrate." For a minute we were silent, then Diaghilev got up, made the sign of the cross over me with quick, small gestures, embraced me, and gave me his blessing "for the coming work and all that is good," and, lo, there was his white handkerchief, waving, waving, as the monotonous, huge, gray tedious houses began to glide past.

CHAPTER II

CREATION OF A DANCER

ONCE IN Turin I immediately had myself driven to Cecchetti's, but, finding him out, went on to the theater. I found him in the middle of a lesson, and at once recognized the small, snow-white, unimposing old man, famous far and wide as the last surviving relic of his tradition in Europe. I found him sitting in one corner of the stage, instructing a girl and two boys. Going up, I mentioned Diaghilev's name, whereupon a happy smile of childlike joy lit up his features. However, he said nothing, but motioned me to wait for the end of the lesson. I waited, but now it was no happy and kind old man that I saw, but an angry, irascible maestro, who, whistling the melody, and emphasizing each beat with his stick, would suddenly jump from his seat and begin not only abusing, but striking his pupils. And the pupils . . . the pupils responded by tenderly, respectfully, kissing the hands that chastised.

Next morning, at nine, I myself was attending my first lesson, a lesson which lasted three interminable, painful, exhausting hours, for Cecchetti had decided we should work three hours a day, one hour in private, and two in a class with the others, but since, with Nijinska, I had not been accustomed to such hours, at first I was literally dropping with fatigue. That lesson, from which I returned covered with bruises, remains in my memory as one of horrible torture. Cecchetti was horrified by the manner in which I held my arms. According to his tradition, the turned-outness which the classical school demands of the feet must be maintained by the hands also. Gazing at my posture, he said: "You like young husband old Nijinska. You no good at all. You not taught right. Your hands been maimed," [1] and began to hit those "maimed hands" with his stick.

In Paris I had dreamed only of Italy and Cecchetti, but in Turin I found there was solely Cecchetti, and an incredible, tormenting boredom. There I lived, without friends or acquaintances, without speech, on a dusty, breathless plain, scorching hot under the July sun. Sometimes I took long, boring walks through the Turin streets, but generally I sat at home, or at Cecchetti's. At home I should have had nothing to do but for a large parcel of books which Diaghilev had given me in Paris. Besides the works of Tchekhov and Aksakov, I found it contained much by contemporary Russian writers, Blok, Kuzmin, Ehrenburg, Remisov, Sologub, Biely, Yessenin, and even works on Pushkin, besides many others.

---

[1] Cecchetti talked in a queer jargon of broken Russian, interspersed with words from other languages.

Never since, have I had either the time or opportunity to read so much Russian fiction, and I must always be grateful to Diaghilev for this present, since it made it possible for me to adorn my tedious, my dejected, life in Turin, and acquaint myself with the landmarks of contemporary literature. But I spent even more of my time with Cecchetti, talking to the infirm, unhappy old man. He was frequently ill throughout this summer, and often I would have to take him home from some lesson during which he had felt faint and put him to bed, though the very next day he would appear as usual, only, as often as not, to feel faint again.

Soon, both Cecchetti and his wife became my great friends. They loved me as though I were a grandson, but Cecchetti loved me also as a pupil, of whom he had great, perhaps too great, hopes. Feeling how short a time still remained to him, and that with him his old classical traditions would depart, he was anxious to make me their repository and thus, through me, transmit all the experience he had so laboriously accumulated. Cecchetti had not much general culture, and but little interest in anything save the ballet and his small garden, yet, where dancing was concerned, his philosophy was complete.

"Never forget," he would often repeat to me, "that in our divine art, to be 'perseverance itself' is a virtue, but if one is excessively fanatical about it, one runs the risk of becoming a maniac. Work always with love, with a will to succeed, but never 'exaggeratedly'!"

In work he would never permit his students "to go full out": for "a dancer," he said, "must always have a reserve in hand" in order to yield himself wholly upon the stage. In this, he was one with Diaghilev.

"Work as I teach, but dance as you can and want to dance," was the old man's perpetual advice. "Moods" and "sentiments," as expressed in dancing, were almost sacred to him, for the way the "soul expressed itself" on the stage, seemed to him something to be handled with great delicacy and tact.

His dream was to die in the theater, and I was often to hear him say that, feeling his last moment near, he would take a taxi, hurry off to the theater, and hang himself there. That end seemed most desirable to him, because then with his last breath he would be breathing its air, and merge at length into the life and soul of that to which he had consecrated all his long life. Even then he was preparing to die, though his wife, with devoted care, managed to preserve his life some short while longer.

"Listen, Serge, I'm getting very old"—he was seventy-four—"and, as you see, am desperately ill. I shall be dying soon, very soon. Our art is on the decline, and I haven't the strength to raise it again. There is only one way it can be done, and that is by preserving the 'annals of the dance.' But those annals are the professor, none other exists. Those I have been to you, up till now. They are all open to you, you read in them as in a book, but when everything has been read your duty will be to make them available to others, so that our beloved art may not die. To you I am transmitting the efforts of a lifetime." And, indeed, in Milan, two years later, he handed me, with my diploma, all the notes he had accumulated through many years, together with a collection of the music he considered most valuable for practicing dancing.

About a week after my departure, Diaghilev's first letter reached me from Venice. It touched and moved me by its solicitude for my well-being, and by the "little bit" of Diaghilev I detected below the surface. He wrote:

"Only yesterday did I arrive in Venice, where I found your nice letter. It was a great pleasure to me to receive the good news you give in it. One thing, however, I do not like, and that is, where you say you are dissatisfied with the food. You must be well fed: that is a matter of prime importance, and you must not neglect it. Please let me know how you are getting on with your reading? Are you returning the books to Paris in order to get them exchanged, and are you getting the Russian papers? Three-hour lessons are certainly long, but one must take the bull by the horns, and, as you know, time is precious. I am hoping old Cecchetti will be able to come to Monte Carlo this winter, but meanwhile, get out of him everything you can. Have you yet written to your colleagues, and what are they writing to you? How did they take your flight to Cecchetti? As I've already said to you, write often: I want to hear all your news.

"About myself, all I can say is that my departure from Paris was one long headlong rush in which I left numbers of things undone. Had I stayed a moment longer I should never have got away at all. Here in Venice, as ever, everything is divine. There is no place on earth like it for me, both for restfulness and because here I conceive all my ideas, which are afterwards shown to the world.

"I shall be delighted to see you again, but that, for the moment, must rest with the future. Don't forget to let me know how you are getting on with Cecchetti. With my blessings for every good fortune.

"Yours, S. D."

Every letter that Diaghilev sent sought constantly to fire me in two directions: one, my work with Cecchetti, whom he was trying to persuade, through me, to come to Monte Carlo; the other, my own instruction, for that he considered indispensable to the formation of a real artist. Thus he wrote in one of his letters:

"I am so glad you are reading so much, do go on, and even more actively if possible, for it will immensely improve my chances of winning my bet! I also spend all day reading, but only French fiction. They have such a number of remarkable authors, such as de Lacretelle, Kessel,

Radiguet, Proust, etc. It is a pity that for the time being, you can't tackle them, but you shall begin in Monte Carlo."

In the same letter I came on a sentence which made my heart beat faster with new hope. "By the end of this month I shall have to visit Milan with my agent, with regard to certain engagements, and then we shall certainly be able to meet. That should be in some 8 to 10 days. I shall let you know the exact date later: meanwhile I shall expect to hear from you *more often*. My blessing for every good fortune...."

Finally, the day came, which, for the past three weeks, had been all my expectation. On July 26th, a short note arrived from Serge Pavlovitch, containing his typically clear and exact instructions:

"Dear Seriozha,

"I shall be reaching Milan on *Tuesday, the 29th*. I leave here by the 9:25 A.M., arriving Milan 3:05 P.M. Get yourself a *second-class* ticket, and leave Turin at 10:50 A.M. You will arrive at Milan at 1:30 P.M., get your lunch at the station, wait for my train, and meet me. I am sending what is necessary for the ticket. Acknowledge immediately receipt of this letter.

"I received your last. Many thinks and au revoir for the time being."

"Yours, S. D."

I hardly know how I got through these interminable three days. It seemed that the twenty-ninth would never come, and that there would be no journey to Milan. And when, on the twenty-eighth, a telegram arrived confirming the arrangements made by letter, I was positive, as I opened it, that Diaghilev must have put off our meeting.

Next day, following Diaghilev's instructions, I reached Milan, and lunched at the railway station. Then at last there was his train, and out of a first-class compartment stepped a rejuvenated Diaghilev—for Italy always rejuvenated Serge Pavlovitch, made him look fresher and somehow lighter. Embracing me, he said he wanted to show me Milan, but, as two days were all he could spare, time was valuable. Whereupon, we began walking to the enormous glass-covered Galleria, stopping to look at La Scala Theater, and the monument to Leonardo and his pupils. All the way, and in the Galleria, where we took coffee, Serge Pavlovitch questioned me in detail as to my life in Turin, my lessons and Cecchetti, but said no word in connection with himself.

Then we went on into the square of the dazzling white Duomo, and entered the Cathedral. Nothing I could say would adequately express what I felt once I was inside—all I can say is that I was more powerfully affected than by anything else that happened to me in this Italian epoch. The very fact of being with Diaghilev induced a state of prayerful tremor. In his presence I felt eternal longings, a yearning to seek the very sources of religion, the well-spring of the divine. It was as though we were both about to respond with a common accord, with the same impulse, and the same breath, in a communion which sanctions the eternal alliance of two lives.

From the Cathedral we went on to Sta. Maria della Grazia to see Leonardo's "Last Supper," but on the way wandered off into various churches to see numbers of frescoes. The result was that we only arrived about six. I was tired and dragged along at Diaghilev's heels, feeling that the mere fact of his presence made me blind to everything else. Serge Pavlovitch was in summer clothes: white trousers, ending at the ankle, tight in the leg and shortened by frequent washings, white shoes and an ordinary straw hat, which he was constantly removing to wipe the perspiration from his brow. There was the inevitable tuberose in the buttonhole of his usual dark jacket, and he was wearing, too, his usual stiff white collar, for he never wore one that was soft. Helping himself along with his cane, not merely swinging it about, he puffed, sniffed, and kept easing his neck, as if trying to rid himself of his dreadful, tormenting horse-collar, and, nevertheless, marched on. I was fearfully tired with the heat and the emotions I had already experienced, and so had but little energy to spare for other churches, or all the things Diaghilev explained. Nevertheless, even under these conditions, Luini's frescoes in San Maurizio, and especially St. Catherine's torments, could hardly fail to move me deeply. And indeed, his were the first paintings to touch me at all in Milan.

But when, eventually, we reached Sta. Maria della Grazia, after what seemed our endless journey, I suddenly seemed to find myself in the very atmosphere of Leonardo's time. All my weariness vanished. There in front of us was the "Cenacolo," and peacefully, reverently, we gazed at it together.

Speaking generally, I observed that Diaghilev's presence either galvanized me, and in some wonderful way raised me to a higher level which sensitized my perceptions, and so enabled me to penetrate into the Holy of Holies of whatever we might be contemplating; or, on the contrary, paralyzed me, and made it impossible for me to perceive anything whatever. There were times when Diaghilev's long explanations would convey absolutely nothing; and yet, two or three words, a hint only, or silence, particularly his silences, would make me take in some work of art joyfully and deeply. Now we sat down in front of the "Last Supper." At first it left me unmoved. And yet, the longer I gazed and strove to visualize it as it must have looked when newly painted, the more deeply did it begin to affect me. Possibly Diaghilev's own feelings and thoughts may in some way have been communicated to me, possibly there were regions in myself which I had never suspected, possibly the great genius himself was speaking to my soul: however that may be, the longer I gazed the less able was I to tear myself away, until at last I entered into a condition of utter calm and delight.

Thus our first day in Milan came to an end. Next day we rose early, and Diaghilev led me to the enormous and very lovely Scala Theater, a theater "in which you, and I hope soon, will be dancing." After which we went to the famous Brera Gallery. Here Diaghilev "showed" me the masters he loved, "showing" them with hardly a glance. He himself already knew them by heart, and so they could give him but little that was new. Besides, he was clearly nervous of the way I should respond. Would I like them enough, feel and value them enough? But naturally, my knowledge of painting was somewhat limited, and I must have disappointed so exceptional a judge.

We began with some frescoes by Luini, whose work I had so much admired the previous day. Refreshed by a night's rest, I gazed at each picture with the greatest attention, though somewhat superficially I must say, seeing that Diaghilev was hurrying me on all the time. Apart, however, from Luini's "Madonna with Saints," nothing in the first four rooms much impressed me. In the fifth room what impressed me most deeply was a head of Christ ascribed to Leonardo, and even more a terrifying "Crucifixion" by Mantegna. I had noticed it the moment we entered the room and, dumfounded, cried:

"Serge Pavlovitch, what is that over there? Surely it isn't an old Italian painting?"

"Of course! Why, what's troubling you?"

"But it seems such present-day realism. Christ is dead, so dead he cannot possibly ever rise again. Can Mantegna possibly have been an atheist?"

"When you have seen more of his religious paintings, you will understand that he was not an atheist, but a man deeply, strongly devout, though an individual, if ever there was one. It is certainly very different from the saintly, näive, prayerful and purely religious cerulean painting of Angelico."

Again I stood amazed in front of Luini's "Women Bathing."

"Is it possible that this, too, is sixteenth-century Italian? Why it's a Picasso, a genuine Picasso!"

"Yes, if you like it's a Picasso of the sixteenth century, if in Picasso you see a manifestation of art violating and destroying accepted canons. In that sense, the Italian art of the fifteenth and sixteenth centuries had much in common with Picasso."

Of the rest of the Brera I have but little recollection. After a prolonged lunch at the Galleria, Diaghilev led me to the Ambrosiana. But my mind was still full of my impressions of the Brera, my head and my feet felt fatigued, and all I remember of what we saw is the "Codex Atlanticus," a collection of drawings and manuscripts by Leonardo da Vinci.

Sadly, I left that evening for what to me was an empty, tiresome, moribund Turin. In the interval I had profited much: I had been with

Diaghilev, visited Milan, Lombardy, seen the works of Leonardo, Luini, Mantegna, and yet I could not help feeling sad and discontented. Somehow I had expected more from Serge Pavlovitch and Milan and, above all, from myself. It seemed to me, I had not been able to assimilate or understand enough of what had been offered me, that perhaps Diaghilev would be disappointed in me, too. Back in my solitude again, and feeling my dissatisfaction even more keenly, I wrote him a somewhat disjointed, unsatisfactory letter about it all, and a few days later came his reply. I quote it here, not so much because it relieved my mood, and drove away every doubt, but because it is typical of Diaghilev's views on the education of an artist:

"My dear Seriozha, I am not too pleased with your letter. There's a sort of unnecessary melancholy about it, a feeling of things left unsaid. These were not at all the sort of impressions I wanted from you.... My own, on the contrary, are cheerful and brave. To me, it seems, that for you to gain acquaintance in this manner with all that is best in this world, is not only useful but indispensable, if you aspire to become a *real artist*. I would very much like to show you France in the same way. That was how Massine's entire activity began, there it was he realized at last all those essential and imponderable things that made him a creative artist (though, unfortunately, but for a short while). I expect there will be a possibility between August 15th and 20th. I shall write about it again...."

About August 10th Diaghilev sent me a parcel of books, the contents of which disturbed me no little, and the following day a letter from Monte Carlo, in which he urged me yet again to go on persevering with my artistic education. "Coming from Venice, I stopped in Florence for three days, and once more was able to convince myself that no artist can lay claim to any culture unless he be intimately acquainted with this holy site of art. It is indeed God's dwelling, and if, perchance, Florence should ever perish in an earthquake, the real art of the world would perish with it. For me each of my visits to Florence is like a pilgrimage to some holy shrine. I have seized the opportunity to send you a small present, ten booklets containing the work of ten of the greatest masters, those of the holy Raphael, portraits and other important works, Botticelli, Mantegna (you remember his Christ?), Piero della Francesca, Donatello, Filippa Lippi, Francia, Masaccio, Michelangelo, and our Milanese Luini. And I consider it your duty to memorize all these reproductions so that you will comprehend the differences between each of these masters, and learn to know them by heart. That would make a good preparation for a possible excursion; very necessary if you are not to lose your bearings. Take the books with you, if you do go to Florence. Please acknowledge their receipt, and also the dancing slippers. I am very pleased that you spend so much time with the Maestro, and help him with his little garden; that is all very good."

If Diaghilev had only known how much his present tormented me! As I looked into the ten booklets I felt at first utterly lost, hardly knew where to begin, or what was meant by "comprehend the difference between each of these masters, and learn to know them by heart." True, I made an effort to read the introductions to each of them, but, my Italian proving inadequate, and the reproductions being monochrome, I made little headway. What on earth was I to reply to Diaghilev that would not give me away? ... Meanwhile, though busy in Monte Carlo with preparations for the new season, his constant search for new talent, and recent discovery of Dukelsky, Diaghilev nevertheless found time to enquire in each of his letters whether I had received the books from Florence, whether I liked and was interested in them, and to ask me to write "sensibly about them, and in full detail."

Having with difficulty reached some conclusion about the booklets and their contents, I wrote a lengthy missive to Diaghilev setting out my impressions, and then, in some apprehension sat down to await his reply, certain my stupidity and ignorance would be most severely reprimanded. However, no answer came from Diaghilev, and it was only later, when we met, that he told me I had seized many of the essentials, and that certain personal observations, jotted down casually and, as it were, unthinkingly, had pleased him greatly and convinced him that I possessed an unusual degree of artistic sensitivity and showed great promise as a true artist.

Thus, I was awaiting a reply from Diaghilev, though to my growing astonishment nothing came, when, on August 18th, late at night, a telegram arrived containing a totally unexpected message: *"Vous ai envoyé 500 liquidez tout à Turin soyez mercredi soir Milano hôtel Cavour avec toutes vos bagages."* Clearly this decision must have been sudden enough for Diaghilev, for that very day he had sent me a short note by express from his Monte Carlo Bank, which seemed to foreshadow no such sudden departure: "Sending check. *Shall write today or tomorrow.* Received today all your four letters together. Thanks and handshake.—S. D."

"Liquider tout" in Turin, in a day, offered no difficulties, since I had nothing to leave save Cecchetti. Our parting was touching and tender, and he promised that that winter he would join me and the Ballet in Monte Carlo. By the twentieth I was in Milan, where Diaghilev met me, and we went on immediately to Venice. Here we arrived late at night, and, as we were leaving the station, Serge Pavlovitch asked:

"How would you like us to go to the center? By cab, or in a gondola?"

I implored him, above all things, to take a gondola, at which he began to laugh merrily, quite in his Italian manner, though I failed to see why. ...

Thus we floated along through the town of vast silences: magnificent Venice of annunciation and night, with its deep dark sky reflected in softly gleaming water: and from that moment I became forever its slave.

Everything took on a totally different aspect. And Serge Pavlovitch changed too. As he was now I had never known him, yet thus he was always to be in Venice, as though a veritable doge, who proudly, joyfully, parades his native, miraculous city. Five days we spent there, five perfect epoch-making days, with Diaghilev all smiles and in a perpetual good humor as he nodded to right and to left, with a *bon giorno* for all, since all seemed to know him. Or else we sat in the square of St. Mark, the most joyful square in the world, as though he were verily at home. As I looked at him, I too would be infected by his smile, his joy. An oppressive weight seemed to have been lifted, and now, at last, I felt I had found in him that for which I had so long sought; a trustworthy, firm and faithful support.

Next day we spent seeing the life of the city. That day Diaghilev made no attempt to show me the museums or galleries, but tried to make me enter the very spirit of the town, though already I felt it was part of me, by recounting tragic tales from its history, by walking me through the city, and by an excursion in a gondola along the Grand Canal. Later that day I took a swim at the Lido, though alone, for Serge Pavlovitch never bathed, since for nothing in the world would he ever have appeared naked. But always we somehow found ourselves back in *the* Square, though, superstitious as he was, Diaghilev, having once mistaken a sign, never himself crossed, and never allowed me to cross, between the two flagstaffs.

That evening we listened to *The Barber of Seville* in the Venice Theater, and after the performance had supper with Yessenin and Isadora Duncan.

The third day Diaghilev began to parade Venetian art in front of me, and with such thoroughness that, however often I might find myself in later years in Venice, there was never anything to add to my knowledge of, or feeling for it. The remaining days were just sufficient, with not an instant wasted, and ample time for everything of any importance: the Doge's Palace, the Academy of Art, all the churches, and all the *palazzi* to which we could gain admittance.

From Venice we went on to the calmness, the intimacy of small Padua of the arcaded, narrow streets—a journey I shall always keep in thankful and reverent rememberance, as one of the chief events in my outer, and inner, life. Here in Padua, my rebirth in beauty and art was finally accomplished: here in St. Anthony's town my eternal pact with Diaghilev was concluded. There I drank from the very sources of Italian art, of all *Italy* itself, from the fathomless deeps, the eternal truth of the great Giotto. What had been only a hint in Milan Cathedral, here, in front of Giotto's frescoes, seemed welded together in one harmonious whole. By the side of the nineteen-year-old boy-youth, untutored and totally inexperienced, now stood the wise, the omnipotent Diaghilev, and by some

With His Troupe in England, 1928
*Desormières, Diaghilev, Lifar, Kokhno, Danilova, Tchernicheva,
Doubrovska*

Lifar, Nouvel, and Diaghilev at Venice, 1926

inexplicable, incomprehensible miracle was seeing Giotto with the same eyes, with an identical feeling of the soul winging heavenwards towards the beautiful and eternal: towards God and loveliness. Liberated, I seemed dissolving, my whole being merging into his, one single breath pulsated in us both, and we were one more closely than in any earthly union.

Serge Pavlovitch was no less moved than I. In some way there was a kind of prayerful luminosity about him, that is the only way I can put it.

Diaghilev was not, in the accepted sense of the word, a particularly religious man and his faith was, perhaps, not strong, but he adored occasions of pomp, church ceremonial, and the ritual of religion, such as the lamp burning before the icons in his room. These he valued greatly. Yet too, he knew moments when the soul prays to some unknown god. In him the practice of religion was intimately bound up with a leaning towards superstition; the latter playing a great part in his life. Thus, he particularly adored St. Anthony of Padua, and always carried a medallion bearing his image in his waistcoat pocket.

After praying at the tomb of the Saint, Serge Pavlovitch embraced me, and told me he believed in me, and would take upon himself to care for me and help me through life. From that moment dated my entire concentration on dancing and Serge Pavlovitch: from then on, no matter what I might be doing, he was ever present in my thoughts. Even when dancing, my thoughts were still of him, as I strove for utter perfection to make myself worthy of his friendship and justify his faith. Avidly I read, or sat for hours in Italian galleries studying paintings, frequented concerts, and was rewarded by unimaginable raptures, in which the soul soared into regions I had never imagined could exist. But even more intent was I on my spiritual improvement. Then, more fully myself, I should be able, spiritually and emotionally, to approach, to understand, to think and feel as deeply as he, Diaghilev, Serge Pavlovitch, Seriozha, my namesake....

Another talk in Padua moved me still more deeply, and raised me on the fluttering wings of hope:

"I have not the slightest doubt left now that, not only shall I win my bet against Nijinska, but I am certain I have won it already. I know absolutely that some day soon, you will be ballet master in the Russian Ballet, and now I am anxious to see your creative activity functioning as soon as possible, so that I may be proud of you, and myself, and share your happiness...."

These words not only moved me to new hope and expectation, but, as by some magic power, they communicated a new impulse to my innermost being, a new conflagration of the creative urge, which from that day has never left me.

From Padua we went to Milan, and there took leave of each other.

Diaghilev went on to Monte Carlo, I to Paris, where on the 1st of September the whole company was due to reassemble.

On August 31st Serge Pavlovitch arrived from Monte Carlo with Dolin and Kokhno, and immediately I felt that a wall had risen between us, a wall that was to keep us apart for months. I could not meet him informally, found no opportunity of talking to him, and once more was doomed to my solitude, but now how infinitely more difficult to endure.

That day, as prearranged, the whole company assembled and were much astonished to see how I had changed, for they now saw a civil, elegant young man, where before they had known an uncouth, rude and somewhat boorish youth. The day after, Nijinska gave her first lesson, which turned into a wonderful personal triumph for me, the more impressive since few in the company suspected I had been working under Cecchetti, or had been living in Italy. Once I had changed, and was standing by the practice bar, I suddenly felt I was breathing just as I ought to breathe, and could hear the song of my body. That moment I knew myself as through and through a dancer, that I was surpassing myself, that I was a changed man. And that the whole company realized too. Immediately, I took the lead of the class, and all admitted it as my due. Yet there was no one more impressed by this transformation in my dancing than Diaghilev himself: from that moment he began to consider me his first dancer.

On September 9th, Serge Pavlovitch gave me a part in *Cimarosiana,* and next day another in *Flore et Zéphyre* . . . Everybody took my rise in Diaghilev's esteem with the utmost good nature, and not only made no effort to "shoulder me out," but, on the contrary, and as it were casually, disappeared the moment Serge Pavlovitch arrived, in order to leave us alone. . . .

On the 14th, the whole company left for Munich, though without Diaghilev, who did not join us until the 21st. Although we spent just a fortnight in this city, and left on the 30th, our performances proved very successful, a success which was generally repeated throughout Germany. I danced with enthusiasm, and seemed but to live for dancing and visiting the museums. Diaghilev I could meet but seldom, and so was forced to content myself with admiring him from a distance, an admiration mingled with pride in the man I imagined the one colossus of the twentieth century, and with tender thankfulness I would remember Italy and how close our relations had been. In church, while praying for my relatives left behind in Russia, I would always add his name to my prayers, would put his name down on the list "for prayers to be said for his health," and have *prosfiras* [2] consecrated for him.

In Munich I would often visit the old Pinakothek and Gliptakothek, to look at the primitive Apollos and my dear Italians. But the Memling's,

---

[2] A certain bread used in the Orthodox Church for this purpose. (Ed.)

Dürer's and Cranach's seemed strange to me, and one day, at a chance meeting, I said to Diaghilev:

"Serge Pavlovitch, who is this Cranash?" (pronouncing it as though it were French, since I knew no German).

Whereupon Diaghilev began laughing, but then gave me a long, interesting and most substantial lecture on early German painting, and himself accompanied me to the Pinakothek to "show me" Cranach and Dürer.

My last joy in Munich came just before our departure, when he gave me the shopwalker's part in *Les Femmes de Bonne Humeur*. Then on October 1st, 2nd and 3rd we appeared in Leipzig, on the 4th, 5th and 6th in Chemnitz, and afterwards left for Berlin, which we reached on the 9th, having visited sundry small towns on the way. Here we stayed until the 27th.

On the 26th, we gave our last performance in Berlin and left for a grand tour through Germany, spending a week (October 27th to November 3rd) in Breslau, five days (November 4th to 9th) in Hamburg, and three days each in Mainz and Cologne. We had a certain amount of artistic success, but it was by no means the triumph to which we were accustomed, and the financial return was far from encouraging. I, myself, was not dancing, owing to an indisposition.

From Cologne the whole company left for Hannover and thence via Ostend for London, while I with Kokhno and Diaghilev journeyed via Paris. About this time the dancers Balanchevadze, Yefimov, Danilova and Gevergeyeva, who had fled from Soviet Russia, happened to be in Paris, whereupon Diaghilev, hearing of their plight, asked them to come and see him, and received them with the utmost kindness. Much moved, the runaway dancers asked him to give them an audition, and were granted one that same evening. When they arrived we took them to Mme. Sert's, where they danced items from their repertoire, much to all our delight. Diaghilev then and there engaged them in his *corps de ballet,* and soon after Balanchevadze, as Balanchine, was promoted ballet master to Diaghilev's Russian Ballet.

But now our great London season was approaching. The opening date was November 24th, and we had contracted to dance at the London Coliseum, twice a day, for seven weeks. So it was necessary to hurry.

One episode of my life in London remains particularly in my mind: namely, my first experiments in choreography. The arrangement was that *Flore et Zéphyre* should be produced by Nijinska but, having for some reason taken offense because Diaghilev had entrusted me with the part of Boreas, she left the company. I vividly recall how astonished, how shaken I was, when Diaghilev, in the presence of all, turning to me, said I was to be responsible for the choreography of this ballet, for I knew well the importance attached by Diaghilev to the new ballet, in which Dolin and Nikitina were to appear; knew too how much he admired the music of the young Dukelsky whom he had recently discovered. All this only made his decision the more overwhelming. If he gives me *Flore et Zéphyre* it must mean ... and my head swam with happiness and hope. ...

Thus I became ballet master to Diaghilev's Russian Ballet, but not, however, for long.

Enthusiastically, and with immense though spasmodic zeal, I took on the task of producing the new ballet. New steps and postures thronged through my mind and at times so tumultuously as completely to banish sleep. One of my ideas at this time was so to build up the part of Flore (Nikitina) that not even for a moment, in the whole course of the ballet, would the ballerina's feet touch ground, sustained, as I meant her to be, on the men's arms. Having thoroughly gone into the details with A. J. Trusevitch (then quasi-secretary to the Ballet) who had been attached to me for special duty, I began work in Astafieva's studio, after which followed two trial rehearsals with Savina[3] as Flore, Turau as Zephyre, and the brothers Khosrami. Thanks to the strenuous efforts I had made, and Diaghilev's tender, attentive support, good progress was registered. Nevertheless, in the early days of the New Year, 1925, I began more and more to feel irresolute and somewhat doubtful of the whole thing—not, indeed, because I had lost interest in the creative possibilities of choreographic art, but as it seemed, because I feared that, by wholly devoting myself to a new art, I should fall behind as a dancer, just when I was beginning to succeed. Strongly influenced by this motive, I did my best to persuade Serge Pavlovitch to be reconciled with Massine, in order that the latter might return as choreographer to the Ballet.

A period of long and painful indecision followed, but finally Diaghilev's love for his Ballet prevailing, he yielded, and Massine began to work on *Flore et Zéphyre,* whereupon an arrangement was made by which Massine was to join us in Monte Carlo for a fortnight at the end of March, in order to put the finishing touches to this ballet. Meanwhile, the rest of the company had reached Monte Carlo on January 11th, where between January 17th and February 1st we gave a number of performances.

Our first performance, that of January 17th, was a gala night, attended by the Prince and Princess of Monaco, the Duke of Connaught and many celebrities. Nevertheless, it almost provoked a tremendous scandal. That very morning certain members of the *corps de ballet* had circulated a round robin demanding an increase in pay. For some unknown reason I and some four or five others were not approached. But the leading dancers, including Mlle. Shollar and Vilzak, sympathized warmly, and Vilzak even undertook to act as go-between, by way of Grigoriev, our producer. Diaghilev, however, through Grigoriev, categorically refused to grant any increase, whereupon the whole cast resolved to go on strike

[3] An Englishwoman, formerly Massine's wife.

at the gala performance. That evening I went to the theater as usual, where I was joined by a few of the dancers. Diaghilev was excessively nervous, for the audience was beginning to pour in, while at the back of the stage, only five dancers were present. Pallid, and with his nervous twitch particularly marked, Serge Pavlovitch went up to the Royal box and approaching the Princess of Monaco, informed her that neither *Les Tentations de la Bergère* nor *Cimarosiana* could be given, and that it would be necessary to substitute individual numbers. Finally, the curtain went up, long after time, and we began to dance our separate numbers.

Meanwhile more dancers had arrived, though Shollar and Vilzak still continued absent, for having decided to stand by the *corps de ballet,* they had quietly remained away, totally unaware of what was happening. . . .

It was Kokhanovsky who saved Diaghilev and the performance, an act for which Serge Diaghilev remained ever grateful, for, in a speech to the cast, he implored them to remember they would be ruining not only a vast enterprise but Diaghilev and themselves. By degrees the dancers were won over, and eventually threw themselves enthusiastically into their parts. Not till next day did Shollar and Vilzak, dismissed from the Ballet, discover how they had been deserted by the rest of the company; what must have made it still more painful, was the fact that neither had had the slightest personal interest in the strike, nor had desired any increase in pay.

Soon after, Cecchetti arrived, and we had a touching reunion. Sometimes I would appear with both him and his wife on the stage.

But now Massine arrived to give the last all-important touches to *Flore et Zéphyre.* The work was by no means easy, for though Dukelsky's music proved very refreshing, its rhythmic design was somewhat difficult, and but little helped by the manner of its scoring.

As we worked, however, something strange seemed happening inside me. Actually, I was not creating my part, for it seemed to be creating itself. Though I studied its every aspect with the most intense application, attaching due weight to every direction, every indication, assimilating and elaborating them all, outwardly there appeared no sign of the inner development of what I was doing. I retired into myself, and in imagination danced a great deal, though following my own bent. Yet at rehearsals I was languidly mechanical, and indeed to such an extent that the rest of the cast began to feel deeply concerned and wonder whether I would not prejudice the success of the whole ballet.

Massine, who left before our first performance, and Serge Pavlovitch, both adopted an attitude of commiseration, for both had been expecting something original, and both were exceedingly disappointed, for what they saw was the dullest mediocrity.

But at the dress rehearsal, something like a miracle came to pass, for

I went soaring over the stage in such a way that the whole cast stood as though dumb and enchanted. All dancing ceased as every one watched me, and when it was over I heard a burst of thunderous applause. Whereupon Serge Pavlovitch, delighted and profoundly moved, came through the wings and, with a face transformed with joy, hardly able to control his rapture, cried:

"Seriozha, my dear, how you danced, how you flew! How you amazed me! You have filled me with joy! I was pinching myself. I could hardly believe I was not dreaming that I was watching a miracle, an extraordinary ... but I can't find the word to describe it. ... Even now I can't be positively certain I actually saw it all, that the dream, the enchantment won't pass, that I'll have to come back to earth. If it really and truly isn't enchantment, then you're the greatest dancer I've ever seen! But if it only turns out to be enchantment, if I've imagined it all? ... I must see you do it again to make quite sure, once and for all. Let the whole ballet be gone through again, from the very beginning!"

They obey, and once again the "miracle" happens. I soar, I soar. Boreas has flown from the north, over the ocean, and then, following my own variation, I gather myself for my last high, long leap into the wings ... I thrust off from the stage, I fling forward my body ... behind are the nymphs, with Danilova, pirouetting and gazing up as I fly through the air ... and then I fall heavily, dislocating both ankles. The whole stage freezes in the immobility of terror. I try to jump up, but my feet fail, and I drop like a stone. Then I am hurriedly picked up and carried to my hotel.

Serge Pavlovitch, in mortal terror, spent a sleepless night at my bedside, while my ankles were being set. Next day, however, in some embarrassment, he appeared and said: "Seriozha, I must ask you to let me transfer your part to Slavinsky. My contract forces me to produce a new work in Monte Carlo this season, and the season is drawing to its end, and you are in no state for dancing. I know that the fault is mine entirely: why did I insist on repeating the rehearsal? But if you insist on dancing, I shall have to cancel *Flore et Zéphyre* and so shall violate my contract. Still, I do beg you most earnestly not to let me down, and to agree to allow, temporarily, only temporarily, Slavinsky to deputize for you. But the Boreas Paris will see, I assure you, shall be you!"

"No, Serge Pavlovitch, I cannot give up my part to anybody. Make *Flore et Zéphire* our last performance: I shall either dance in *Zéphire* or throw myself from the rock of Monaco, but I will never allow another to do my Boreas."

Diaghilev realized then that my decision was unalterable, and postponed *Flore et Zéphyre* to our last performance, a week thence. Days passed, and doctor after doctor averred that fully six weeks must elapse before I could dream of dancing. Diaghilev was in terror, and Pavel Georgievitch refused to leave me for a single moment. Utterly determined to dance, whatever else might happen, I took my own cure in hand. For a whole week, one of my feet being in splints, I made myself fomentations of boiling hot water, immediately followed by icy cold, and combined both treatments with continuous massage. In three days the swelling began to go down, but being unable to move my feet, I went on practicing with my hands. Then, at last, the fateful day, April 28th, arrived, and with my right foot tight in a rubber sock, I was borne to a cab and driven to the theater. When Diaghilev came into my dressing room he could hardly believe I intended to dance, and was obviously in a state of great anxiety, both on account of my mad decision and the ultimate fate of the whole performance.

The curtain went up, and again I danced exactly as I had danced at the dress rehearsal. Nobody in the audience had the least idea of the state of my feet, nothing at all was noticed. Very few of the artists even knew that, during the performance, one ankle was dislocated three times, and on each occasion had to be reset. Nevertheless, this ballet was the first of my triumphs. After the show, Serge Pavlovitch wrote the following inscription for me on a program: "To dear Boreas, the young and irresistible wind, on the day when he first swept through Monte Carlo." All the same, my triumph cost me dear, for my "cure" laid me low soon after our arrival in Barcelona, to which we had gone on leaving Monte Carlo. A sore throat, with a rapidly rising temperature, began to make it impossible for me to breathe. In mortal fear, Diaghilev had me seen by the best specialists, who diagnosed septic tonsils. For a week I hovered between life and death. My memory preserves an image of Serge Pavlovitch in tears by my bed, and, somewhere near, the plaintive whining of Kokhno's little dog. Meanwhile Diaghilev was constantly veering from hope to despair: one moment thinking my time had come, the next detecting some gleam of improvement, at which he would begin to build wonderful prospects for my future. To those around him he would say: "He'll either die, or live to fulfil all his promise...."

My recovery was, as it were, quite accidental. I made a sudden movement, was violently sick, and the moment after was well again. It seemed I was not suffering from tonsilitis at all, but from an abscess in the throat, due in the first place to the extremes of heat and cold to which my feet had been subjected. Serge Pavlovitch was overjoyed at my recovery, and, weak and thin as I was, I found his attentions and kindness infinitely touching.

Altogether we remained in Barcelona for a fortnight, during which I remained in bed, did no dancing and saw nothing. On May 15th we started for London by way of Paris, where on the 18th we were due to open our important season at the Coliseum, scheduled to last two months.

I was now saddled with an immense amount of work. Vilzak having been discharged, all his parts fell to my province (among others those in *Les Fâcheux* and *Les Biches*); but what made them particularly onerous was my excessive weakness. However, in time, I not only overcame these difficulties, but enjoyed great success both in London and Paris.

On June 17th we gave our first performance of *Les Matelots* in Paris, a performance especially memorable to me. For this ballet, invented by Kokhno, with music by Auric, Serge Pavlovitch had again invited Massine to arrange the choreography, and allotted the parts of the sailors to his very best dancers, namely, Woizikowsky, Slavinsky and myself, mine being the most lyrical of the parts. In London, Diaghilev would often ask me to lunch at some restaurant and, on one of these days, happening to be kept rather late, rehearsing, I heard Serge Pavlovitch, as I drew near the restaurant, shouting angrily and excitedly to Kokhno:

"I gave those parts to Woizikowsky, Slavinsky and Seriozha, and I will not alter my decision in your favor. As I have said, so shall it be. You are the author of this ballet, but I am the director of the Russian Ballet, and I know what I want, and what orders I have given." At which Kokhno left, whereupon, becoming aware of my presence, Diaghilev, completely transformed, turned kindly and tenderly to me, saying:

"I say, you must be hungry, Seriozha! Sit down and eat! Not tired, are you?"

All through lunch, with friendly solicitude, he tried to persuade me to throw off my feeling of weakness, to make an effort to begin dancing again; for, with the possibility of Dolin resigning, he felt it necessary to convince me that the whole future of the Russian Ballet rested with me, and that I must prove worthy of the great future in store.

Dolin's contract was due to expire on July 1st, and it was common knowledge to us all, including Dolin, that the contract would not be renewed. I was as well aware of the fact as anybody, for Diaghilev had already told me of it in Padua. Then, on June 1st, part of the company left to fulfil a week's engagement in Paris.

Meanwhile Diaghilev was insisting that Dolin must observe the full letter of his contract, much to the latter's annoyance, and so he accompanied us. On board the steamer, however, Dolin, happening to buy some French newspapers, saw that although the forthcoming season in Paris featured my name, there was no mention of his at all.

"I shall not go to Paris!" was his immediate reaction.

Nevertheless, Woizikowsky and Sokolova were able, though with great difficulty, to persuade him to continue, bow to the inevitable, and conscientiously fulfil his contract. My own dilemma was a painful one. On the one hand it grieved me deeply that, though involuntarily, I was the cause of the situation, yet, on the other hand, and that seemed most important of all, I felt frightened. An invincible dread of the future took possession of me: dread of the responsibilities with which I was being burdened, in having the Ballet's fortunes thus linked so closely with my own. Then and there I decided, that the moment the train ran into the Gare du Nord, I should desert and seek the unknown.

But when the train pulled in, there on the platform were Pavel Georgievitch and Kokhno, who had arrived the day before with Diaghilev, and who at once took me off to the Grand Hotel where Diaghilev wanted to see me. There, I implored him to release me from the responsibility he was thrusting upon me, reiterating that, come what might, I should never be able to see the engagement through, that I would be bound to break down, and thus have to abandon the company.

"Nonsense, that's all pure foolishness! It's far too late to think of that now. This whole engagement rests on you, and yours is the sole responsibility, both as regards myself and Paris."

On June 15th we opened at the Gaîeté Lyrique with three ballets, *Pulcinella, Flore et Zéphyre* and *La Boutique Fantasque,* with myself dancing in the two last. One of our best dancers, Slavinsky, had been allotted a part in Stravinsky's *Pulcinella,* but for some reason, being unable to appear, Diaghilev intended to substitute Dolin. He did not, however, make the request himself, but through the intermediary of a friend, the impresario Wolheim. Dolin began by refusing indignantly, but eventually agreed to help his comrade. The ballet over, Dolin came into my dressing room, and with delicate, tender fingers, in a way I found comradely and touching, and which lingers in my memory as a most beautiful gesture, adjusted the wreath I was wearing as Boreas.

On this occasion Paris took me to her bosom, as it did Nikitina, a dancer all grace, and the very soul of the music. Our third night, that of the seventeenth, was the première of *Les Matelots.* It was a jolly ballet, with a sort of saucy tunefulness about the music, and the Press and public liked it immensely. And indeed, this ballet had many of the qualities of success, as, for instance, the bravura of the variations, which incited the dancers to vie with each other, its uncommon freshness and youth, and, I would say, a sort of choreographic ingenuousness, as though the dancing were solely for dancing's sake, and for the delightful interest in it.

Each variation had its own individuality to suit the temperaments of each of the three sailors. Mine was the most lyrical, the most lilting, part of the three, the only part in which Massine had employed the steps of classic dancing, which thus threw it into especial prominence. Special to my part were a series of *pirouettes* in set postures, with one hand thrown up, and the other supporting the knee of a raised leg, after which I would do four *pirouettes en dedans,* and repeat exactly, with the other leg off the ground. In the variations of the two other sailors (Woizikowsky and Slavinsky) tap dancing predominated. A most interesting feature were Slavinsky's *sauts,* his part requiring sixteen *sauts* made in a horizontal position, with one leg immobile *en arabesque* against his body, while he leaped along on his other leg.

The décor in black and white, and the costumes, all designed by the Spanish painter Pruna, were fresh and joyful and well suited the general atmosphere of the ballet. Indeed, the moment the three young sailors appeared, the house was already smiling. But that first night a remarkable incident occurred in connection with the *ensemble* danced by the sailors on chairs. The first to appear on the stage was Woizikowsky, the second Slavinsky, and the third myself. I was busy pasting a small moustache on to my lip in the wings, and was about to take hold of a chair, when that very moment Woizikowsky tries a chair, then quickly exchanges it with Slavinsky, who in turn takes my chair, handing me Woizikowsky's. I seize it, and, to my dismay, find it completely loose in the joints. We begin our dance with the chairs, and first the seat of my chair falls out, and then one of the legs goes.... Nevertheless, I jump on my chair, but only to find a second leg drop off, leaving me with the back, the frame and two diagonal legs.... With a more cheerful smile than possibly my part demands, I jump on my chair yet again, by some miracle preserving my balance, then drop on my seat as the last chord is struck; at which the whole thing collapses with a sound like the crack of a whip, and I fall to the stage amid the wild applause of the house.

On the twentieth our last performance took place, the program consisting of *Les Fâcheux, Flore et Zéphyre, Les Matelots* and *Le Train Bleu*. It was a sad day for Dolin, who, with tears in his eyes, was, for the last time, dancing in Diaghilev's ballet. As we were about to leave on our journey to London I said good-by to my late rival. We parted friends, and friends we are still. In after years Dolin was always present at my performances, and would generously, unrepiningly, congratulate me on my successes, and be glad for my sake....

We resumed our important season in London on the 22nd of June. During this second half of our season the whole ordering of the Ballet was left in my hands, and I was inundated with flowers, objects, fruit and letters. Diaghilev especially was lavish with flowers after each performance. The season was a brilliant and impressive success. On July 7th the London Music Club gave a reception in honor of Diaghilev and the Ballet. Serge Pavlovitch awaited it with immense trepidation, for, though a fascinating speaker and companion in private, or at small gatherings, he felt lost amid crowds, and would often sit in gloomy and total silence from beginning to end. On this occasion, however, the reception went off very well. Serge Pavlovitch's speech "On the Russian Ballet, not Omitting Russian Art" had been carefully prepared some time beforehand, and he delivered it perfectly and to the admiration of his audience, even though he began by attacking the lack of taste, and general ignorance, of the English in matters concerning the ballet. Earlier, on July 2nd, Diaghilev had given a gala performance at the Hotel Cecil in aid of the Russian Red Cross, which proved another of our triumphs.

On August 1st our big and happy London season came to an end with *Le Mariage d'Aurore* and the company broke up for a two months' holiday. In the book of my life a new page was being turned.

CHAPTER III

ALYOSHA

NOW WE left for Italy, and so began that part of my life in which I was most closely associated with Diaghilev, a connection that continued uninterrupted until Serge Pavlovitch's death. In those four long years, each so different from the other, at times joyful and happy, at times troubled, painful, even tormenting, the image of this great man—in all its complexity, its human incalculability—engraved itself forever on my mind: became, and will forever remain, the mainstay of my existence, so much part of me indeed that now it is difficult for me to treat it as a different entity.

But how is one to build up an image of a relation compounded of so much that is trifling, uncapturable, barely apprehended: words, gestures, and imperceptible variations in the movement of the muscles of the face and hands?

As ever, when real intimacy exists, people only talk frankly, revealingly, to each other at the very outset of their acquaintance. It is only as they enter upon a common path that people pour themselves out to each other, seek to discover each other. But the deeper their intimacy progresses, the more they learn to express themselves to each other, not in words, but half-words, to apprehend by hints and half-hints, till at last, having ceased to unburden themselves, having indeed lost that need, they cease also to understand each other, as each retires into his own shell. Such is the cruel law. Deep friendship and great intimacy must always begin by seeking to stabilize themselves in terms of propinquity, or sure spiritual ties, which often singularly remind one of a convict's chains, till, as a result, only estrangement can ensue: and thus the lovely, vital, vibrant emotions of affection are doomed to final destruction. Between such as are linked by the forms of *domesticity,* real revelation ceases to take place. There is something ludicrous in expounding one's views and convictions to that other self which shares one's existence. It would indeed be far more revealing to listen to that other talking to some *outsider,* but even so, any such revelation must arouse a feeling of distrust, a feeling that it is pride or affectation which speaks. That is why the reminiscences of a great man's relatives—his wife, brother or sister, say—are, in the majority of cases, so pale, so utterly devoid of interest. It is not only because these relatives are unable to distinguish between what is important or trifling, between fundamental and superficial, inextricably mingled though they may be, but because they have nothing really to tell. True, they may know every practical detail of the great man's life: but the rich, the abundant inner world is a closed book. And so the reminiscences of a wife, to all intents and purposes, may differ not at all from those of a housekeeper. To the one, as to the other, was revealed only the great man's commonplace, ordinary, everyday life.

If such a law may be generally applied, how much the more is it applicable in Diaghilev's case, seeing how greatly he feared all affectation, and thereby taught me to fear and avoid it too. For Diaghilev, though fond enough of gossipy talks, felt not the slightest need to reveal or explain himself, nor needed words from another, to know, to feel, and love him as a friend. Nevertheless, towards the end of our life together, my links with him had somewhat weakened, and I developed a more independent existence. Yet it contented him sufficiently to go on loving me, in the knowledge that someone he held dear was close at his side. I, on the other hand, at twenty-two and twenty-three, wished to be able to share my every experience, and wished him, too, to share with me all that was in his soul, and all he lived by. But since the communion of our souls grew ever more rare, to me it seemed we were drifting apart. And indeed, so it was, but for reasons other than those of the law of friendship, about which I have written above. Nevertheless, the effect was similar, and I will come back to it in due course.

Diaghilev had received me as an Alyosha Karamazov with a blind, unswerving faith, and as though it were a refuge. The thought of any change was anathema to him, I was always to be his Alyosha, the creature he had loved from the first. Often, in moments of tenderness, and there were many, particularly during 1925 and 1926, when it seemed our friendship was eternal, when neither had as yet thought of death, or sorrow, or the end of our friendship, when the world still seemed as though the gods had created it for us, and us alone, my "Kotushka," my enormous and tender "Kotushka" as though rapt and motionless and unbreathing, would exclaim:

"Seriozha, you were born for me!"

And, indeed, every thought I had was for him. Meanwhile, desiring to keep me forever his, and as though fearful I might need him less, and perhaps depart, he sought to wall me off from others by interposing his own huge self, limiting me to one friend and one only, his cousin P. G. Koribut-Kubitovitch, whose devotion and crystal purity he solely trusted. Soon I found, however, that Serge Pavlovitch was less interested in my spiritual development than in my sartorial elegance, but I did not seek to oppose his plans, having by now put aside my dream that together we should achieve some miraculous spiritual perfection. There were treasures of tenderness in "Kotushka," treasures of solicitude for those whom he loved. Then the great promoter of the Russian Ballet would change into the touching "Varlamoshka," and, were I sad, would begin dancing, doing small *tours* and *pirouettes* in the hope of cheering me up.

"Have a look, Kuksa, at your Kotushka doing small *tours* and *pirouettes!*" and Serge Pavlovitch, the burly, ponderous Serge Pavlovitch, would begin "pirouetting" or imitating ballerinas *sur les pointes,* looking amazingly like "Varlamov,[1] the immense," from which I drew my nickname "Varlamushka."

Serge Pavlovitch, always a late riser, when at last compelled to get up, would remain for a considerable time wandering about in soft felt slippers and a nightgown, reaching below the knees, dating back to his time in Russia. This was the garb in which he usually performed.

"What else would you like me to show you? Would you now like to watch your Kotushka dancing your own variations?"

At which Serge Pavlovitch would begin dancing my variations, knocking against wardrobes, tables, armchairs, which would then go crashing over.

To watch these ballet "exercises" was sheer physical delight. I would roar with wholehearted laughter, while inwardly I would be deeply touched, knowing it was all for me, to cheer me and make me smile.

My "Kotushka" had many nicknames, but of all those I invented for him, the most suitable was undoubtedly "Othellushka."[2]

Diaghilev was jealous of everyone and everything: of the Countess from Kiev, my childish love-dream, though separated from me by many frontiers; of the girls in the *corps de ballet,* of my dancing partners, of casual acquaintances, and of my stage successes. Always he demanded the whole of a person, and in return would shower back everything it was in his power to give, *everything.* But on one condition, and one only, that all should come from him, be given by or through him. All else was anathema to him. This tyrannical jealousy was part and parcel of his being: it appeared in all his personal relations, but became unbelievably intense wherever his nearest and dearest were concerned.

In the past I have been *her* slave, and it had been a long, arduous business liberating myself, for the wound went on bleeding for years; yet, though at that time she no longer existed for me, nor reigned over my dreams, Serge Pavlovitch, nevertheless, continued to be jealous, suspected I was breaking my word, and was still corresponding with her. Always in terror lest I might abandon him, he would torment me with his jealousy. True, there were many temptations: our women dancers, other women, and especially ballet enthusiasts, in the theater and out, agitated and tormented my imagination, but that was all, for there it rested. I remember how once, after a new ballerina had been engaged, and we had been working together, Serge Pavlovitch said to Grigoriev, the producer: "Sack the girl, why does she flirt with Lifar?" and how it had needed considerable effort to get the order rescinded.

---

[1] Varlamov, a comedian of immeasurable girth, was one of the leading and most popular actors of the Alexandriinsky Theater in Petrograd. (Ed.)

[2] Russian diminutive of Othello. (Ed.)

In his solicitude for my artistic career, and in imagination seeing the most famous ballerinas my partners, Diaghilev would engage them for me, and expect them to see my "genius" exactly as he did; nevertheless, the moment they sought to show any personal esteem for the mere man, apart from dancing, or seemed to the jealous eye of Diaghilev to give the slightest sign of so doing, he would immediately begin to frown, to rage, and be perfectly prepared, at any moment, to pick a quarrel and send them packing.

Having admitted me to the circle of his friends, and gone to considerable effort to make me better acquainted with them, a deep gloom would nevertheless descend on him when, as he thought, his friends seemed too attentive to me, or appeared to be trying to neutralize his influence and alienate us. He also disliked seeing them encourage me to stand on my own feet, for that, he feared, might make his friendship seem less essential to me.

Even more contradictory was his attitude to my stage successes. Though Serge Pavlovitch had done more than anyone to further and make them possible, and though no one delighted in my triumphs more, he was immensely jealous of those very successes, jealous even of the very applause for which I had worked so hard, because he himself was not there on the stage to share it with me.

This jealousy at times led to some exceedingly stormy scenes from my "Othellushka," the first soon after our arrival in Italy. Diaghilev was showing me the north, Stresa, and the lakes, and for some days we stayed at the Villa d'Este on Lake Como. The year 1925 had been an exceptionally happy and fortunate one for Serge Pavlovitch and, as a result of the London season, which had been brilliant in every sense of the word, he was in an especially exalted condition, kindly, endearing, and full of affection and solicitude. Indeed, our life on the enchanting lake, under the friendly, calm, pale blue skies, seemed to me a veritable idyll. Nevertheless, the merest of incidents almost destroyed it completely. Some friends of Diaghilev's happened to be living nearby, and one day the lovely Mme. D. invited us to go over to dinner in their house at Cernobbio. Though she conversed at table with Serge Pavlovitch, her eyes kept turning to me, and her manner was particularly kind and attentive. Soon I was aware that Diaghilev's good humor had begun to alter, that he was fast losing his temper, and only just managing to keep himself in control. But when, after dinner, our beauty proposed we should go for a trip on the lake, Serge Pavlovitch, superstitious and mortally afraid of water, refused, saying:

"No, I won't: have your trip with Seriozha, and I'll go home."

We spent a charming half hour on the lake, merrily talking. Delighted with the beauty of our surroundings and that of my companion, with whom moreover I could talk Russian (a pleasure that but seldom came my way, for my ignorance of other tongues condemned me frequently to silence) I momentarily forgot Diaghilev's black mood, and having accompanied my partner home, returned to our hotel, totally unconcerned, and in the best of spirits. But as I was going upstairs to Serge Pavlovitch's room, the concierge stopped me with the words:

"Monsieur Diaghilev est parti, et vous a fait dire que vous pouvez passer ici toutes vos vacances."

I rush to his room, but Serge Pavlovitch is gone, and all his things with him. Whither? Nowhere but Milan, I tell myself, and hastily packing, hurry off to the Milan hotel at which he usually stays.

"Monsieur Diaghilev?"

"Monsieur Diaghilev vient d'arriver il y a dix minutes."

I had little difficulty in persuading Serge Pavlovitch how little it had been my intention to offend him, my most convincing proof being doubtless the speed of my arrival. Besides, Diaghilev himself was beginning to fear that by his departure he might have rendered me more vulnerable to the charms of Mme. D.; was indeed already beginning to regret his haste.... How many such scenes did I not endure in those four years!

In Diaghilev, the confirmed bachelor, there was, nevertheless, a love and urge towards a patriarchal existence. Perpetually he dreamed of a home of his own; he, the eternal wanderer, longed for a settled life! My first blow to his hopes dates from 1925, when I refused to fraternize, over a glass of wine,[3] with one of his most intimate friends.

Nevertheless, a thousand ties indissolubly bound me to him, the mightiest of which was art, and our service to it and the theater. It was our cloister, our life. And every performance invariably found Serge Pavlovitch in the same calm, though tense, mood of excitement.

"Seriozha," he would say, "we have distinguished guests in the house today: there's Rachmaninov in the stalls, Briand in one of the boxes, the Princesse de Polignac and the Comtesse de Noailles in the first row of the stalls, Ronché in the third. Now, don't let me down!...Please, darling, do your best, and don't fail us all!"

Coco Chanel and Misia Sert would already be in the house, discussing yesterday's rehearsal. Behind the scenes, though closed to the public, one would be sure of meeting a number of "adepts," among others, Stravinsky, Prokofiev, Cocteau, Picasso, and Tristan Bernard. London was the same, though there it was "Bernard Shaw, Lady Cunard"...or "Lady Eleanor wants to watch from the wings, it's all right"; or "Marconi would like to see you"...or, "here come Chaliapin and Pavlova."

Royal personages would be greeted by our leading artists in their boxes, sometimes with a gift of flowers. Very distinguished guests would be personally welcomed by Serge Pavlovitch, and during the intervals he

[3] By Russian custom, you drank a glass of wine to pledge eternal friendship. The outward result was that you then "thou'd" each other afterwards. Under certain conditions it was considered a mortal offence to refuse such a pledge. (Ed.)

would present our principal artists to them. It was all letters, invitations, flowers, requests for photographs, autographs, interviews, dressing-room receptions after the performance, questions—half understood, and vaguely answered—in the still hovering glamor of the footlights, a sort of un-earthliness all about one; then supper, speeches. . . .

I was enraptured with my life in the theater, my dancing, my appear-ances in front of the footlights, and no sacrifice was too great to demand of me, such was my devotion to it. Soon after this London season began, for instance, Serge Pavlovitch happened to make a casual remark that my make-up was not entirely satisfactory, and that my nose needed to be "put right." Whereupon, without the least hesitation, I immediately decided to have my nose operated on, for once the stage seemed to require it, there remained no alternative. The operation itself took ten minutes, but I did not achieve my Grecian profile. Somewhat disappointed, I was willing to have the operation repeated, and at the same time get my ears "put right," but Serge Pavlovitch would not hear of it. Later, he much regretted having been the cause of my first operation since, in his opinion, its shape had been better before. I still have the program on which he wrote: "With sincere wishes that a silly boy will become a wise boy, and long-nose, snub-nose!"

Diaghilev would never permit his personal relations to interfere with theatrical matters. Though he might have weaknesses in his personal life, where art was concerned his verdict was final, and without recourse. In all my seven years with him, I only remember one occasion in which he was swayed by personal considerations. It happened in this way. The representative of a firm selling patent milk offered me £50 for a signed testimonial, but when I consulted Diaghilev on the matter, he said:

"You mustn't on my account agree to such a price. I could understand your accepting an offer of, say, £100, or even £75, but £50, no, it's not worth your while, you must have a proper idea of what your name's worth."

Meanwhile I had discovered that another leading dancer, as well as a prima ballerina, had done what was wanted for £50, and came to the conclusion that I had been foolish to go on refusing, particularly since, at the time, my salary was exceedingly modest. When next I saw Diaghilev, therefore, I was able to show him my check for £50. But immediately there occurred something I could never possibly have imag-ined. Serge Pavlovitch flew into a tearing rage, began shouting abuse, and finally slapped my face. Equally annoyed and deeply offended by the injustice of it all—for had he not suggested I might accept £100, or even £75?—I, too, lost my temper, locked myself in my room and smashed the whole of the contents. . . . Next day we were reconciled, but nevertheless it was clear that Diaghilev still bore me a grudge. A few days later we were about to give *La Pastorale* and I was pumping up

Picasso and Lifar

my bicycle tires in readiness for the show, when Serge Pavlovitch approached me crossly:

"I say, have you changed your variation in the *Pastorale?*" (referring to his wish that I should do thirty-two *entrachat-six* instead of thirty-two *entrechat-quatre,* a suggestion we were considering for the future, but which had by no means been finally decided upon).

"No, I haven't, and anyhow I can't do anything without Balanchine."

Diaghilev said nothing and went out into the auditorium.

La Pastorale began. Well in the middle of my variation, with horror, I heard the orchestra beginning on a long *ritenuto* and thus, after all, I was forced to dance the thirty-two *entracht-six* so that I almost scorched the soles off my feet. Blazing with nervous excitement I left the stage, but in the wings seized my ballerina partner by the neck, began attempting to strangle her, and was only pulled off with the greatest difficulty. After which I attempted to rush to the orchestra, intending to thrash Desormières, the conductor, for executing Diaghilev's orders without giving me the least warning. The performance over, I found some flowers from Serge Pavlovitch, with a card bearing but one word: "Peace."

All this, indeed, was hardly serious, and never led to any really bad blood. True, there were days when Diaghilev would look surly, be morose and apathetic; days when nothing would please him, when anguish and distress would seem his sole portion. Again, there were days when we would feel estranged and discontented one with the other, but there was nothing in all this of a festering or rancorous quarrel. The nearest approach to anything of the kind was an incident I well remember.

The whole thing started in the most ridiculously trivial way with Serge Pavlovitch wanting me to buy him something, and my refusing, simply because I did not want to go out.

"So my kitten doesn't want to do what I ask him to? Well, if that's so, then I'm going to jump out of the window."

Whereupon Diaghilev went to the window, and with a smile threw one leg over the sill.

"Serge Pavlovitch, for Heaven's sake, stop joking. I tell you I won't go, whatever you do." Diaghilev, however, went on smiling, and actually made a sudden movement as though to throw himself out, as he said: "I really mean it!"

"You're mad, Serge Pavlovitch!" and, with a bound I seized him from behind and pulled him to the floor, struggling desperately. Any moment, it seemed, Diaghilev would crush me under his enormous body, but by some miracle I managed to escape and with one dexterous twist got both his shoulders touching the ground.

Serge Pavlovitch, though tamed, was still formidable and, paling, glared at me furiously.

"You must be absolutely mad."

Such intense and helpless anger glared at me from those eyes, so much injured dignity in one accustomed to command though never to submit, that I would infinitely have preferred defeat than to have caused that look....

For the first time the lion's nature in Diaghilev had revealed itself to my eyes, whereas before I had only vaguely suspected its existence.

These digressions, however, have somewhat interrupted the chronological sequence of my story; I return, therefore, to my Italian holiday of 1925.

For two months, August and September, I enjoyed the perfect rest of traveling through Italy with Diaghilev for my guide, and M. and Mme. Legat as our companions. Such care, such solicitude enveloped me, that there were times when tears of happiness and joy would force themselves unbidden from my eyes. My memory will always hold this trip as one of the most important happenings in my life, one that did most to foster my spiritual development.

The moment he found himself in Italy, Diaghilev immediately became benign and carefree. All care dropped from his shoulders as he plunged into his Italian happiness. Everything that was Italian gave him infinite delight—even the pickpockets. According to him, cheats and pickpockets were often admirable people, among whom perhaps more talent might be found than among decent, honest people; for in Diaghilev's eye talent justified all things.

"Only compare the Italian pickpocket with the French. The Italian is cheerful, likable, he makes a merry joke while cheating you, or pilfering your belongings, and if you catch him in the act, has such a charming way of saying 'Scusi, Signore,' or 'Scusi, Eccelenza,' (for all Italians addressed Diaghilev as 'Eccelenza') that you can't help forgiving him, whereas the French thief glowers surlily at you, and would think nothing of robbing you and then breaking your head."

There was some truth in these words, for up till 1922, Diaghilev's favorite valet had been an Italian named Beppo, a cheerful, impertinent villain, who ended in jail for theft. Diaghilev knew that Beppo was dishonest, insolent, and could not really be trusted; nevertheless, because he was by nature cheerful, full of quaint saws and quips and pranks, he grew to be quite fond of him in time. This Beppo was also married to a woman whom Serge Pavlovitch esteemed highly. When he spoke of her, it was as "that saintly woman," and his attachment to her was nearly as great as to his stepmother. When, in 1920, Serge Pavlovitch fell dangerously ill (his first attack of diabetes), she literally nursed him back to life, and thus won his eternal gratitude. Always he visited her, and always, as he left, would ask her to bless him with the sign of the cross.

One strange mania I must refer to. So very meticulous was Diaghilev in verifying all his bills and accounts, and so long did he take to pay his cab-drivers, that any onlooker would have thought him a very miracle of miserliness. The truth was that Diaghilev could and did squander money, and had spent thousands upon thousands of pounds without a second thought, as it were; nevertheless, even the smallest error in a bill, possibly even the fraction of a penny, would make him immediately suspect he was being cheated. Whereupon his rage would flash up, and he would become almost ill with fury. The year 1925 was a particularly bad one in this respect in Paris, and endless difficulties would arise with hotel managements because of this strange "meanness" of his. Bills would arrive, and be laid aside, because he was busy and preoccupied. After a time, a second bill would arrive, whereupon he would remember receiving a similar account, and feeling certain it was paid, create a furious scene, and refuse to listen to any explanation. The upshot would be that he paid "again" as he thought, then left the hotel boiling with fury. Thus it was that in 1925 alone he fell out with the managements of the Continental, Wagram and St. James's hotels.

Quite unexpectedly we found that enough members of the cast had assembled in Venice to provide a performance, for in addition to us three, Diaghilev, Kokhno and I, there were also Legat, Alexandrinea Trusevitch, Sokolova, Woizikowsky and a few others. Serge Pavlovitch decided to give a private performance in the Palazzo Papadopoli, at that time inhabited by the Cole Porters. It was not to pass off, however, without two thunder storms, one from the skies, the other from Diaghilev. The first burst with tremendous violence while we were performing, and sank a number of gondolas; but the second burst when the performance was ended. The whole thing had been tremendously successful and our grateful, enthusiastic hosts had added to our usual "envelopes" a few presents, though what they were I don't remember. For some reason or other, however, this fact produced an incredible outburst of rage from Diaghilev, who cried: "How do they dare give presents to my artists—my artists have no need of such paltry sops!" Then, like a raging lion, Diaghilev rushed off to the Piazza San Marco to storm and rave at our hosts, and as a result, created a first-class scandal which soon spread through the town.

Not till the beginning of September did we leave for Florence, and all the time we were with the Legats. Meanwhile, I went on with the lessons I had begun in London under M. Legat, lessons which were continued in Florence, Rome and Naples. Through Diaghilev I learned to understand and love both Florence and Rome, but more particularly Florence, his beloved, holy town. Five consecutive days we spent in the Uffizzi—five marvelous days that eternally enriched my imagination with one revelation after another!

Diaghilev was indefatigable in his enthusiasm to show me his Florence, Florence as he knew and loved it. It made him happy and proud to be transmitting his understanding and love, and I accepted it all with gratitude and due humility, listening, learning, assimilating, growing.

I remember well one expedition to Fiesole. Not that we visited any particular place, for we merely sat talking on the restaurant terrace, as we watched the darkness creep up over distant Florence. . . . Nothing at all stands out in my mind of this drive to Fiesole, yet somehow it made me love Florence even more dearly, and remains in memory as one of the few perfectly luminous moments in my life.

After Florence, Rome! Of this first visit to Rome, all that remains are fragments and chips of impressions garnered in its museums, and an overwhelming impression of a vast accumulation of the treasures of art. An impression natural enough, considering the shortness of our stay. In all this, too, Diaghilev felt somewhat lost, puzzled to decide what was most important to show me. And besides, I was still saturated with my impressions of Florence, and somewhat weary of the ceaseless round of museums, intent on seeing everything they had to show. Fortunately, Diaghilev had no intention of showing me "all Rome" on this, my first occasion, and though I saw but little, that little I saw well.

Our two months' tour in Italy ended in Naples, amid strident, motley crowds, for the whole populace appears to live solely out of doors, and I brought away memories of that lovely bay and of Pompeii and Herculaneum.

On October 1st, the whole company was again assembled in Paris, and but for a four-day tour to Antwerp, there we remained rehearsing until the 24th. Much work needed to be done, for our old repertory had to be gone over, and the new "creation" *Barabau* to be prepared. The music to this ballet was by Rieti, the sets and costumes by Utrillo. Also we had acquired a new choreographer, Balanchine, who, as a test of his powers, was entrusted with the new ballet. The experiment proving successful, Balanchine remained ballet master to the Ballet throughout the rest of its existence.

Utrillo's sets, however, proved somewhat difficult to adapt to the stage, and Serge Pavlovitch was kept busy, therefore, modifying them to his requirements. As a result, he became for the nonce a sort of decorator-dressmaker, besides helping in other ways, as, for instance, suggesting that the chorus should be masked by a partition, so that only heads should be seen.

On October 26th we started our two months season at the London Coliseum. Between that date and December 19th, we gave in all ninety-six performances, including a daily matinée, and all with the same unvarying success. Then, on December 11th, we gave our first production of the new ballet *Barabau,* which was received with immense acclamation.

This happy year in the lives of Diaghilev and myself, in which I achieved my ambition of becoming a *premier danseur,* was now drawing to its close as joyous and untroubled as it began. Nineteen hundred and twenty-six, however, opened more obscurely, and was to bring not a few reverses in its train; reverses which were eventually to pave the way for Diaghilev's retirement from the ballet. How exactly, I cannot say, but in some way they helped to direct his thoughts into other channels, and led him to find another occupation, one not connected with the stage. But this did not happen until 1927.

From December 22nd until January 6th we were performing in Berlin. Yet, though our productions, and especially the new ballets, *Les Matelots,* and *Flore et Zéphyre* proved a remarkable success, the Press praising us up to the skies, the big Künstlertheater remained, nevertheless, three-quarters empty, and the Ballet sustained a huge financial loss. Indeed, its whole material future was put in peril by this season.

The only happiness that fell to Diaghilev at this time was the Christmas tree I set up for him on December 24th. The thought, and the tree itself, moved him deeply. He even wept tears, as he said that it was the first, the very first Christmas tree he had had since childhood, after which he began to recount memories of this, the happiest time in his life, as a schoolboy in Perm, mingled with reminiscences of that Russia of which he could never speak without tears. Nevertheless, the tree brought its own touch of sadness and reawakened his dreams of a hearth of his own, inaccessible though it seemed.

Here in Berlin there occurred an event of the greatest importance to the ballet, namely, Nemchinova's decision to leave. Unknown to us all, she had signed a contract to appear in London under the management of C. B. Cochran.

Hurrying from Berlin, we reached Monte Carlo in time for January 17th, the Principality's annual fête. A week later, the twenty-fourth, a great gala in honor of the Prince was given, with Nemchinova and myself dancing in *Le Lac des Cygnes.* From this moment, I could consider our whole classical repertoire my own. Some time later, Nemchinova got permission to absent herself, but did not return when the period ended.

Serge Pavlovitch was exceedingly disturbed and highly indignant over Nemchinova's behavior, and said, with an air of finality:

"Vera Nemchinova is never going to dance in the Russian Ballet again!"

He kept his word.

Nemchinova's flight opened the way for two young ballerinas, Nikitina and Danilova, but this in itself led to fresh complications. . . .

All through the early part of 1926, after our Berlin disappointment, Diaghilev was subdued, oppressed, and unsettled. There were the Paris and London seasons to prepare, money was lacking, and there seemed no one to whom to turn. I remember how, while the opera season was in full swing, Serge Pavlovitch would lie abed for weeks, busy with "little talks and thinks" (as he termed it). Cheerless indeed these "talks" and "thinks" must have been, for his nerves had gone completely to pieces, and his diabetes had taken a turn for the worse and constantly plagued him. And here I must mention something of which I have always been proud, the fact that it was I who cured Serge Pavlovitch of the drug habit. Since he hated smoking, with no great effort I gave up cigarettes for his sake. This, however, provided me with some justification for "worrying" him to stop his drugging, which was undermining his physique and ruining his well-being.

"I have given up smoking for you; you must abandon this filthy habit for my sake. . . ."

"Do you know, Seriozha, a strange thing happened to me this morning! I woke up and suddenly felt a strong repulsion to this powder. Really, I feel almost as though I'd never had the habit. I'm going to give it up once and for all now. I'm positive I don't need it any more."

Serge Pavlovitch's "little thinks" led him, in the end, to stake his all on Lord Rothermere, who, at that period, was keenly interested in our ballet and ballerinas. Rothermere, theoretically speaking, was perfectly ready to provide financial support. But oh, the distance between theory and practice, and how agitated, restless, and wretched Diaghilev became under the almost intolerable strain. I well remember Diaghilev's suppers to Lord Rothermere, and the state in which he would return, at times full of hope, and again as though relentlessly driven into some drear blind alley. Equally well do I remember the *perpetual* telephonings, during which Serge Pavlovitch, sweating profusely, and quivering with nervous agitation, would call up Lord Rothermere every thirty minutes, hoping to find him in. And when at last he did succeed in speaking to him, making an appointment, to his chagrin the meeting would be either postponed or canceled. Meanwhile Nikitina, our dear and talented Alice Nikitina, regardless of the damage to her artistic career, was beginning to make all sorts of extravagant demands, to which Diaghilev was forced willy-nilly to submit, however it went against his artistic conscience. As time went on, the friction between them became more and more pronounced, till at last it ended in an open quarrel. Indeed, she several times retired temporarily from the company.

Eventually, and after innumerable delays, a sufficient amount of money was advanced, costly though it was, and sadly as it encroached upon the season's harvest, and Diaghilev hastily, nervously, set to work preparing a Paris season which was to include a new ballet entitled *Romeo and Juliet,* for which a young Englishman, Constant Lambert, had written the music. That February I happened to be absent, for Serge Pavlovitch had sent me, with Pavel Georgievitch, to Milan, to go on working under Cecchetti, and when I returned in March, the preparations were already in full swing. Meanwhile, Diaghilev was negotiating with Kshesinskaya, though nothing came of it, had invited Karsavina to join the Ballet, and had engaged Nijinska to produce *Romeo and Juliet*. I stayed but a few short days in Paris, then left for Monte Carlo with Kokhno, in advance of the others. The day we were leaving, Serge Pavlovitch sent us up to Montmartre to look at a show by a group of surrealist painters, including Ernst and Mirò. Having reached the studio, we walked round in silence, and in silence looked at the pictures, of which we could make nothing.

When he was seeing us off at the station: "How did you like the surrealists?" asked Diaghilev.

Kokhno said something about "all this nonsense not being worth the time spent on it." Though inwardly entirely of the same opinion, I nevertheless, influenced by a sudden thought that perhaps there was something important underneath it all, which neither Kokhno nor I was capable of seeing, more cautiously said:

"I didn't like Ernst and Mirò, and I didn't understand surrealism at all, but you'd perhaps better go and see for yourself."

A few days later Diaghilev arrived in Monte Carlo ... with Ernst and Mirò, whom he had commissioned to paint the sets for *Romeo and Juliet*. He was wholly wrapped up in his new friends, bothered practically not at all about the season, hardly ever attended rehearsals, or even noticed what was going on. Far more than in the coming ballet season, was he interested in discussing art with Ernst, talks which began at evening and often went on till five next morning. This reawakening of an old interest seemed actually to rejuvenate him again. In gratitude for my advice to go and see the surrealists for himself, Diaghilev had brought from Paris some paintings by both Mirò and Ernst which had particularly taken his fancy, and these he presented to me, thus laying the foundation of my collection. He had done the same once before for Massine, presenting him with a collection of first-rate pictures, including an excellent Matisse, Braque, Derain and a number of works by Italian futurists. Thereafter, my own collection grew also with each first night and every holiday.

Now the company began to collect in Monte Carlo, increased by the addition of Karsavina and Nijinska....

Nijinska, however, discovering that Karsavina and I were to dance in *Romeo and Juliet*, declared:

"I insist on our holding an examination for M. Lifar. I would never consent to his dancing the part of Romeo without such a test."

The reader may picture my indignation. What? Make the company's first dancer pass an examination as though he were merely some unknown super! But Serge Pavlovitch quickly reassured me:

"It's all right, Seriozha. Don't fuss, and don't get angry. Nijinska wants an examination; well, she shall have it. *Tant pis pour elle!*"

Examination day came. Our teacher, Legat, was at the piano, and, noticing how nervous and agitated I was—I had gone as white as a sheet

—he did his best to reassure and encourage me. Whereupon Serge Pavlovitch, Pavel Georgievitch and Kokhno appeared, and after them Nijinska. . . .

My "examination" took half an hour, and I danced as I had never danced before. Legat began by setting me small variations, then, noticing how enthusiastically I soared, and the ease with which I accomplished my twelve *pirouettes,* my three *tours en l'air,* led me through more and more complicated steps. The "examination" ended with Legat abruptly leaving the piano and kissing me in his delight, to be followed by Serge Pavlovitch, who also embraced and congratulated me, saying: "Tomorrow we begin the production." Nijinska herself was obviously troubled.

On the "morrow" I began rehearsing with Karsavina. At first I felt lost: I could hardly believe I was dancing with the glorious, the famous, "Tata" Karsavina! With all the ardor of youth (I had just celebrated my twenty-first birthday) I was already kissing the earth at her feet, already desperately in love. And Karsavina took to me, treated me kindly and indulgently, much to Serge Pavlovitch's delight.

At last we gave our première of *Romeo and Juliet.* . . . I danced in great exaltation, covered the stage as on wings—something was singing and soaring inside me . . . I knew I was dancing as never before. Our success was tremendous: applause and masses of flowers, and among them some from Diaghilev, and a bouquet of magnificent roses with a charming note: "Most heart-felt wishes for a brilliant success. Tamara Karsavina." These roses I took to my room, and returned to await my partner, whom I was to accompany to the supper celebrating our première. But, as I was waiting, along came Serge Pavlovitch:

"What are you doing here?"

"I'm waiting for Tamara Platonovna."

He said nothing, and went away, visibly irritated, an angry frown on his face. All his good humor had vanished. A few moments later Karsavina appeared, we all had supper, and then, having accompanied her home, I returned buoyant and cheerful to my hotel room. One glance, and I saw that my roses, the roses given me by Karsavina, no longer stood on the table. Throwing open the window, I saw them littering the courtyard. A piercing pang, followed by furious rage, took possession of me. Was it possible that Diaghilev could have flung my roses away, the roses of my triumph? Like a second Romeo, I swiftly knotted my towels into a ladder, and was already beginning to climb down, when Serge Pavlovitch appeared like a whirlwind, grabbed me by the hair, and pulled me back into the room.

Whereupon there ensued a scene, remarkable even in the annals of such scenes, at which the whole hotel seemed to wake into life.

"How dare you permit yourself to behave so indecently in front of the members of my company? I will not permit my theater to be turned into a den of vice, I'll turn out all these women who hang round the necks of my dancers in front of everyone's eyes. And you, my 'first dancer,' have nothing better to do than fall for the first woman's smile. Trust me to clear you both out of the theater...." After which, as impetuously as he had entered, Serge Pavlovitch left, slamming the door with such force that every door in the corridor rattled.

As I was waking next morning, I overheard a conversation in the next room between my faithful old friend and nanny, my best and most charming Pavel Georgievitch, who had arrived to "reason" with Diaghilev and restore peace. Diaghilev was saying:

"It isn't him so much I'm accusing, as her. He's still a boy, much too innocent and inexperienced yet, and that's why it's easy for any experienced woman to lead him astray. But what about Karsavina! How could I possibly imagine that any nice-looking youngster would tempt her? Of course, Lifar melted like butter at once, and now he's head over heels. You'll see, Pavka, he'll desert us all for her: they're beginning a serious affair, you'll see how it's all going to end...."

"What nonsense you're talking, Seriozha: as if you didn't know our Seriozha, and how utterly inaccessible Tamara Platonovna is. What a romance you're inventing! You yourself wanted Karsavina to be kind to the boy and encourage him, to give him faith in himself. And now when Tata so kindly, so charmingly, gives him his due, and even sends him flowers, you imagine God knows what, and fill your head with things that never were and never could be true.

"Seriozha, too, I understand perfectly well," Pavel Georgievitch's voice went on reasonably and quietly. "Only think of the effect on him of becoming Karsavina's partner, the world-renowned Karsavina, who not only dances with him as an equal, but also sends him flowers! It seems to me rather touching in him to value her flowers so highly, and be so determined to get them back. It isn't he, it's you who are at fault, Seriozha, what with unjustly offending him, and making him aware, by your scenes, of things he would never have given a thought to else...."

Whereupon Serge Pavlovitch gradually calmed down, and asked me to lunch at the Café de Paris. On the way, looking at me in sad reproach, with a deep sigh, he said:

"Yes, indeed, Seriozha, things have come to pass which I would never have expected of you.... You really should give a thought to the way you're behaving and what you're doing. Even so good a friend as Pavel Georgievitch, who always defends you warmly, feels seriously annoyed with you this time."

It was impossible not to burst out laughing, whereupon Serge Pavlovitch gave me the kindest imaginable smile, which instantly sealed our peace.

That Easter was "greeted" in Mme. Kshesinskaya's villa at Cap d'Ail. Some forty in all had been invited to partake of the Easter breakfast, and what a banquet it was! Never have I seen so princely a meal.[4] First we attended the midnight service in the Russian church at Mentone, and then motored over to Cap d'Ail. There I "broke my fast" so lavishly at the groaning, cheerful table, that soon enough the wine went to my head, and by the time dessert was being served I was bold enough to pluck a rose from the table decorations, rise, and to the astonishment of all, take it round to our hostess:

"Mathilde Felixovna, let me present you with this rose!"

A moment of indecision was followed by loud cries of "Bravo, bravo!" After which Mme. Kshesinskaya, touched by my strange and improvised greeting, rewarded me by opening the subsequent ball with me as her partner in the traditional polonaise. Later events I remember as little now as I did then, my mood being far too festive to notice anything much. How it happened I have no recollection, but some time or other I discovered myself behind a sofa flirting with Karsavina: she, on the floor, signing Kshesinskaya's golden book, and I scribbling my signature over hers. Everyone was dancing and thoroughly enjoying themselves. . . . I felt merry and buoyant . . . when suddenly I heard Serge Pavlovitch saying in a stern, threatening voice:

"You seem much too gay, young man, isn't it time you were at home?"

And the young man, though much against his will, was driven off to bed. . . .

Having given our last performance at Monte Carlo on May 7th, we left for Paris on the thirteenth, bringing with us four new ballets: *Barabau, Romeo and Juliet, La Pastorale* and *Jack in the Box*. I had parts in each of these ballets and so, with some justice, could consider the approaching season as my own.

Not only the rather pallid *Jack in the Box,* but even the colorful *La Pastorale* were left comparatively unnoticed, relegated to the background by the real *clou* of the season, *Romeo and Juliet,* a *"Répétition sans décor en deux parties."* Long before the first night, on May 18th, the new "surrealist" ballet had provoked an immense amount of discussion. The police had also informed Diaghilev that both surrealists and communists intended to stage a demonstration, at which they meant to thrash that "bourgeois" Diaghilev, as well as the traitors Ernst and Mirò, who had sold themselves to the "bourgeois," and offered to provide a special guard. To this Diaghilev replied that his confidence in the police was unbounded, and that he approved of any measures they proposed to take; but, nevertheless, he would be very grateful if no uniformed men were placed in the theater.

As a result we were all in a keyed-up, nervous condition, especially Diaghilev, as was shown by his pallid face and the increased severity

---

[4] After the midnight Easter service, Russians usually broke their fast with a sumptuous meal, which often lasted well into the early hours, and at which many jolly old customs were observed. This festive occasion was called "greeting Easter." (Ed.)

Pavel Georgievitch Koribut-Kubitovitch

of his tic. Finally the day of the performance arrived, whereupon, begging Diaghilev to entrust the whole matter to me, I assembled the company and told them that we must now consider ourselves shock troops, and that, if any demonstrators should try to climb the footlights, we must attack in our turn, and let nothing stop us making cripples of them all.

It was May 18th. The performance began. Not a vacant seat was left in the whole of the Sarah Bernhardt Theater. The first ballet, Stravinsky's *Pulcinella,* went off calmly, and was received with universal applause. But after the interval, the curtain went up on ... "a curtain" which, as the critic V. Svetlov describes it, "disclosed only a few commas and smudges, which any scene painter's assistant could have produced, without in any way claiming relationship to the surrealist community." We, the dancers, were discovered in our working clothes, busy at a dancing lesson on the stage, when suddenly such a din of howls and whistling was heard that not one note of the music could pierce through. Nevertheless, though met by this perfect hurricane of mad cries and incredible yells, we began our performance. Nobody, however, paid the least attention to the stage, while from the gallery white leaflets, proclamations,[5] began fluttering down till the house looked as though there had been a snowstorm. Meanwhile, in the auditorium, a pitched battle seemed to be raging. I saw one of Diaghilev's great friends, Iya, Lady Abdy (daughter of the dramatic artist and playwright and granddaughter of the painter Gué), slap a man's face, and at the same moment someone tore her dress. Then plain-clothes policemen began to appear from all sides, seized hold of the "demonstrators," and removed them from the house. During all this, someone was trying to lower the curtain, but I managed to push it aside, heavy though it was, the management's orders being that on no account was the curtain to be lowered. Desormières, the conductor, had stopped the orchestra.

It only took two or three minutes for the Paris police to quell the "riot," after which the curtain went up, a new start was made, and the ballet was safely enacted.

All this had but one result, that Paris did nothing but talk of the new ballet, so that whenever it was given (May 20th and 27th) we played to crammed houses.

I recall, about this time, what seems to me a very characteristic and revealing incident as to the manner in which both Diaghilev and Stravinsky analyzed dance rhythms. It took place in connection with our revival of *Les Noces,* the sole male parts in which had been assigned to Balanchine and myself. Just before the performance, while still in the rehearsal room, both of us began inventing dance steps, which, though they responded to the general lines of the music, by no means followed the tempo. Actually, it would have been physically impossible to do so in the ten minutes at our disposal, when to fit our steps exactly to the tempo would have

[5] A surrealist manifesto. For text see Appendix B. (Ed.)

necessitated quite a month's hard work. Meanwhile Diaghilev, Stravinsky, and the whole Ballet were watching us. But whereas the company could not restrain their laughter at our efforts, Diaghilev and Stravinsky, on the contrary, nodded approvingly, and said:

"Well done, boys, very well done!"

Such indeed was our virtuosity in our art, that what to others seemed obvious discrepancy between the dancing and musical rhythms, to these specialists appeared as perfect musical sense and "expert syncopation," and it was in the same manner that later we treated the *Sacre du Printemps*.

Our Paris season having ended, we set off immediately for London, where we were scheduled to appear from June 14th to July 23rd. Our star ballerina in this city was Karsavina, and it was while I was dancing with her that, for the first time, I felt I was no longer merely the ballerina's physical support, but something that sustained her with every other faculty in my possession. In all my connection with the Ballet I cannot remember a more brilliant, more triumphant season than this, with, perhaps, the exception of the very last, in 1929. The public literally carried us shoulder high, smothered us with flowers and presents. Every one of our ballets, the old as well as the new, were ecstatically received with unending storms of applause.

Very successful, too, was the exhibition of my own collection of paintings at the New Chenil Gallery, which opened on July 4th, and included ten Derains, eight Max Ernsts, three Picassos, nine Prunas, and six Miròs.

The season over, the company broke up for a three months' holiday, though holidays of such duration were rare in Diaghilev's ballet, and dispersed in all directions. Still, we had worked very hard, and we all deserved it.

And again I went to Italy, but now I was most of the time alone, or with Pavel Georgievitch and Cecchetti. Now and then Diaghilev would put in a brief appearance, only to depart again for Paris or Monte Carlo, where he was busy with preparations for the coming season. Only in August did we "travel" in any real sense of the word, revisiting Florence and Naples. Then, at the end of the month, Pavel Georgievitch and I established ourselves on the Lido, after which I left for Milan, and, throughout October, once more worked under Cecchetti. While in Florence I made the acquaintance of an old friend of Diaghilev's, the English poet, Sacheverell Sitwell. Serge Pavlovitch became fired with the idea of producing a new, important ballet, the "little talks" began, and Sitwell began working on the libretto of *The Triumph of Neptune*. Balanchine was called in, we met in Naples, and Lord Berners set to work on the music. Thus our holidays became, instead, a period of strenuous effort.

By November 1st the whole company had reassembled in Paris, and, time pressing, began rehearsals for the approaching season at the Lyceum. With Nikitina's departure, the Ballet was somewhat in need of more prima ballerinas, since the whole work had to be borne by Sokolova and Danilova, though chiefly by the latter, for on her mainly depended the success of our most strenuous month in London. As a result Diaghilev invited Lopokova to appear in *L'Oiseau de Feu,* which she did amid veritable storms of applause. A particularly magnificent, triumphant performance of this ballet was that given on November 27th, attended by the King of Spain.

On December 3rd we gave our first performance of *The Triumph of Neptune,* but it might as well have been called the "Triumph of Diaghilev's Russian Ballet" or the "Triumph of Danilova, Sokolova, Lifar, Idzikowsky and Balanchine," so remarkable was the public's behavior. Flowers, hats and objects of one kind and another were showered on the stage, there were innumerable recalls, and it was impossible to lower the curtain.... This ballet was subsequently repeated nightly, and each time with equally remarkable success.

It was during this season that I was all but involved in a serious accident. We were giving *Le Lac des Cygnes* in which I had to dance with Danilova, but while I was practicing steps with Balanchine in the wings, awaiting my cue, I leaped in the air and struck the concrete ceiling with great force. Fortunately I was wearing my wig, yet, nevertheless, blood began oozing out, while I was due to go on the stage at any moment. I have no recollection at all how I managed, my head bleeding and painfully aching, to go on and dance my part. But the performance ended, I was hurried to hospital, and there underwent a minor operation, which kept me in bed several days.

On December 11th our last London performance took place, comprising *L'Oiseau de Feu, The Triumph of Neptune* and *Le Mariage d'Aurore.* Next day we left for Paris, and thence for an Italian tour of a fortnight in Turin, from December 24th to January 6th, and three nights in Milan (January 10th, 12th and 16th, 1927). Meanwhile, Serge Pavlovitch had again invited Massine to join us as choreographer, and Olga Spessiva to join us as prima ballerina for both our modern and classical repertory. I found it very pleasant to work with her.

One performance of *Le Lac des Cygnes* stands out with especial vividness in my mind. Massine had thought fit to rearrange the old ballet and, without warning either Spessiva or myself, instructed our conductor, Inghelbrecht, to introduce certain modifications in the tempo. As a result, the famous *pas de deux* was played at about half the speed we had got used to taking it, which meant almost slow-motion dancing. Meanwhile, the whole company, with bated breath, waited to see how we should acquit ourselves in this most difficult dilemma, for then and there we were forced to recast our parts, and change the whole manner of our dancing. As we were dancing to a full house, in front of many of the leading figures in Italian society, much hung on how we acquitted ourselves. But, to our relief, when the *pas de deux* came to an end, a tumult of cries and enthusiastic applause broke out. Then Spessiva began to dance her own variation, that too at half its tempo, while my heart seemed to contract with amazement, beatitude and rapture.

I was watching Spessiva, and admiring her performance; but, as my own entry drew near, a feeling of rage began to master me, for I realized that Inghelbrecht meant to continue his slow-motion tempo, and that would inevitably destroy the effect of my own variation. Whereupon, I leaped out on the stage, and clapping my hands, gave the conductor the right time. My clappings and beats had their effect, and soon Inghelbrecht was conducting at a terrific tempo.

The performance ended, I got the company together, and we worked out a petition asking for Inghelbrecht's removal and replacement by some other conductor, and this was submitted to Diaghilev through Grigoriev, though, truth to tell, Inghelbrecht could hardly be considered responsible in the matter. Serge Pavlovitch, however, observing that the petition was covered with names, tore it up, unread, saying: "I don't accept collective demands and protests."

This illegitimate and, considering my relation to Diaghilev, somewhat inexplicable act, was nevertheless comprehensible, for I had been driven to it by mad fury: so too was the way in which the whole company reacted, and the warm support they gave me. Having begun myself in the *corps de ballet,* and risen to be first dancer, I did not, in spite of my altered circumstances, turn away from my former colleagues, or treat them with scorn. On the contrary, I did my best to modify Diaghilev's, and the first dancers', attitude to them. In the past it had been perfectly usual for the first dancers to send the boys in the *corps de ballet* on errands, for cigarettes, matches or a bottle of beer. It was a sort of arrogance which seemed to me not only insulting, when I had been in that position, but quite unjustifiable. I, therefore, sought to establish our relations on an equal footing, and succeeded. My efforts, however, were less successful where Diaghilev was concerned, for though Serge Pavlovitch really enjoyed being present at parties in which, on festive occasions, the whole company would come together, and be as kind and friendly to one as to the next, he inwardly despised the *corps de ballet* as sheep, and would often say to me:

"I can't think what it is you want, and what you're making all this fuss about. Let them stew in their own juice; all they want is to be fed and clothed. Sheep will always be sheep, and no one will ever succeed in turning a hen into an eagle."

Nevertheless, as time went on, I did improve Diaghilev's attitude a little.

Our Italian tour ended in Milan. We gave *Cimarosiana, L'Oiseau de Feu, Le Lac des Cygnes* and *Le Mariage d'Aurore.* It was my first appearance at the famous Milan Scala, and it was made memorable for me by the touching scene which took place after the performance. My Maestro, and director of the Scala ballet school, Cecchetti, had been sitting in the audience, and now, profoundly moved, he came behind the scenes to congratulate both me and Serge Pavlovitch. He was delighted, too, with Spessiva's dancing, and Idzikowsky's *sauts* and *tours* in the *pas de trois* in *Le Lac des Cygnes,* and swore that not even Nijinsky himself could ever have danced that variation with such perfection.

Though we had given a matinée performance in the Scala on January 16th, we were back in Monte Carlo on the seventeenth. All February and March were taken up with the opera season, during the last days of which we appeared both in Marseilles and Cannes. Meanwhile we were exceedingly busy preparing our Monte Carlo, Paris and London season, rehearsing our new ballet *La Chatte* to music by Sauguet, and working on *Le Pas d'Acier,* the outline of which we already had. Though *La Chatte* was one of Balanchine's best and most perfect creations, *Le Pas d'Acier* assumed enormously greater importance in Diaghilev's life. Through it, and Prokofiev, Ehrenburg and Yakulov, certain threads were spun, which began to lead Diaghilev towards Soviet Russia. Nevertheless, that *grand seigneur* and aristocrat by birth, education and nature, could never have been a revolutionary, or feel anything but contempt and hatred for Marxism with its clumsy, utilitarian approach to aesthetics.

Diaghilev, where art was concerned, was a forerunner. In *The World of Art* he had fought against old beliefs, against academic and other routines, against traditional, reactionary responses. Nevertheless, though "tomorrow" was the watchword of all his activities, that "tomorrow" was instinct with a sort of aristocratic conservatism, which revealed itself in the attraction that old masters and schools of art exerted over him, and in his eclecticism. Yet therewith, deep in the secret places of his seigneurial nature, lay hidden anarchic seeds, ready to blast out of existence that deep-rooted culture to which no one was more devoted than himself.

It was a kind of momentary revolt against a weary civilization, the self-sufficient bourgeois world, bourgeois forms of enjoying art and every other of life's precious gifts, a sort of worm that gnawed at the very roots of his being. Diaghilev himself was well aware of it, and so would never venture to discuss certain subjects. Not that I am attaching any undue importance to that incident of the "red flag," which occurred at the 1917 Paris performance of *L'Oiseau de Feu* in the very throes of the Russian revolution; for the red infection, at that time, had seized the whole of the Russian intelligentsia. Still, I do believe that this incident, to some extent, does reveal Diaghilev's iconoclastic nature: and I may add, too, that anyone who persists in ignoring that side of Diaghilev knows nothing of the *whole* man.

Soon, however, nothing red was left in Diaghilev, and in due course the Scythian was ousted entirely by the good European. Much suffering, though, was still to be endured by that European, both on his own account and that of his country, for the Peace of Brest-Litovsk had made Diaghilev hate and despise "the Soviets," though he did not thereby cease to love Russia. Instead, a sort of mawkish sentimentality mingled with that love, as though a lament for Holy Russia, and those immured within its frontiers. Such refugees as came his way he would receive with open arms, and ply with questions, though he knew well he would never return to that land which was locked to him as though with the seven-fold lock of a curse. Yet, though he would treat them with the greatest affection, for the wretched and persecuted always moved him to tears, he always retained a slight sense of distrust, an apprehension that they might be spies.

But in 1926 his attitude to the Soviets began to change, and a new interest to awake in its developments. The chief responsibility for this change no doubt lies with his friend Seriozha Prokofiev—who had finally deserted Mme. Zeitlin's Paris salon for Moscow—and Ehrenburg: though earlier he had been able to meet, and talk with, his old friends Lunacharsky and Krassin. Now, what he heard of the new Russia, its search for new ways of living, new forms of art, interested him deeply, and its "seeking" spoke to his soul.

Thereupon Diaghilev entered into correspondence with Prokofiev, with the idea of producing a new Soviet ballet for which Prokofiev promised to write the music, while suggesting that Yakulov might come to Paris and help with the production. The new ballet was to be called *Le Pas d'Acier,* and would illustrate the concepts of the "constructivist" school. The Moscow ballet master Gailizovsky, it was hoped, would collaborate in the production.

Far greater than his difficulties with Moscow were those of Diaghilev in overcoming the inertia of his own "Art Committee." A special meeting was convened to discuss the matter, at which both Pavel Georgievitch and Valetchka energetically attacked the idea, arguing that Diaghilev would alienate not only the emigrants, but their aristocratic patrons, and that the production of anything even faintly resembling a Soviet ballet would provoke fearful opposition and lead to the worst repercussions on Diaghilev's own ballet. For the first time, at a meeting of the Committee, Diaghilev asked my opinion, whereupon I expressed my disagreement with that of his friends, gave him my warmest support, and emphasized that we had no right to shut our eyes to anything constructive in the way of artistic achievement in Russia, whatever the source of its inspiration. I also said that since constructivism was the outstanding artistic phenomenon of the '20's, and marked an epoch, it could not be ignored and that I, personally, had, not only no fear that it would prejudice our existence, but was ready to welcome it even.

Now we began to work concurrently on both *La Chatte* and *Le Pas d'Acier,* Massine being entrusted with the choreography of the latter. By April *La Chatte* was ready, and the first performance took place on the thirtieth of that month, the other ballets in the program being *Le Mariage d'Aurore* and *Le Lac des Cygnes*. On May 5th our Monte Carlo season ended, and next day we left for Barcelona, before returning to Paris. Here we arrived on the twenty-fourth, three days before we were due to open at the Théâtre Sarah Bernhardt. We all felt that a great deal depended on this season, and could not help wondering how Paris would take our Soviet ballet. Our repertory consisted of a number of classical items, starring Spessiva; the new opera-oratorio by Stravinsky *Oedipus Rex; La Chatte* and *Le Pas d'Acier;* but it was on our most recent items that everything was staked. We were also reviving Massine's *Mercure* and Stravinsky's *L'Oiseau de Feu*. However, in order to prepare the Parisian public for Spessiva, Diaghilev published the following article in *Figaro*.

"The first night of the Russian Ballet, which opens tomorrow, will see the début of a new dancer, Olga Spessiva. True enough, a dancer bearing almost the same name has recently been dancing at the Opera House, but for some reason or other it so happened that the Mlle. Spessivtseva of the Opera House failed to attract the most sensitive audience in the world, namely, that of Paris.

"I have always held it to be axiomatic that no man's life can contain more than a certain quantity of joy, that only the enjoyment of one Taglioni is allowed to one generation, or the hearing of a single Patti. Having seen Pavlova in my youth and her own, I was certain that there was the Taglioni of my existence. Imagine my amazement, then, on meeting Spessiva, a nobler and more talented artist even than Pavlova. That is saying a great deal.

"That great master of dancing, Cecchetti, to whom we owe Nijinsky, Karsavina and so many more, was saying only this winter, during a lesson at the Scala in Milan: 'One apple came into the world; and when it was cut in two, one half became Pavlova, the other Spessiva.' And I would add that, to me, Spessiva is the half the sun shone upon.

"I hope I may be permitted to speak thus after an effort of more than twenty years in the poisonous atmosphere of the theater. It makes me happy to know that, even after so long a time, when hundreds of dancers have passed in front of me, I can still present such artists as Massine, Balanchine, Woizikowsky, Idzikowsky, Danilova, Tchernicheva and Sokolova in Paris.

"And still greater joy do I feel when, remembering how I began twenty years back with Pavlova and Nijinsky, I come to Spessiva and Lifar. The former seem mythological. The latter, immensely different from their predecessors, stand now before us, awaiting their turn to enter the realms of legend. That lovely, too flattering, legend associated with the glory of the Russian Ballet."

This article appeared in *Le Figaro* for May 26th, and that very day Spessiva, by some accident, hurt her foot. It was impossible to cancel the première of *La Chatte* announced for the next evening, for that would certainly have compromised the whole of our Paris season. Meanwhile Balanchine was insisting that Danilova (who knew the part) should take her place while Diaghilev held that Nikitina was the only adequate substitute. As I had always been, and still was, on very good terms with her, I offered to get her to agree to stay with us through the season. Then, with no more than a single day in which to rehearse, I took her right through her part in *La Chatte*. At the performance she acquitted herself to perfection, and scored a deserved success though, it is true, I helped her greatly by carrying her, most of the time, on my arms.

This first night went off most auspiciously, triumphantly inaugurating the rest of the season. But now the 8th of June was approaching, the date for our première of *Le Pas d'Acier,* and we were all in a state of extreme nervous tension.

The "Soviet people" had arrived in May, and we now began to receive such unusual visitors as Ehrenburg and Yakulov, whereat P. G. Koribut-Kubitovitch and V. F. Nouvel would ostentatiously refuse to carry out their secretarial duties, or have anything to do with them. This, however, only made Diaghilev, if anything, kinder and more polite. Every moment he could spare was spent with them, not only because of the new ballet, but because anything and everything in connection with the new Russia, to which Diaghilev was now longing to go, most keenly interested him. He even took steps, at the Soviet Embassy in Berlin, to make the necessary arrangements for a visit, and was granted both passport and visa. However, he finally found that he lacked the courage to go without myself and Kokhno. True, the Soviet ambassador did his best to persuade him, and gave every guarantee that whenever he liked he would be free to return to Paris, but he also added, *sotto voce:* "You must take this as a personal guarantee, that of an ambassador: but what I cannot be absolutely sure of, is that *Moscow* may not change its mind, and withdraw all it has promised."

There was still a great deal to do in connection with the new ballet, the theme of which was the story of a steel flea, taken from Leskov. Though Diaghilev, Massine, Yakulov, and Ehrenburg in turn went to considerable trouble to adapt it for the stage, nothing much came of it, and finally it was decided that the new production should be staged under the title "1920." This, however, pleased nobody, because it already sounded antiquated, and was likely to go on sounding more so with every year that passed. Only at the last moment was the title *Le Pas d'Acier* invented, and that by Diaghilev himself. He it was, too, who at the dress rehearsal introduced a feature whose origin was purely accidental. We had come to the end of one of the rehearsals when a few dancers in the *corps de ballet,* as a joke, began to tap out the rhythm with their hammers as they sat about the platform. Serge Pavlovitch was delighted with this

La Chatte, with Lifar

happy invention, and ordered it to be incorporated in the ballet, and in-deed it made a striking and most unusual finale.

Finally June 8th arrived, heralding the première of *Le Pas d'Acier*. It was an anxious day for Diaghilev, since he felt certain that there would be a terrific uproar, and that the Russian *emigrés* would stage a mass protest. Nevertheless, he awaited the event calmly, and even with a sense of pleasurable expectation. What he feared, what really made him uneasy, was a feeling that the white Russians might begin shooting and so kill me. However, the performance was received calmly, even tepidly. There was some applause, some catcalls, but there were no bursts of enthusiasm, nor indignation either. The new ballet simply did not appeal to Paris audiences, unaccustomed as they were to ballets in which the dancing took second place. The house therefore preferred to manifest its per-plexity and displeasure by shrugging its shoulders rather than by creating a riot. All in all, Diaghilev was deeply disappointed, and assured us that our audience "had no backbone" and that it was pure cowardice which made them afraid to protest. Nor did the Press pay much attention to our venturesome new ballet. For the most part they coldly praised it, as though it lacked all trace of originality. And though they mentioned its *"splendide révélation,"* no one took the least trouble to explain in what that *"révélation"* lay.

On June 11th we gave our last performance in Paris, and on June 13th, our London season started. Serge Pavlovitch was in no haste to put on *Le Pas d'Acier* again, and it was July 4th before the first English première took place. Indeed, he had already several times postponed its perform-ance, and was even beginning to doubt whether he should stage it at all, being well aware how risky it was to produce such a ballet in London, since it might easily prejudice the whole fate of the Ballet. Eventually the first night was announced, and we danced to a packed house, with the Duke of Connaught in the audience. Anxious moments passed as the curtain went down on the finale, and, for the first time in our experience, we listened to an absolute dead silence. Meanwhile, all eyes were turned on the Duke's box, for no one seemed courageous enough to express an opinion. Diaghilev had gone pale with nervousness and anxiety. Could the ballet have proved a failure? At last, however, the spare, small old gentleman rose, approached the ledge of his box, leaned over and began to applaud; whereupon, as though obeying a signal, the whole house im-mediately did likewise, to loud cries of "Bravo. Bravo." The Duke of Connaught had saved our honor, and thenceforth *Le Pas d'Acier* en-joyed an incomparable success whenever we gave it. In all we presented it eight times more, the dates being July 6th, 8th, 12th, 19th; with two performances on both the 20th and 21st. Nevertheless, its success was as nothing in comparison to that of *La Chatte*. The conductors in London were Goossens, Sargent and Lambert.

Our rooms in London were situated in Albemarle Street, where we were under the same roof as Igor Stravinsky, whom we would often meet for long and friendly conversations. One night, I remember, while supping with him after the première of *La Chatte,* he expressed his delight with my dancing, and added: "I've a surprise for Serge." Later we went home, but Stravinsky and Diaghilev sat up in the drawing room, talking for another hour and a half. At last Diaghilev came in, in great delight and excitement, woke me, and said:

"Let me congratulate you, Seriozha. Stravinsky has been saying the most astonishing things about you. He's so pleased with you that he's going to compose a ballet especially for you, even though he's working overtime on a commission for America!"

Igor Stravinsky, the author of our *Sacre du Printemps* meant to compose a ballet especially for me! Need I say how joyful, how proud I felt at that moment?

And indeed, Stravinsky there and then began composing the new ballet, so that on September 30th Serge Pavlovitch was able to write—I happened to be in Milan, he languishing alone in Monte Carlo—"Here I am sorting out books, covered with perspiration, dust and cockroaches, the place full of an uncanny silence, not a soul about...."

"My dear, arriving here I found a note from Stravinsky, in which he says that he had come round, intending to ask me to dinner, but had been told I was not yet back. As next day he was leaving for London, I went over to Nice in the morning, not having seen anybody in Monte Carlo, to catch Igor before he left. I spent the whole day with him, and at five saw him off at the station. It was an eminently satisfactory meeting. He himself had only got back from the mountains the day before I returned. He had gone to the mountains for the sake of his wife, who is by no means well, looks much older, and has got very thin. I went to see him *alone.* After lunch he played me the first half of the new ballet. It is, of course, an amazing work, extraordinarily calm, and with a greater clarity than anything he has so far done; a filigree counterpoint round transparent, clear-cut themes, all in the major key; somehow music not of this world, but from somewhere above. It seems strange that, though the tempo of all this part is slow, yet at the same time it is perfectly adapted to dancing. There is a short, fast movement in your first variation—there are to be two for you, and the opening is danced to an unaccompanied violin solo. Very remarkable! On the whole, one feels it is part Glinka and part sixteenth-century Italian, though without any intentional Russianizing. He played it over to me three times running—so that I have the clearest idea of it now. The *Adagio pas d'Action* has a broad theme very germane to us today; it runs concurrently in four different tempos, and yet, generally speaking, the harmony is most satisfactory. I embraced him and he said: 'It's for you to produce it properly for me: I want Lifar to have all sorts of flourishes...'

"When the train was already moving out, he shouted to me: 'Find a good title!' But all the same, there is really no subject. And very soon this 'good' title was found: *Apollon Musagète*." [6]

During the summer of 1927, Serge Pavlovitch spent much time traveling all over Europe, but these journeys were not so much connected with the Ballet as with his new hobby, book collecting, which by the autumn of 1927 had, from my point of view, taken an unhealthily strong hold on him.

This decline of interest in the ballet was, given Diaghilev's nature, inevitable. In any case, that "episode," important though it may have been, having taken up twenty years of his life, had lasted far too long. War, revolution, and then emigration, had so determined Diaghilev's activities as to fix him in one occupation for the greater part of his life. Nevertheless, it constantly irked him, and there were often occasions when he wished to break free. Even in the seven years of my association with the Ballet, there were several occasions on which he was prepared to relinquish the whole thing (in 1924, for instance, and again in 1926). Diaghilev, the aristocrat and *grand seigneur,* looked down with contempt, good-natured it is true, on the crowd, the masses, though he always dreamed of discovering new Americas for them, of blazing their trails, of teaching them to love what he himself admired.

Yet, though to the end he retained all his youthful enthusiasm so that some picture, some symphony, some plastic movement would move him to tears, and though he was able to discover new worlds for himself and others, the final miracle of absolute faith was lacking in him, and thus utter and absolute satisfaction always eluded him. Possibly that was why his eyes smiled so sadly, a sadness that deepened with time, in spite of the irresistible charm that radiated out from them and conquered whomever he met. No activity could ever absorb him completely, somewhere there was a vacuum in his soul, a spiritual desert, and, strangest of all, a sort of despairing inertia. Hence, the recurrent periods of unutterable anguish, hence his innumerable wild enthusiasms, and his passionate yearning to people his desert. But, in addition, Diaghilev was afflicted with a mania for collecting, which almost imperiled his very existence by instilling its poison into his soul, and severing the solitary slave of his

[6] A very different account of the creation of *Apollon* is given by Stravinsky in his *Chronicle of My Life.*

For some time, Stravinsky says, he had been interested in the idea of writing a ballet on material derived from ancient Greek mythology. It seemed to him that the plastic qualities characteristic of such a subject were admirably suited to what is commonly called "classical dancing."

A contemporary music festival was being oganized about that time in America, and the Library of Congress at Washington asked Stravinsky to write a ballet for it. Seeing an opportunity to carry out his long-felt ambition, and having little other work on hand, Stravinsky gladly accepted the invitation.

He chose, he says, as his subject, *Apollon Musagète,* Apollo, the leader of Muses, but, for various reasons, made use of only three Muses, Calliope, Polhymnia and Terpsichore.

The discrepancy between Diaghilev's contemporary and absolutely trustworthy account and Stravinsky's memoirs, which were not written till some years later, reveals how fragile is human memory and how little it is to be relied on.

passions from the joys of his fellows. My first realization of his mania occurred in 1926, in connection with an almost insignificant incident, though serious diseases often begin thus.

Kokhno had acquired a gramophone which he would play to us at times, when suddenly, for no apparent reason, Serge Pavlovitch became one of its most extravagant enthusiasts. From that moment no one could have been more devoted to that instrument. He would search all Paris and Europe for some record (and, Heavens, the time he wasted!). His special enthusiasms were recordings by Tamagno, Chaliapin and Fleita, and he would literally tremble with joy on finding one he had long sought. It was gramophone mania at its intensest, adumbrating another far more serious illness, in so far at least as the Ballet was concerned.

That other illness began quite casually also. Diaghilev had always busied himself collecting, but for the benefit of others. Thus, he had first collected pictures for Massine, then for myself; then, too, he often bought books for Kokhno, who was gathering a library for himself. But in 1926 a "little book" happened to come his way, interested him ... and off he went on the track of his new hobby, which inaugurated a new epoch in his life, and, threatening to oust all else, endangered the very future of the Ballet. Whereupon a new life began for Diaghilev, that of the book collector; new friends appeared, and the "ballet" notebook began to fill with the addresses of booksellers, antiquaries, booklovers and experts. Diaghilev's immediate friends did not attach much importance to his hobby, and some even laughed at him a little (how offensive that was!) behind his back, and with condescension, as though anyone had the right to look down on Diaghilev, or his infatuation! Meanwhile, with jealousy and dismay, I observed this passion gradually dominating all else in Diaghilev's mind and soul, and gnawing at the very heart of the Russian Ballet.

"Serge, get me granddad Sopikov!" or "Boris, do you happen to know where Levin has got to?" he would say as, lying fully dressed on his bed, he would spend hours poring over booksellers' catalogues, or working out journeys, not to find some ballerina or dancer, or arrange some contract, but to buy books. All was agitation, which rose to fever heat at times. Some expected book would be sure to get lost, or damaged in the post; or he would accuse himself of having committed the unpardonable sin of refusing to pay some bookseller's price, and as a result "it would give him the slip," had, in fact, done so already, and was now sold to another. It was a hobby which cost him considerable sums, and placed a heavy burden on the Ballet's resources, even though Diaghilev succeeded in securing his rare editions very cheaply. Or again, Serge Pavlovitch would be in a turmoil about what that "great Pushkin expert," Professor Hoffman, might have to say about some miniature by Jukovsky, an unpublished letter of Pushkin's, or some Lermontov manuscript. "For suppose it turns out not to be by Pushkin or Lermontov at all?" Thus the arrival of a parcel of books, especially one expected for some time, would become an event rather more important than the première of a new ballet. In a state of nervous exaltation impossible to describe, he would open the parcel, and take up the books, his priceless treasures, one by one....

Serge Pavlovitch's collecting was that of a dilettante, catholic and uncritical; yet, in this hobby too, that magic wand endowed him by fate helped him to discover buried treasure. Among the books that "came his way" were some exceedingly rare and valuable items. A *Book of Hours,* for instance, printed by the father of Russian printing, Ivan Feodorov, and perfect in every respect, though a defective copy, having the first few pages missing, was preserved in the Public Library of St. Petersburg as its most treasured monument of Russian printing; two copies of A. N. Raristchev's *Journey from St. Petersburg to Moscow* burned by the hangman's hand in the reign of Catherine II, holograph letters from Lermontov, Glinka and Pushkin....

To give some idea of but one of the elaborate entries in his catalogue, I quote the following:

"Azbuka [A-b-c-]—Printed by Vassili Feodorov Burtzev in the royal city of Moscow, by order of him the Lord Tsar and Grand Duke Mikhail Feodorovitch and the blessing of ... the Patriarch Ioasaph of Moscow and all the Russias, in the twenty-fourth year of the reign of Mikhail Feodorovitch, i.e., in 1637. The postface which gives these details also states that the printing was begun on January 29th, and finished on February 8th of the same year.

"The book is in 12mo and contains 108 leaves, i.e. 216 pages and an engraving representing a schoolhouse and the thrashing of a schoolboy.

"Sopikov (v. I., p. 57, No. 160-163) mentions four editions of this book and considers the one printed in 1637 to be the first (*our* copy). He cites also the full title: *A Primer in the Slavonic language,* i.e., the beginning of learning for children who desire to learn to read the Holy Scriptures, with prayers and a short catechism on Faith added; Compiled and written by Vassili Burtzev. Moscow, 1637—in 8vo.

"In our copy this full title is absent and this is in accordance with the description of the book given in the *Survey of Slavonic-Russian bibliography* by Sacharov (p. 109, no. 335), where we find: 'A-B-C. Printed by Vassili Feodorovitch Burtzev. 108 leaves. With picture of schoolhouse. At the beginning: short introduction (11s 1—10) and at the end: "The history of how St. Cyril the philosopher compiled the A-B-C.'" According to Sacharov, then, there is no title as quoted by Sopikov. But Sacharov, in contradiction with Sopikov, holds the 1637 edition to be the *second,* placing the first in 1634 (idem, N.—0310). *A very rare* book, but in a state in perfect preservation." [7]

[7] For some particulars of Diaghilev's collections see Appendix C. (Ed.)

A tradition connected with this particular copy has it—as Serge Pavlo-vitch told me—that it was used to teach Peter the Great[8] reading.

Meanwhile, his collection was becoming ever more inclusive, and to the books proper began to be added autographs and portraits. Diaghilev also began to buy and commission the manuscripts of contemporary authors. In imagination, he was already laying the foundations for a new flowering of Russian culture, organized on the large scale of *The World of Art* days, which was to find expression in a monumental exhibition of Russian portraits and material dealing with Russian opera and ballet abroad, and next in the establishment of an immense Russian library and manuscript collection for the use of Russian students abroad, and as a focus for a cultural renaissance. To himself, Diaghilev justified his new activity by claiming that thus he would help to preserve for *Russia* its great cultural inheritance. As time went on, however, it became clear that he was collecting for collecting's sake, and developing all the manias of the collector.

I have a letter dated September, 1927, from Florence, to which Serge Pavlovitch had gone after a short stay in Rome, though not, of course, for the sake of the "rotten opera" or to enjoy the company of Vyacheslav Ivanov, with whom he spent his evenings, but on account of "the little books." But the moment the bookshops shut for the holidays—"the most important 'bookman' has put up his shutters until October 12th," he wrote—Rome suddenly proved "intolerably empty" and he left. The letter continued:

"In Rome everything was fine...I dug up a beautiful, tremendous Russian book, and other things too...."

And, indeed, the book did turn out to be "tremendous," the vendor evidently having not the least idea what it was, a Slavonic book being obviously as unintelligible to him as one in Chinese. In fact, the only clue he might have had to its value was its inclusion in a collection of thirty exceedingly rare volumes, in several languages. It turned out to be the first Russian grammar ever printed, and a product of the presses of the first Russian printer, Ivan Feodorov. Until this "tremendous" find came to light, only six works from this press had ever been listed; Diaghilev found the seventh and most important to Russian bibliography. This book alone was a complete and final vindication of his hobby. With burning eyes, though Diaghilev's eyes very rarely lit up, and then only for a barely appreciable moment, he recounted with rapture the details of his find.

Next, Diaghilev went off to Munich, again a most satisfactory expedi-tion, naturally from the book fiend's point of view, and mentioned the results in a letter from Paris:

"My dear, thank you for your nice little notes. I am very pleased you took a ticket for the second Toscanini concert too. I should like you to

[8] On separate leaves.

go to *all* the concerts given during your stay in Milan. I imagine you've enough money, but, in any case, don't stint yourself. I'm glad, too, that nothing has happened to interrupt your lessons. *I won't say a word about books: I've got stacks, and spent whole days at the 'bookmen,' with divine results.*

"Good news is, that in Vienna, we are going to appear in the *Grand Opera House,* a building both famous and beautiful, and in which I heard my very first opera. Pavka [Koribut-Kubitovitch] knows well what a marvelous building it is.... Alice [Nikitina], they say, cannot dance at all any more, she's leaving the stage because of 'her marriage to R....'! I hope to be able to arrive on Sunday or Monday, though there's a great deal of work still to be done. Hoping for further 'letters from Milan,' I embrace and bless you...."

Serge Pavlovitch had said he was glad "nothing has happened to interrupt your lessons," but that was hardly the truth, for I had ceased having them for some time, though fearful of letting him know lest it should pain or divert him from his eager activities, which left him not even the time to come and visit us, for P. G. Koribut-Kubitovitch was with me in Milan.

Meanwhile, our lives had flowed peacefully on in concerts conducted by Toscanini, visits to museums, lessons with Cecchetti, interminable talks.... Then, one day, I happened to be practicing some difficult exercises, threefold *cabrioles* with double *tours* on one leg, when suddenly I felt as though my leg had disappeared into the ground, and found it so much damaged that it had to be put in splints. Thus I was obliged to remain in bed for a long, anxious, most boring month, during which not a word of the accident was allowed to leak out. Occasionally Serge Pavlovitch would telephone to inquire how we were, but only to hear: "All's well and satisfactory, the lessons are going on, thanks for inquiring...."

Now the time came to return to Paris, but my leg had not yet healed, and I was forced to use crutches. You may imagine Serge Pavlovitch's shock of bewildered surprise on seeing me descend from my carriage!

Then the time came to set out on our important tour through Germany. At Freiburg the masseurs who were treating my leg and back had me on my feet again in a wonderfully short time, and I was able to begin dancing as though nothing had ever happened to me. It was an interesting tour, and tremendously successful, though not in Dresden, which proved a complete failure, both as regards the public and the Press. At Brünn, in Czechoslovakia, after we had given *La Chatte,* the Russian students rewarded us with an ovation which lasted a whole half hour. Nevertheless, the tour had been badly organized, and the material result was nil. Serge Pavlovitch's moods throughout this tour were exceedingly unstable, and he was constantly fluctuating between extremes. At one moment he would be thoroughly displeased with the whole cast, and consider us all responsible for our lack of success; the next, for no particular reason, he would be cheerful, amiable and full of hope. What especially delighted him was a certain sleigh ride and the sound of its tingling bells. He seemed positively to melt with joy as he said how much it reminded him of his youth and Russia, for which, at that moment, he was feeling especially homesick. Then he recalled memories of our Russian snows, and carnival time. "But the Russian carnival doesn't exist any more. . . . Our, my Russia, is no more. . . ." he sadly ended. In picturesque Budapest, however, his spirits rose, for the motley gypsy crowd delighted him, and all the time we could spare was devoted to going from one cabaret to another, listening to gypsy songs and the clashing cymbalon. Here we stayed from November 19th to December 17th, and gave five performances in all, with literally staggering success.

We reached Vienna on December 9th, where, for the first time in our acquaintance, Serge Pavlovitch began to manifest openly a certain jealousy of my stage successes, a kind of resentment and even fear of my growing fame, for as time went on he took less and less trouble to mask it. "The hero of our times," as V. F. Nouvel had nicknamed me, was evidently becoming too independent. . . . All this weighed me down, and just at this time something occurred to distress me profoundly. From 1925 on I had begun to have many admirers. Far from welcoming them, however, I sought to ignore them, well aware of the jealous eye Serge Pavlovitch turned on my "conquests." But one admirer, a perfect beauty, a girl of good German family, it was impossible for me to ignore, for she followed us everywhere, always sat in the front row of the stalls, sent me flowers and notes, and did all she possibly could to put herself in my path and make my acquaintance. I was always running into her in Monte Carlo, whether in the park, the post office, on the terrace or at the Café de Paris. At restaurants her table would always be next to ours, and she took care always to sit facing me. It annoyed Serge Pavlovitch intensely, and he took no pains to hide his displeasure, often expressing it loudly enough. In spite of the fact that the girl dressed well and in perfect taste, and moved in good society, Diaghilev would loudly proclaim, obviously meaning to be heard:

"On voit encore une fois cette grue!" [9]

If we happened to pass her walking, Serge Pavlovitch would either turn away, or make rude remarks about her. Nevertheless, she bore it all with patience, and went on sending me flowers and frequenting such spots as offered a hope of meeting me.

We were staying at the Hotel Bristol in Vienna at the time. It was November 9th. We had given our performance, and I was returning home, when I saw a large crowd assembled outside the hotel, waiting to give me an ovation. But my elation disappeared the moment I saw my lovely German girl in the crowd. "She's here again," I thought, and

---

[9] There's that tart again. (Ed.)

turned gloomily away, ignoring the applause. In the hall, however, I found Diaghilev waiting, when, without a moment's hesitation, he burst out:

"You really amaze me, Seriozha, by your lack of manners. Don't you realize that such an attitude of contempt is gross discourtesy, and merely shows you've been badly brought up. Go out and thank them properly!" I therefore went out, bowed and smiled pleasantly, the girl still being there! After supper I went up to my room, and to bed.

In the middle of the night, however, I half woke in a strange, dimly excited condition, feeling I was not alone, that another presence was by me, that I was holding it in my arms, and being covered with kisses ... in the penetrating odor of scent.... That perfume brought me completely to myself. In sudden terror I switched on my bed lamp, and saw my beautiful German girl at my side....

"Why are you here? What do you want? How did you get in? *Partez immédiatement...*"

Whereupon she explained that she had booked the adjoining room and bribed the floor-maid to give her the key to the communicating door. Nevertheless she remained where she was, and only clasped me more closely to herself. Tearing myself away, I jumped out of bed, but all she said was:

"If you refuse me I'll scream, make a scandal, then everyone will come rushing in and find you here with me!"

What was I to do? With sudden inspiration I felt all would be well if only I could persuade her to go to her room.

"Allons dans votre chambre!" I said, and drew her in my arms to the door, when, with a sudden push, I swiftly shut it on her and as immediately locked it.

I had only just time to return to bed, and switch off the light, when in rushed Serge Pavlovitch.

"What is it? What's happening? What was that noise? Who's been here?"

I pretended to be asleep.

"I'm asking you, Serge, what's been going on in this room? Someone has been here! And what's that?" Serge Pavlovitch went pale. "Your bed's all rumpled? There's been a woman here, yes, I swear there's been a woman here, I know by the scent.... Answer, Serge, who's been here with you?"

Utterly taken aback, I hardly knew what to say, and remained sunk in a deathly suicidal silence. Then another inspiration flashed through my brain. Some time before Serge Pavlovitch had given me a pint bottle of Chanel scent, which I had not yet opened: this would explain everything.

"It must have been that bottle of scent you gave me. I was using some just before going to bed, and must have spilled it."

"What scent? What's all this nonsense? Where is it? Show me your scent!"

Whereupon I went to the bathroom, but, oh horror! so soundly corked down and sealed was the bottle that there was no way of opening it quickly. At which, I flung the bottle crashing into the bath.

"There, now all these whims and fancies of yours have made me smash the bottle! It's all the fault of these eternal whimsies of yours, your perpetual suspicions of one thing and another . . . this is the sort of thing it leads to!"

Whether Serge Pavlovitch was satisfied or not, I cannot say; nevertheless, it reduced him to silence. Luckily, he did not go into the bathroom, or he would have discovered that I had smashed a still unopened bottle.

Thus, I managed to keep myself "pure" and "innocent" from the temptations of womanly charms.

Next we gave four performances in Geneva, and on December 23rd arrived in Paris, where we appeared twice at the Opéra. It was my first experience of that stage, and coincided with the première of my version of the *Faun* (following tradition, I had kept the seven nymphs in the cast), which was received with great applause. Serge Pavlovitch, too, was delighted with it.

This momentous, critical and difficult year of 1927, a year of great significance in Serge Pavlovitch's life and my own, was now drawing to its close. In this year, Serge Pavlovitch's passion for book collecting had increased to the point of mania; and I, for the first time, had seen N. P., who was destined later to enter my life. . . . It also marked the beginning of a critical period in my relation to Diaghilev, for, realizing how I was maturing, both in my artistic appreciation and as a dancer, Serge Pavlovitch was beginning to resign himself to the thought that I would leave him, having taken all I needed, as each of my predecessors had done.

The year 1928 began with a tour in Lyons, where we gave four performances, and Marseilles. Then, at the end of January, we were back once more in Monte Carlo, and gave our last performance on February 1st. That night I gave a dinner to celebrate the fifth anniversary of my association with Diaghilev's Russian Ballet, to which I asked, in addition to my contemporaries, Alice Nikitina, A. Trusevitch, Tcherkas, the brothers Khoer, Kokhanovsky, Prince Shervashidze, Serge Pavlovitch, P. G. Koribut-Kubitovitch, and all the soloists of the company. At this dinner Serge Pavlovitch made a most deep-felt, moving speech.

At one of our charity galas in Nice, that of March 30th, I made the acquaintance of Pushkin's granddaughter, Countess Torby (who had arranged the whole thing). Countess Torby fell at once under Serge Pavlovitch's charm, and promised she would leave him, when she died, a letter written by Pushkin to his betrothed, N. N. Goncharova. This letter she had jealously preserved, not only refusing to allow it to be published, but even refusing to let it be seen. In conversation, she told Serge Pavlovitch that, on her marriage to the Grand Duke Mikhail Mikhailovitch, when, as a result, the Emperor had banned him from Russia, she had sworn an oath that not only she herself, but her grandfather's letters, should never again see Russia. She was as good as her word, for, though the Russian Academy of Sciences, on several occasions, sent representatives to England to see her, Countess Torby firmly refused to have anything to do with them. In addition, the late President of the Imperial Academy of Science, the Grand Duke Constantin Constantinovitch, had written to her, urging her to return this heritage of all Russia to its native land.

"I wish you could have seen his letters! He actually dared to write, to me, that my duty was to hand these letters over to the Academy, that they did not rightfully belong to me but to them, because they held the memory of their illustrious poet in such great honor, and so it was not his descendants but his country that had the right to them. 'Such great honor' indeed, when, just because the Grand Duke marries the granddaughter of that Pushkin they honor so greatly, he must be driven from Russia as though he has done something disgraceful. Never, I swear, will they get a single line written by my grandfather. But you, Serge Pavlovitch, will have something worth having, and fairly soon, too, I imagine, for I feel I haven't got long to live."

Countess Torby proved a good prophet, for she died only a few months after. But this conversation had made a profound impression on Serge Pavlovitch's mind. As a result, he developed a mad enthusiasm for Pushkin, and determined to get, not only the one autograph letter he had been promised, but all the eleven letters comprising the correspondence. A year later, shortly before his death, that dream came true. The Grand Duke Mikhail Mikhailovitch needed money, was continually ill, cared little what went on round him, and his daughters fell wholly under Serge Pavlovitch's charm. Thus, for a ridiculously small sum (if I am right, only some 30,000 francs), Diaghilev acquired this priceless treasure.

That February I left Monte Carlo for Milan, returning at the end of March. On April 4th our season in Monte Carlo was due to begin. How well I remember an incident which occurred during a performance of *Schéhérazade*—our *Aïda,* as it were. Watching this ingenuous, somewhat antiquated ballet, Serge Pavlovitch burst into such uproarious laughter that two aisle seats crashed under him. Though he continued to present this ballet for another season, it was reserved solely for Monte Carlo, since Diaghilev did not dare to revive it in Paris or London. Meanwhile, both Nabokov and Stravinsky had arrived, for we were at work on two new ballets, Nabokov's *Ode* and Stravinsky's *Apollon Musagète.* The *Ode* frankly bewildered Diaghilev, both in its music and choreography, and he could hardly decide to allow us to put it on. Nevertheless, later, in Paris, I was able to persuade him to allow us to include it, which he did for my sake, though it did not interest him at all. He spent the night before the première at the theater, and helped to get the production into shape; but he never, in fact, got to like the ballet himself.

But where the *Apollon Musagète* was concerned, both he and ourselves were most enthusiastic. Indeed, in his last years, Diaghilev was inclined to consider this his very best ballet.

I led all through the Monte Carlo season, which lasted from April 4th to May 6th, and meanwhile worked on *Ode* and *Apollon*. On May 9th we left for Paris, but did not stop, and on the 11th began a tour through Belgium. For three days we stayed in Brussels, the minimum time necessary for our performance in connection with the opening ceremony of the Palais des Beaux-Arts. It was a most brilliant function, and reminded me of that we had given in 1923 at Versailles. But as Diaghilev was expecting some parcels of books in Paris, he left immediately after.

Our Belgian tour took us to Antwerp, Liège, and back again to Brussels. There, at the Théâtre de la Monnaie, on May 23rd, we suffered a spectacular and scandalous failure, the program consisting of *The Triumph of Neptune, Le Sacre du Printemps* and *La Boutique Fantasque.* We had had no dress rehearsal, and danced shamefully badly; *The Triumph of Neptune,* for instance, which should have taken but forty-five minutes, went on for a whole hour and a half.

On June 2nd and 3rd we were in Montreux for the traditional *Fête des Narcisses,* where we gave *Cimarosiana, Les Sylphides* and *Prince Igor.* On the fourth we were back again in Paris, and on the sixth started a two weeks' season at the Théâtre Sarah Bernhardt. We opened with our first performance of Nabokov's *Ode,* and both the public and Press proved very friendly. Every part of this ballet, the music, setting, the use of the cinematographic apparatus and, especially, the performers, won warm praise, and this seemed somewhat to reconcile Serge Pavlovitch to it. Nevertheless, the *clou* of the season proved to be *Apollon Musagète,* which we performed on June 12th, and subsequently repeated on June 13th, 14th, 19th, 21st, and 23rd. Reserved in regard to the *Ode,* Diaghilev wrote of *Apollon* as follows:

"Stravinsky's ballet is an outstanding event in the world of music. I, personally, consider it one of his major works, a product of true artistic maturity. Stravinsky has striven for, and reached, a majestic calm.... The choreography, arranged by Balanchine, is in perfect accord with the spirit of Stravinsky's music, a classicism of today; the muses in specially cut *tu-tu's.* The sets are by André Bauchant, the French artist, a painter closely allied to a group which claims to derive from the *douanier* Rousseau, at present exhibiting at the Mejeulan Galleries. A somewhat naïve, sincere approach characterizes his work, in sharp contradiction to the generally accepted Greek product ... the dances I consider to be exceptionally well conceived."

All artistic Paris was present at our première of *Apollon,* and for some

Lifar in *Apollon Musagète*

unknown reason all Soviet Paris too—possibly Moscow may have been courting Diaghilev. The success was *fantastic,* and my own reward an enormous ovation. But what pleased me more than this ovation on my feast day was my joy at having earned the right to be satisfied with my artistic achievement. That meant infinitely more to me than the loudest applause, or Stravinsky's or Diaghilev's approval. Stravinsky himself sent me a few very kind lines; Serge Pavlovitch, profoundly moved, impulsively kissed my leg after the performance.

"Remember it, Seriozha, for the rest of your days. I am kissing a dancer's leg for the second time in my life, the last was Nijinsky's after *Le Spectre de la Rose!"*

To reward me for having created *Apollon,* Diaghilev presented me with a golden lyre. This lyre I dedicated to, and left with Coco Chanel, my "godmother," at the ball she gave after this première, as she had done for each of our others.

My triumph, which began in Paris, continued in London, at His Majesty's Theatre, where we began to dance on June 25th, finishing on July 28th. In that period we gave, in all, thirty-six performances, dancing *Apollon* eleven times, and *Ode* six. Serge Pavlovitch was then in his ballet "stretch" as he called it. Throughout 1928 the ballet and book "stretches" were perpetually alternating, but the book "stretch" was visibly gaining the upper hand. Two more performances were given in Ostend on July 29th and 30th, after which our ballet-grind, for the time being, came to an end, and the company broke up for a long vacation.

With sorrow in my heart I could not but see how Serge Pavlovitch was gradually receding ever further from the Ballet. In August, as usual, we went to Venice, and once again Diaghilev began planning both in regard to book collecting and the Ballet. For September we had arranged to visit Greece. Diaghilev fussed a great deal about this visit, and collected numbers of letters of introduction, including one from Venizelos. The project itself, and the necessary preparations, absorbed him completely; but, of course, it was neither the Acropolis, nor the Dipylon Gate, nor the Olympic Hermes, nor the Lion Gate of Mycenae which most attracted him; it was Mount Athos, where "little books" and manuscripts in Russian and Church Slavonic might possibly be found....

Even then, he was planning to find a large flat on his return and later a house—indeed he had one already in view—there to install his book treasures to-be, and forswearing the world, to devote himself utterly to those silent, true and faithful friends....

As for the Ballet, a great change was about to overtake it, for Diaghilev had decided to split it up into two unequal portions. One, a small group of about twelve, with myself at the head, was to concentrate on artistic research, and devote itself exclusively to the pursuit of the purest art forms. For this group Diaghilev meant to erect a small theater on the Lido, and had already presented me with curtains and sets designed by

Picasso, Matisse and Derain, on condition I had them copied for him.

The larger group was to derive its artistic sustenance from the discoveries of the small studio-theater, and would provide for the material needs of both studio and library. Nothing else would be required of it, and Diaghilev would have no further interest in it. Monte Carlo would be its center, from which it could radiate out on world-wide tours, in particular to America. But these plans seemed only to make clear that the Russian Ballet was heading towards deterioration and eventual break-up, which could not now be long postponed.... Serge Pavlovitch's health was also beginning to fail; certain swellings began to appear on his body, which finally turned out to be boils.

Not one of these plans materialized, however. And news of an epidemic made Diaghilev postpone our visit to Greece time after time, so that in the end we never got there.

Soon after the season ended, we went for a short motor tour round Italy and visited Venice, Padua, Mantua, Ferrara, Ravenna, Perugia, Arezzo, Siena, and ended our journey in Florence. Ravenna, the ancient, rich in Italian primitives and pre-mediaeval relics, impressed me deeply. The pagan Christianity of the fifth century, the mosaics in the Baptistry were a veritable revelation to me. I was touched by their naïve realism, and childlike power. A new aspect of Italy was revealed to me, totally unlike the Italy of the Renaissance, something I had never dreamed of. Especially was I impressed by the images of the Christ I saw, a pagan Christ, heavily bearded and with all his nakedness unveiled, for un-Christian and ungodly though they might be, they were incredibly forceful.

In Arezzo, far more than by the painters of the Sienese school, was I affected by one unique painter, about whom, for a time, I literally raved; the severe, profound and searching vision of Piero della Francesca whom, with Diaghilev, I "discovered."

From Arezzo we went to Florence, but Diaghilev was anxious to be moving, and soon left for Poland—"in search of artists"—alias "books."

On October 3rd I received a letter written from Warsaw:

"My dear, the landscape as one nears Warsaw, with its little copses, its women with kerchiefs round their heads, reminds one of our little mother Russia, but Warsaw itself is a not-too-bad little German town, which I cannot visit properly because of the dreadful cold. It's cold in the streets, and not too warm in the rooms. I, of course, began by starting a cold in the head, which, however, today, is very much better. In addition, the swelling in the armpit proved to be neither more nor less than a painless boil, which burst last night. All this is of no importance, rather boring, in fact. As for theatrical matters, tonight I visit the principal theater. They are doing an opera, *Casanova,* for which a whole company of ballerinas has been engaged. I shall certainly see something, but the really serious performances only begin on Saturday with a new ballet-opera, *The Siren,* and *Giselle* on Sunday. I've already seen a number of people; they all recommend the same three ballerinas and three dancers, and say they're quite good. Mme. Nijinska has taken on four men for the *corps de ballet* [10] but, they tell me, not the best. I see a great deal of Dobetzky, Novak and Kurillo, who're very helpful. I shall be seeing, too, Petrova, who is just back from touring the Polish provinces. Tell Pavka I am seeing Dima, and shall tell him in detail all about it. My arrival passed unnoticed to begin with, but now the whole ant heap is beginning to sit up. I've visited the smaller theaters; everything is capably produced and in a very lively manner; there are some excellent actresses, too, but not our *genre,* though most of them are Russian.

"As to books, nothing out of the way. Any number of antiquarian bookshops, but no one here handles Russian books. Levin is in London, but his brother sold me some good stuff, useful for the library. What is really amazing here, is the *food,* absolutely first class, though expensive. Everywhere you find Russian cooking, and the gorging is terrific.

"I am thinking of going for a day to Vilna, the train service is excellent, one can return the same day. Here, generally speaking, everyone dances. There are schools of ballroom dancing at every street corner; not to mention the private schools for teaching acting, though all they do teach is 'plastic poses and acrobatics,' in their provincial eagerness to be 'modernistic.' The dream of the principal theater is to be able to engage Chaplinsky, the famous ballet master, at present choreographer-in-chief to the Royal Opera in Stockholm. I repeat, I haven't as yet seen any real ballerinas, but they've warned me that here they like fat women, and that Petrova is considered thin and exceptionally plain! On the whole, it seems a very far cry from the Warsaw of the eighteenth century, in which Cimarosa, Casanova, and Canaletto stayed. You have to stay in a place like this to realize how much of a metropolis Berlin is. Nevertheless, everyone's exceedingly civil, they try to understand you and answer in Russian, but the younger generation doesn't talk a word, though, of course, it's not to be wondered at.

"One doesn't feel the vicinity of Russia in the least, and the Russians who live here are poor folk, who have nowhere to go, and haven't any money. All this is very interesting, but rather drab. Yesterday I heard a talented chansonette singer, in a cabaret, singing a Russian song, called *Sunflowerseed.* They said the pleasures of the Soviet Paradise would be displayed. She was more genuine, more touching and pitiful than the whole of Tairov's troupe put together. They applauded her tremendously. I had quite a lump in my throat, and for a long time couldn't get off to sleep.

"God keep you both: I embrace you, my dear.

"SPDK."

[10] For Ida Rubinstein's ballet.

In this long letter, which seems to me of great importance for a proper understanding of the subject of this book, one sentence needs emphasizing: "Tell Pravka I am seeing Dima and shall tell him in detail all about it." And indeed Serge Pavlovitch did relate to Pavel Georgievitch and myself, in the greatest detail, a narrative shot through with considerable bitterness, how he had found and met his Dima.

Many years had passed since their last meeting, but now, not only was it impossible to find a common language in which to converse together, but Diaghilev had, in addition, to listen to much that was strange and unexpected, for the fanatical political journalist Filosofov did nothing but attack Diaghilev for busying himself with entirely "useless" and "unwanted" activities at a time when ... etc., etc. ...

Serge Pavlovitch, before departing for Poland and Germany had, as heaven alone knows how often before, "entrusted" me to Pavel Georgievitch's care. After a few days more in Florence, we left for Milan, where I was to continue studying under my old teacher Cecchetti, whose classes opened on September 24th.

In Florence I had spent my every moment in the Uffizzi, starting at the paintings, and striving with everything in me to thrust down the resentment, the irritation and apprehension I felt at being again doomed to that solitude from which Diaghilev himself had rescued me, though only to make the succeeding contrast all the more painful. As a result, I retreated into myself, and though to all appearances I remained unmoved and submissive, my allegiance to him began to waver. I made no protest, no accusation, and endured in patience; but that calm was purely superficial, as was proved by my growing neurasthenia, my memory-lapses, and most important of all, the utter silence in which I was sunk, for days would pass without my uttering a word. Boundless as my devotion might be, somewhere I was already beginning to mutiny against him. And my mind was perpetually occupied with grandiose plans, with passionate protests, and solutions of all the deep problems of life and of art. Yet all my cleverness, my eloquence, were merely mental, and I said nothing of my thoughts, my "finds," or the "bold schemes" I conceived. A deep-rooted exasperation took possession of me; a feeling of separateness, of being different from other men.

In October, Serge Pavlovitch arrived for a few days, but then left for Paris in order to prepare his twenty-first season.

In November our important English season began, and from November 12th to 17th we were dancing in Manchester. The thirteenth I remember especially well, for that night my heart was heavy with sorrow as we danced Les Sylphides, and I wore a black ribbon instead of a white. That day "my" maestro, and I feel with justice I may call him mine, Cecchetti, had died. I had taken my last lesson on October 31st, but leaving, I knew I should never see him again, that his teaching days were ended, that his time was near. Yet, though I was prepared for his death, the news overwhelmed me. On the twelfth he had gone as usual to the school, and there a heart attack struck him down. He lingered for a day, and next morning passed away peacefully, conscious to the last, and to the last one with that art to which all his life had been devoted, for his last words were of his pupils and the ballet. . . .

On the eighteenth we left Manchester and visited in turn Birmingham, Glasgow and Edinburgh, while Serge Pavlovitch departed for Paris, not on this occasion in search of books, but to witness the season Ida Rubinstein was giving. It was a moment that coincided with one of his ballet "stretches," and these performances did much to inflame his enthusiasm. He attended them all and wrote of them to me in detail. The first, in response to a letter of mine, was dated November 25th.

"My dear: Paris is an awful town, impossible to find five minutes for a couple of words even! . . . Everyone seems to have collected here, it's the most awful muddle! Let me begin with Ida. The house was full, but there was a good deal of paper about, mostly her friends. Not one of us, though, were given seats, neither myself nor Boris, Nouvel, Sert nor Picasso. . . . We only just, just managed to get in. *All our people were there,* Misia, Juliette, Beaumont, Polignac, Igor [Stravinsky] and other musicians, not to mention Mayakovsky, etc., etc. The whole thing was astonishingly provincial, boring and long-drawn-out, even the Ravel, which took fourteen minutes. It's a big company, but totally lacking in experience: they were just making fault after fault and seemed not to have the slightest notion of ensemble. And the hosts of solo dancers! Shollar was supposed to be representing a baby, in the heart of a cabbage, but looked more like an old woman in the green rags she was wearing. Nikolayeva had her hair sweeping the ground, wore a yellow dress, and pranced about in a classico-bacchanalian manner on her toes. The best dancer turned out to be Rupert Doone, the little Englishman we both know. And then, in the middle of the ballet, something really wonderful happened, for a certain gent in an open pink shirt with blue trimmings and a short red velvet cloak, wearing a red wig and a bright green wreath on top of it, made up to look like the worst sort of coxcomb, suddenly appeared borne triumphantly on his colleague's arms, and began dancing *something that vaguely resembled a classical variation:* it was Unger, yes, Unger!

"Benois seems to have lost every atom of color and taste. He seems exactly where he was thirty years ago. But now, much, much worse!

"Singaievsky also came on, naked, and in a gray beard and property helmet. But neither he, nor the show as a whole, had any success. The Press is pretty lukewarm about the whole thing. Stravinsky was seen in Ida's dressing room, where it appears he said: 'Delightful: I say it from the heart, charming.' Argutinsky himself told me the story. But the morning after the show Stravinsky rang up to say how disappointed he had been, how indignant the whole thing made him.

"All this you can read during supper to the principal dancers. I've exaggerated nothing. Tomorrow we have the second performance."

After which he concludes characteristically with a typical Bakst ending, except that Bakst put it more strongly: "It is very useful to look at *rubbish*: it makes one think." And indeed Ida Rubinstein's "rubbish" stimulated Diaghilev intensely, and roused all his competitive spirit. Thus we find him writing:

"Rieti played over his ballet to me: he has improved considerably, and may possibly turn out something agreeable. What's more important is that Prokofiev had already composed a good half of his ballet. A lot of it is very good. As yet he hasn't got the female part quite right, but is quite prepared to rewrite it. Tomorrow I'm lunching with both him and Meyerhold, who seems to be courting me pretty assiduously. At present I feel I'm deep in the ballet 'stretch,' and not in the 'book.'"

The new Prokofiev ballet was *Le Fils Prodigue*, the libretto for which had been suggested by Kokhno in October, when Prokofiev had at once begun composing the music. As a result of this lunch, and Meyerhold's blandishments, a plan was evolved for a joint season, soon after which Diaghilev wrote to me:

"It's possible I shall be giving a joint season with Meyerhold in Paris this spring; his company and ours on alternate days. The arrangement is that he'll do Ostrovsky's *Forest, Revisor* and *Le Cocu Magnifique,* but there's to be absolutely no politics. In my opinion it should be of the greatest interest and importance. I am convinced of his talent, and am sure that this is just the moment for it: tomorrow may be too late.[11] The only protest comes, of course, from Valetchka, who's against it body and soul . . . that can't be helped, however! People such as he and Pavka are very pleasant, but if one took their advice one might as well go straight to the cemetery. That's why Ida's performances turn out like 'charity bazaars' (as Tchelichev says). She listens to her 'Valetchkas' but lacks the small amount of talent it needs to pass over their heads. . . ."

On November 28th, the "second Ida Evening," for so he headed his letter, Diaghilev, still worried, though less fearful she might spoil our season, wrote:

"I'm just back from the theater, with a fearful headache, as a result of all the horrible things I've been seeing. Stravinsky's was the only new ballet, the other promised novelties not being ready, so that I shan't be able to see either the Auric or Sauguet. All in all, it's doubtful now whether they'll be given at all. In the first ballet, *Bach,* I noticed this evening a little *pas-de-deux* which I missed the first time, danced by Nicolaeva and Unger, and which is well worth seeing. After which came Igor's ballet. It's difficult to say what it was meant to represent—tiresome, lachrymose, ill-chosen Tchaikovsky, supposedly orchestrated by Igor in masterly fashion. I say 'supposedly,' because it sounded drab, and the

---

[11] How very typical of Diaghilev this last remark is.

whole arrangement lacked vitality. The *pas-de-deux,* however, was quite well done to a beautiful theme from Tchaikovsky, based on the song 'No, only he that knows!' That, and the coda in the style of the *Apollon* were really the only bright spots (though the latter, too, was somewhat melancholy). But what went on on the stage, it is impossible to describe. Suffice it to say that the first scene represents the Swiss mountains, the second a Swiss village on a holiday, accompanied by *Swiss* national dances, the third a Swiss mill, and the fourth back again to mountains and glaciers. The heroine was Shollár, who danced a long *pas-de-deux* with Vilzak, to Petipa's choreography, or at least a *pastiche* of his work. Bronia [12] showed not the least gleam of invention, not one single movement that was decently thought out. As for Benois' décor, it was like the sets at the Monte Carlo Opera House: these Swiss landscapes were worse than anything by Bacharov or Lambin (Grigoriev will be sure to remember them). The theater was full, but as for success—it was like a drawing room in which someone has suddenly made a bad smell. No one pretended to notice, and Stravinsky was twice called to the curtain. The whole thing was stillborn, and all our friends merely shrug their shoulders, except Valetchka, of course, who, when it was written, could 'find no music' in *L'Oiseau de Feu,* though now he finds it interesting, and even managed to convert Sauguet, no difficult matter seeing that the latter is on 'the Jewish ballet's' salary list. But what use is it all? In the second performance the *corps de ballet* got so completely out of hand, that not one movement was in time to the music, or with each other: and that in spite of the fact that there are some quite decent dancers among them, though still quite green."

After which came one of his typically anarchistic utterances. "All the time I was asking myself the same question: 'What use is it all? No, far better let the Bolsheviks, or some Napoleon—it's all the same—blow up all their old barracks.' "

This sentence, I must confess, affected me deeply. For, I thought, if, indeed "all the barracks" were to be blown up, possibly Diaghilev's ballet would be equally destroyed, and then what would happen? Why, Serge Pavlovitch would be left with his books. Continuing this train of thought, my mind ran on: Here, with the utmost cruelty, he attacks these rivals of his, not only Rubinstein, but any one who dares work with her, Stravinsky, Sauguet, Benois, Massine, Nijinska, Vilzak, Shollar and even Unger. Yet all these people once worked for him, too; even Rubinstein herself began with him, and he more than any one, raised her to fame! Thus it was inevitable that I should begin to ask myself whether Diaghilev was not, in his way, striving to wipe out the whole past of his ballet, and his connection with it.

Later, when I was able to see her ballets for myself I got my answer: for miraculous indeed, and infinitely potent, must have been Diaghilev's

[12] Nijinska.

influence, so to force and spur on each of his co-workers, to give of the best in them. Indeed, the same artist under, or away from, Diaghilev, was two quite different beings. But it was not only her ballets which taught me this lesson, but other things too.

Next day yet another letter arrived, again dealing with these same performances, now stimulating him to renewed interest in the ballet, and to a more critical view of his own. This letter, however, was intended for me alone, and not as before, "calling all stations."

"My dear, I am afraid I shall have to stay on longer than I expected, to see Ida Rubinstein's last performance. They are doing the *Sauguet* and perhaps the *Auric,* i.e., both the Massine ballets, or in any case, one. By then, however, we shall know more about the King's illness. If, God forbid, the worst should happen, the tour must stop that very day, and all must return to Paris immediately: you, of course, will go Dover-Calais. But, if all goes well, I'll meet you in Edinburgh, which will suit my plans perfectly, to reassure myself as to the way the company's dancing, and cast an eye over the new arrivals.

"I've any amount of work to be got through, what with our projected novelties on the one hand, and the season at the Opéra on the other. There's all the advertising to be seen to, and a number of sets that need renewing, bad though they be. Ida Rubinstein is dancing to full houses, every seat *bought and paid for.* If we're to rake in the money we need, and which will be absolutely essential, if our English tour should come to an abrupt end, we've really got to pull ourselves together in every way we possibly can. These performances are like those little pictures about which Bakst used to say: 'How useful it is to look at this trash.' To-morrow two more of Bronia's ballets are going to be done, *Tsar Saltan* and Borodin's *Sérénade.* But we've got to prove to this bourgeois crowd how immeasurably superior we are, in spite of the fact that our sets weren't painted yesterday, that our costumes aren't quite so fresh. All the time I'm on the boil about next season's productions...."

Again, on November 30th he wrote me another wicked, slashing criticism.

"Yesterday was Ida's third performance. As novelties they had *Sérénade,* music by Borodin, arranged by Tcherepnine; and *Tsar Saltan.* The beginning was better than usual. A moonlit scene, Spain, really a great improvement on the rest, firstly because moonshine is always lovely, and secondly because it was dark, and there was less to be seen. The first dance, an *ensemble,* was better than anything else, and for once the costumes weren't so vulgar and the dancing was better. At last we saw something of Lapitzky, a shortish, i.e., fattish Lapitzky, it's true, with his legs going through the floor, but nevertheless dancing well, and very much in the Bronia manner. It really began to look as though the whole thing would turn out better than any of the other ballets, but the moment Unger, who had one of the leading parts, appeared, impersonating an old gouty marquis and trying to be fearfully comic, though he certainly wasn't, the whole thing began going downhill. And then, what finished it off completely was the appearance of Ida, with her interminable classic *pas-de-deux*. It's impossible to describe such dancing, or her tousled red hair blown in every direction. As for Tcherepnine's arrangement, it's simply shocking. Imagine getting a *tenor* to sing the 'cello part of that famous quartette. Why, it's like turning Borodin into restaurant music. After which came *Tsar Saltan,* turned into a bad sort of *L'Oiseau de Feu*. As for the set, that must have come straight from the *Casino de Paris* plus a postcard or two by E. Boehm and Solomko, both of which Grigoriev will no doubt remember. The changes aren't bad, but why the Smolny nunnery should rise from the bottom of the sea passes understanding. The Russian national dances were produced à la the Brothers Molodzov, though without their technique and success; and Unger and Lapitzky stagger through the *prisiadka*.[13] The only original touch was provided by the Tsarevitch (Vilzak) who dances a wild variation in a crown and mantle, and gives one the impression of having got so drunk that he just could not help dancing. Ida did more dancing in this than in any of her other ballets. She appeared dressed like a Pavlova swan, specially got up for some Moulin Rouge performance (her bodice one mass of false diamonds, and her wings all covered with spangles). In both ballets the curtain came down too soon, so we did not really see the finales: it came down also right in the middle of the Schubert ballet. They say the Auric won't be produced at all, or the Nabokov, but they're doing the Sauguet at the last performance, Tuesday's. Massine couldn't wait for the première, and left for the States. Now I hear that Bronia is busy rearranging Sauguet's ballet. Everyone's cursing and disappointed— except, it appears, Bronia, who keeps on telling Ida she's a genius."

As in all of the "Rubinstein" letters, Diaghilev in the next and last tells me of his plans for the Russian Ballet:

"Yesterday I signed the Chirico contract for Rieti's ballet (*Le Bal*). The sketches are to be done in oils, so that a certain collection will be the richer by a number of good things." That "certain" collection, i.e., my own, was even then a very rich one.

On December 1st, Serge Pavlovitch again heard Prokofiev's music for *Le Fils Prodique*: "Much of it is very good. The last scene, the prodigal's return, is beautiful. Your variation, the awakening after the orgy is, for Prokofiev, quite new stuff. A sort of profound and majestic nocturne. Good, too, is the tender theme of the sisters, and very good, in the genuine Prokofiev manner, the pilfering scene: three clarinettes performing miracles of agility."

Having finally "buried" Ida Rubinstein, Diaghilev at last appeared in Edinburgh on December 4th for the tail end of our brilliant English tour.

[13] Russian National Dance, based on a deep *plié* with alternative *jetés* of both legs either forward or sideways.

Here we all stayed another few days, and then left for five days in Liverpool.

On December 15th we gave our last performance, composed of *Les Sylphides, Le Mariage d'Aurore* and *Les Dieux Mendiants,* a most charming ballet by Balanchine to music by Handel, the première of which had been given on July 16th, during our summer season. Though Serge Pavlovitch thought nothing of it at all, everywhere we went, London, then Birmingham, Glasgow, Edinburgh and Liverpool, it proved an immense success, almost a triumph, both for the ballet and the leading performers, Danilova, Tchernicheva, Dubrovska and Woizikowsky. Nevertheless, all through this period in England Serge Pavlovitch was in a surly, hostile mood, and was perpetually scolding the company. In particular he was excessively rude to Nikitina, and sharply reprimanded her in front of everybody, ending with the words: "I must ask you to dance properly if you want to remain in my Ballet."

Neither in Paris did Diaghilev's temper improve, where we gave four performances at the Opéra on December 20th, 24th, 27th and January 3rd, which included our première of *Les Dieux Mendiants, Apollon, La Chatte, L'Oiseau de Feu, Petrouchka* and *Soleil de Nuit,* from *Snegourochka.* Meanwhile Serge Pavlovitch was becoming continually gloomier, detaching himself more and more from the Ballet. That short ballet "stretch" which had begun to set him afire in November was ended, and, as it seemed, forever.

The end of 1928 seemed filled with approaching thunder, with hurrying storm clouds, tense and electric—one's breath came with difficulty and the heart was oppressed: 1929 loomed on the horizon!

CHAPTER IV

THE LAST SEASON

NINETEEN-TWENTY-NINE. The last and tragic year of Diaghilev's life had begun, and with it the final and twenty-second season of the Russian Ballet. It began with difficulties, a sense of oppression; a feeling that it was doomed to be the last.

For February 4th I find the following note in my diary: "I predict that this will be the last season of 'Diaghilev's Russian Ballet.' Serge Pavlovitch is tired of it, is detaching himself, has lost all interest in it. The discovery of some old Russian book is of more importance to him than the production of a new ballet. Our hero, our Ilya Murometz, is no longer the same."

Serge Pavlovitch had spent his whole life in flaming, volcanic activity, in ever-recurring enthusiasms. His life had been that of the eternal wanderer, always in hotels, always public, and now in his fifty-seventh year he, the wanderer and tourist, felt wearied and alone, lonely as King Lear. And indeed there was much of the king about him, a majesty, a royal charm, a royal smile and ... a royal impotence.

His whole life had been spent surrounded by people. He could not, he would not, live in any other way, despite the bitter and ofttimes profound disillusion it brought in its train, despite his ill-health; and now in the last year of his life a void seemed to surround him.

He had cast off all his old friends. Of the friends of his youth and *The World of Art,* one only remained, Valetchka Nouvel, and of those made in Paris only two, Stravinsky and Picasso. But Picasso, whose wife was then exceedingly ill, he could see but rarely, while as for Stravinsky— that "genius" Stravinsky, who, after *Apollon,* he had presented with such pride and joy to the world—they had begun to drift wider and wider apart, that very *Apollon* and Ida Rubinstein's season being the main reasons.

Thus, Diaghilev was left with only his family, a Karamazov family, it is true, composed of myself, for I was his Alyosha Karamazov, Pavka (P. G. Koribut-Kubitovitch), Valetchka (V. F. Nouvel) and Boris Kokhno. Pavka and Valetchka were dear to Diaghilev, "But if one took their advice," as he said, "one might as well go straight to the cemetery." Pavel Georgievitch, a most excellent creature, was a first-rate nanny to whom I could always be entrusted, but in no way a help or adviser in matters of art. In addition, Serge Pavlovitch was at times irritated by the way in which he had constituted himself a sort of unofficial "attaché" to the Russian Ballet after his arrival from Russia. Nevertheless, he needed to have him about, feeling that Pavel Georgie-vitch would be available, not only as my nurse, but also as his; and that it would be comforting to have him about at the end of his days. Indeed, just before his death he sent for him, but Pavel Georgievitch could not manage to arrive in time.

Valetchka Nouvel, that old friend and one-time confessor and artistic adviser, eventually lost all his authority in Diaghilev's eyes for failing to keep abreast with what Diaghilev believed to be his *chefs-d'œuvre:* the *Sacre du Printemps,* and *L'Oiseau de Feu,* in which the former had "found no music." Neither had he been able to accept the constructivism of *Le Pas d'Acier,* and had strongly opposed establishing any connection with Soviet art. This was why Serge Pavlovitch had said of Ida Rubin-stein: "She listens to her Valetchkas, but lacks the small amount of talent it needs to pass over their heads. . . ." Leaving questions of art altogether aside, however, what was clear was that Serge Pavlovitch in the last year of his life, though not deliberately avoiding "that bosom friend" who had accompanied him through life, yet seemed to admit him less and less to that heart, which, caught in a tragic impasse, had closed to him as to others. . . . It may be that Serge Pavlovitch was seeking to hide, refusing to see, what he had only realized too late, the faults and errors, or rather *the error,* of his life, in which nothing took precedence of his own wish. Perhaps, too, Valetchka Nouvel sensed something of all this: or else had decided that his own peace of mind and philosophic tranquillity were more precious to him, for in 1929 we see him, though we do not know why, seeking, as it were, to remain aloof and indifferent to this inner drama in Diaghilev. On several occasions, even before this last and tragic year, I had observed a sort of triumphant, even mocking smile on Valetchka's face when anything happened likely to diminish Serge Pavlovitch in my eyes. Nevertheless, it must be said that Nouvel was very frequently of my mind, and that this was the only way in which he dared express his disagreement with Diaghilev.

Thus there was left my devoted, faithful self, who had vowed to be faithful to him to the end, in all humility, patience and obedience. Never-theless, my devotion, my faithfulness, inspired no confidence in Serge Pavlovitch; for he feared that very patience of mine. All it seemed to him was a sort of calculation, a watching for the propitious moment. . . .

This spiritual drifting apart stirred me profoundly. I did not realize how superficial, how fleeting, and indeed, how much the product of my own imagination it was. Nevertheless, the acute distress which it caused me was all too real. Still, I went on loving Serge Pavlovitch, and as was proved by later events, there had been no diminution in his love for me, though, absorbed as each of us was in his inner life, his own activities, no need arose for that profound mutual interchange which had so enriched our lives in the past. Serge Pavlovitch felt no need to express, and so assure me of, his feelings; and I, by then, should have known how much he disliked revealing himself. But I "minded" Diaghilev's apparent diminution of interest in me, his incuriosity about my life, and paid no heed to what might be happening inside him.

It was a year that ushered itself in, for him, with great spiritual and physical fatigue, a profound apathy and indifference to all things. His whole desire seemed to be to remove himself, as far as possible, from the bustle and noise of the stage to the peace and calm of his books.

However, his nature being what it was, fatigued and ailing though he might be, Diaghilev still continued to seek for new men, new ideas: a search that came to fruition in the discovery of a young musician "genius," Igor Markevitch, then still a pupil at the *lycée*.... Yet complementary, as it were, to this urge towards new things, something was pulling Diaghilev back into the past, to long forgotten enthusiasms, the memory of old friends, reminiscences of childhood and youth.

I well remember the visit we paid Nijinsky in January of that year, a visit motivated by Serge Pavlovitch's impossible dream of restoring that great dancer to normal existence. At the time Romola Nijinsky was in America and so it was necessary to get the required permission from Nijinsky's sister-in-law, Tessa Pulszka.

As we journeyed to the mental home in Passy I was overcome by a longing to turn back, such was my embarrassment and anxiety. I feared we might do some irreparable harm by thrusting ourselves into that life which had ceased to belong to this world, and questioned my right to seek out that which could only inspire me with terror and dismay. Surely, I thought, it would be best to return immediately to my own active, normal life.

However, when we reached Nijinsky's flat, what struck me most was the hospital atmosphere, the hospital smells, and particularly the hospital silence—that deathly silence—in which the servants were wandering about in white overalls, like hospital attendants. Our hostess happening to be out, the servant said he would "announce" our arrival, though I realized all he wanted was to make sure that Nijinsky was in a fit condition to receive us. As the servant entered his room, no, not his room, but a prison cell, I saw, through the half-open door, a man reclining on a low, very wide mattress, clad only in a loose open dressing gown and a pair of stockings. And there he lay all through our visit with legs crossed and outstretched, either biting his nails till the blood came, or somewhat affectedly playing with his wrists.

Meanwhile, the servant had gone up to Nijinsky, telling him that some friends had called, and would like to see him; whereupon, in a voice as calm as that of a sane and normal person, we heard him reply: *"Faites entrer!"*

We entered. The moment I crossed the threshold all my uneasiness vanished, leaving me only with a feeling of strong compassion for an unhappy fellow creature. Going up to him, I put my lips to his hot hand. For a moment his eyes glowered at me from under the knitted brows, with the wild, suspicious glance of a hunted animal, then quite suddenly, a wonderful smile lit up his face: a smile so kindly, so childishly pure, so luminous and undimmed, that I fell utterly under its charm.

For the first few moments he paid no attention to Diaghilev whatever, but soon it became clear that, with every minute we stayed, he was growing more and more conscious of his presence, as though indeed some chord of recollection had been struck, for, from time to time, like a normal person, he appeared to be listening intently to what Diaghilev was saying. But when Serge Pavlovitch told him that I was a dancer also, Serge Lifar, and that I loved him, Nijinsky, he said abruptly, on a questioning note:

"Loves me?" These were, however, the only words he said in Russian, for everything else was said in French.

"Yes, Vatza, he loves you, and so do I, and all of us, as ever.'"

Whereupon Nijinsky began laughing, and responded: *"C'est adorable!"*

Diaghilev then began to talk about dancing, hoping that memories of the past might rouse Nijinsky to a sense of reality and his own achievements, when dancing had been his whole universe. But the latter listened indifferently, though some associative process must have been going on in his mind, for he suddenly looked at me with perplexed curiosity, and even apprehension, as though trying to understand who I might be. And again, Serge Pavlovitch said I was a dancer, and had specially come to greet him, the great dancer. At this the muscles in his face began to quiver, just as they had always done whenever he saw other dancers who seemed likely to threaten his fame. This was not, however, envy, but that instinctive, insuperable urge which arose in him to surpass what he saw and move on always to greater achievements.

"Il saute?" suddenly and rather startlingly cried Nijinsky, at which the set muscles of his face relaxed, and he laughed that wonderful adorable laugh, a laugh so appealing, so gentle, that it masked completely the withered, ageing, pitiful body. Diaghilev went pale. That unexpected note of interrogation in Nijinsky's cry, a suddenly resuscitated Nijinsky, frightened him; but immediately, making an effort to master his emotion, he began saying:

"Mais oui, Vatza, il saute: il saute très bien, tu le verras!"

And at that an inspiration flashed through his mind; he would take Vazlav to the Opéra, for that very day *Petrouchka* was being given, in which Karsavina, his own former partner in his favorite rôle, would be dancing. According to Diaghilev, his only object was to get Nijinsky photographed with the cast of this ballet, but by the way his eyes had lit up, I could see how much he was expecting, a very miracle in fact. Once at the Opéra, amid scenes so intimately evocative of his life, of all he had lived for, what else could happen? Meanwhile, Madame Pulszka having returned, Diaghilev made his suggestion, which was accepted with alacrity, as though she too had been infected by the hope in Serge Pavlovitch's sad eyes.

By the way in which Nijinsky was looking at Diaghilev it seemed obvious that, by now, he was well aware of his identity. It was clear, too, that it pleased him to see us in those dreary rooms, where such a visit was an important event; for, in the two years that his wife had now been absent in America, no one had ever come to visit him. Thus, he was forgotten and alone, with all the heavy thoughts he could neither clarify nor solve for himself.

Now we began to prepare him to go out. When I asked him to get up he did so with pleasure, whereupon I was amazed by the seeming short-ness of his stature. He got up rather strangely also, first sliding from his mattress on all fours, and only then rising to his feet. Generally speaking, it seemed to me he was diffident of getting too far away from the floor— even his mattress lay on it—and that he felt a need for support. When he walked, it was with a floorward stoop, as though he could only really feel comfortable when lying down. Diaghilev measured us, and I turned out to be taller by half a head. His legs were those of a great dancer, with immense globular muscles, though so flabby now that one wondered how they could possibly support his body. Then we took him to the bathroom, where I ministered to him as though to a child, and by the power of my will made him obey me. While I shaved him with a some-what inefficient Gillette, he sat patiently, making faces or smiling a kind, gentle smile; but he was obviously afraid of the servant, and looked very much scared when the latter began cutting his hair.

Altogether we stayed with Nijinsky for a couple of hours. Then at nine I returned, to take him to the theater, for I had plenty of time before my own appearance in the last ballet, *Petrouchka,* in which I was dancing the part of the negro.

When I went in Nijinsky was sitting in a strained attitude with a dull upward stare. I was leading him downstairs by the arm, in a mutual silence, when suddenly he said:

"Faites attention!"

Apart from that short sentence he said nothing. He had retired into himself, had shut out the world, and I no longer existed for him. He got quietly into the car, and sat perfectly still all through the drive to the theater.

As I led him by the arm across the stage, I could feel a nervous tremor in my muscles. Serge Pavlovitch and Rouché met us, led us to a box, and there Diaghilev stayed with him all through the performance. Nijinsky looked at the house and the stage—the first ballet was in progress—but he was not with us. Outwardly, he gave the impression of someone entirely absorbed in some deep, grave, besetting thought, which made him oblivious to all around him. What was he thinking? I do not know; indeed, who could? But what I do know is that he was somewhere far, far away, and quite unaware that he was in a theater.

Soon it was known that Nijinsky was present, and during the intervals various people came to pay their respects, to greet, and speak to him. However, he continued to remain utterly unresponsive, stared upwards, and answered with gentle, kind, yet dull, inarticulate words. In the second entr'acte, just before *Petrouchka,* Nijinsky was led on the stage, and photographed with us all: Karsavina "the Ballerina," I "the Negro," on the right; Diaghilev, Benois, Grigoriev and Kremnev on the left; and in the midst, unaware of it all, one who till late had been a divinity. When the camera was focused on him, reacting to an ancient reflex, he smiled as he had always smiled in the days of his triumph.

The photographs being taken, he returned to the box, but now, as Diaghilev told us later, quite flushed and hot. Finally, the ballet being over, he was asked to put on his overcoat in readiness to go home, but *"Je ne veux pas!"* he said, and had to be led out by force....

On February 10th, 1929, I find myself writing to my permanent correspondent, Pavel Georgievitch, from Bordeaux, during our first visit to that town:

". . . As you see, with God's help, Serge Pavlovitch is in a good mood and keen on work. He is enthusiastic about his twenty-second season, and very busy with preparations for it. I myself am feeling exceedingly well, and pleased with my 'cup of life,' now full to the brim. I practise a lot, the work makes good progress, and I feel that though my shoulders are weak, they will be adequate to support this season. As you know, practically the whole weight falls on me. I often attend concerts, and nearly every night visit the theater or cinema, which latter attracts me more than ever. I live in an atmosphere of warmth, contentment with the present; it is all dear, peaceful and good. The future seems unclouded and full of hope . . . I have everything, it seems . . . my 'cup is full' . . . and yet, a vague anxiety oppresses me, a sadness which will not allow me to feel at one with life, or those about me, and which separates me from our 'family.' God grant that it be only imagination! How often I recall our dear and peaceful conversations in Milan. I miss you keenly . . . with you here, how much more hopeful, confident and stable everything would seem."

Two days later it became clear that my sadness and anxiety were no mere passing mood, but a vague dark premonition foreboding the wrong that would be done to me.

Not for nothing was I unable to feel at one with our little family, or had the sensation that something had risen between; something that turned out to be premeditated, and indeed a stab in the back. For many

On the Stage at the Paris Opéra, 1929

Kremnev, Benois, Grigoriev, Karsavina, Diaghilev, Nijinsky, Lifar

matters at this time were being discussed unknown to me, their sole object being to widen the rift between Serge Pavlovitch and myself.

Now Diaghilev, yielding to persuasion, decided to re-engage Dolin, and had the "Englishman" sent for. Nothing was said to me, no one asked my opinion, and, principal dancer to the company though I was, I only heard of it on the dancer's arrival. Small wonder, then, that our company, and Paris, began buzzing with rumors, "I was leaving the Ballet," "my star had set," "the 'Englishman' was superseding me." And indeed, such was the degree to which these rumors were credited that my arrival in Monte Carlo to dance as usual might have been called almost sensational.

On February 13th I wrote to my old, and only remaining friend, Koribut-Kubitovitch: "That depression about which I wrote you three days ago, that vague discomfort which seems to have dogged me of late, turns out to have been a premonition. That subconscious inner self of mine, which has never deceived me, that secret and greater self, greater than my I, greater than my conscious understanding, seems to have been living in hourly expectation of bitterness and scorn, and now both have descended on me, and it is as though I had died, as though all that was deepest and most sacred in me had been murdered, and as though the faith I had built up through so many years, in our family, had at one moment been scattered to the winds. My friends are gone, and now I realize they were never mine, that we were just creatures which circumstance had momentarily brought together. . . . It is not my pride that is hurt, nor my self-love, but something deeper has been cruelly, painfully wounded by the engagement of this Englishman. I repeat, it is not any false pride that is hurt, but something of which I might justly be proud, the better part of myself, the mainspring of all my creative activity, all my heroic efforts in the arts, that urge which inspired me with the strength to sustain the whole Ballet with my own feeble forces, when everyone of our principal dancers had left us. As witness the season, when neither Massine, Idzikowsky, Slavinsky, Dolin or Vilzak were with us.

"You know, and *they* too know it, whether they admit it or not, that everything of which I was capable, I gave to the Russian Ballet; they cannot ignore the fact that, though I had broken my ankles, still I went on in *Flore et Zéphyre* rather than let it down.

"Outwardly, everything will remain unchanged. I shall go on as before, even though I shall smile more seldom. But from now on my heart will be locked. This ordeal has not destroyed me, for I feel strong and sure, positive I am entering a new stage in my life. I shall build up my life anew, but this time in solitude, and for myself only.

"And yet, if you only knew what agony it is to carry about in my heart the realization of a truth that no other, possibly, understands. The truth that *the impossible is possible, and only achievement is transitory.* Ah, how unhappy I am, dear Pavel Georgievitch."

Soon, however, great happiness befell me, though not unmingled with
a certain bitterness.

It was in Paris, some few days later. Serge Pavlovitch, Nouvel and I
were discussing our program for the spring.

"We've two 'creations,'" said Diaghilev. "*Le Bal* and *Le Fils Prodigue,*
but we must absolutely have a third. I don't want to entrust any more
ballets to Balanchine, he's only with us a few more days now; I'll soon be
sending him packing. So what's to be done?"

Whereupon there followed a frigid silence. But then, addressing me,
Serge Pavlovitch continued:

"After all, Seriozha, couldn't you try to do us a ballet? I used to have
great hopes of you once as a choreographer."

"Used to have great hopes!" Had he abandoned them, then; had he
forgotten all my ambitions?

His words wounded me deeply, not so much by what they said, as by
the tone in which he said them. It sounded so indifferent, so cold, as
though it hardly mattered to him or myself, when in fact it was a
matter of the deepest moment to me, something which had been my
consuming ambition all through the four years since my first timid
efforts in *Flore et Zéphyre.*

But Diaghilev went on listlessly turning the leaves of his notebook,
looking for some ballet he might possibly revive.

"Ah, here's something ... Stravinsky's *Renard*. We could do *Renard*.
Well, Lifar, can you or can't you do this ballet? Would you like to have
a try?"

His tone, as I say, wounded me deeply. Was this the way to talk to
me of something round which all my creative fire, all my burning
ambitions, had so long centered? But sternly controlling any sign of
feeling, I replied with an equal indifference:

"Well, I don't mind trying, if that's your wish, and you think it
might interest you."

After which we went off to lunch at a near-by restaurant.

That, then, was how I turned "choreographer." It marked a new stage
in my life. For me, however, there was naught of love, solemnity or the
sacred tremors of friendship, to meet me on the threshold—earnestly and
heartfully though Diaghilev might love to inaugurate in this way each
new phase or landmark in the life of his friends.

How different it had all been in 1924, when he so ardently assured
Nijinska that a great future as dancer and choreographer awaited me,
when he told me I should study Italian painting, live in an atmosphere
of art, acquire all the knowledge I could, to refract it again through the
prism of my creative genius. But then his faith in my creative genius had
been strong. Then, too, it was, he had urged me, prematurely as it proved,
to try my hand at *Flore et Zéphyre*. Before *Zéphyre* I had only dreamed
that some day I might become a creator, yet my first attempts, timid

though they were, gave me confidence that some day I should emerge as chore-author. I therefore went on studying in secret (no one knew of it, save Diaghilev, for often, alone in his presence, I would work out dance steps and variations), certain the day would come when I should either prove myself a master-choreographer, or be forced to relinquish my aspirations for ever. Now the day had arrived, chill and overcast.

During lunch Diaghilev, coldly confident of my approval, suggested that my name, as choreographer, should be included in the season's posters.

"No, not yet, Serge Pavlovitch, let me think it over. When I've gone through the score I'll give you a definite answer. It will take only a few days now, and then I'll let you know definitely whether I feel able to accept your offer!"

I took the score, studied it, and almost immediately conceived the idea of constructing the ballet round two parallel themes, one expressed in dancing, the other acrobatically. My idea was so to build up the movements and develop them as to create a sort of skyscraper of dancing, in line with Stravinsky's music and Picasso's cubism. I told Diaghilev how I saw it, and he fully concurred. But then Kokhno intervened, and began to argue that, though he considered the introduction of the acrobats a sound and happy idea, he nevertheless thought it undesirable to split the spectator's attention, and that therefore one should confine oneself solely to acrobatic action. Meanwhile Diaghilev was listening in silence, but suddenly he cut the discussion short by saying:

"It's no good arguing now. Let Seriozha work on his ideas, and give us a few illustrations for us to judge what it is he's driving at. Then we shall be in a position to discuss it. But you, Serge, don't listen to anybody, and follow your own artistic instinct."

I set to work, alone, in one of the studios of the Salle Pleyel, and after a few days' rehearsals had prepared my outlines of the dances of *Le Renard*. At times I was on the verge of despair, so isolated did I seem. Hope as I might for aid, no one came to my assistance, no one offered the least moral support.

On February 23rd Diaghilev said he would look in next day to see what progress I was making, a moment I awaited with fear and trembling, for was it not to decide my whole fate? My critic would not be my "Kotushka," with whom so many "little talks" had united me through the past five years, but Diaghilev, the director of the Russian Ballet, the most eminent, the only great critic and arbiter of twentieth-century art; that Diaghilev who was both wizard and prophet. Should he disapprove, it was my sentence of death so far as art was concerned: should he approve, a great future, a rich creative existence would open in front of me. And the fact that this critic was my best and only friend did nothing to allay my fears. For I knew that, whatever verdict he pronounced, it would be utterly dispassionate; that neither for pity, love, nor any regard of the links that bound us, would he hide the truth from me. Even though my failure, my shame would be his, he would make no attempt to veil it from himself: that I knew better than anyone.

On the twenty-fourth, as arranged, he came to the Salle Pleyel, and there approved the outlines of the dances I demonstrated to him, though he expressed no particular enthusiasm or praise. Next day he returned, this time, however, following my work with more interest and approval. Finally, he declared he would reserve his final decision until March 1st. That would be my "Day of Judgment."

Now I gave myself up body and soul to the creative urge within me. Suddenly, I found myself in a world that was utterly new; a world which in feeling, thought, I never had known before. As though possessed, everything in me seemed at white heat, and as though I were burning with high fever. So keyed up were my mind and senses, so fiercely did they burn, that at times terror would overtake me, for it seemed the mind could not endure such strain, must burst, or suffer some incalculable change which, spelling delay in the production of the ballet, must bring catastrophe in its train. I was terrified I might die before the ballet was completed . . . oh, if only I could see it through!

But what if I were unable to complete it; what if the artists proved incapable of expressing that with which I was brimming over, that which, with such urgency, demanded expression in me? If that were the case I should hate myself forever, I should abandon dancing, all hope of success, become a wretched weak-willed outcast, and sink back once more into nothing.

I was burning with creative fire, and yet I was deeply wounded, offended, by the way "they" (my family) behaved. Little did they care what I might be doing, feeling or thinking. Sometimes I would hear them laughing together in the next room, and then the tears would start to my eyes, and I would clench my teeth with fury, and the effort to restrain myself from entering the room and breaking up their comfortable lives and laughter.

On March 1st my "Day of Judgment" arrived, and, angry and with no hope of success, I made my way to the studio. My "judges" were Diaghilev, Larionov, who had designed the sets, and Kokhno.

Helped by an accompanist at the piano, I sketched out my dances for *Le Renard* . . . but not one answering word or movement came, and nothing broke the stony silence. To rest myself and recuperate my powers (or rather to summon up new strength) I went out to the dressing rooms, from which I heard a heated discussion immediately break out. Listening intently, I could hear Serge Pavlovitch's raised and protesting voice . . . the words of which still ring in my ears.

"Since the *Sacre du Printemps* . . . simply unbelievable. . . ."

On which I returned, and demonstrated another fragment. But now my mood had completely changed, and my knowledge of the satisfaction felt by Serge Pavlovitch made me jubilant.

As we were returning by taxi Diaghilev addressed me, and declared:

"I shall have your name put on the posters, I shall give you the best artists and *carte blanche* for the production. What you showed us was excellent and very important."

Thereupon I set to work in earnest.

Though everyone had left for Monte Carlo, I stayed on in Paris for a few more days to utilize the opportunity of working in peaceful surroundings, and the joy of creation made me somewhat forget my trouble of mind. Indeed, such was the faith in myself which it gave me that I was even at times alarmed.

Meanwhile, Serge Pavlovitch seemed to live in the train between Monte Carlo and Paris. Sometimes he would look in at my rehearsals, express his pleasure and say, "Excellent, remarkable," and depart as though fearful of being drawn into discussion. Wider and wider seemed to grow the distance between us, though he was kindness itself to me and my ballet, and seemed exceedingly moved when I dedicated this, my first choreographical work, to him, my maestro. Then, at the end of March, I too reached Monte Carlo, and began to rehearse with the rest of the cast.

The news that I had been entrusted with the choreography of the new ballet was received with the greatest kindness, and the whole company followed the progress of our work with the friendliest interest. Mainly I worked with Woizikowsky (Fox) and Yefimov (Cock), and was delighted with their efforts. To this day I hold them in grateful remembrance, for both (but especially Woizikowsky) answered my every demand with such ease and promptness, so justly appreciated and executed my ideas, and so true and comradely was the spirit in which they sought to ensure our success, that every rehearsal was a great joy to me and helped to lighten the depression into which I had sunk. Thus the work made excellent progress, helped by the company's whole-hearted support.

About this time Diaghilev appeared at one of the rehearsals, accompanied by Rouault, Stravinsky and Prokofiev, and in his pride at my achievement began to say how fortunate he considered himself to have the co-operation of such talented young forces, and so excellent a new ballet master.

Later, he began to talk of two new ballets he intended to commission Markevitch and Hindemith to write, for which I was to provide the choreography. The latter's work he particularly admired.

On April 4th we began what was to prove our last ballet season in Monte Carlo, and on May 12th it came to an end. The whole season had proved brilliantly successful, and the program had been both varied and impressive. It had included the new Kokhno-Rieti-Chirico-Balanchine production *Le Bal,* performed on May 7th, which enjoyed a remarkable reception.

On the thirteenth the whole company left for Paris in good time for the season which, on the twenty-second, opened with two new productions, *Le Fils Prodigue* and *Le Renard*.

This season got under way with Diaghilev in both lethargic and difficult mood. At one moment he would be all aflame and full of his old activity, but the next he would be cold, inert, apathetic. It was clear he was far from satisfied with *Le Fils Prodigue* as it revealed itself at rehearsals. Somehow, the ballet refused to take shape, and the work progressed lethargically, with myself possibly the most indolent of any. Before *Le Renard* I had always worked closely with Balanchine, and had done my best to help him, but now all my energies were absorbed by my own creativity. As a result I contributed nothing, and confined myself to merely attending rehearsals. Meanwhile, our slow progress added considerably to Serge Pavlovitch's depression. Time and again he would refer as though casually to this ballet, and try to draw me into conversation about it. It was as though he were seeking to prompt, to influence me in some way.

"I say, Seriozha, don't you think it might be possible to put more life into the way *Le Fils Prodigue* is being interpreted?"

Or: "Don't be afraid to put more feeling into the part of *Le Fils Prodigue*. And don't be afraid to dramatize it, either, if you see it that way."

I confess, I was profoundly astonished to hear Diaghilev talk to me thus, so strong in the past had been his opposition to all dramatization, to anything "intense" in our miming.

Nevertheless, I maintained my silence and refused to be drawn, and Serge Pavlovitch would leave me distressed.

For this ballet the sets and costumes had been confided to Rouault, whom Diaghilev had earlier prevailed upon to join us in Monte Carlo. Rouault stayed with us a month, a month mostly occupied in lengthy discussions upon art. Thus, when it was time for the painter to return to Paris, it was suddenly discovered that practically nothing had been done. Luckily, the situation was saved by Diaghilev himself; for, persuading the hotel management to unlock Rouault's door, he thus gained access to the painter's sketches, and from these was able to choose the sketch for the first scene of the ballet. The second—the tent scene—he designed himself, and, managing to find Rouault, set him to work on it the same day. After which he busied himself with the costumes, and in developing such preliminary sketches as were ready.

Generally speaking, the production caused us all much trouble and disappointment. Prokofiev was very dissatisfied with it, and his relations with Balanchine proceeded from bad to worse. Meanwhile Diaghilev had heard that Balanchine was secretly helping Pavlova to prepare her ballets, and that he was also negotiating with Balaieff. The upshot was that Diaghilev finally decided not to renew Balanchine's contract (this was canceled at the end of the season) and to transfer everything to his new ballet master—myself.

Troubled and depressed, Diaghilev took his new ballets to Paris... and our own spirits, too, were but little better. Then, on the morning of the dress rehearsal, having as usual spent the night at the theater, supervising the final details, Serge Pavlovitch came to me, and for the first time begged, nay, implored, me to help him.

"Seriozha, I beg of you, please save my twenty-second season in Paris. Never yet have I had a failure, but now I feel we might, if you will not consent to help me, if you go on refusing to treat *Le Fils Prodigue* more dramatically, as it should be treated, instead of in this cold academic manner. I am relying absolutely on you, Seriozha!"

That day at lunch I drank a good deal, and spent the rest of the day in a state of exaltation and over-excitement. Then, after the rehearsal, accompanied by Pavel Georgievitch, I returned to the Hôtel Scribe, at which, with Diaghilev, we were staying.

In the evening a telephone message came from Serge Pavlovitch to say he would not be returning before the performance, that I was to go to the theater with Pavel Georgievitch, and would we send on his dress clothes by Kokhno? All this was most unusual, for our departure for a first night had always been treated with the utmost solemnity, and we would always prepare for it as though about to set out on some lengthy journey, all sitting down in silence for a few moments. Then Serge Pavlovitch would get up, embrace me and make the sign of the cross over me. Whereas now!... Had he really been prevented from coming, or had he wished not to do so, seeing that all the last days he had avoided me so sedulously? Or was it, just, that he now felt the whole procedure to be pointless and futile?

I, however, went to bed, declaring to Pavel Georgievitch:

"I can't go to the theater today. I don't feel I'm in sympathy with the part of the Prodigal Son, and so I'm afraid I may turn it into a failure. I can't understand what sort of way they want me to treat the part. Let them act it themselves. I can't, and I don't want to, and prefer to stay here at home. Even if it is a failure, they can't blame me."

Pavel Georgievitch was dumb with terror. However, he made no attempt to reason with me, knowing that persuasion would only increase my obstinacy. All he knew was that it was not sheer caprice or obstinacy on my part. Picking up a paper, he sat quietly at my side, though glancing from time to time at his watch, and occasionally at me over his paper.

"You know, Seriozha, it will soon be half-past seven."

I remained silent, motionless. Another quarter of an hour passed, and Pavel Georgievitch could stand it no longer.

"Seriozha, my darling, do make an effort. Dress and let's go to the theater."

"I can't go...."

Eight o'clock ... five past ... ten past ... Pavel Georgievitch had gone as white as a sheet, as though slowly dying of anxiety. I was looking at him. Suddenly I began to fear he might have a stroke. I wanted to rise if only for his sake, but something made it impossible for me to do so. Some force, obstinacy, or consternation at what I was doing, seemed to be pinning me down.

A terrific struggle was going on inside me. Somberly, sadly, I thought of Serge Pavlovitch, he who was my spiritual father, and of our relations together. I thought of the past, that life I had offered up as a sacrifice to him, uselessly and so unnecessarily. Why? To what end? Then visions out of the remote past came thronging round me. I saw myself in Kiev, on my father's threshold, returning from my first, unsuccessful effort, to fly abroad ... I, a prodigal son, waiting for dawn to dare enter my home.... The love, tenderness and care Serge Pavlovitch had lavished on me, the manner in which, through him, I had become an artist; all, all rose before me again, and a feeling of intolerable poignancy, of pity for the ailing, weary, aged old man—for suddenly he had begun to seem much older—sent a wave of endless commiseration pulsing through my being. Was it possible I could betray him? ...

The memory of things past, my sudden vision of the old man, merged into one image of ... The Prodigal Son. I *am* that prodigal son of his.... In my ears there sounded Prokofiev's music. Suddenly I saw light, I began to understand. From out of the depths of chaos and turmoil emerged the creative instant of clear and calm perception.

I leaped out of bed.

"Let's be off to the theater. I have created my Prodigal Son.... It is myself."

In all haste we reached the theater, and in a few moments I was ready. I danced *L'Après-Midi d'un Faune,* but Serge Pavlovitch was nowhere in sight. Then came *Le Renard;* but search as I might, I could see no trace of Diaghilev. The ballet proved an immense success and received a veritable ovation, to loud cries of Stravinsky, Stravinsky, Lifar. Stravinsky took the call with the artist and bowed. But the calls for Lifar went on increasing, drowning the applause. Stravinsky hurried out to fetch me, and strove to draw me on the stage ... but I refused to follow him.

"If you do not come now, I swear you'll make an enemy of me for life!"

"I refuse absolutely!"

At this the whole cast began to applaud me and try to force me to take the call, but in spite of Grigoriev's agitation and peremptory "Lifar, go out immediately," I steadfastly refused, and clinging to an iron bar, finally succeeded in having my way.

An interval followed, succeeded by *Le Fils Prodigue.* And still Serge Pavlovitch remained undiscoverable. At last we reached the final scene. I was as though possessed, ecstatic, practically improvising the whole

Le Renard, 1929

scene. It was myself I was acting, I was that Prodigal Son, it was I whose faith in his friends was shattered, I who had been abandoned, and left weary and alone to the torments created by those in whom I had so blindly, childishly, placed my faith.

Everything through which I had lived in the past six months, the solitude, the anguish, the suffering and disappointment, I, as though under a spell, dramatically, plastically, enacted, in my five or six minutes on the stage. It was more than acting: it was my life itself flung there on the stage. I had acted as never before, and as I shall never act again.

When the curtain went down, pandemonium broke loose. Numbers of people were crying, though no one had realized it was my self, my life, that had been enacted. Only the great soul of one man might have suspected it.... He! And that man was possibly not even in the theater. But where could he be? Perhaps disgusted with my performance in *Le Renard* he had gone from the theater and not even seen my Prodigal Son.

Meanwhile Valetchka Nouvel had burst into my dressing room, and embracing me warmly was crying:

"Bravo, Lifar, wonderful, terrific!"

My dressing room was full of people, many of the women had arrived in tears, everyone was congratulating me, embracing me, clasping my hands, but still there was no sign of Serge Pavlovitch....

I began to take my make-up off, and only then did I perceive Serge Pavlovitch in a corner, masked by the crowd. Everything turned over inside me, to see him stand there so motionless and make no attempt to approach me while heavy tears fell from his eyes. Had I hurt him? Was he mourning for me? It was not emotion, it was rather some terror which moved me, and a great anxiety took possession of my soul.

If Serge Pavlovitch stays there, I thought, if he continues to avoid me, it can only mean he is ashamed of me for sacrificing my art to a personal triumph, for barnstorming, for revealing all the pettiness of my nature. In that case, everything's over. Now there is no alternative for me but to bid farewell to Diaghilev and the Ballet.

Then Serge Pavlovitch moved slowly out of his corner and towards me. Only then did he realize I was at the end of my nerves, in a state of feverish exaltation. But still he said nothing to me, though he asked my visitors to leave the dressing room. I know now that Diaghilev had given strict orders that no one was ever to enter my dressing room, and had even quarreled with Maurice Rostand one day on that very account. Only Valetchka Nouvel and Abel Hermant stayed on—for the latter liked sitting about with me, and was a privileged intruder.

I finished removing my make-up and by degrees began to grow calm. Then I heard from Nouvel that Serge Pavlovitch had gone off to *Les Capucines,* and was expecting me for supper. But somehow I could not decide, fearful lest, perhaps, he might reprove me in public! How deeply

I repented my "play-acting" and cursed myself for always doing the wrong thing.

Finally Nouvel and I departed for the restaurant. There it was as difficult as ever to push a way in, so crowded was it—as always—after a first night. However, I was immediately greeted with cries of approval, admiration. But still I felt downcast, and heavy-hearted sat myself opposite Diaghilev in the seat of honor between Misia Sert and Chanel. "What's the matter, Lifar?" they said, seeing my drawn face.

"Oh, it's nothing ... only, I feel very tired...."

Champagne was brought, I raised my glass, and gazing at Diaghilev, said:

"I beg to raise this glass to you, Serge Pavlovitch, and your twenty-second season. And whatever may have happened to others," I went on, as though in apology, "no doubt could exist as to your success...."

Serge Pavlovitch raised his glass, gazed at me for some time and then his eyes dimmed with tears:

"Thank you, thank you, Seriozha. You are a great, a true artist. There is nothing more I can teach you ... I can only learn from you now...."

Meanwhile, the season at the Sarah Bernhardt Theater continued to enjoy the same brilliant success. But the very last performance of all left me with a most disagreeable impression. It was June 12th, and as was his custom, Diaghilev, the performance over, left for *Les Capucines* while I, with Tchelichev and Kokhno, remained behind to remove my make-up. Dressed at last, I was reaching up to pull down the portfolio of Rouault's rough sketches presented to me by Diaghilev, which were lying high on a cupboard, when a mirror, placed by someone on top, suddenly dropped on my head, and crashed to atoms at my feet.

"That settles it! We shall never play in this theater again ... it's our last performance."

Immediately we set to work to collect the pieces, hoping to ward off ill-luck by throwing them into the Seine, and as a result were much delayed in reaching the restaurant.

"What's happened to you? Why so late? And why so pale, Seriozha?"

Whereupon I told him our adventure. As Diaghilev was profoundly superstitious and believed in every kind of sign and omen, this incident obsessed him for days, and his friends, in particular Nouvel, reproached me greatly for having told him. I, too, reproached myself bitterly, and especially because Diaghilev, at that moment, was afflicted with the huge boils which had first attacked him in Warsaw during that October visit of 1928.

A little before he himself left Paris, Serge Pavlovitch invited my elder brother and myself to dinner, *chez Cabassus*. But all through the meal his attention was entirely given to Vassili, whom he plied with questions on politics, life in Soviet Russia, his wanderings in Slavonic countries, and what he thought of me, his brother....

Day by day, the distance between Diaghilev and myself seemed to widen. I had grown up, was maturer, more myself and independent, but with it more morose. Besides, after that glorious burst in *Le Fils Prodigue,* a great loneliness possessed me, for Serge Pavlovitch was more and more engrossed with his most recent discovery—that new musician—who seemed to him on the verge of achieving something extraordinary. And indeed there was much that was remarkable in Igor Markevitch, not only for the rhythmic saturation and scant thematic content of his music, but because of his own musical immaturity. Full of a youthful—though shy—aggressiveness, proper enough to his sixteen years, the Stravinskys, the Prokofievs meant nothing to him, possibly because he knew little of their music, his only allegiances being Johann Sebastian Bach and himself, Igor Markevitch. It shocked us all to see how high was the opinion he held of himself, and the categorical manner in which he disposed of others. Diaghilev, however, claimed that with time and a profounder musical culture, all this would vanish. As so often before, he now dreamed of revealing all the riches of music to this boy, of ripening his taste and judgment, of converting him into a first-rate musician. How often would he not repeat: "My dear Igor, you should do all you can to acquire a musical culture. Then it will be easier for you to discover in yourself that true musical feeling which corresponds to today, and if God wills, to tomorrow."

To discover the man of tomorrow, to help him bring his gifts to fruition! Yet again we see Diaghilev surrendering to the seduction of that vision, which he had once described as being unable to live "without the hope of seeing in the dawn, the rays of tomorrow's sun." Markevitch, for him, was now the rays of that sun, but alas, there was to be no "dawn" for Diaghilev. That, he could sense himself, and a yearning grew in him to recover what had once been. But alas! now it was too late.

The season over, the Ballet left for its tour in Berlin and Cologne, and I remember there was a violent scene between Diaghilev and Nouvel in the former city. We had gone for a walk, and returning with some indignation, I thus addressed Serge Pavlovitch:

"Have you seen the posters?"

"No, what's the matter?"

"The matter is, that it seems I'm rated the last artist in the company. The town's all plastered with posters announcing the appearance of Woizikowsky, Idzikowsky, Dolin ... and Lifar!"

Whereupon Diaghilev sent for Nouvel, and such was the fury of his anger that a little more and Nouvel would have been flung out of the window. Kokhno, too, came in for a severe rating.

The Berlin performance proved immensely successful, and generally speaking, this season was one long triumph for Serge Pavlovitch ... though fated also to be his last.

From Berlin we went to Cologne, but unaccompanied by Diaghilev, who had left for London to prepare the forthcoming season. There in July we foregathered again, to be joined by Markevitch and Rieti, who had orchestrated the former's *Piano Concerto.* This season, presented at Covent Garden, and scheduled for a month (June 25th—July 26th), had Markevitch and myself for its high lights, and both our names are mentioned together in the last article Diaghilev was ever to write. It was written during a period of illness when Serge Pavlovitch was confined to his bed and is quoted on pages 330-4 of Book One.

This appreciation pleased me greatly, but I was under no illusions as to what had caused it, knowing full well that the London public had to be made familiar with Markevitch's name, and that my own, since I was clearly well known and a favorite, was introduced merely to give that of Markevitch more weight. On this occasion—for the first time in his life—Diaghilev, after the dress rehearsal, held a cocktail party, this too for Markevitch, and invited the Press and a number of influential society people.

Our joint première took place on July 15th, the program including my *Renard,* and Markevitch's *Piano Concerto,* but he was nervous, played badly and unevenly, and missed many of his entrances. Such was the success of *Renard,* however, and so thunderous the applause, that the orchestra could hardly be heard, and we all found it almost impossible to get on with our dancing. The performance over, I was presented with a gold crown of bays—the last present Diaghilev was ever to make me—which I piously cherish to this day. Then, late that night, Diaghilev gave a supper party at the Savoy "In honor of the ballet master and Markevitch."

All this time Diaghilev was becoming more and more deeply attached to the young composer, and now began to think of accompanying him on a trip to Salzburg.

Meanwhile Diaghilev was ill in bed, and suffering from his boils. Yet at moments he would appear in my dressing room—I now had the dressing room used by Chaliapin—sit down, and immerse himself in silence. Here it was that he would listlessly receive his visitors ... but the slightest effort tired him, it was difficult to rouse him out of himself, and even his momentary interest soon relapsed into indifference. His strength seemed visibly ebbing and it was obvious that his vital functions were declining.

I remember how pained he was at my refusal to dance *Le Spectre de la Rose.* Yet, when his friend the impresario, Wolheim, happening to be there, suggested:

"After all, Serge Pavlovitch, if Lifar refuses, why not let Dolin dance the *Spectre?*" he sharply retorted:

"Please do not try to teach me who is to dance," and so I never did dance this ballet.

Serge Pavlovitch's lassitude, his illness and our estrangement oppressed me deeply. Besides, I felt that he was only making a semblance of accepting me, that he was content with our superficial calm, fearful of outbursts and anxious to avoid any pretext for a frank talk. It was as though he was weighed down by his feelings, as though he knew all too well what difficulties, what gloom environed him, and how inevitable was his approaching end.

That season proved one long round of triumph, and the success of *Le Sacre,* in particular, gave Diaghilev immense joy. Because of his illness Diaghilev had decided to leave London before the others, having it in mind to consult Dr. Dalimier in Paris. I remember that the farewells were particularly moving, and how tenderly and at length he took leave of all the veterans of the company, particularly Kremnev and the faithful Vassili. With Grigoriev, however, he had fallen out. Tchernicheva and Balanchine were about to leave, and ten or so of the dancers. Some sort of reconstruction could be felt in the air, and thus the company dispersed with distinct feelings of alarm and apprehension. They were saying that Serge Pavlovitch's nerves had given way completely, that he had become quite impossible to approach.

On July 27th, feeling as though we had already lost him, we left for Vichy via Ostend, where we gave two performances. We had already arranged that we were to meet in Venice, and Diaghilev had promised to write so that we might both arrive on the same day.

In all, we gave four performances in Vichy—on July 30th, August 1st, 3rd and 4th. This last performance consisted of *Cimarosiana, Le Tricorne* and *La Boutique Fantasque,* and though we did not know it, proved to be the last performance in the twenty years of the annals of the Russian Ballet. With the final scene in which both I and Woizikowsky appeared, the Diaghilev curtain descended for the last time. Dolin had departed somewhat earlier, and thus was not dancing on this memorable night. Then the company dispersed for its usual vacation, Kokhno, as ever, going to Toulon, Nouvel with Stravinsky to the Cantal, and Koributut-Kubitovitch to stay in Paris.

Meanwhile Diaghilev had twice been visited by Dr. Dalimier (on July 25th and 27th) and following the second visit, wrote me as follows:

"Dearest, my congratulations on the end of your brilliant season in London. I am overjoyed with the success of *Le Fils Prodigue.* What flowers and bays! Who can possibly have sent them?

"I am leaving today at two. My health is better, but the wound not yet healed. Dalimier was dumfounded at the sight, and says I've had a lucky escape. Yesterday I signed for Spain, i.e., Barcelona. I think that ought to please you. Write me at Munich, Regina Palace.

"Embraces and blessings,

"Your friend S.D." (Follows a sketch of a cat—for so Diaghilev nick-named himself.)

"Be a good boy now you're turning six."

Dr. Dalimier had done his best to dissuade Diaghilev from going to Germany, urging the necessity for a serious cure; he also protested against the choice of Venice, for the humid atmosphere, he said, might exacerbate the boils, and lead to a fatal termination.

Nevertheless, refusing to heed Dalimier's warnings, Diaghilev left for Germany, to pick up Markevitch, as he had already arranged. Together they proceeded to Baden-Baden (July 28th—30th), Munich (July 30th—August 5th) and then to the Salzburg Festival. At Baden-Baden, the Princesse de Polignac met him by chance at a concert, and says she found a very changed man. There, too, he met M. and Mme. Nabokov, and "Though he looked a sick man," wrote the former, "it would have entered nobody's mind that the end was so near."

All this time Serge Pavlovitch pursued his bibliomania, visiting antique booksellers and making extensive purchases. He also met Hindemith and Richard Strauss, and the latter presented him with his score of *Elektra*. Chiefly, however, he spent his time consulting diverse specialists. At this period music had an extraordinary softening influence on him, and particularly the works of Mozart and Wagner. Not long before, Serge Pavlovitch would have attacked Wagner unmercifully, but at *Tristan and Isolde*, on August 1st, "burning tears gushed from his eyes." What moved him most, however, what gave him the deepest happiness at this time, was Tchaikovsky's *Sixth Symphony*. By now, too, Diaghilev had begun to find his young companion's immaturity in matters of music somewhat fatiguing, and the *cure musicale* not having succeeded, he felt too weary to make a new effort, rest, above all, being what he needed.

Now rest and quiet were his great longing, and the desire to be with old friends. On August 7th, we find him writing to Koribut-Kubitovitch, giving instructions in regard to the things he wished brought to him in Venice, including a bottle of Guerlain's Mitsouko, from the shop in the Champs-Elysées, at 100—150 francs. On the whole it is a business letter but we find in it the following sentences, "I have sent you a wire asking you to join me in Venice. I want very much to see you, particularly as I am still ill, and it would be a great boon for me to have you recuperating here also. The wound has healed over, but I'm now full of that beastly rheumatism, and it is giving me a great deal of pain."

"If Seriozha has not taken the parcel from Levin"[1] (the Church—Slavonic Gospel), "be sure to bring it with you.

"Impatiently expecting you,

"Yours, Serge D."

---

[1] An antiquarian bookseller.

No longer does he need others. The only people who matter to him now are his "Pavushka" and myself, his "dearest" as he addresses me from his bed of pain in touching letters and telegrams that beseech his "kitten" not to forget its old "cat."

I had myself not written to him for some time, when suddenly a veritable shower of telegrams descended on me. At once I dispatched a telegram to Munich, and Serge Pavlovitch almost immediately replied, in a letter dated August 2nd.

"Dearest, your telegram made me feel easier in my mind. I haven't, however, had the tiniest little note from you. Why didn't you write? Forgot, Kotja? Did you get my letter from Paris?

"The Hindemiths are very nice, but so far he's done nothing. But he's full of goodwill and hope. His *Cantata* is a strange piece of work, but you can see it was rushed, and the show that goes with it is pretty poor. I've seen masses of friends from Paris, not to mention Mme. de Polignac, Mme. Dubost, etc. My sustenance here is Wagner and Mozart. What geniuses, and how well performed here! Today, at *Tristan,* I shed bitter tears. Books take up a lot of my attention. Thank Boris for his first letter. It was alarming, but by the telegrams, everything seems to be right now.

"Don't forget your 'cat' who embraces and blesses you." (After which, in place of the signature, follows a sketch of a cat with its tail in the air.)

It was the last letter he was ever to send me; thenceforth, one telegram succeeded another.

On August 7th Serge Pavlovitch left Salzburg, and I, Paris, en route for Venice, where I arrived the following day. The moment I stepped from the train my eyes sought for him, but there was no Diaghilev. Troubled in mind, I had myself taken to the Lido, where I knew he was staying at the Grand Hotel. But I did not see him on the porch, waiting to greet me as was his custom. Then, looking up, I saw him waving from his window, an infinitely aged Serge Pavlovitch. Indeed, my first glance failed to recognize him, so terrible was the change which the past fortnight had wrought; for now he was pale with a waxen pallor, aged, enfeebled and bedraggled.[2] My heart fell, and I trembled. What could be wrong with Serge Pavlovitch?

Almost running I hastened to his room, and Serge Pavlovitch, curiously changed, clasped me with tears to his breast, and then with trembling hands touched my body as though assuring himself I was really present, so anxious had he been for my coming, such was his fear I would never arrive.

"What is it, Serge Pavlovitch, are you ill?"

"Yes, yes. I don't feel well at all, and the journey tired me dread-

[2] Serge Pavlovitch was always forgetting his ties, handkerchiefs, underwear in hotels. On this occasion he had left almost everything behind in Germany, and now lacked most necessities.

fully. Altogether I feel tired out, and terribly weak. The German trip was a failure; it took too much out of me altogether. Suddenly, for the first time, I felt a terrible pain in my back, and it's gone on, now almost a week, without interruption. I can't sleep, or move, or eat anything. I don't seem able to digest anything, and last week I swallowed a tooth, and now I'm afraid it may give me appendicitis. I was so tired out, I felt so bad, that when I tried to go down to meet my Kotja, I just couldn't do it—my knees gave way, and I couldn't walk. The German doctors say it's all rheumatism, but I'm afraid, I feel it's a lot more serious. But you, how are you?"

"How was I?" Full of pain and unspeakable terror to find Serge Pavlovitch in such a condition, and my heart went out in pity. But it was no longer for him—my only Serge Pavlovitch—but for a sick and ailing old man in his suffering, a feeling accompanied by a sort of half-felt repulsion, no doubt physical—as though for a corpse. That feeling harassed me to the day of his death. It was as if my own instinct of self-preservation had turned me into an automaton in order to deaden the anguish of my inevitable loss.

Hurriedly changing, I took him off to his doctor. The latter examined him carefully, listened to the tale of his woe, and ended by saying that nothing serious was the matter, that it was all due to rheumatics, overwork and the after-effects of the boils. Then jokingly, and with a slap on Serge Pavlovitch's bare back, he said that the boils were definitely healed now, advised leg-massage, and, above all, absolute rest. All this somewhat reassured Serge Pavlovitch, but not me. What terrified me was not so much his illness as his utter depression and nervous collapse. After leaving the doctor, however, we went off to the Piazza San Marco, where we spent the rest of the evening, Serge Pavlovitch sitting by me in a quiet and strangely beatific mood, though complaining constantly of his tiredness.

"How tired I am, Oh, *God,* how tired!"

Back at the hotel Serge Pavlovitch engaged a huge double bedroom, which he then begged me to share with him. Obviously, he was in panic fear of being alone, terrified that, if he remained alone, he would die, and in his fear clung to the idea that anybody with him would help to keep death at bay.

This was to be the first of my many long sleepless nights, for not until August 20th was I again to enjoy a whole night's uninterrupted rest. Meanwhile, the days dragged by, overcast, wearisome and oppressive. I had become a nurse, a sister-of-mercy, as I sat there for hours, massaging his legs, giving him medicine, or helping him get up and dress, for he could do neither without assistance. And every hour he seemed to grow weaker, a symptom which alarmed me more than all else. Diaghilev, too, was equally alarmed. Meanwhile, I was doing my best to hasten the arrival of Koribut-Kubitovitch and discover traces of Kokhno: when would they appear?

"Why do you sit here all the time," said Serge Pavlovitch one day, forcing me away to the beach to get some tennis, "as though I were dying?"—afraid though he was of being alone. Then, sometimes, I would allow myself to be persuaded and go, but only to hurry back in anxiety. And still the sky remained overcast, and never for a moment did I see the joyous sun of Venice.

Then, too, there were times when he would begin discussing the company's future, and the manner in which he hoped to reorganize the whole thing. At such moments he would declare that I was its new ballet master, in charge of the whole choreography. Yet, when I sought to withhold my consent, urging that he should again resort to Massine, he would say:

"No! With Massine, everything is finished for good and all. I am content with what was before, and what there is now."

And Serge Pavlovitch's thoughts would rove off to other friends, friends who had broken faith, to return to myself. Whereupon, with an infinite tenderness, and the phrase still rings in my ears, he would say:

"You are the best of us all: how grateful I am to you for everything." Did Serge Pavlovitch know, I wonder, did he ever realize, how, during these last fearful days, he was alone, utterly alone in the world: that throughout these days (but only then—and I was miserably to repent before his dead body) so estranged from him did I feel, that it was as though he no longer existed for me? True, I was prepared to do all in my power to save him, preserve his life, and more than ready to sacrifice not only my sleep but everything in my power that might have helped him. His sufferings were mine, I was unspeakably sorry for him, utterly wretched, but yet I was only his nurse: nothing linked me to him, a gulf existed between us. At times, it was as though his gaze turned to me imploring for friendship, real intimacy and feeling—but what could I do? Sometimes—especially at night—Serge Pavlovitch would recall the days of his youth, his student years, and say how that was the happiest time of his life. Then he would talk of how he had journeyed down the Volga, to the Caucasus, and weep, remembering that loveliest of Russian rivers, and how Levitan had painted it. He was yearning for his fatherland, the country he would never see again, the student years he could never relive, the youth he would never recapture, the rapturous days when the world lay at his feet, and life seemed full of magnificent promise and future fame. And tenderly and with affection he would remember the first visits to Italy, to Venice and Rome; those halting steps on the path to manhood.

Again the eternal wanderer, eternal creator, he relived his scattered existence and, could it all have been again, would have wished for a different life, more fixed and settled. He was afraid to die, and desired only to stave it off a little while longer, so deep was his anxiety to make amends for everything false and theatrical in his life, his actions. Possibly, at the last, he realized, too, his imperfections, that nothing lofty had ever guided his feelings, that he had never sought to control the blind urge of his own egotistical impulses, and possibly, too, for the first time, he was now repenting. Often he would draw me into long discussions upon music, as though they, too, might hold death at bay, and then he would speak in melting words, and gather comfort and strength from them. With tear-filled eyes he would recall Tchaikovsky's melodies, those trailing Russian melodies of ours, and then, profoundly affected, begin to sing to himself themes from the *Symphonie Pathétique,* and say, with tears in his eyes, that music had never produced anything finer than Tchaikovsky's *Sixth Symphony,* or Wagner's *Meistersinger* or *Tristan.*

"And what about your Glinka?" I said, Diaghilev having always admired and extolled Glinka above all other Russians.

"Glinka is something different. Yes, he's great, truly great, but his importance is national and historic, whereas Wagner and Tchaikovsky soar above nationality, they are universal, and will always remain so as long as men desire music, the greatest of the arts."

After which he would begin to hum bits of *Tristan,* utterly absorbed and carried away by the amorous longing of the second act, as though his soul were ready to abandon its fleshly trammels.

I remember how, after that horrible sleepless night of August 9th, Serge Pavlovitch, lying in bed in a state of intense nervous excitement, began singing aloud in that unattractive and inflexible, though incredibly strong, voice of his, and how for a long time he went on in this way, making the window-panes rattle—till at moments it was almost a yell—and I began to shiver with terror and apprehension.

But mostly his thoughts and his talk were of death.

"What do you think, Seriozha...? Surely I can't be going to die: is my illness really so dangerous?"

And I, I did my best to calm him, assuring him that no one had yet died of rheumatism, that his boils were quite healed, and that the doctors had not found anything wrong, or seriously the matter, with him. But what frightened me was to see the degree to which this man—in whom I saw all the great legendary figures of our past unshakable in soul and body—was terrified of death, and how with all the timidity of a woman he anxiously implored some new lease of life.

I remember another conversation. It took place on August 14th, towards nightfall, and after he had taken finally to his bed.

"I've still such a number of unfinished schemes, there's so much to be done, that I don't want to die: and yet, death seems near. Terrible thing, death! All my life I've been terrified of it—and always shall be— I think, even to the very last moment. And you, Seriozha, are you afraid of dying?"

"No, Serge Pavlovitch, though I love existence, I am prepared to die at any moment, prepared even to take my life, if necessary, and so depart of my own free will. Perhaps our generation is different from yours: we seem to want less and care less about what lies in the future. In any case, death does not frighten us, and we can look it stoically in the face. Say the word, and I will shoot myself now. . . . If there is any fear of death in me, that fear is metaphysical, impersonal, as it were; but I, my I, my being, is indifferent to it. What frightens me is the thought that there is an end to everything, but not that I myself may come to an end."

"How strange, how very strange! Yes, it's so clear that we belong to different generations, different periods, a different culture and beliefs." After a silence, he said in a very quiet voice: "Thank you, Seriozha, for coming to me in my most difficult moment. You knew everything and yet you came . . . *Serge, tu sais, tu mais dominé.*"

On August 12th Diaghilev took finally to his bed, never to rise. And from that moment, as it were, he began to burn up. Day by day his temperature mounted, soon, almost vertiginously. Where would it stop? On the morning of the twelfth his temperature was 98.6° Fahrenheit, and at 11, 99.7°. Next day it was 101.3° (in spite of the aspirin he was taking), on the fourteenth it was 103.1°; on the fifteenth and sixteenth it fell slightly, thanks to the effects of aspirin and quinine, on the seventeenth it rose again to 103°, on the eighteenth to 105° and during the night to 106°. Meanwhile Doctors Vittoli and Biduli were constantly in attendance—the latter visited him five times on the sixteenth—but were at a loss to explain why his organism was burning up in this way, and what steps were necessary to stop it. Several blood tests were made, but nothing could be gleaned from them.

At this point Boris Kokhno arrived, but Serge Pavlovitch barely recognized him, for he had greatly changed his appearance by shaving his beard. Indeed, Diaghilev hardly noticed he was present. And now he seemed to be raging with fever, was often delirious at night and suffered from choking fits. These nights, like that of the sixteenth, spent watching him with Kokhno, were terrible, for Serge Pavlovitch would begin sobbing aloud, then violently shout that he wished his bed changed and to be given mine. An old superstition in my family has it that when someone is ill and wishes to be put in another person's bed, it is a sure sign of approaching death. Profoundly superstitious as he was, Diaghilev must have known this legend, and for that reason his demand filled me with terror. I therefore absolutely refused to humor him, for—voluntarily or not—it seemed to me tantamount to murder.

"You're mad, Serge Pavlovitch, it's impossible. I refuse to allow it."

"No, no, I must have another bed," he would go on demanding with the utmost vehemence.

I remember how on the morning of the seventeenth, his temperature back at 101°, Diaghilev said he was feeling better, and bitterly regretted never having had a family of his own. He added:

"I know it, you are too different, you two; you'll never manage to get on together."

Later, Kokhno and I went down for lunch, after which we played ping-pong together and—for the first time—carried away by our game, made no effort to hurry back.... Suddenly a page boy handed me a message ... the last Diaghilev was ever to write ... in trembling, distorted characters:

"Tell the doctor my pulse is frightfully uneven. If he could only look in for a moment after lunch, he'd see."

Sending for the doctor we hastened to his room. But a fearful spectacle awaited us, for Serge Pavlovitch, choking, and with infinite effort, had crawled over the floor to my bed, which he had just managed to reach. He was trying to pull himself up on it, in spite of his fruitless efforts. He had evidently tried to reach the bell, to summon a valet to help him, but had overbalanced with the effort, fallen out of bed, and begun crawling to mine.

Then I realized that this was the end; that Serge Pavlovitch had himself gone out to meet it.

Yes, he had gone to meet it, in spite of his terrible fear. Two days before the end I remember he said to me:

"Do you think I may be going to die now, Seriozha?"

I remember, too, painful as it is to recall, another talk we had together.

"Tell me, Seriozha, if I'm taken to hospital, will you send me flowers?"

"No, I won't!" I answered abruptly.

Serge Pavlovitch was deeply hurt.

"And you, Boris?" he asked Kokhno.

"Why, of course; I shall bring you flowers every day!"

I could hardly go on enduring the horror of those sleepless nights, I was infinitely weary of my own enslavement to my feelings, and wrote to V. F. Nouvel urgently asking him to come.

Soon after a telegram arrived: *"Heureux arriver lundi 18 santé mieux,"* whereupon Serge Pavlovitch, smiling sadly, half jokingly said: "Pavel, of course, will be late, and arrive after I am dead...." He was right. Not knowing how serious it was, Koribut-Kubitovitch decided, as usual, that one day more or less "hardly matters" and so arrived only when all was ended. But others appeared, dear friends of his who, with their heartfelt compassion and loving kindness, helped to comfort his last conscious instants.

Quite unexpectedly, disembarking from the Duke of Westminster's yacht, Coco Chanel and Misia Sert arrived, and I was overjoyed, not only for Serge Pavlovitch's sake, but for my own.

Together they visited him and remained by his bed for an hour. But while the yacht was at sea so great was their anxiety for him that on the

Diaghilev's Cortège at Venice, August, 1929

evening of the eighteenth they returned. Serge Pavlovitch had not been expecting them, indeed he was in no condition to think, he was delirious and his temperature was over 105°; but when they appeared in their trim white clothes he recognized them at once and said:

"*Oh, comme je suis heureux!* How well white suits you, Misia, you must always wear it!"

Even when his speech had already left him, Serge Pavlovitch still cared about his personal appearance. Critically ill as he was, and in high fever, he insisted on wearing his plate and when, in his delirium, he would happen to lose it, instinctively he made infinite efforts to restore it to its place. To the very last he strove to appear clean and trim, and the neglected condition of his beard and whiskers worried him greatly.

Two days had elapsed between the visits of the ladies, and they were profoundly shocked to observe the vast change. On the sixteenth there had still been hope of recovery, for no really dangerous symptom had appeared. But now they decided to send for a German specialist, Dr. Martin, who, too, proved equally nonplussed to say what was wrong. According to him Serge Pavlovitch's illness was due either to acute rheumatism or, possibly to an attack of typhoid fever (for which the temperature curve with its steady rise seemed to provide some justification). A telegram was therefore sent to Dr. Dalimier, requesting a supply of antityphoid vaccine, impossible to obtain in Venice; and, in addition, a nurse from the American Hospital was engaged.

Just before sundown, at about seven, another great friend, Catherine d'Erlanger, appeared with some flowers.

"*Oh, Cathérine, que vous êtes belle, que je suis content de vous voir. Comme je suis malade—je suis très, très malade.*"

Tenderly, soothingly, Catherine d'Erlanger stroked his head, and under her caress he dozed off into oblivion. When, for the last time, he regained consciousness, his words to Misia Sert, sitting beside him, were "that she was his one true friend, the only one he had ever had." Then, surprisingly he added in Russian:

"It seems to me as though I'm drunk...."

Soon after, the doctor arrived, told us the crisis was approaching, and that provided his heart did not fail ...

"But be ready for the worst, his condition is grave, and there is really not much hope."

Meanwhile Serge Pavlovitch was oblivious to all things, and in his delirium only unintelligible sounds escaped from his lips. Then again he would groan aloud: "Ah—ah—ah," and after falling calm, be aware of what he was saying. But while I was sitting at a table, copying his temperature chart, and glancing at him from time to time, I noticed he was having great difficulty in breathing. Then, at about eleven, the nurse came to me.

"Send for the doctor quickly, his heart is very bad."

Rushing into the next room, where Kokhno was asleep, I implored him to hurry for the doctor, and Misia Sert. The doctor arriving, further injections were ordered, but we were immediately told that his condition was desperate, and that it would be as well to send for the priest. This, however, I refused to agree to; to me it seemed equivalent to renouncing our last hope, tiny though it might be. Nevertheless, I had in the end to admit its necessity—for it was clear that death was inevitably at hand. Towards midnight the priest, Father Irenius of the Orthodox Greek Church, appeared in the room, and began to read the prayers for the dying in Church Slavonic. Serge Pavlovitch, however, was by now unconscious, and knew nothing of what was going on. At 2 A.M. his temperature had jumped to about 106°, and he was suffocating. The death agony had begun. Until this moment, I had still preserved some gleam of hope and was continually urging the nurse to give him fresh injections while I myself poured eau-de-Cologne over the dying man's head. But then the nurse refusing to repeat the injections as often as seemed to me necessary, I took the syringe away and myself repeated the injections almost every ten minutes. In the old days Serge Pavlovitch would get furious and shout if any of the eau-de-Cologne I dabbed on his brow trickled into his eyes. But now, although my clumsy shaking hands spilt so much that quantities ran over his face and into the wide staring eyes, Serge Pavlovitch felt nothing and did not blink even. My last injection had no effect at all, for the nerve centers had ceased functioning.

All my life I shall remember that dreadful night in which I sat there, supporting the dying man on one side, Kokhno on the other, with Misia sitting at his feet and the doctor and nurse silent by the window.... Slowly the night dragged on.

Now, because his mouth was parched, we helped him, at first, to drink through a straw: then, when he was no longer able to suck up the liquid, we poured the water into his mouth. Even the touch of his body was dreadful, for every fold was burning hot, while the skin itself streamed with ice-cold sweat, as though he had just stepped out of water.

About five in the morning, in the false dawn, he began a hurried precipitate breathing, five or six breaths a second, but no air seemed to enter those lungs. No, I shall never forget the sight of those fearful efforts. At 5:45 every sign of breathing stopped. In sheer terror, I began to shake him, and so twice restored him to life. Then, for the third time his breathing stopped, stopped forever, without warning, with no convulsion or outward sign, save for the last motion of the head dropping forward. Tiptoeing, the doctor approached and said: *"C'est fini."*

At that moment the first rays of the rising sun flashed forth, glittering on the dead man's face, and the huge tears that were still trickling down it....

And then, before the mind had even learned to realize this was death,

before it was even conscious that Serge Pavlovitch was gone—and forever—a startling, almost incredible scene took place. On one side I, on
the other Kokhno, threw ourselves on Serge Pavlovitch's body, I striving
to thrust Kokhno away, he striving with me, and both struggling over
the dead man's body. It was necessary to remove us forcibly from the
room. Outside, Serge Pavlovitch's old friend Landsberg began to reason
with us as though we were babies.

When we again entered the room my mood had changed completely;
I was calm and remote from all things. My mind was now perfectly
clear, and everything necessary to be done was clearly before me. First,
I arranged that photographers and artists should be sent for in order
that the death mask might be taken. It was a terrible sight to see how
the sculptors smote away at Serge Pavlovitch's head, to remove the mask
when it was finished. Meanwhile, Kokhno had gone off to arrange for a
plot in the cemetery, and I was left alone with the body. For a full
twenty-four hours I stayed with the body, and while making his last
toilet, refused to allow anyone to enter. I shaved him, trimmed his
mustache (in the clipped "Peter the Great" manner he always affected),
parted and arranged the hair (I kept a lock as a memento), made up the
face, and tied the jaw with a towel. Then, having dressed him, I
fastened his tie and slipped into his cuffs the links which he himself
had given me in Italy (keeping his own links for myself and later having
them made into three pairs, all with the "fern" emblem, for, according to
Serge Pavlovitch, the Russian word "diagil," i.e., fern, was the origin
of his surname). Then I folded his arms, and put a tuberose, his favorite
flower, into his buttonhole. And when the others entered the room they
could hardly credit what they were seeing. For now, so handsome, so
fresh, did he look, that his death, and the long unending nightmare of
the last nights, seemed hardly credible. Then we covered the body with
flowers, and put ice under the bed, and the windows were thrown wide
to temper, as far as possible, the tropic heat of the Venetian summer.

Meanwhile a second telegram had arrived from Pavel Georgievitch,
saying he would be arriving at 4 P.M. Some force, however, superior to
my will, kept me chained to Serge Pavlovitch's body—and it was Kokhno
who went to meet him and prepare him for his fearful ordeal. The first
panikhida [3] had been arranged for 5 P.M. at the bedside (an old nun
had begun to read the prayers for the departed an hour before, but
greatly irritated, I made her retire into a corner), and at the appointed
hour all Serge Pavlovitch's friends then in Venice were assembled. Meanwhile, the priest had arrived, but I begged him to wait for Pavel Georgievitch before beginning.

And then I saw Pavel Georgievitch and Kokhno slowly approaching,
and a wave of anguish swept over me for him; for how would he manage to endure it? And at this I begged the priest to go with me, so

[3] Memorial Service.

that I might meet and prepare him, only to find, however, that Kokhno had already "prepared" the unhappy man at the railway station....

Pavel Georgievitch, a pale, snow-white old man, came into the room, approached Serge Pavlovitch's body, and for a long, long time gazed at it in silence. My heart bled for him, and an inward trembling took possession of me lest the shock should prove too much for him. But then he sank upon his knees, and slowly crossed himself with the broad Russian gesture and, after a momentary concentration in prayer, arose and stood aside. The service began....

All three of us, Pavel Georgievitch, Kokhno and I, remained with the body through the night. An unquiet night, broken by a terrible thunderstorm (an earlier storm having broken about two when I was alone with Diaghilev's body), a veritable hurricane marked by uprooted trees and vivid lightning flashes which strangely lit up the room and the dead body. All day I had been obsessed with one idea: "Suppose Serge Pavlovitch has not really died?" and now the lightning gave an illusory life to the still body. Strange hallucinations took possession of me, and several times it seemed as though Serge Pavlovitch was resuscitated, was staring at me. I was almost pertified by that stare....

Before dawn the coffin arrived, and Serge Pavlovitch was laid in it, with the little crucifix which Misia Sert had put into his hands as he lay dying. Then, for the last time, we all kissed him on the brow, and the coffin was screwed down. On our arms we carried it down the main staircase and into the hearse, to be taken to the jetty. It was a strange procession, for the whole journey was made over a green carpet of boughs, twigs and leaves, strewn by the storm of the night. Then, when the coffin and wreaths—I had ordered two, one from myself, with the inscription *"Au grand Serge,"* another in the name of the "Russian Ballet"—were placed in the large black funeral gondola, we all moved off, bearing Diaghilev's remains to the Greek church in Venice—*"La Venise de nos consolations...."* And now the prediction that Serge Pavlovitch would die on the water had come true—he had died on an island amid the lagoons.

Up to the moment that Serge Pavlovitch's coffin was about to leave the church for the cemetery, I had kept myself well in hand; but, from then on, the nervous strain to which I had been subjected day and night from August 8th, began to tell on me. That strain had manifested itself in various ways, from the cruel automatism at first, to the unnatural, yes, and even supernatural, presence of mind and resolution I had shown in tending the dead Serge Pavlovitch's body and amid the hallucinations of our storm-night vigil....I was overstrung, full of a nervous electricity which imperiously demanded release in some form of nervous discharge.

I was near, dangerously near, insanity: to some profound mental and psychic disturbance: even to breakdown....

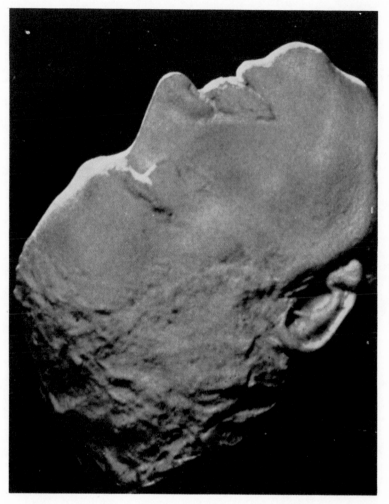

Diaghilev's Death Mask

In Venice, Misia Sert made us welcome, for by then we could hardly move or stand from fatigue. For the life of me I could not have prevented myself stretching out on her bed, and immediately fell into a profound slumber. About ten she woke me, and together we went to the funeral service. But when we came to the church, San Georgio dei Sciavoni, now full of people, though I was supported on either side by Misia and Coco, I found it utterly impossible to enter the church, for at every effort some unknown force seemed intent to prevent me. It was as though a wall had risen in front of the church which I was utterly unable to pierce. With every ounce of my will I strove to master the spell cast over me—but unsuccessfully. I was terrified: What could it be—was I about to go mad? And this thought paralyzed me still more completely. After a number of efforts, however, I finally succeeded in making a rush that forced me through the portals, as though I were crashing through something hard and indestructible which had raised itself like a barrier: then racing down the whole length of the church, I collapsed with a terrible scream by the altar, behind the *ikonostasis,* as though I had gone completely out of my mind.

After the service the procession, wonderful in its solemn, silent beauty, re-formed, led by the magnificent black and gold gondola, bearing the coffin smothered in flowers, followed by that containing Pavel Georgievitch, Misia Sert, Coco Chanel, Kokhno and myself, and a whole string of others, full of friends and mourners. Then, over the smooth ultramarine surface of the Adriatic, sparkling with golden sunshine, the body was wafted to the island of San Michele, and there borne on our arms to the grave.

I hated the idea of approaching the grave and was terrified of seeing the coffin lowered into it. Turning aside, therefore, I stood remote and unmoved as it were, but half insanely moaning to myself. Pavel Georgievitch, however, came for me: "Seriozha, my dear, they are about to lower the coffin. . . ." I followed him, almost crouching as I went, for my knees had turned to water, such was my insane fear, and my feeling that the nearer I was to earth, the less I should see, the less horrible I should find it all. Trembling with the same inward fear, I listened to the last words of the priest, trying to suppress, to smother something that was rising in me. Then, picking up a small trowel, the priest cast a handful of earth upon the coffin. How fearful was the sound it made! And I, too, took some earth, meaning to follow his example. But suddenly it was impossible to hold myself back. I was swept away by some unknown force which surged irresistibly up in me, which swept away all restraint, and I hurled myself into the grave. . . . Whereupon a dozen hands seized me, and with immense difficulty managed to drag me back, for my maniac delirium had endued me with herculean strength. Then I was led from the cemetery.

Quiet, solemn quiet, reigns on the island of San Michele, where the mortal remains of Serge Pavlovitch Diaghilev rest forever—

"Venise, inspiratrice eternelle de nos apaisements." [4]

[4] The words on Diaghilev's tombstone were taken by me from a notebook which he gave me to be used during my lessons with Cecchetti. They are written on the first page: "I hope that these notes, drawn from the teaching of the last of the Great Masters in Venice, will remain as unforgettable and eternal as Venice itself, eternal inspirer of all that brings peace. S. de Diaghilev, Venice 1926."

VISIT TO NIJINSKY IN JUNE 1939

SINCE 1929 Nijinsky has been lost to the world—alive and yet not in being. He has been under the permanent care of a Swiss mental clinic, excellently looked after and given the most modern curative treatment.

At one moment the news spread through the world that he was on the way to recovery and that the doctors were confident of bringing him back to normal life. It inspired in me—as in many others—a slender and fragile hope that perhaps a miracle was still possible. I made up my mind to repeat Diaghilev's experiment: to provoke a shock which would bring the past back to Nijinsky's consciousness, would dispel the twenty years of dreadful obsession and lift the dark curtain which separated him from the world and from the Nijinsky of the past. I began timidly to believe that if I succeeded even for an instant, that one dazzling moment would work the miracle.

In June 1939 I organized a gala performance at the Diaghilev Exhibition in aid of Nijinsky. By that time his means of support had been entirely exhausted and it was urgently necessary to do something to make it possible for him to continue being treated in the Swiss model clinic. Just before the performance I went to see him in Switzerland. This was my third meeting with Nijinsky—as different from the first two as the present Nijinsky was unlike the Nijinsky I had met ten and fifteen years ago.

My first impressions were satisfactory and hopeful. When I had met him ten years before he was on the way to becoming fat in a disagreeable, flabby manner; now he was more fit again, more supple in his movements. He had become more sociable—less shy than formerly, less like a hunted animal. His face had lost its hopelessly timid and downtrodden expression, and he would readily respond to a question or command. He no longer tore his nails to the quick. The nervous movements of his hands had found a quite different mode of expression. They had something of the dance, of the genuine dance—very beautiful at times. He never ceased playing with his hands, and his movements—especially round his head—were reminiscent, every now and then, of the plastic of Siamese dancers. But gone was his shy and childlike smile, a smile of confidence and good-natured benevolence. Its place had been taken by a hoarse laugh, deep and convulsive, which shook his whole body and threw it into sharp and angular plastic poses. In these, too, something of the dance was subconsciously expressed.

When we entered his room Nijinsky was talking to himself. He is always talking to himself, in a language of his own, quite unintelligible to others—a mixture of the most unexpected combinations of Russian, French and Italian words.

I asked him, "Do you remember Diaghilev, Vatza?" and Nijinsky instantly answered—his reflexes are exceedingly quick, much quicker than those of normal people—"Remember ... yes, yes, he ... remarkable ... how he ..." and suddenly the hoarse, terrifying laugh convulsed his whole body, jerked it hysterically into sharp, angular contortions.

He answers questions at once, but without understanding them, as if guessing or sensing their meaning from a stray word or other, which he repeats incessantly. They seem to evoke in him fleeting associations that vanish immediately. What for the moment promised sense and coherence fades instantly into nonsense. Ideas pass through him like the eternal swell of the ocean without tarrying for a moment. It is useless to repeat one's questions—he does not know what he has said the moment before and there is no logical sequence either in his ideas or words, no *continuity*. He lives only by momentary reflexes; to a proffered hand he responds merely by a similar movement. Nevertheless, when he perceives a gaze directed at him, at first frightened and watchful, he quickly resumes his placidity and soon returns the look not merely with confidence, but even kindly.

My brother offered him some strawberries. Nijinsky loves them and pastry more than anything. The way he eats strawberries can only be described as exquisite. He took up a strawberry with a smooth, rounded gesture of his outstretched fingers—not without a certain elegance—plucked off the stalk, put it aside, and ate the fruit, repeating delightedly: "How good! How good!"

It was then that, compelled by an irresistible inner urge, I decided to dance before and for Nijinsky. Having put on his dancing tunic and his slippers, I began to go through exercises at the *barre* (which had been installed in the hall in the hope that Nijinsky would some time or other make use of it) when suddenly I heard, "You might fall into the air," followed by other obscure exclamations.

I continued, and rhythm—to which every living creature is subject—began to act on Nijinsky. At first he only nodded his head, then began to tap with his foot and finally to count, "One-two, one-two ..." then, suddenly, "Ferma!"

I asked him: "Do you remember Cecchetti, Vatza—*maestro* Cecchetti?"

"*Oui, Cecchetti grand, très grand ...*"

My words had touched something within, but the thread was immediately broken. Again the convulsive laugh, and the body writhed, as if ready to fall apart into the sharply angular lines of its movement.

A gramophone was brought in with the records of the *Faune* and the *Spectre de la Rose*. First the *Faune* was put on. Nijinsky watched me for a considerable time intently and steadfastly, following my movements; became afraid and tried to hide, and finally followed my slightest movements with his eyes, like a cat stalking a mouse. But it was obvious that the rhythms of the *Faune* had made no impression on him—he somehow turned away from it.

I started on the *Spectre de la Rose*—and the miracle began. The rhythm of the *Rose* conquered and infected Nijinsky. He did not, of course, recognize Weber's melody, nor was he aware that I was dancing the *Spectre,* but the rhythmic persistence of the sound-accent began to act on him.

At first he said: "Oh, how good ... look, look ... very good, very good, excellent!" and then—as if in response to my *entre-chats six*—without any visible effort or preparation, without *plié* even, Nijinsky began to rise from the floor. His high-soaring jump was such that no one of those who witnessed *that Spectre de la Rose* will ever forget it. His wife and my brother Leonide paled and stood as if transfixed—Romola Nijinsky because of the miracle she saw again after twenty years, my brother because of a miracle he now saw for the first time in his life.

In soft shoes, with insteps only slightly arched, Nijinsky continued his absolutely faultless classic *entre-chats six*. I saw how Nijinsky was gradually being drawn into my orbit, into my dance, into my curve of the *Rose*. I could discern in his dance perfect *cabrioles, pas de bourrée....*

The record came to its end and stopped. Nijinsky was breathing heavily.

In ecstasy I went down on my knees before Nijinsky—and suddenly the fabulous dancer of the great past, as if repeating my gesture and my inspiration, went down on his knees before me and, pointing at my feet, exclaimed, "Good, yes.... Very good...."

The miracle was over, insanity prevailed and again the mad laugh interrupted the last words of the god of the dance.

The shock I had arranged was successful, far beyond my hopes. I had in fact been able to resurrect for one fleeting instant the old Nijinsky, but that instant could not be held, did not light up and dispel the dark night which surrounds the soul of the great dancer of the past. I realized that nothing can ever give back Nijinsky to mankind; that he is condemned to solitude—eternal, sorrowful and senseless.

THE SURREALIST MANIFESTO

IT IS intolerable that thought should be at the service of money. Yet not a year passes which does not bring the subjection of some man, whom one believed unconquerable by the powers he had so far opposed. The individuals who abandon everything to such a point as to ignore social distinctions matter little, the conception of that which they demanded before abdicating, subsists irrespective of them. That is why the participation of the painters Max Ernst and Joan Miró in the forthcoming production of the Russian Ballet, can never imply that though they themselves have abandoned their class, the surrealist conception has done so likewise. Essentially subversive as it is, it could never come to terms with similar enterprises, whose purpose has always been to domesticate, for the benefit of the international aristocracy, the dreams and revolts of our present-day physical and intellectual famine.

Possibly Ernst and Miró may have thought that their collaboration with M. de Diaghilev, made legitimate by Picasso's example, could never have had such grave consequences. Nevertheless, because of it, we whose function it is, regardless of the cost, to maintain the advanced posts of the spirit out of reach of every sort of slave-driver, are obliged to denounce, irrespective of persons, an attitude which puts weapons into the hands of the most rabid partisans of an equivocal morality.

It is well known that we do not attach an exaggerated importance to our artistic affinities with x and y. Will people do us the honor of believing that in May 1926, we are more than ever incapable of sacrificing our sense of revolutionary reality!

IT MAY interest the reader to know some of the titles of the rare editions in Diaghilev's collection, and now in my possession:

Triode of Lent, published 1561, Venice. *Apostol* (Acts Apost.) Moscow, 1564, by the first Russian printer Ivan Feodorov and Peter Mstislavetz. *Book of Hours*—printed in Moscow "in the year seven thousand and seventy-four. Begun the second day of September, completed the twenty-ninth day of October, in the thirty-first year of the reign of the Lord Tsar and Grand Duke Ivan Vassilievitch, and in the second year of office of the Metropolitan Athanasius." Until the discovery of this copy it was believed that only *two* copies of this *Book of Hours* existed (one in the Russian State Public Library, the other in the Royal Library at Brussels). I take this opportunity therefore of stating that mine is a *third* copy of this most rare edition. It should be noted also that the first leaf of the Leningrad copy is missing, whereas the Diaghilev copy is complete and in perfect preservation. Diaghilev acquired this volume in 1927, in Rome, from an antiquarian bookseller who was unaware of its great importance. *Biblia Ruska*—an extremely rare work in Slavonic-Russian, published Prague, 1517-19, by Fr. Scorna. Also included in the collection were two leaves from the *Book of Kings.*

Later publications were: *Sluzhebnik* [1]—very rare—printed by Andronicus Timofeev, Moscow, 1602; a Lvov *New Testament* (1636); *Poluustav* (Kieff, 1643); *Eucologion,* by Peter Mogila (Kiev, 1648); *Slovonic-Russian Dictionary,* by Pamva Berynda (1653).

Triode of Lent, printed, Moscow, 1658; the *Sermons of Grigorius of Nazianz* (Moscow, 1665); *Synopsis* (Kiev, 1674); a very rare Moscow edition, 1680, of Simeon's Polotzky's rhymed psalms *Psaltir Rithmotvornaja; Grammatika Rossiiskaja,* by Hendric Wilhelm Ludolff (Oxford, 1696).

The epoch of Peter the Great is also well represented. Suffice it to mention the *Slavonic, Greek and Latin* grammars (Moscow, 1701); the famous *Arithmetic,* by Magnitzky (Moscow, 1703); *Trilingual Lexicon* (Slavonic-Greek-Latin), by Theodore Polikarpov (Moscow, 1704); and the famous publication *Symbols and Emblemata,* printed in Amsterdam in 1705 at the wish of Peter the Great.

Among later works of especial interest I mention *The Rock of Faith,* Stephan Javorsky (Kiev, 1730); *German, Latin and Russian Dictionary*

[1] Church ritual.

(St. Petersburg, 1731); *Ukases of Peter the Great from 1714 to 1725* (St. Petersburg, 1739); *Ukases of Catherine I and Peter II* (ibid, 1743); and a copy of the very rare *Apologia or defence of the order of Freemasons* (Moscow, 1784), banned and burned by the hangman in 1792 in the reign of Catherine II.

Particularly representative is the collection dating from Catherine's reign, as may be seen from this short selection of titles: *Satires,* by Prince Antioch Kantemir (St. Petersburg, 1762); *Fables—Political and Moral,* by Volkov (St. Petersburg, 1762); *Works and Translations of Lukin* (St. Petersburg, 1765); Kheraskov's *Numa Pompilius* (Moscow, 1768); *Rossiada* (Moscow, 1786, printer, P. I. Novikov); the comedy *Oh, Times!* (St. Petersburg, 1772); *Instruction* (St. Petersburg, 1767) and *In Imitation of Shakespeare* (St. Petersburg), by the Empress Cartherine II herself.

Of later publications I should like to mention the very rare Moscow edition, 1795, of an *Onomatology* (Lexicon of natural magic) and the *Heroic Poem of the Field of the Prince of Novgorod, Seversky Igor Svitoslavovitch against the Polovtsians,* composed in old-Russian at the end of the twelfth century and transcribed into contemporary speech. (Moscow, Senate Printing Press, 1800, to. viii—46—I—I). Bound Morocco (cover preserved).

I shall not enumerate here the first editions of Pushkin and those of lesser contemporary poets, or Diaghilev's very comprehensive collection of nineteenth-century Russian literature and works on art.

The collection also includes many unpublished manuscripts and holograph letters by Pushkin, Lermontov, Viazemsky, Tolstoy, Turgeniev and the whole of Diaghilev's own documents.

The space is lacking to do adequate justice to Diaghilev's musical library; but it included practically everything by Glinka, Wagner, Rimsky-Korsakov, Stravinsky, Prokofiev, Debussy, Ravel and Falla—besides the manuscript scores of all the ballets.

INDEX